To the Memory
of
S. PARKES CADMAN

JOHN WESLEY

FRANCIS J. McCONNELL

GOD IS LOVE

LONDON: THE EPWORTH PRESS

First Published in 1939
Printed in U.S.A.   Bound in Great Britain
All rights reserved.   Copyright 1939

Published   in   Great   Britain

by

THE   EPWORTH   PRESS

25-35 CITY ROAD, E.C.1

CONTENTS

PART I

THE BRAND PLUCKED FROM THE BURNING

PART I

THE BRAND PLUCKED FROM THE BURNING

Epworth

JOHN WESLEY lived from June 17, 1703, to March 2, 1791—practically the whole of the eighteenth century. Of all the great English leaders of that great century probably more has been written about Wesley than about any other, except possibly three or four statesmen, five or six scientific thinkers, and a general or two. Substantially all is known that it is necessary to know to form approximately just judgments about him.

The opinion of virtually all students of his life is that he stands out above the other religious leaders of his time for two qualities—his God-consciousness, or awareness of God, or devotion to what appeared to him to be the will of God, or whatever we mean by a God-filled spirit. On the other hand, the students concede to Wesley a talent for practical administration amounting to genius.

The Godward side of the life of Wesley, or of any religious leader for that matter, has to be taken as we find it, or as it comes to men as a gift. The wind bloweth where it listeth. The realm of practical affairs lies more within the reach of ordinary understanding. It ought to be possible to consider the two phases in their relation to each other, especially the relation of Wesley's practical activities to what we think of as the deeper phases of his life. It is a commonplace to all students of Wesley that he took expedients wherever he could find them, that the class meeting and the lay ministry and the system of Conferences were adopted as at hand in the actual circumstances, or were inevitable outcomes of those circumstances rather than deliberate creations. Consideration has been given to all such concerns as if they were details of a useful sort, valuable for a longer or shorter period. May it not be, however, that this practical bent of mind had an influence upon Wesley's idea of God, and of conversion, and of what he called Christian perfection, and of the Church? At any rate, it is with questions like this in the background that the present author asks his readers to look again at Wesley's life and career. It is most significant for our purpose to get firm hold of the fact that the most practically-minded churchman of the eighteenth century was the most persistent seeker after the highest spiritual ideals for himself and others. It was not possible for him to keep separate these two phases of his life and thought. The practical activities interpreted the ideal of perfection and the ideal of perfection influenced the activities.

We have all heard many times of the burning of the Rectory at Epworth when John was about six years old, of how John escaped by being plucked as a brand from the burning by one neighbor's standing on the shoulders of another and rescuing the boy who appeared at an upstairs window with the flames raging all around him. This experience evidently made a deep impression on the mind of Wesley, for he often referred to himself as a brand plucked from the burning, and once, when he had gone far into years, stopped a public service when he recalled that the day was the anniversary of that boyhood event.

If one allows one's mind to play around the suggestiveness of that incident of the fire, it is found to be quite full of meaning. Wesley's own feeling was sentimental. The spectacular and dramatic features made him look upon it as providential deliverance from death. From that point of view, its significance has possibly been overstressed. The young Wesley knew exactly what to do when he saw the fire in his room: he moved a chair, according to his father, a chest, according to himself, up to the window and called for help. If he had presence of mind and will to do that much, he would probably have had the alertness of mind and will to drop the ten or twelve feet to the ground if he must. Still, events move quickly at a fire: Wesley's father says that the boy was scared, and thus lost time when the neighbor's face appeared at the window; a few minutes after Wesley had touched the ground the roof and possibly the wall of the house fell. I have even called this section: "The Brand Plucked From the Burning," for the suggestiveness of the expression. At least up to Aldersgate Wesley's life was tried and molded as by fire.

Moreover, quite as meaningful a question for Wesley as the saving of his life by Providence was that as to the actual cause of the fire itself. He in after years spoke of it as the deed of an incendiary, though he does not give his evidence, but he knew that attacks upon his father had been common enough during the earlier period of the life at Epworth. Samuel Wesley favored the draining of the marsh land on which Epworth was built. The dwellers on that island of Axholme, a district of forty square miles surrounded by rivers, thought of their livelihood as in some way dependent on the marshes, and resented furiously Samuel's advocacy of improvements. So they did burn his barn, and did attempt to ruin his stored crops, and did mutilate his cattle. The elder Wesley suffered much for his convictions. The recollection of what Samuel Wesley endured for his principles remained with his son all through life. When we read that in the days of his field preaching ruffians threw clods and stones and clubs at Wesley and that he took all this as a matter of course, we may remind ourselves that he had seen his father before him take outrages against himself as a matter of course. There is not any indication that Samuel Wesley ever trimmed his views to avoid unpleasant consequences. Part of the rage of his neighbors against him was due to his adhering stiffly to his own political opinions when all his community was against him. I repeat that the significance of the famous fire was largely in its being of the type of opposition the convictions and conduct of Samuel Wesley called forth.

If we look at the Wesley family at all closely, we may raise question as to whether Samuel Wesley has ever had justice done him by the writers who tell of the greatness of his son. Susanna Wesley herself is partly to blame for this injustice—or, at least lack of justice—because of that well-known and oft-quoted sentence in the letter to her son that it was part of the misfortune of the Wesley family that her husband and herself could not often completely agree. Because of the almost incredible honor in which Susanna Wesley is held in Methodism, the ordinary Methodist forthwith assumes that this sentence leaves Samuel in a very bad plight indeed. There evidently were divergences of opinion between the Wesleys, but that does not necessarily mean that either was wrong. John Wesley is himself on record as saying that when Samuel noticed that Susanna was not responding with an "Amen" when he prayed for the king because she was a Jacobite, and not for William, he said that if there were two kings there would have to be two beds—and left his wife for over a year, while he betook himself to London, that there was a long interval between the birth of John Wesley and the child who immediately preceded him. Nobody ever would have believed this story if it had not come from John Wesley. It would suggest an element of heartlessness which nothing else in the facts known about Samuel Wesley bears out. How reliable a witness is John Wesley here? Admittedly, he is dealing with a period before his own birth. It is common enough in long-established families for all sorts of legends to get started, especially when there is a flavor of the dramatic or sensational about them. The trouble with the story is that it does not fit into the record. There is no way to adjust such a period of absence of Samuel Wesley as that required into the dates as we have them. The children came along at the same intervals as when Samuel was at home. John was born when Anne was twelve months old. Moreover, an examination of Samuel Wesley's correspondence shows that he was never away from Epworth, even at the "Convocation," as long a time as the story assumes. Whatever basis in fact the story had the telling must have been incredibly exaggerated, not to say distorted.

Samuel Wesley was stubborn enough, with the stubbornness of one who could hold fast to a plan year in and year out. He wrote a commentary on the book of Job which called for almost illimitable persistence and patience. We smile at it today, but it was taken seriously and admiringly enough by the clergymen of the Church of England in his day, scores of whom bought the book. Samuel Wesley was of indomitable will. Mrs. Wesley is authority for the statement that her husband was not skilled in financial management. Maybe so, but how anyone could have made so little money go so far is an insoluble mystery, explicable perhaps by the carefulness with which Samuel kept his records. Every shilling received and set down was accounted for. He worked his way through Oxford, beginning with two pounds and six shillings and leaving with ten pounds fifteen shillings. The trouble was that he did not have money enough to meet burdens which were not of his own creation and seeking. John Wesley, when near the close of his life, ceased keeping accounts, stating that he had kept accurate record of his funds all his life, from childhood on. He had the example of his father before his eyes. It is true that Samuel Wesley went to prison as a punishment for debt. The debt laws of the time were very stringent. There is no sign that anybody found serious fault with Samuel Wesley for debt. Nobody hinted that the unfortunate clergyman was guilty of any moral fault in his financial shortcoming. He spent too much on others, attaining, however, to the satisfaction of being able to say that he had given his sons the best educations to be found in England.

So much has been said about Susanna's influence upon her son that it is just as well to think of the influence of the father. Nobody has ever questioned his courage. There is a well-authenticated story to the effect that when a brigadier-general sitting near

Samuel Wesley in an inn fell into obscene speech, Wesley offered the brigadier a glass of water with the suggestion that he wash out his mouth.   Friends restrained the irate militarist, who, according to the story, afterward apologized.   Dr. Umphrey Lee has forcefully showed us that Samuel Wesley was a strict disciplinarian in ecclesiastical requirements.   It gives us a glimpse at times far different from ours to read that he imposed a penalty upon an adulterous church member which compelled the penitent to walk upon a public street clad in a garment of contrition.   Such a demand today would meet with nothing but ridicule, but at the time it was anything but ridiculous.   It bore witness to the power of the old church to command and punish its members.   Now, let our minds step ahead about thirty years to John Wesley's much-questioned and much-denounced treatment of a member of the church in Georgia during his work there in 1738—the exclusion of Miss Sophia Hopkey from the sacrament of the Lord's Supper. This regrettable episode was complicated by the fact that it had been commonly supposed that Wesley was to marry Miss Hopkey and that the engagement had ended unfortunately.   Wesley's disciplinary treatment of Miss Hopkey has often been looked upon as arising from resentment, or personal pique.   It would be impossible completely to exonerate John Wesley from blame in this matter, but it would be negligent indeed for a student of Wesley's life not to see that he was acting in the spirit and manner of church discipline as he had seen it administered in the parish of Epworth.   The young woman in question had failed in requirements of the Church —of no vast consequence indeed—and Wesley was dealing with the situation as he thought he should in loyalty to the Church.   This does not make the action of Wesley any wiser or more sensible, but it does make it more intelligible to an age which, without such explanation, cannot understand it at all.

In spite of a stern, unyielding character Samuel Wesley must have been a likable human being.   Some features of the picture that has come down to us show that under all his systematic persistence in whatever he undertook was a fine devotion to his family. We do not read of his ever punishing any of his children.   He insisted on being obeyed, even by his wife, but all through the variegated correspondence which he left behind him was a considerateness and regard for all with whom he came in contact.   In collecting the tithes due him from those who cultivated his land, he found one renter stealing from him and marched the offender down in the market place and made him disgorge. Shocked and outraged though he was, there is something almost whimsical about his telling of the attempted theft. Again he found that his parishioners were neglecting the christening of their children till these infants were grown into big lubberly boys, whom he had to take into his arms for the ceremony, the scene suggested being irresistibly funny, since Samuel Wesley measured only five feet and five and one half inches in height. Once again he declared that Jack was so much given to reasoning that he wondered that the boy would attend to the most pressing necessities of nature unless a reason was possible for so doing. When John was at last made a Fellow of Lincoln, the father's pride could not contain itself, since, come what may, his Jack was a Fellow of Oxford. His letters about his debts, in all their careful statements, reveal a touching anxiety and distress.

Another incident, or series of incidents, by which light is thrown on the character of the father, and of all the family, for that matter, consisted of the famous noises heard in the Epworth Rectory in the winter of 1716. Knockings upon the walls and floors, rustlings as of the garments of an unseen passer-by, and the swift scuttling along of some indefinite animal form upset the calm of the family. Quite a mass of written testimony survives to us describing the experience. Some who knew of the noises were sure they were made by rats, others that they were pranks played by young men who might have come to call on the Wesley girls (a curious commentary on the notion that there was never anything but a somber spirit in the Wesley home). Others, including Samuel Wesley and his wife and John—who, by the way, was not at home when the disturbances occurred—were positive that the sounds were supernatural. The spirit must have been a rowdy sort of poltergeist, for when Samuel Wesley would pray for the king the rappings, interpreted as expressive of disgust, were almost furious.

Now, no one can read such accounts without feeling that the writers were utterly sincere in their conviction as to supernatural origin. The pertinent question for us is not whether the disturbances were supernatural. Some of the Wesley biographers gravely tell us that we do not know what the causes were, with a hint at implication that they may have been supernatural after all. We do not indeed know what happened in that Epworth Rectory two hundred and fifty years ago, so far as concerns the noises, but we do know that all the persons in the house, and probably most outside the house in the village, believed in ghosts. The time was just a century later than that of Shakespeare, the significance of whose ghost scene in *Hamlet,* for example, lay in that theatergoers in Shakespeare's time believed in the return of departed spirits to visit the haunts of men. Now, since the Wesley household believed in ghosts, we find something quite noteworthy in the attitude of the family to "Old Jeffery," as they called the supposed spirit. Did they seek to move out of the house and abandon it as haunted? They did not. No ghost, real or imagined, could scare, after the first few disturbances, the Wesley children. They took the noises as they came—tried at first to get into communication with the spirit, and finally treated "him" with an easy familiarity bordering on amusement. Samuel tried to devise a scheme of return knocks to the tappings, with apparently as cool a rationalism as if he belonged to a psychical research society of our modern type. The girls used to believe that they felt Old Jeffery holding a door shut when they tried to open it. Instead of running and screaming in terror, they pulled harder on the door, and when they got it free indulged in ejaculations of contemptuous defiance at the rude visitor from the realms of shade. There have been those who have declared that the two most determinative incidents in the boyhood of Wesley were the fire and the uproar caused by Old Jeffery. It is not easy to see just how one could accept such an extreme conclusion as this, but it is perhaps worth while to note that the attitude of John to the disturbances was essentially that which he took throughout his life to all reports of such phenomena. On the one hand he accepted them as supernatural, on the other he had toward them the temper of a rationalist. He would travel long distances to see and talk with the subjects of what seemed to be extraordinary spiritual visitations, and then question the persons after the manner of a scientific inquirer. He never lost interest in such phenomena. The last reference to Wesley in Boswell's *Johnson* has to do with a not altogether satisfactory answer of Wesley to a question of Johnson about a famous spiritualistic medium, as we should say today. There is something pathetically tragic in that John, and his mother for that matter, seemed to bolster up their faith in the supernatural by these wretched noises.

Augustine Birrell has made a list of three or four "purges" which reveal the unsettled religious state in which Samuel Wesley worked. The first purge was that which drove the Roman Catholics out of power during Henry the VIII's reign. Second, under the Commonwealth the Puritans expelled as many as they could of those believing in episcopacy and High Church. Third, when the Stuarts got back under Charles II they enacted an Act of Uniformity which sent two thousand more out of their livings. Fourth, William and Mary came and brought dissension into Wesley's own household. There was no telling who was who and what was what in the religious period through which Samuel Wesley served.

We leave Samuel Wesley for the present with the remark that he was utterly devoted to the service of God, that he gave himself to incessant study of religious themes that we should not consider important today, that he expected obedience from his wife and children, though he always dealt with them in a spirit of respect for them, a respect which they fully returned. Making all due allowance for the notions of the times as to parental authority, Samuel Wesley seems to have been on terms of frank intimacy with his children. Speaking after the manner of a believer in heredity, Samuel Wesley showed himself the worthy son of a father who sacrificed virtually all hopes of ecclesiastical preferment for the sake of his convictions, being himself a dissenter. Samuel Wesley revealed himself in nothing more worthy of his ancestry than in his returning to the fold of the Church of England against which his father had dissented so vigorously at such cost.

We come now to look for a little at Susanna Wesley, about whom an almost unassailable tradition for perfect handling of children has been built up. The more closely we look at Susanna the more wonderful she appears, though she loses something of the halo put upon her brow by those who believed her perfect in everything. So far as family descent is concerned, she was a thoroughbred both on the father's and mother's side. Intellectually she was a marvel. At the age of thirteen she had gone over the arguments of dissenters and of believers in the Church of England and had decided for the Church. Her letters to John on matters of church doctrine and religious experience show amazing discernment and acuteness, while the more intimate communications like that describing the fire, like that telling of the shortness of the Wesleys' material resources in response to a question of an archbishop, like that to her wealthy uncle about the state of the family finances, are worthy of a place in any collection of fine specimens of English prose.

Probably the best-known letter of hers was the one to John describing her bringing up of her children: of her teaching them to "cry softly"—if they were to cry at all; of her success in bringing each child (except one) to the mastery of the alphabet in a single day— two achievements of most doubtful value; of her inculcation of correctness in manners; the difference between her training and the lack of it in other homes of the village as shown in what the children brought back with them in rudeness and crudeness of word and deed after they came home from the sojourn with friendly neighbors made necessary by the famous fire.

Mrs. Wesley was system throughout. It is not possible to see how she could have done anything at all if she had not been so. Every hour, every minute of the day had its duty. In a home where, first and last, nineteen children were born, just about everything had to be duty. Between the orderliness of the father and the system of the mother, the natural tendencies of John to like system got too much encouragement. The effect of system on young Wesley's development was more decisive on his character and religious experience than any number of fires and ghostly noises ever could have been. The oft-quoted remark of Samuel Johnson that Wesley would never stretch out his legs before the fire and have his talk out, dealt with a peculiarity that was fully developed before Wesley left Epworth. There was not much chance for stretching the legs in easy relaxation in the home of Samuel and Susanna Wesley and not much chance either of having a talk out. The whole situation would have been one of intolerable strain if it had not been that every minute, like every penny, was saved.

Some of Mrs. Wesley's advice about children we insist was of uncertain value. With all her astounding abilities, it is to be questioned if there was much that was genial or amiable about her. Possibly one should not look for amiability in a mother of nineteen children, nine of whom she had seen die in early infancy. Think of the sheer mass of grief thrown upon a mother's heart by such a stunning succession of calamities. Anything would have seemed possible in somberness of view after a total of distresses like this. Of course such woes were taken in those days pretty much as they came, for they seemed part of the regular ongoing of nature. Not much was known of the care of infants. The increase of a nation's population was purchased at a terrible cost in the death of children that did not survive the first two years of life, the chief distress falling on the mothers. To bring ten children to maturity out of nineteen was a notable achievement.

When all this is said, however, we still have considerable of a problem in getting Mrs. Wesley's point of view about the proper rearing of children. She told John that one must break the child's will in order to save its soul—grim method which hosts of Methodists have acted upon, and other hosts had followed since the beginning of time. There was one will she did not break—that of John. There is no indication in the letters of her children that she broke the will of any. Those who, after the jargon of modern psychology, speak of John Wesley as a type of mother-fixation, would do well to point out to us just where this fixation showed itself fixed. Wesley did indeed follow his mother's advice in many, many instances, even after he had come to full manhood—one of the worst instances being his attempts at the Kingswood School virtually to break the wills of his pupils, but he himself never followed his mother's judgment just because it was his mother's judgment. He insisted upon having reasons. If Mrs. Wesley herself succeeded in breaking the wills of her children, the wills must have been terrible before they were broken, for each went forth from the home with a will all but inflexible.

President Eliot, of Harvard, once said that the best legacy a father could leave his children was the memory of a character they could respect, even if they might not be able to feel much emotional affection for the father. The element of truth here is probably as valid for mothers as for fathers. The children of the Wesley household loved their mother as they did their father, but the dominating element seems to have been respect. Even after he had come to manhood, John Wesley preached that children should obey their parents as long as their parents were alive. He seems to have forgotten that in the one outstanding instance in which it was possible for him to obey his parents after he himself had become a man, he was positive in his refusal. The instance was that of his denial of his father's request that he (John) follow him as rector of Epworth. John did at last say he was willing to do so, but only after a long correspondence and persistent refusal. When he did yield, it was too late. His reasons were good enough for himself but not for his father. John felt that he could do more good by remaining at Oxford than by working among the virtual barbarians at Epworth. That was not just the way he put it, but that is what he meant. As for his preaching about obedience, that was a queer manifestation of the ultraconservatism which was at times dominant in Wesley. He himself had no children, but more and more he came to look upon Methodism and Methodists with the eyes of a parent and to desire to guide them in all things.   The preaching is significant, more-over, as showing the respect which Wesley cherished throughout his own life toward his own parents.   Both father and mother must have been remarkable indeed to have won such respect from a mind like that of John Wesley.   His mother lived till long after the Methodist movement was in full sweep, and in many important directions, notably in that of lay preaching, helped by her advice to mark out its course.

I have spoken of the community around Epworth as virtual barbarians.   I do not think this opinion is unjust or overharsh. Incendiaries, crop-destroyers, cattle-hockers they manifestly were in their relation to the Wesley family, or more particularly to Sam-uel, its head.   It is a wonder that the children ever looked back, as did John, even to the natural beauties of such a place with any fond-ness whatever, though the view from the churchyard is most impres-sive in the sweep over the low-lying landscape.   Now, in such a com-munity Mrs. Wesley won a striking spiritual victory.   Her husband belonged to what in those days was known as the Convocation, an ecclesiastical assembly which sat in London while Parliament was in session, to act upon church matters.   This required Samuel Wes-ley to be absent from Epworth for weeks at a time.   During one of these absences Mrs. Wesley called her children together on Sunday evenings for religious instruction, consisting chiefly of the reading of such fine religious literature as her exquisite taste might select. Then a few neighbors asked permission to come in, and then more, till finally the Rectory was at every meeting overcrowded.   Prob-ably not many of the houseburners were in these audiences, but that there was any audience at all was a noble tribute to the instructions given by Mrs. Wesley and to her surpassing moral qualities.   What she was doing, however, seemed to the ecclesiastical type of mind, including Samuel's, little short of scandalous, and she had to yield to her husband's positive orders to cease such irregularity—not, however, till she had gone to the utmost to get her husband's con-sent to her ministrations.   The stupidity of Samuel Wesley in this matter is almost beyond belief, or would be if we were not aware of the way the ecclesiastical mind works.   The obvious good effects of such a course as that of Mrs. Wesley were not obvious to Samuel. It would have seemed to the unsophisticated intelligence that what was needed was eyesight if insight was not available.   The simple fact that scores of hearers in a community like Epworth were getting something they could not get anywhere else ought to have been enough for anyone except a true-to-form ecclesiastic.

The children of the household at Epworth were all of distinctive and separate quality. The daughters were fearfully pinched by poverty, without much chance to get out, as the sons could, and earn a little money for themselves. To their credit be it said that they were not of the docile, submissive sort who bear the afflictions of life without protest. Their marriages were not notably fortunate. Susanna, the younger, married a ne'er-do-well, bore with him patiently for a time and left him and would have nothing more to do with him. Kezia, the youngest of the family, probably felt the pinch of poverty most. She was the only one of the daughters who did not marry. Her letters show a delicate richness of feeling, deserving of a better chance than she ever got. Martha married a preacher named Hall, a queer, twisted soul who finally gave up Methodism and took to preaching and practicing polygamy. Mrs. Hall was a strong nature of a high intellectual cast. Her somber figure stands now and again across the pages of Boswell's *Johnson*. Johnson evidently had genuine admiration for her, and, it appears, at one time asked her to become a member of the little circle that lived more or less continuously under his roof. Another of the daughters, on rather strong evidence in a realm where strong evidence is often nothing more than gossip, is supposed to have been betrayed by a lover. There are passages in Wesley's *Journal* which seem to bear this interpretation. Arthur Quiller-Couch's *Hetty Wesley* is founded on this assumption, an assumption which Quiller-Couch maintains as fact. Stevenson, who seems to have known more about the facts than anyone else, is authority for the statement that the scandal reached its climax when Hetty "stayed out" all one night with her lover. Stevenson claims to have seen the correspondence in which this was established, and that is all there is. In the *Journal* passages the father and mother seem determined to exclude the unfortunate daughter from the home as "ruined." No matter what her fault, it was not bad enough to warrant the attitude of her parents. In this crisis John stands out in a moral strength and fineness above Samuel and Susanna, both of whom were equally merciless. It is to be regretted that in *Hetty Wesley,* though the author's chief prejudice was against the father, he did not find it possible to soften his prejudice against John Wesley also enough to recognize adequately the justice and kindliness of John. In any event, Samuel insisted that the daughter, against whom suspicion had been directed, forthwith marry another suitor for her hand. So the unhappy woman passed into a companionship in which she could find no joy, and met increasing sorrow with the years. The artificiality and severity of Hetty's home training appear in that she was reading the Greek Testament by the time she was eight years old. The marriage of Mary—herself semi-invalid—to John Whitelamb, rector at Wroote, seems to have brought a degree of satisfaction though her husband never fully made adjustment to the Wesley household—but who could? On the whole, the lot and fate of the daughters arouse mingled feelings of sympathy for souls in frustration, of regret that the opportunities did not allow free play and development of talents which, under more favorable material circumstances, might have flowered into exceptional beauty. Emilia at first was interested in a Quaker, who sought her hand, but after a while got through "with all followers of George Fox." Emilia once wrote reproachfully to John for spending the money to visit the Moravians at Herrnhut while the family at Epworth was in such distress—one of those tragedies which the actors in them can never understand. John wrote back with unpardonable severity, telling Emilia that her letter showed a sinful temper, and that inasmuch as she had sinned in one point, she had sinned in all and was as bad as a murderer—and worse. Kezia died unmarried at the age of thirty-two. Like the other Wesleys, she was an excellent letter writer, given, as she said, to "impertinence and simplicity." Mrs. Wesley was once asked by an ecclesiastical superior whether her table had ever lacked for bread. She replied that she could not literally say yes, but that many times the getting of the bread cost so much effort that it did not seem to make much difference after she got it as to whether she ate it or not.

Of Charles we shall have abundant occasion to speak later. Samuel, Jr., the favorite of his mother, was possibly the solidest and steadiest of the Wesley family. He came to be a man of thorough scholarship, rather hardheaded in his practical affairs, without much sympathy with what he called the "enthusiasms" of John.

When we look at the difficulties under which the Wesley family lived, we wonder that they achieved so much. Poverty was always at hand, though probably there were never more than eight of the children at home at any one time—not more than the number in many a Methodist parsonage in America, today with no more money than the Wesleys had to live on. There can be no doubt of the height of attainment in Christian character in any one of them.

The whole atmosphere is one of devotion to lofty religious ideals and to fineness in human contacts. There is not much suggestion of anything sordid or contemptible in any records which have come down to us from the Epworth Rectory, and many records have come. The excellent breeding and self-nurture of the parents repeated themselves in the children. It would not be possible to find a coarse expression in any letter, or diary, or reported conversation of any member of the Epworth household, though they certainly possessed the ability to speak frankly with one another. We must remind ourselves that nobody knew that through the after-centuries the Wesley name was to be proclaimed to the ends of the earth. What records have reached us were made on the assumption that the household of the Epworth Rectory was like that of rectories elsewhere. Nobody was acting in the belief that the later ages would carefully treasure every scrap of information about the Wesley family. This is, indeed, a commonplace reflection, but one worthy of being constantly kept before us.

A further consideration is also important. The eighteenth century was a period of serious decay in religious interest and moral conduct, but there were some bright spots. We must not forget that the Rectory at Epworth, apart from the exceptional native endowment of the parents, could not have been the only such rectory in England. The children at Epworth certainly did not think that the conduct prescribed for them was different from that to be expected of the children of ministers anywhere. Diaries of country parsons, put into print in the past few years, have given us intimate glimpses of other rectories—diaries like that of James Woodforde and William Jones, for example. Both these diaries reveal most human qualities in their authors—without the extraordinary spiritual vigor of Samuel and Susanna Wesley—but they tell of lives devoted to pastoral service if not to profound theological reflection. Not much was then being done for the people as such through legislative or concerted social action. This must have increased the sense of responsibility in scores of English rectories. We cannot believe that such centers of spiritual vitality as that of the Epworth Rectory were idle and futile. In the after years, after his father had passed away, John paid tribute to the effectiveness of his work. There were at any one time about eighteen hundred to two thousand lives for whom the Epworth rector must feel himself spiritually responsible. There were indeed sporting parsons in the eighteenth century Church of England; there always have been such. They lent color to the spectacular charges of the age as dissolute, but they were not all. There were other centers of righteousness like that at Epworth. The sons of Samuel Wesley reveal an unfaltering devotion to religious interests from the first. They went out from home with a feeling of religious trusteeship and stewardship. It was this that helped make them such devotees of system. They must account for every penny that came into their hands and for every minute of time. The somberness of spirit that we often see in them was due to the feeling that the service of the divine called for all their resources, and they did not have much, for all their time, and the time was short. Burdens like these were put on their shoulders at Epworth and remained there till the end.

To the patient industry of Dr. James R. Joy I am indebted for the following item, which suggests manifestation of genius in the Wesley family, not hitherto recognized among Methodists: "John Wesley Jarvis (1781-1840), a self-taught artist, who was considered the chief American portrait painter of his generation, and whose work is represented in the principal American collections, was a lineal descendant of Samuel and Susanna Wesley. His mother, Nancy Lambert, was the granddaughter of Anne Wesley (b. 1702), a sister of John and Charles."

CHARTERHOUSE SCHOOL

Before following John Wesley to school and college we would do well to look at the educational training he received from his mother, who taught all the children in her own home. We can judge pupils by at least one test which is of surpassing importance, namely, their command of their native tongue. It is true that the style is the man, but nothing requires harder and more persistent application than does style. We are fortunate in having specimens of the English of almost all the Wesley children. In simplicity and forthrightness all are much alike. Some of the daughters attempted verse, with no noteworthy poetic success, indeed, but still with enough to indicate knowledge of poetic meters and more than ordinary skill in phrasing. If Hetty, long after she had come to maturity, did attempt to make "tear" fit with "beer" in her most pretentious poem, she did not sin more grievously in this respect than her brother Charles did upon occasion.

The foundations of John Wesley's written style must have been laid under his mother's training. From the time he began to write at all we recognize the signs of clearness, directness, and force which were his for seventy-five years. A distinguished student of English literature has said that to get vigor of direct expression like that of Wesley anywhere but from Wesley, we have to read the dispatches of the Duke of Wellington for objective and steady gaze upon facts as they are, for the concise and summary statement of things done. It has been justly remarked that Wesley shared the sentimentalism of his age, which is true enough, but he succeeded marvelously in keeping the sentimentalism off his written pages. There was, indeed, quite a lot of somewhat florid stuff in his correspondence with Betty Kirkham and Sally Kirkham, young women in his Oxford days, but, that aside, the writing seemed, indeed, of the kind with which later the Iron Duke wrote from the campaigns in Spain.

John Wesley went straight from his home to the Charterhouse School. Not much has come down to us about his days there. There could not have been more than fifty boys there in Wesley's time. He was about ten when he entered and about seventeen when he left. In an entry in his diary covering that period of his life he says: "From ten to fourteen I had but little but bread to eat and not great plenty of that. I believe this was so far from hurting me that it laid the foundation of lasting health." He appears to have studied Latin and Greek, with some Hebrew. He also came in contact with Tooke, a noted teacher of mathematics at the school. Samuel told his son to be sure to run around the school yard three times every morning for exercise, which John did. The quality of the instruction seems to have been high enough, as schools went in those days.

It was concerning the life at Charterhouse that Wesley wrote the famous passage about his entering school in a state of grace and coming out a sinner. The passage describes adult experience, or is put in adult terms, for Wesley had no notion of the difference between a child's religion and a man's; or, if he did, he never saw fit to describe it in writing. Tyerman, far and away the most important of Wesley's biographers so far as collection and assembly of fact-material is concerned, took Wesley's statement of his sinful condition at full value and added to it, forgetting that Wesley had not given a single serious instance of what the sin was, and that Wesley was chronically given to self-depreciation in telling of his spiritual states. As the case stands, the best course to take with all this period of falling away is to forget it, or at least to give it no appreciable weight. We know what Wesley was when he went to

Charterhouse and we know what he was when he came out. He went in a well-trained boy, physically and mentally sound, and he came out with both physical and mental soundness intact. His own statements about his loss of religious experience at school and Tyerman's statements, which were stronger than Wesley's—Wesley says that his sins were not scandalous in the eyes of the world—are the result of the attempt to fit the boy's experience into a dogmatic system. Wesley had in his Epworth days a stiff religious training. It was not to be expected that he would find such training anywhere else, certainly not in a boys' school. He would at once notice the difference. Charterhouse boys were given to the fagging system that prevailed at the time all over England—the older boys' compelling the younger to render them menial and even degrading services, a most excellent device for creating and developing bullies and yet of some worth as teaching youngsters to take care of themselves in outwitting the bullies. In an atmosphere like this the boy Wesley would probably find new trials and temptations. He probably reacted against bullying as any boy of spirit would. To take a self-depreciating statement, however, as if it meant a lapse into sin, under such circumstances, is absurd. The early Methodists laid such stress on conversion as a turning from evil after experience of evil, that to deal with a conversion without such emphasis on knowledge of evil was difficult for them. So, if one had committed no transgressions externally, one must have committed them inwardly. Wesley left Methodism a worthy statement of the ideal in the religious training of children, but his own practice and his own statements have done harm. He probably had the yeasty ferment of soul which marks all adolescents and construed this as a lack of assurance of salvation, or, worse, the loss of it. To Tyerman at least Wesley simply had to be a sinner in order to be afterward a Christian. Tyerman could not see that a Christian could have lofty ascents into the upper air of religious experience without necessarily starting from the mire of a swamp. Wesley's experience started from a plateau of high living. Here is how Wesley wrote about the Charterhouse life in after years: "I believe until I was ten years old I had not sinned away that washing of the Holy Ghost which was given me in baptism, having been strictly educated and carefully taught that I could only be saved by 'universal obedience,' by keeping all the commandments of God in the meaning of which I was diligently instructed. And those instructions so far as they respected outward duties and sins I gladly received and often thought of. But all that was said to me of inward obedience or holiness, I neither understood nor remembered. The next six or seven years were spent at school, where outward restraints being removed, I was much more negligent than before even of outward duties; and almost continually guilty of outward sins, which I knew to be such though they were not scandalous in the eyes of the world. However, I still read the Scriptures and said my prayers morning and evening. And what I now hoped to be saved by was (1) not being so bad as other people, (2) having still a kindness for religion, and (3) reading the Bible, going to church, and saying my prayers."

I seek to put stress on all this because the religious experience of Wesley is regarded as classic among all students of the method of the human seizure of the divine. Deep as may have been Wesley's distress over his spiritual condition, a distress which recurred until in his wide campaigning he became too preoccupied to dwell much on his own spiritual condition, he does not seem to have gone through a darkness of soul like that of Bunyan, for example. He said repeatedly that throughout all his life he had never lost a night's sleep from any physical or mental pain until far along in years. Statements like these, which slip into the *Journal* almost inadvertently, give us a hint of a background in our reflection on his experiences of spiritual distress. Coming back for the moment to Charterhouse, Wesley throughout his life used to make it a point to visit the old grounds at least once a year. There is nothing to indicate that he did this with any other purpose than to revive old memories, certainly nothing to hint that he did it with the purpose of brooding over a period of sin.

One further consideration makes us chary of accepting Wesley's own interpretation of his adolescent days. There can be no doubt as to the thoroughgoing rigor of the Epworth training. From the date of the fire Susanna Wesley had felt a special responsibility for the religious nurture of the brand plucked from the burning. It is not easy to suppose that Wesley lost the effects of this training as soon as he got away to school. It was not the type of training easily lost, unless by reaction or revolt against overstrictness, and the extreme strictness was in the formal and systematic regularities. There was too much of this, but the harm was that Wesley never cast any of it out. He was oversystematic to the end of his life. System nearly ruined him. His father once said to him that not everything in this world was settled by logic. It would have been well for John if he had learned earlier to weigh what his father had said. Mrs. Wesley evidently had nearly systematized the life—at least in the phase of liveliness—out of herself. There is not much that suggests sprightliness or buoyancy in what we know of her. A son at all like herself would likely have had moments of unhappiness at Charterhouse, but not necessarily because of sin. It is from the Charterhouse period that the good story about Doctor Sacheverell dates. Sacheverell was the High Churchman for whom, according to John Wesley's *History of England*, Samuel Wesley wrote a speech by which Doctor Sacheverell profited. John went to Doctor Sacheverell for a small favor and got a mental bullying. When the little Wesley stood before the bully, he was met with: "You are too young to go to a university. You cannot know Latin and Greek yet. Go back to school." "I looked up at him as David looked at Goliath and despised him."

Oxford

At seventeen Wesley entered Oxford. Here again we find an institution of the eighteenth century which has been a favorite object of attack. To read some authors one would suppose the eighteenth century to have been hopelessly sunk in iniquity, and the universities of the time to have been idling places of dissolute young men, who counted upon their wealth or their social position to give them whatever support they needed through life. Relatively speaking, Oxford University probably did its work as well for its time as it did for later times. Gibbon has written drastically of the Oxford of his day, but Gibbon got his training there. It is quite common for brilliant students to go far beyond what gave them their start, and then look back superciliously on the beginnings. The educational institutions of the eighteenth century appear quite infantile to us of today, but that is because we look back through a larger educational experience than that of the teachers of two hundred and fifty years ago. We forget that the knowledge of today is the result of the labors of the men who came up through the older training. Most of us have merely entered as beneficiaries into the present-day treasures, whereas the strugglers with the older knowledge were working toward the present knowledge as discoverers. The older knowledge was at least provocative enough to start men toward something better. Wesley was critical of the college training of his day, but Wesley was to a degree the product of the training itself. He had by native endowment an enormous curiosity of the stamp we call scientific, and came out of Oxford with that curiosity livelier than ever. Oxford never has laid the chief emphasis on the natural sciences, but she is surely entitled to credit for what her sons have done in the field of such sciences. She has given them an ideal of the things worth while in life—a basis of thoroughgoing method, an enthusiasm for learning on its own account, a wide framework of general understanding. If we are to study profitably the influence of Oxford on Wesley, the sensible course would seem to be to look at Wesley as well as at Oxford. Even if we grant that Oxford gave him nothing that he did not have before, it certainly provided the conditions under which what was in him came out into expression. It will not do to say that Wesley became what he was in spite of Oxford. Here again we have to look at Wesley's own attitude toward Oxford. He was glad enough to live and work there. Even when his father and brother urged him with all their persuasive power to apply for the parish of Epworth, he preferred to stay at Oxford. Both Samuel, Sr., and Samuel, Jr.—remarkable for forthrightness of speech— seized upon this desire as proof of John's eagerness to remain in circumstances and environment which he liked best. John made no pretense of denying that he liked Oxford better than Epworth. At the time he thought of his father's parishioners as a rough set. He did not foresee that all his own life was to be passed in dealing with rougher sets than any he would meet around Epworth, and he did feel that much of his training could be used to better advantage at Oxford than at Epworth. We have noted his father's anxiety to have him become Fellow at Oxford. John showed no slackness in seeking the honor and opportunity, and having secured the post remained at Oxford till he was well past thirty years of age. The time came when Wesley bade farewell, virtually forever, to academic shades. We are not on that account to minimize the truth that those same circles put something into his life, or brought something out of it, for which the world cannot be too grateful.

Just one further word about getting a just perspective on institutions like Oxford. We cannot go into details of Wesley's life there, a residence which covered a period of possibly three generations of college students. We cannot judge any institution by the content of what was taught alone, the vital question always being as to what use was made of that content. Benjamin Franklin, in whose experiments with electricity Wesley was always interested, would for a few minutes be an object of mirth if he were to reap-

pear on a college campus with his kite and key. To find Franklin's
real contemporaries of today, however, we should have to go into
the laboratories where the most advanced experiments are being
performed. Something of the same is to be said of Oxford in earlier
centuries. The content of the teaching was not itself considerable,
but that content was awakening some minds and putting them on
the path of larger truth. Wesley took with him to Oxford an
insatiable intellectual curiosity and came away with it more marked
than when he went in. It is true that in his later years he professed
to value knowledge for the use that could be made of it for the
help of men, but the other motive of knowledge for its own sake
is clear enough. For example, he said in his later years that the
study of medicine, or of medicines, had been the chief avocation of
his life. It was out of such researches that his appalling book of
prescriptions came. Now, whenever Wesley deals with this field,
the insatiable restless curiosity of the born knowledge-seeker is
apparent. Likewise with what we today should call religious psychology. Then there were his reflections on the Copernican theory,
which can hardly be said to have had a practical aim. In a word,
Oxford deepened, if anything, Wesley's knowledge for the sake
of knowledge itself, and that has been one of the aims of Oxford
from the beginning. Or perhaps the aim would be better stated as
the pursuit of knowledge for its larger cultural results without
overemphasis on the immediately practical.

Yet in dealing with John Wesley we no sooner say this than
we have to turn at once to that ruling passion for, or slavery to,
system which ruled him every minute of his waking life, a system
which would have to be called chiefly practical. As it happened,
Oxford did something for that too. While at Oxford Wesley served
as a chairman or moderator of a debating society which was an outstanding feature of the institution. It was the duty of this func-
tionary to sum up the discussions and point out fallacies and inade-
quacies of statement. We cannot imagine any student who needed
such exercise less than did Wesley, for it increased an orderliness
of mind which was by this time fast getting too orderly. Wesley,
however, then and afterward thought differently. He attributed
his power to detect weaknesses in an opponent's argument to the
training in this Oxford group. He would have done well to have
kept constantly in mind his father's word that not everything in this
world is settled by logic.

The foundation laid at Oxford in formal intellectual training must have been solid. For years the two brothers, John and Charles, used to do a large share of their conversing with each other in Latin. That means much for the training of their minds in exact scholarship. Who in these days thinks of studying Latin with any notion of mastering it well enough to speak it? If John set out to master Latin, he probably mastered it down to the last possible detail. Anybody who will glance through the Greek grammar which he prepared while he was working at his Methodist enterprises will marvel at the exactness of the scholarship. The basis of all this type of achievement, as likewise for the conquest of German, French, Italian, and Spanish, was laid in the Oxford days. Whoever taught John Wesley to study did so by arousing in him an appetite for knowledge which never could be satisfied, or, at least, did not so teach him as to dull that appetite. Wesley once declared that he had to give up geometry because it was costing him too much in the time taken from spiritual exercises. He spoke as if this were a veritable sacrifice.

All such considerations we have to remember when we read later Wesley's disparagements of learning and his contemptuous word about the futility of the British Museum. A good deal of such disparagement in all times has come from those who have not been themselves learned, and has been a symptom of an inferiority complex. Wesley, on the other hand, knew what learning was, knew it even in its limitations. His disparagement came out of his preoccupation with the work of the divine in human lives. He saw the possibilities before the untrained mind which sought to open itself to the will of God. He saw too the hindrances which intellectual pride sometimes puts in the way of understanding of the divine. As soon, however, as the untrained—even illiterate—life turned toward the divine, Wesley sought to put before that life all treasures for the dawning spiritual intelligence. The fifty volumes of the Christian library which Wesley edited are sufficient witness and testimony at this point—full of selections, for the most part, of the best of all the ages of religious thinking.

One result Oxford did not achieve for Wesley. It developed his tendency to system, taught him the necessity of the widest possible reading, especially in the pursuit of historical subjects, and helped him to a wonderfully clear power of comprehensive summary. It did not, however, make him a brooding thinker, with ability for sustained attention upon a problem to which he might set his mind. Wesley's intellect was notable for the movement

toward decisions.   On all the questions which came before him he
seemed to think he had to take a vote.   He did not like to leave
anything open.   To be sure, his mind did move by slow ripening to
mature convictions through the years, but ripened usually under
the pressure of events.   He used to say of himself that he was more
by himself during his periods of travel, and had more time for study
than any other man whom he knew.   It is significant though that
when he acquired a "chaise" in his later years, he sealed up one side
of it to be used for book shelves and writing desk.   He had to have
something in his hands—a book or a pen.   A statue of the under-
lying conception of Rodin's "The Thinker" would never have been
appropriate for Wesley.   System!   System!   System!   Every hour
had its allotted task.   It is not too much to say that if he was considering the arguments of his Calvinist friends, he would probably
reflect on predestination from ten in the morning till eleven, and
on free grace from eleven till noon.   At Oxford he reached the
determination not to see any would-be companions in conversation
who would not turn their attention to the same serious themes in
which he was interested.   There must have been a season along in
those years when, except to a few friends, he was almost intolerable.
Yet it seems strange even to suspect this.   Of arresting presence,
with fine features, with a lithe body kept supple by such splendid
exercises as walking and swimming, he was of the type to attract
attention and to win friends.   He must have missed a good deal at
Oxford in not learning to talk in haphazard conversation with all
sorts and conditions of men.

We do not wish to anticipate, but we cannot help letting our
minds play a little with the idea of what a conversation between
Wesley and Samuel Johnson would have been like—if it could have
been carried through to an end.   In some respects the minds of
these two were similar; both were men of wide-ranging observation though they were not likely to look long at the same objects.
The conversation probably never would have come to a natural
end. Wesley could not have stood Johnson long enough; he could
not have endured Johnson's lack of system, to say nothing of an
untidiness which is forever associated with the memory of Johnson.
It is to be feared that Wesley would have thought Johnson's inner
man untidy, though he did respect the essential greatness.

All these points of view seem important to me for the basis
they supply in the consideration of Wesley's religious experience.
We are about to come to the Holy Club, and the beginnings of

Methodism. Whatever the religious life and career of John Wesley, it did not make him anything other than he had been from the beginning so far as his fundamental qualities are concerned. The contribution which Wesley made on the side of religious experience was largely in his teaching about what he called Christian Perfection. As we look back now we can discern pretty clearly that, however we ourselves may interpret this experience, or way of life, or ideal, it was what Wesley was seeking for from the beginning of his serious religious strivings at Oxford and long before, though his own aim did not become sharply manifest till later.

A certain form of perfection Wesley strove after in everything he did, and that from the boyhood years at Oxford—the perfection of doing the best possible in whatever he undertook. I say "doing the best possible," for everything significant in Wesley's life was something that could be put into practice, or about which something could be done. Even in the mechanical phases of his work he could not endure to have anything left at loose ends. Admittedly, this may lead to leaving some of the most important matters at loose ends, but the passion for orderliness can have marked spiritual outcomes. It can be described as a passion to go the full length, to do all for the ideal aimed at, the temper being that of the scientist or the artist, who will not stop short of perfection so far at least as his intention and determination are concerned.

Before leaving the more intellectual side of the life at Oxford, I wish to call attention to a letter written by John to his mother at Epworth from Oxford. The date is 1725, the theme is the idealistic philosophy of Berkeley. John was at the time about twenty-two years old. On a previous page I mentioned the fact that some writers on Wesley will have it that the relation of John to his mother was what the present-day psychologists call "mother-fixation"—the life of the son being so controlled by the will of the mother and by such responsive dependence on the mother that the son all but lives in the life of the mother. Here in this letter is an instance of complete companionship between a mother and a son, a companionship the like of which it would be hard to find in accounts of such intimacies, but a companionship for which "fixation" is not a happy term. For there is no suggestion here of anything but what might be called a lofty friendship—a son of twenty-two talking to his mother on a plane of mutual understanding. Understanding of what? Of a philosophy which, though this may not have been surmised at the time, was indelibly to mark the idealistic course of philosophy for generations. Berkeley is today, philosophically speaking, a vital figure, so vital as almost to be called a contemporary of many teachers in foremost philosophical chairs. The son simply assumes that the mother could understand philosophy—as indeed, she could—and the mother receives the letter as if it were entirely in the customary course of ordinary events. There is indeed nothing remarkable about John's criticism of Berkeley as to its content. Berkeley moved in deeper channels than John fathomed, but that is not quite to the point. His criticism is quite as sound as most of such criticism of Berkeley. It has all the marks both of John's and of Susanna's form of reasoning—strict logic where logic may fail because of its strictness, or just because it is logic. What we have is two persons communing on the plane of reasoning of about the same high order as that which Newton and Halley had together when Halley was urging Newton to seek a mathematical proof for Kepler's discovery about the courses of planets as ellipses in their travels around the sun. It would not have argued mother-fixation if Newton had been a woman and Halley his son. That is to say, we are dealing here with an intellectual communion in which there is nothing in the content to suggest any of the modern psychological lingo. We have two minds —John Wesley and his mother—meeting together on a theme in an unusual realm for such discussion; the two minds united, not in a queer fixation, but in mutual assumption by each that the other knew what he was talking about.

Christ Church, November 22, 1725.

Dear Mother,—I must beg leave to assure you that before I received yours I was fully convinced of two things,—first, that Mr. Berkeley's notion, which at first sight appeared very plausible—as, indeed, an ingenious disputant will make almost anything appear—was utterly groundless; and that he either advanced a palpable falsehood, or said nothing at all: . . . Mr. Berkeley's reasons on a second reading I found to be mere fallacy, though very artfully disguised. From one or two you may easily judge of what kind his other arguments are. He introduces Hylas charging Philonous with skepticism for denying the existence of sensible things: to which Philonous replies that, if denying the existence of sensible things constitute a skeptic, he will prove those to be such who assert sensible things to be material; for if all sensible things are material, then, if it be proved that nothing material exists, it will follow that no sensible thing exists; and that nothing material can exist he undertakes to demonstrate.

Matter, says he (by which you must mean something sensible, or else how came you to know of it?), you define as a solid extended substance, the existence of which is exterior to the mind and does in no ways depend on its being perceived; but if it appear that no sensible thing is exterior to the mind, your supposition of a sensible substance independent from it is a plain inconsistency.

Sensible things are those which are perceived by the senses; everything perceived by the senses is immediatly perceived (for the senses make no inferences, that is the province of reason); everything immediately perceived is a sensation; no sensation can exist but in a mind; *ergo* no sensible thing can exist but in a mind, which was to be proved.

Another of his arguments to the same purpose is this: Nothing can exist in fact the very notion of which implies a contradiction; nothing is impossible to conceive, unless the notion of it imply a contradiction. But 'tis absolutely impossible to conceive anything existing otherwise than in some mind, because whatever anyone conceives is at that instant in his mind. Wherefore as matter is supposed to be a substance exterior to all minds, and as 'tis evident nothing can be even conceived exterior to all minds, 'tis equally evident there can be no such thing in being as matter.

Or such: Everything conceived is a conception, every conception is a thought, and every thought is in some mind; wherefore to say you can conceive a thing which exists in no mind is to say you conceive what is not conceived at all.

The flaws in his arguments, which do not appear at a distance, (may be) easily seen on a nearer inspection. He says, artfully enough in the preface, (in) order to give his proofs their full force, it will be necessary to place them in as many different lights as possible. By this means the object grows too big for the eye; whereas, had he contracted it into a narrower compass, the mind might readily have taken it in at one view and discerned where the failing lay.

How miserably does he play with the words "idea" and "sensation"! Everything immediately perceived is a sensation. Why? Because a sensation is what is immediately perceived by the senses—that is, in plain English, everything immediately perceived is immediately perceived; a most admirable discovery, the glory of which I dare say no one will envy him.

And again: all sensible qualities are ideas, and no idea exists but in some mind—that is, all sensible qualities are objects of the mind in thinking, and no image of an external object painted on a mind exists otherwise than in some mind. And what then?

Rather jaunty criticism this, with its imputation of falsehood to Berkeley, and its summary dismissals of profound reasoning with waves of the hand. Jaunty, but hardly fixation.

Coming back now to the beginning of the quest for perfection, we note that this began in the reading of books on the devotional life by William Law and Jeremy Taylor. It would be a wild misreading of the spiritual plight of Wesley to think of him as agonizing in distress over personal transgressions. It is here that writers like Tyerman have so badly misled us. Such men, looking upon the struggles of soul through which Wesley passed, think they must find some adequate cause for the distress in the recollection of past evil. If souls are in sorrow, such interpreters assume there must be some specific cause for the sorrow. Now, as actual psychological fact, those whose lives have been passed in transgression are not always those who feel the deepest sorrow, for transgression is likely to blunt the sensitiveness out of which sorrow comes. Hence the paradox that those who personally know the least of sin by experience feel most deeply their falling short of the ideal. The man who has made the fewest mistakes may be the one who sees most clearly the distance between himself and the ideal. Wesley's strain and tension came out of a pure mind's realization of how far away was the ideal. His search for the truth meant that he already had it, at least in the realization of its worth. The scientist who strives for the last item of knowledge relevant to his search is not driven by the haunting spell of past mistakes. He is drawn from ahead and from above. The artist who seeks perfection in a curve of beauty is not under the bondage of past errors from which he is struggling to shake himself free. He is under the spell of the perfect curve and will not be content till he can draw or paint or carve it. He may never achieve it, but he will die trying. How utterly absurd it would be to surmise that the artist must have sinned against artistic idealism and be seeking to atone for that sin in his unresting quest for perfect beauty! Now, a reading of what Wesley said and did during the days at the Holy Club is amply explained by this interpretation of an indefatigable, persistent, unrelenting search for the utmost in religious experience. It might be better to say the "utmost attainable," but that would not quite express the Wesley mood. He was determined to have it whether it was attainable or not.

Sir Isaac Newton's famous remark about his own ignorance is suggestively relevant here. Newton said of himself that he was like a child gathering a few pebbles from the shore of the ocean of truth, while the vast ocean itself stretched away illimitably. Newton's spirit was not that of acquiescence with the handful of pebbles.

No more daring explorer ever sailed the ocean of truth itself than Newton. So in the world of religious knowledge Wesley was as humble as Newton before the vastness of the sea of truth, and as determined as Newton to add to his own store.

The theological basis of the search was works like William Law on *Christian Perfection,* Jeremy Taylor on *Holy Living,* in the study of which Wesley was helped by his mother's discerning comments—writings of the Church Fathers, notably those of Clement of Alexandria. In studying Law especially Wesley had a strange experience. By a paradoxical fatality it often happens that the seekers after the most spiritual illumination descend to the use of weapons in controversy which are almost if not quite carnal. Wesley was deeply indebted to Law, but somehow got it into his head that in correspondence over holiness Law had not been quite fair with him, or not faithful in pointing out his (Wesley's) shortcomings. Whereupon he addressed to Law a letter which was impertinent, not to say impudent. In the temper and content of the correspondence Law had the better of it, though he himself later may have wandered far into mystic vagaries. Perhaps, after all, such acrimonies are to be expected. The searchers after the highest religious experience, like those after the highest in science and art, get desperately serious. At first Wesley's striving after holiness was directed more Godward than manward, and more toward himself than toward his fellow men. Anyhow, the squabble with Law was at the same instant genuinely true to Wesley and thoroughly deplorable.

Charles Wesley—not John—was, strictly speaking, the founder of the Holy Club, which at first was nothing more than a group for the study of and development of the higher religious life. Morgan, Delamotte, and Ingham were names afterward to become well known among Methodists, and a little later we find George Whitefield in the circle. An instance of the Wesley democratic spirit appeared in this relation to Whitefield. Whitefield was a servitor at Pembroke College, working his way through college by lowly services rendered to other students more fortunate than himself in social standing and material resources. Wesley came from more favored social surroundings. Never from the first, however, did either John or Charles Wesley show the slightest consciousness of social superiority. The Wesleys were by breeding and conviction Tories, High-Churchmen, Monarchists. Not a trace of the aristocratic aloofness appears in the personal attitude of either of them

toward other men. Here again was a mark of the earnestness of
their search for the highest. They assumed from the outset that
the Divine Spirit could speak through all sorts and conditions of
men. Moreover, they would not allow anything to stand in the
way of the Christian brotherhood in which they both believed. It
is interesting to recall that as a matter of fact Whitefield seemed
in the after years to enjoy most the society of the highborn, while
the personal contacts in which Wesley seemed to take delight were
with the lowlier. This may not be altogether strange. The Countess of Huntingdon made more of an appeal to George Whitefield
than she ever did to John Wesley. It was an advantage to Wesley
in dealing with the masses of people who became Methodists, masses
that never had the advantages of a home of fine culture and high
traditions, to belong himself to what was in the best sense an aristocratic family. He was from the first devoid of all fear, of all taint
of inferiority, in meeting the socially high-placed.

The words "Holy" and "Methodists," given to the little
Oxford group of those seeking after the highest righteousness, were
exactly descriptive and profoundly prophetic. The aim from the
beginning was holiness. It was a happy providence that linked the
suggestion of method with the pursuit of holiness. Religion has
in all times suffered from those who in a mistaken fashion have
waited for the coming of the divine influx, from those who have
wrongly used the passage which tells that the wind bloweth where
it listeth, that men hear the sound thereof and cannot tell whence
it cometh and whither it goeth. To be sure, the genuine mystics in
all periods of the history of the Church have girded themselves for
their task by the most earnest and careful preparation, with a system
almost savoring of technique; but the notion is quite common that
inner religious experience is largely a series of impressions or of
states of soul, which come of themselves. In his work as leader of
Methodism Wesley had through an anxious crisis, or succession of
crises, to meet quietists, who taught that the Christian must not
seek to attain to religious peace or effectiveness by any means whatever, not even by the so-called means of grace. The Holy Club's
career was chiefly a search for the right means of attaining holiness—
regularity of worship, system in study and prayer, persistence in
right living before the world.

It is odd to reflect that the little group at Oxford ran in a kind
of resumé about all the stages by which the Church as a whole has
sought after success in Christian living—study, practice in specific

religious exercises, the creation of situations leading to sudden illumination. Among other practices was something closely resembling Romish asceticism. It is ordinarily understood that Wesley's asceticism was merely extreme frugality, for the sake of better use of money than in customary expenditures, as when he wrote to his mother to tell her how much money he was saving for benevolent uses by not having his hair cut more than once a year.

Wesley, however, seemed to have a positive relish for ascetic sacrifices. It was this apparent relish which later led to the charge that his asceticism had a Romish taint. There was certainly a trace of the abnormal in it. Among the most devout members of the Club was William Morgan, who was at first thought to have died through the severity of the abstention and self-denials which he practiced as a member of the Club. Mr. Morgan, Sr., father of William, at first believed this, but changed his criticism of the Club to enthusiastic praise when John Wesley wrote him a statement of the facts in the case. Still there was enough stress laid on self-denial in itself to arouse suspicion that it had gone to absurd and irrational lengths.

Other exercises of the Club were continued prayer and praise in the meetings till emotionalism broke all barriers. At one such meeting an almost terrifying burst of feeling swept everything before it. The members broke at once into the *Te Deum,* which has likely never been sung with more sincere fervor than on that occasion. The account of the meeting, though, does not suggest the healthiest methods or the soundest results. We must concede, however, the measurably well-regulated expression of the ecstasy in the singing of the *Te Deum.* It would not have been surprising if the feeling on such occasions had found vent in incoherent ejaculations without any spiritual worth whatever.

More important still were the positive works of human helpfulness and relief to which the members devoted themselves. We repeat that they never lost sight of the demand upon pure religion and undefiled, to visit the widows and the fatherless in their affliction as well as to keep oneself unspotted from the world. The visits of the group were chiefly to those in prison, many of them under sentences of death. The report of what the Wesleys were doing reached the Epworth Rectory, with the hint that perhaps John and Charles were touched with fanaticism. Samuel, Sr., at once responded with his entire approval of the course of his sons.

It has been objected that the intention of all these visits of mercy was the salvation of the souls of the visitors, rather than the good of the visited. Avowedly the aim of the young men was their own spiritual welfare. It is true that the chief work of Wesley began after his regard was directed more away from himself to the needs of other men, but it is also true that, if these seekers were trying to develop their own religious forces by ministering to the needs of their fellow men, they were on the right track. Not all searchers for inner life thus seized so unerringly upon the true path.

Inasmuch as the men of the Holy Club were striving to aid the distressed, some wise instinct or wise advice set before them the sufferers worst off. The laws of England against criminal offenses were in the eighteenth century indescribably severe, and some offenses then, such as indebtedness, would not be called offenses now. Jails are never pleasant, and the jails then could never by any stretch of charitableness be called humane, or even decent. When John Wesley came in the later times to commend the work of John Howard in prison reform, he could speak unsparingly of the terrors of jails, out of his own experience in visiting them from the days of the Holy Club on through many decades. Possibly, with the exception of John Howard and hardened criminals, John Wesley knew more about the inside of jails than any man of his time.

The kind of experience the early Methodist leaders used to undergo can be at least glanced at from a passage in Charles Wesley's *Journal* under date of July 19, 1738. This was long after the period of the Holy Club, but it does show something of the task the young men set themselves, something of the social conditions of England, and something also of the frightful limitations of the understanding of Charles and presumably of the others also as to the implications of the gospel. Charles had become interested in the spiritual state of a Negro and of prisoners named Read, Newington, and Hudson who were under sentence of death. He went with one or two friends to the place of their execution. Following is the exact quotation:

The black had spied me coming out of the coach and saluted me with his looks. As often as his eyes met mine he smiled with the most composed, delightful countenance I ever saw. Read caught hold of my hand in a transport of joy. Newington seemed perfectly pleased. Hudson declared he was never better, or more at ease, in mind and body. None showed any natural terror of death: no fear, or crying, or tears. All expressed their desire of our following them to paradise.

I never saw such calm triumph, such incredible indifference to dying. We sang several hymns: particularly

> "Behold the Saviour of mankind,
> Nailed to the shameful tree,"

and the hymn entitled "Faith in Christ," which concludes,

> "A guilty, weak, and helpless worm
> Into Thy hands I fall:
> Be Thou my life, my righteousness,
> My Jesus, and my all."

We prayed Him, in earnest faith, to receive their spirits. I could do nothing but rejoice; kissed Newington and Hudson; took leave of each in particular. Mr. Broughton bade them not to be surprised when the cart should draw away. They cheerfully replied they should not: expressed some concern as to how we should get back to our coach. We left them going to meet their Lord, ready for the Bridegroom. When the cart drew off not one stirred, or struggled for life, but meekly gave up their spirits. Exactly at twelve they were turned off. I spoke a few suitable words to the crowd; and returned, full of peace and confidence in our friends' happiness. That hour under the gallows was the most blessed hour of my life.

Now, just a remark or two about all this. We have here an instance and illustration of work like that of the Holy Club during all the time the Club existed. To begin with, the picture here is very vivid, though some of the phrasing is queer. What are we to make of encouragement to criminals about to be hanged not to feel "surprised" when the wagon should be pulled from under them and they left dangling in the air? Or what are we to make of the statement that these dying men were so at peace with God that they did not struggle in throes that are entirely beyond the control of the will, being involuntary muscular contractions? The story is one of the complete absorption of Charles Wesley in producing what he thought of as a personal spiritual result.

We have here an example of the length to which an individual emphasis in religious experience can go. It is a legitimate charge against the Wesleyan Revival that, so far as its direct and avowed aim was concerned, the stress on the personal aspects was wholly out of proportion. There is not the slightest sign of any qualm or question here or elsewhere as to whether the doomed men were unjustly condemned or not. Charles Wesley was presumably as kindly a man as was to be found in England. Yet he took the social

callousness as a matter of course. The assumption here is that the
men were dying justly. Perhaps they were, but, with the enormous
list of capital offenses at the time, we cannot help wondering why
question never seems to have crept into his mind. The acquiescence here in a barbarous system almost passes belief. Moreover,
that presence of a crowd at the execution is indicative, though public executions are not even yet altogether a thing of the past. The
worst of the story, however, is yet to come. The earlier part of the
entry from which I have quoted is as follows: "By half-hour past
ten we came to Tyburn, and waited till eleven: *then were brought
the children appointed to die.*"

Remember that the close of the entry was, "That hour under
the gallows was the most blessed hour of my life." Take this entry
in its context as a revelation of the spirit of the times—with its overemphasis on a strained emotional state, with the casualness of the
reference to the children who were to be "turned off," and it ranks
high as a narrative of horrors.

The brighter side is that the souls of condemned men stand
out as having such value in the sight of these workers. Of course
those about to be hanged had the opportunity of receiving the
last rites at the hands of regular chaplains, but these victims seem
to have refused such services. Probably the services were perfunc-
tory enough. In any event, the object lesson of men like Charles
Wesley and his companions, standing by to help men about to be
executed, proclaimed a message of no small importance. This was
part of the Methodist contribution to democracy, this assumption
of the worth of anybody's soul. Only I wish Charles could have
found some other expression than "the black."

GEORGIA

We come now to one of the most perplexing and, in a way,
distressing periods in the life of Wesley—his sojourn in America
from November 10, 1735, till February 1, 1738, including the time
taken to go out and return. The journey outward required till
February 4, 1736. To get the true perspective on this period we
may perhaps not go far astray in calling it an enterprise of the Holy
Club. The Rev. Dr. John Burton, a trustee of the Georgia enterprise, to be further mentioned in a moment, had it in mind to try
to persuade the Holy Club of Oxford to go out to Georgia. After
some wavering consideration three men—John Wesley, whose
mother approved the plan; Charles Wesley and Benjamin Ingham,

all intimately familiar with the Holy Club—accepted the invitations and set sail for Georgia.

The Georgia movement was the outcome of the interest of James Oglethorpe in prison conditions of his day, and in the general economic situation in England, at bottom responsible for those conditions. Oglethorpe was a member of Parliament for thirty-two years and had become aroused by parliamentary investigations into the conditions of prisons, especially those in which honest debtors were confined. He became convinced that the problem of these debtors could not be fully solved until something had been done to deal with unemployment. The debtors discharged from prison could not find work, and so, through walking the streets, were likely to yield to temptations to steal. A company was formed with the purely philanthropic purpose of establishing a community at what we now call Savannah which would give these persons a new start and a fresh chance. It is not fair to say that Georgia was colonized by "jailbirds." The colonists were jailbirds in the same fashion that Samuel Wesley, Sr., had been—in prison for debt—and there were others besides discharged prisoners who sought opportunity in the new colony, among them Protestants who were seeking ampler religious freedom. The plan was, on the part of the benevolently-minded persons who started the enterprise, to give the adventurers free passage out and to help them get a foothold in various forms of agriculture, including cotton and silk culture. The rum traffic was to be strictly controlled, the Indians dealt with fairly, receiving the same justice as the Englishmen. Slavery was at first prohibited, the prohibitory action dating from 1735. Oglethorpe all his life stood against slavery, but by 1750 the act was repealed. John and Charles Wesley went as ministers of the Church of England to give the colonists the kind of religious service to which they had been accustomed. At no time during the stay of John Wesley did the community or communities—for there was another settlement at Frederica, one hundred miles from Savannah—number more than a thousand persons. The chief task of Wesley, according to his understanding before he left England, was spiritual supervision of the colony and a ministry to the Indians. In addition to all this, after the return of Charles to England he served after a fashion as a sort of secretary to James Oglethorpe, the governor. Georgia was founded with as pure unselfishness as any colony in America. The ideal was noble, but did not take account of practical difficulties. We are interested especially in what Wesley encountered and in the effect of Georgia on the development of his religious leadership and experience.

Wesley said he went to Georgia to save his own soul—an expression which has led to no end of misunderstanding. The word is sometimes treated as if Wesley were like a penitent undergoing some difficult task for the sake of working out an atonement for a wrong or sinful life. Wesley usually talked of himself in terms of artificial and forced self-depreciation. There were two poles to his religious life, the inner and the outer, with the inner at the outset almost frightfully overemphasized. Let us remember the long background of the religious struggles of one whose ancestors for generations had sought for the best in religion, that best being conceived of as what might almost be called an immediate experience of God. Wesley's "saving his own soul" meant primarily the search for the utmost possible in the knowledge of God and the emotional warmth and glow which he was sure would come with that knowledge. The story of the earlier years of his ministry is that of an effort to get the two poles of the experience into right relation to one another—love of God balanced with work for men—or of the events by which these two poles were brought into right adjustment. Wesley, indeed, said that he went to Georgia to save his own soul, but he also said that he went that he might labor wholly for the glory of the Lord.

The voyage out lasted from November till the following February. At once Wesley gave himself to systematic improvement of himself for the tasks ahead of him. Every minute of the day had its assigned duty—prayer, meditation, study of German, Latin, French, Italian. A record of times at prayer was kept in a diary, which afterward formed the base for the *Journal*. I have counted through page after page the recorded periods of prayer in specimen days: the entries were seldom under four and often went to seven. I admit that the exercise of counting thus was not healthy; it was about like counting the times in a day a man might avow interest in his best friend, or express love for his wife.

The ship was well fitted out as ships went in those days. The adventurers for the Holy Club—for that is what these young men were—could not have got through what they did in study and in instruction to the passengers if they had not been in fair comfort. In a storm, however, there was discomfort enough, and danger enough. It is supposed by those who have been best able to understand the Wesley psychology that John had a fear of the sea, amounting to something like what we should today call an obsession or a complex. Just how Wesley conquered that complex is not altogether clear, but we can at least guess that he won by going ahead in sea journeys, complex or no complex. By the time he had in the later years taken over forty journeys across the Irish Sea, some of them in extreme peril, he had certainly got rid of the complex. On this point of the fear of the sea probably too much stress has been laid anyhow. Whatever the cause of the fear, it was natural enough. There was not sufficient reason to make the fear a sign of lack of reliance on God. The sailors had to do their work whether they were half-crazed with fright or not. As for the Moravians, their quiet self-control, their singing in the storm were admirable, but not any more admirable than Wesley's attempts at the same crisis to help those scared or sick. At this stage of his life as well as ofttimes later Wesley seemed to have a veritable zeal for disparaging himself. We note that in spite of his word that he had come to America to save his own soul—leaving us with the unpleasant suggestion that he was not thinking of anything or anybody except himself—he was spontaneously helpful. It was wholly natural for him to seek to be of any aid, and all forms of aid, to his fellow travelers. Some of the difficulty into which he got in Georgia came out of this irresistible desire to be of help. All of which must be reckoned in the account when we are inclined to construe too literally that statement about going to America to save his own soul.

Here, then, was this member of the Oxford Club, just a little beyond thirty years of age, going to a new land to set the principles of the Club—for that essentially was the aim of Wesley—with what might be called the real world before him. At Oxford he could at evening time retreat behind the shelter of his college doors, no matter how terrible the events he had passed through during the day. As a visitor to prisons he went into a world not his own, and went into it from the outside. In Georgia he had to be himself a part of the world to which he sought to minister.

There were on the vessel two women, altogether designing adventuresses, who, after the arrival in Georgia, gave him his first glimpse at how far such scheming persons can go. Professing desire for religious help, they filled the mind of both Wesleys with slanderous stories against Oglethorpe. They were apparently trying to get Oglethorpe into their own power for their own purposes, whatever those purposes were. The women acted in such irrational fashion that their schemes never have been altogether intelligible.   John Wesley was taken in by them, and for a time doubted the moral soundness of Oglethorpe, who was a straight soul in his personal morality.   In this gullibility Wesley did Oglethorpe a dire wrong and managed to get himself assaulted by one of the women, who attacked him with a pair of scissors.   The difficulty with such breaches of friendship is that they never thoroughly heal.   The good that came out of the experience was the vindication of Oglethorpe, the revelation of the possibility of such evil in women, and the opening of the eyes of Wesley to the fact that he could not trust his own complete good faith as a guarantee of the good faith of all whom he might meet.   The humiliating experience ought to have been at least significant enough to lead to that famous Methodist rule about conversing sparingly with women.

Another phase of experience that, as we look back, was well calculated to prepare at least in a small degree for the after-responsibilities was Wesley's various duties with the governor of the colony. The secretaryship was more properly the function of Charles, but Oglethorpe appears in general to have preferred John to Charles. There are still in existence official papers of Oglethorpe in the handwriting of John Wesley.   For example, on July 26, 1736, Oglethorpe wrote to his trustees: "I shall reduce the expense by all possible means, especially by encouraging the lazy to leave the colony."   Church, in his invaluable work on Oglethorpe, says that this letter is in the handwriting of John Wesley.   Wesley states that at periods he worked for stretches of six hours continuously with the governor, taking intervals now and again for prayer and praise. In spite of various embarrassing episodes due to the overstrain of Wesley's piety, Oglethorpe was a good associate for a member of the Holy Club.   He was of high ideals, ideals perhaps a trifle too exalted for his task as governor, and yet with a fund of sound, practical sense to which Wesley needed to be constantly exposed.   There is something about the character and career of James Oglethorpe which makes him of compelling interest after the lapse of two centuries.   One element is probably the uniqueness of his idea of colonization.   He recognized in his colonial sphere the opportunity of dealing with a social problem at home by handling the poor-debtor difficulty constructively, and of marking out a path for a noble course for England in serving backward peoples in her new lands, peoples like the American Indians.   Considering his long experience in Parliament, his connections with the trustees of the

Georgia Trust Fund in London, and his own remarkable personal qualities, he presented to Wesley an opportunity through daily association which was of the first order as a practical training in statesmanship. To be fully candid, we have to voice the opinion that Wesley must have been something of a trial to Oglethorpe, with his persistent pressure for religious exercises, some of which must, under the circumstances, have seemed artificial. Think of yielding to the request of a secretary that five minutes out of every working hour be given to prayer. Think too of Wesley's listening to wicked stories about the man who was virtually his chief. Oglethorpe recognized Wesley's many excellences but, after Wesley had left Georgia, gave it as his opinion that the coming spiritual adviser to the colony ought to be of mature age. John Wesley got more from Oglethorpe than Oglethorpe from him. In a wholly unconscious fashion Oglethorpe made a contribution to the Wesleyan Movement.

It was understood at the outset that Wesley's work was to be chiefly among the Indians. Here again we have the man of the Holy Club seeking ideal conditions for the spread of religious truth. Perhaps we should better say that he was seeking virgin minds whose acceptance of the gospel might throw light upon the gospel for the sake of the missionary himself. This is indeed warranted by Wesley's own statements, but we must be careful here. This self-centered intention was all within a life which was naturally given to doing good to men. Wesley assumed as a matter of course that he was to help men. We are not to take his extreme words like that of going to America to save his own soul as meaning that he was withdrawing into himself to seek salvation. Self-salvation was the center of his goal, but he was no more independent of the other center than an ellipse is independent of either of its foci when the gaze of the mathematician is fixed on the other.

As to the Indians, Wesley started to Georgia long before Rousseau had made popular the notion of the noble Red Man as the unspoiled child of nature, but he at first made the same mistake that Rousseau made—and made famous—that civilization had spoiled human life by its myriad and manifold shackles. He failed to see that the savage condition is one of conventions and laws and chains that put the savage into a slavery as heavy as that of civilization. From morning to night, and from night to morning, the savage—including the Red Indian—is at the mercy of customs and taboos and superstitions. He is just as much the product of all these

forces as the white man is the product of the social mysteries of
England or France. It was through a mind thus bound and ridden
that the Indians of Georgia had to get what they could out of Wesley's preaching. They did not get much. He spoke of them at first
in October, 1735, as having "no comments to construe away the
text of the Scripture; no vain philosophy to corrupt it; no luxuri-
ous, sensuous, covetous, ambitious expounders to soften its un-
pleasing truths. They have no party, no interest to serve, and are
therefore fit to receive the gospel in its simplicity. They are as
little children, humble, willing to learn, and eager to do the will
of God." In 1737 he wrote of them as "gluttons, thieves, dissem-
blers, liars, murderers of fathers, murderers of mothers, murderers
of their own children."

A good deal has been made of Lecky's statement that the
preaching of Wesley saved England from horrors like the Reign
of Terror in the French Revolution. This is an impressive utterance, possibly more rhetorical than historical. The second passage
above about the Indians, however, did, we may fairly believe, have
something to do with preserving the mind of England from the
wild nonsense of Rousseau about the mind of the savage as a guide
and norm for so-called civilized man. This description of the
Indians is unjust, but it is nearer actual fact than Rousseau's—
probably because founded more nearly on actual factual observation than on the fanciful speculations of Rousseau—though this is
not intended to minimize the importance of Rousseau's other
work. The picture of the Indians which Wesley drew of them
sitting on the banks of streams, looking now at one another, now at
the sky, and now at the bubbles on the water, was about the mildest
Wesley left us, and that was evidently written in contempt.

Wesley was not a success with Indians. Speaking of the total
situation in Georgia, Oglethorpe did more for the Red Man than
did Wesley. We have in the contrast between the two types of work
that between an intense idealism which is impatient of facts, and an
idealism a portion of the intensity of which seeks what is best to do
under given circumstances. Oglethorpe's work had its tragedies—
after Oglethorpe had gone—but it built on a sound basis of knowledge of the Indian character. Like so many other evangelistic leaders, Wesley had to learn that in the proclamation of truth an understanding of the mind receiving the truth is quite as important as
the mind of the one uttering it. This lesson Wesley did learn,
perhaps learned it too well, for we do not find after Wesley's return

to England any overwhelming interest in what we today think of as missionary work, work for the so-called backward peoples. It is true that he complained that he went out to America primarily to preach to the Indians and that he did not get a fair opportunity to do so, but he evidently did not regard Indian communities as a favorable evangelistic opportunity, just as in earlier years he pronounced the inhabitants around Epworth as hopeless from his point of view of himself as a preacher. It is true too that he seconded Coke's missionary enterprises, but not with any manifest feeling of his own responsibility. "Missionary" had a wide meaning in those days. The American Methodists almost immediately after their organization as a Church set aside Freeborn Garretson as a missionary—to Nova Scotia! It is indubitable that Wesley said, "The world is my parish," but this had no reference to missionary tasks whatever. The famous sentence was spoken of his ordinary tasks, and meant merely that he would preach wherever he pleased without regard to any Church of England bishop.

Wesley met obstacles to his unyielding religious demands, not only from designing individuals and from "the heathen," but from the settlers in Georgia. Utterly open himself, with nothing in his consciousness of which he was ashamed, he could not see why, in his capacity as priest, he could not step into the inner personal lives of those for whose souls he felt responsible. The unfortunate truth was that many of the settlers did not care for his ministrations, or for those of anyone else. There were others who resented out of the evil of their own lives the presence of good in his life—and sought to bring him into disrespect in every conceivable fashion.

Theodore Roosevelt, a careful observer and close student of men under frontier conditions, has pointed out the changes in character that men undergo when transplanted from old and established communities to frontier settlements. The man who at home cheerfully bears his share of the social burden becomes heroic in self-sacrifice when he moves to a sparsely populated frontier. On the other hand, the mean man, or the revengeful man, becomes, upon slight provocation, a murderer when in pioneer conditions. The reason seems to be that on the frontier the customary restraining pressures of social sentiment are relaxed and men show themselves for what they are in themselves. Now, the Georgia settlement, when Wesley was there, did not number more than a thousand in population, a thousand people who had to live three thousand miles from all scenes to which they had been accustomed.

The effect on Wesley made him overstrained in his set determination to carry through his religious purposes, but was not otherwise harmful.   Certainly, he kept himself in splendid physical condition if being able to sleep on rainsoaked earth without taking cold is any test.   The effect on those who would have been displeased with Wesley in England was to make them hate him in Georgia.   Charles Wesley, who shared the enmity of the settlers, relates that when he was walking in the outskirts of Frederica a bullet whizzed past his head, evidently intended for him, which is just what is to be expected when in frontier conditions hatred has gone beyond a stage which in an old settlement would find vent in malicious speech, and seeks to kill.   John Wesley was hated even more than Charles.

John kept himself strictly to his hard-and-fast program of daily tasks, thereby increasing the rage of the settlers against himself, and preventing anything like even a touch of homesickness in his own heart.   One can go carefully through every paragraph of his *Journal* during this period and not find a sign of longing for England—quite remarkable when one thinks of the delights of the life which he left behind at Oxford.

A frontier community gets used to the notion of a relaxation of the rules of settled, so-called "civilized" life.   The existence at Georgia was not free from the alarms and terrors of possible dangers from savages and Spaniards, the nearest foreign neighbors, so that every man knew that he had to walk warily.   However, the settler, even though he was "regular" in his support of church at home, could not see why everything ecclesiastical had to be so much stiffer in Georgia.   When Wesley insisted upon dipping babies into the water in baptism, unless physical health was thereby to be manifestly imperiled, it is not to be wondered at that the mothers of children born in a virtual wilderness did not care to have the Church add to the hardships of a life already hard enough.   The picture of Wesley here is not pleasant.   It suggests a life without much balance, not to say good sense.   The Church as a sacred institution in itself was bulking too largely in his thought.   Moreover, all this unyielding rigor suggested a mind not yet sure of itself.   Wesley was not yet strong enough to hold anything in an easy grasp.   He seemed afraid to surrender anything for fear he might have to give up all.

He was not sure of himself.   In Georgia occurred that oft-quoted interview with the Moravian Bishop Spangenburg, in which the bishop laid it down so uncompromisingly that the belief that

Christ died for the world, one's self included, was not enough, but one must have a personal assurance of Christ's salvation for one's own self. This started Wesley anew on a quest for inner assurance arising out of a desperate fear that he was not himself saved. Let us now glance ahead half a century to the day when John Wesley declared that as he looked back to the positiveness with which he and Charles had preached that a man was not saved until he knew he was saved and when he was saved, it was wonder the people did not stone them. That is to say, the definiteness of that early preaching was a mistake, and that includes the ironclad doctrine of the Moravian bishop. This after-statement of Wesley is not to be taken as a sign of the mental relaxing that comes with old age. It was a statement of mature judgment and is not to be passed over lightly. If we seek standards by which to judge Wesley's work, we are fortunate indeed to find some from his own pen. This matter is important because of its significance for the later course of Methodism. There can be no doubt that there are for multitudes of souls just the type of experience that Spangenburg, and Wesley after him, had in mind; but there can be no doubt either that the effect of the unqualified teaching of such experience as a necessity for salvation has to be taken into the account in estimating the religious results of Methodism. Through such uncompromising sternness many souls were left in darkness, if not led into it. Many found refuge in other religious groups who would have been more happy in Methodism. Of course, if we are to judge the truth of a proposition merely by its spiritual effects, we can make out a good case for this doctrine, if in our effort we do not forget the harmful results as well as the helpful. Spangenburg and Wesley, however, were not twentieth-century pragmatists of the school of William James. They thought of truth as absolute in its own right, and sincerely taught it as such. Wesley's statement in later age did not mean that he thought he had used a tool in a bungling fashion, but that he had not hold of the full truth. We have to concede a measure of force to Lecky's judgment that Wesley preached a religion of terrors, though the terrors were not those of hellfire but of requirement upon all seekers to attain a type of assurance without which they were to regard themselves as lost.

We come now to an experience of Wesley which seems strange judged by ordinary human standards, but which is not so strange when we know Wesley, with his intense piety—the story of his relations to "Sophy" Hopkey. It is perhaps worth while to note that the more recent biographers of Wesley make more of this relationship than did the earlier.   Moore, one of the most important of all writers on Wesley, does not seem to know, or to remember, the name of the young woman.   Wesley does not appear to have spoken about the matter to anyone in England.   It may be that with our larger knowledge of the effects of such experiences for the entire after-life, we are wise in paying more attention to this early love affair than did Wesley's contemporaries, though it would be easy to exaggerate the importance of Miss Hopkey in Wesley's life.   The young woman herself was only eighteen years old at the time, though here, again, we must not forget that in those times a young woman of eighteen was commonly regarded as having come virtually to full maturity.   Wesley was fully fourteen years the senior of Sophy Hopkey.

Before Wesley came to Georgia he had not had extensive acquaintance with women outside the Epworth home.   There was indeed some fancy letter writing with the sisters of some of his college mates, most of it as far up in the air as such writing usually is.   It is manifest, however, that Wesley's knowledge of women at the time of his sojourn in Georgia was altogether superficial.   To Wesley there seemed for a long period in his life no realization of any essential differences between children and adults, between the civilized and the savage, between men and women, between different persons.   His conceptions of persons were certainly oversimplified.   To his credit be it said that, until he found reasons for doing otherwise, he treated all whom he met as moved by the same interests and motives as himself.   In the critical juncture in which Wesley now found himself everything was complicated by the fact that he did not know himself.   It appears that he went out to Georgia with the idea that he would not marry.   The possibility that he might fall in love does not seem to have occurred to him.

Now, in circumstances like those in which Wesley lived in Georgia almost any man can fall in love with almost any woman.   Proximity counts mightily.   Miss Hopkey seems to have been an earnest, attractive young woman, with no especially distinguishing characteristics.   Wesley fell in love with her because he was so much in her company, or near her; there were not many other young women near at hand; she seems to have taken kindly to the exercises to which Wesley introduced her for the improvement of her intellectual and spiritual powers.   On some occasions they were thrown into quite intimate relations, as on a trip from

Frederica to Savannah on which they were together in almost complete intimacy much of the time. On that trip the usual course in such intimacies seems to have been followed, automatically, or with the regular psychological sequences. The two fell to talking about a man of Miss Sophy's acquaintance; Miss Sophy revealed that the man had asked for her hand, and next declared that she would not marry him. Whereupon Wesley made what was a full equivalent to declaration of love, and Miss Sophy burst into tears and asked him not to mention the matter again. This is the old, old path that has been trodden by thousands upon thousands of couples since time began, and will be traveled till the end of time. The usual outcome is that a few further interviews bring to clearer understanding and finally to marriage.

From the time of this first interview Miss Hopkey acted much like a normal human being, and John Wesley not like one at all. His conversation with Miss Sophy was, for the most part, preaching. He was clear as to the lines of conduct she should take and not at all clear about himself. We have to remind ourselves that during this troublous season Sophy Hopkey had to deal with John Wesley as John Wesley was then. She did not know what a world figure he was to become, nor did anyone else. He must have seemed to her the strangest person she had ever met in her brief eighteen years. If she put up with all the queerness which he seems to have manifested, she must have been herself quite unusual. There is nothing in the record that indicates that she could have understood what Wesley was about, any better than any other girl of eighteen could have understood a man of thirty-two who was preaching and seeking to practice an ideal of holy conduct almost incomprehensible in circumstances like those of the Georgia colony. So Miss Hopkey suddenly married someone else. Speaking again on the authority of all accounts that have come down to us, there was not the slightest trace of anything reprehensible in her conduct. It would not be strictly precise to say that Sophy Hopkey jilted John Wesley; she merely gave him up as an insoluble problem, possibly in a mood of desperation.

Now the trouble began. Wesley by this time was almost two personalities—a strict and stern ecclesiastical martinet and a man disappointed in love. Acting in both capacities he avowed that the marriage of Miss Hopkey was illegal because of some irregularity about the banns. Just how it was going to help anything or anybody to talk of such a detail as this does not appear. More folly followed, coming to a climax in Wesley's refusing the communion service to Mrs. Sophy because of her neglect of services preliminary to the sacrament of the Lord's Supper. In all this Wesley thought he was acting as a faithful priest of the Church.

In an earlier section we saw that Samuel Wesley, Sr., made an erring communicant do public penance on the streets of Epworth. The offense for which that penance was required was adultery, and was serious enough in the eyes of the community to sustain the rector in the inflicted penalty. Not so with John's attempted punishment. The Georgia community seems to have felt that Wesley's severity was unreasonable.

In any case Williamson, the husband of Sophy, tried to hail Wesley into court on ten charges, one of them being slander. The others were wholly ecclesiastical. John was willing to meet the charge of slander, but denied that a civil court had any right to question his ecclesiastical conduct. In this he was fighting a battle which recurs in every generation, the same battle which is now on the point of breaking out, or actually breaking, in every land in Christendom. All the positions he took in his defense were sound, judged by the wisdom of later centuries. The charge of slander led to a wretched mass of vicious talk against Wesley himself, but had not enough merit in it to warrant trial. John Wesley never was guilty of slander against Sophy Hopkey. He did all he could to get the case into court to clear himself but did not succeed, the energies of his enemies exhausting themselves in annoying him and in seeking to hinder him even when he was trying to leave for England. At last he managed to get away, and reached England on February 1, 1738, after passing George Whitefield, who was leaving the shores of England for America just as Wesley drew near to them—Whitefield who, by the way, on arriving in Georgia found warrant for paying high tribute to the work of Wesley. If Wesley looked longingly back to Georgia and its people, including Mrs. Sophy Williamson, he does not say so in any passage either in a letter or in the *Journal*.

One or two somewhat reckless historians have written as if Wesley had to leave Georgia, allowing the reader to infer that he was forced to go. This is utterly mistaken. Wesley had to go in the sense that he saw that his work in America was done. I have spoken plainly of the impracticalness of many of his plans, and the undiplomatic rigidity of his methods. There was, however, nothing to criticize in his conduct in any moral aspect. We have to write down the fact that his ideals were too high to gain acceptance by the people of Georgia. The most careful perusal of his own correspondence, of his diary and *Journal*, of all available records of his life found in any source, fails to bring to light anything suggestive of self-seeking. At that time money for his services was not forthcoming. Probably he had then to endure a poverty that meant hunger; but if so, he took it all in the day's work. What he did was not productive of serious harm, but taught him lessons that worked powerfully for good in the spread of Methodism in England. The difficulty was that in Georgia he was the knightly Don Quixote, without the good hard sense, coarse good sense, if you wish, of any Sancho Panza.

PART II

THE HEART STRANGELY WARMED

ALDERSGATE—MAY 24, 1738, TO APRIL, 1739

PART II

THE HEART STRANGELY WARMED

ALDERSGATE—MAY 24, 1738, TO APRIL, 1739

ABOUT a quarter before nine, while [someone was reading Luther's Epistle to the Romans] he was describing the change which God works in the heart through faith in Christ, I felt my heart strangely warmed, I felt I did trust in Christ, Christ alone for salvation; and an assurance was given me, that he had taken away *my* sins, even *mine* and saved *me* from the law of sin and death."

Wesley got back from Georgia on February 1, 1738. On May 24, 1738, he had the famous Aldersgate experience. We must seek as full an account as possible of this crisis, which has been almost as much discussed as any in religious history—the so-called conversion of Wesley.

It is important to set the whole scene in its true context. The experiences leading up to Aldersgate are usually depicted as seasons of torment in Wesley's soul. The relief following the experience is usually spoken of as a passage into a depth of peace never known before. Now, all this has to be understood in terms of what Wesley has said of his own peculiarities. The various entries in the *Journal* do not bear out quite such an agony of woe as some statements of some biographers suggest. For example, Wesley was fond of telling of the soundness with which he slept— had slept every night of his life. The *Journal* tells us that he had never lain awake more than fifteen minutes in any night in practically his entire life. This is, of course, one of those offhand statements that men make in after years when they look back on a life in which the usual course seems to have moved regularly from the beginning. Still, the fact is not to be doubted that all his life Wesley reaped the benefit of his regular living in regularity and steadiness of mental processes. Even if in those earlier times Wesley tended to asceticism, the asceticism was not as harmful as even the innocent dissipations of youth are likely to be. Retirement and rising at fixed hours, simple and plain food, vigorous but not excessive exercise—all this makes for the best working of the body. No pictures of Wesley, or accounts of him, carry down to us a hint of a body ever burdened with even a pound of excess weight—witness Leslie Stephen's picture of him as a "human game-cock"—and none of them suggest, on the other hand, the drawn pinched features of the ascetic.   Whatever the experiences through which Wesley passed, we cannot easily think of him as walking the streets at night, or appearing with hair or clothes in disorder, or as gazing off into vacancy.   If we may use a dreadfully mechanical figure of speech, the currents of Wesley's life were pretty thoroughly canalized from the first.   There were not in them many rapids, or whirlpools, or marshy stretches, or cataracts.   The stream did not vary much in depth and moved at an even flow.   Let us get all this firmly before us as we come to Aldersgate.

There was, however, enough in what Wesley had passed through, especially in Georgia, to perplex if not to torment him. Immediately after his heart became strangely warmed he tells us that he began to pray for his enemies.   Who could those enemies have been but Williamson and Causton and the rest of that ilk who had persecuted him in Georgia, with perhaps a stray thought now and then for Sophy Hopkey?   He had put his type of religion to the test and the results in the working out had not been notably gratifying.   No one could have stood more stiffly for his religious conceptions than Wesley had done.   The most he could feel about the outcome was that if he could have a second try at Georgia, he could do better.   The old adage tells us that we are to let justice be done though the heavens fall.   What kind of justice had Wesley meted out to Sophy Hopkey?   Nevertheless, more than one sage has observed that if justice makes the heavens fall, there may be something wrong with the justice.   It may have taken Wesley some time to get around to asking a pertinent question, but he asked it at last: "Is there anything wrong with the type of religion I have been preaching and practicing?"   Wesley was becoming convinced that his type of religion was not doing him much good and was not much helping anyone else.

Consider again the legalistic, formal type of the religion. It consisted in doing things according to religious commandment. The spirit was that of utter devotion to the loftiest conceivable ideal.   We usually think of a legalist as one who, having fulfilled, let us say, his daily stint of good works, looks upon himself as thereafter free till the hour for the next duty arrives.   This form of legalism is rather comfortable.   Now, this was not Wesley's type.   He thought of all his Spartan self-discipline of the spirit as a path to reach an ideal which he would not disobey in the least detail. Instead of leading to peace this course led in the opposite direction. Indeed, ask often enough, "Have I done enough?" and one is headed toward madness.

It is easy to say, as one looks back over the history of a group or an individual, that this or that must have, or not have, been thus and so. There is no mistake, however, in our saying that Wesley must have been disappointed in his religious life in the months between February, 1738, and May of the same year. Allowing for all the tendencies in Wesley himself to iron response to an iron conviction of duty, he could not have found much satisfaction in the type of life he was leading. He craved something more nourishing to the emotional life, something that he could feel. We can hardly call anything life which we cannot feel. It was one thing when the seeker for thrills sought feeling; it was another when Wesley did so, for Wesley's mind and will had been, if anything, overworked in the service of the ideal. He evidently desired something he had never had, and something which he perhaps had never seen anyone else have. We cannot give too much honor to Susanna Wesley for her training of her son, but we cannot forget the almost exclusive predominance of the mind and will elements in that training. Dr. Umphrey Lee has given us a worth-while hint as to a possible suggestiveness in the epitaph which John and Charles prepared for their mother—that strange reference to her having endured a legal night for seventy years. "Night" as a word descriptive of religious experience provokes us to strange musings. Those who coined the expression "legal night" knew the meanings of words and would not have spoken thus if the characterization had not been appropriate. I have already referred to Tyerman's statement that John Wesley entered Charterhouse School a saint and had come out of it a sinner, as a perfect specimen of the result reached when a theologian simply has to make experience conform to theory. Still, it is doubtful if Wesley ever saw at close range any religion that was strongly marked by religious satisfaction. So far as we can make out, Wesley's religious experience had gone stale with him. He had debated it threadbare. To have suggested to him that he ease off a little from the intensity of his grasp would probably have horrified him. Yet he was manifestly feeling after something which he could not get by being always keyed up to highest pitch. Something simply had to happen.

It was shortly after his return from Georgia that Wesley had his famous interview with Peter Böhler, the Moravian, in which Böhler told him that he must purge himself of his philosophy and preach faith till he had it, and after getting it, preach faith because he had it. This advice it was which shocked Robert Southey— whose biography of Wesley never loses charm—as something insincere and tending to hypocrisy. We do not have to suppose that Böhler was urging Wesley to claim to have an experience which he did not have. A man can be convinced that religious experience in any phase is most desirable without saying that he has attained unto it himself. There have been many preachers who have believed thoroughly in mystic visions without ever receiving one. John Wesley came to believe in and preach the doctrine of Christian perfection, without ever claiming to have reached this state in his own life. In any event Böhler's word sank deep into Wesley's mind and has to be reckoned as one of the factors in his conversion.

As we come to look at the conversion itself we have to recognize that there is about all such experiences an element that defies description or analysis, as all vital experiences have at their center a heart of mystery. Still, some things about them can be known and profitably discussed.

We may well be thankful that modern psychological study has done so much in this field, provided we steer clear of dogmatism and scientific pedantry and such cumbersome terminology as "evangelical" conversion. The mind is the most delicate of organisms. Its finer operations are subtle and illusive, only to be caught by the most delicate perceptions. Moreover, processes of the mind fade into one another almost imperceptibly. There is required for their understanding not only the largest and most patient training, but also the acutest sympathy and intuition. It is almost impossible to understand a religious feeling objectively, or from the outside. The critical mood by its nature is likely to prevent sympathetic understanding of religious states of mind.

Yet there are some facts which appear in all psychological investigation, facts which we have all known after a fashion without realizing their universal nature. For example, there is the rhythm in which all phases of life move. There is no such experience as a living soul's ascending to a psychological plateau and staying there. There are spiritual rhythms dependent upon the shorter and longer bodily rhythms. We live not on straight lines but on curves, and the curves are quite as much up and down as to one side and another.

Then there is the tendency of all inner life to respond to thinking which seems to come of itself, out of the subconscious, as we say in today's phrase. So far as the entrance of truth into our minds is concerned, we are stormed upon by all manner of impressions which we do not invite to cross the threshold of consciousness. They come without invitation, and will not leave at our order. They sink below the level of our purposive regard, or they hang around the fringes of our consciousness, always near. In all thinking that we call creative we do best when we adjust ourselves to this tendency of an idea to take care of itself. The classic illustration is the statement of Poincaré, the famous mathematician, that in his handling a mathematical conception he would get it clearly stated to himself, think over it as long as he felt he was getting anywhere with it, and then cease to strain to hold the idea in his attention, letting it find its way about among the other contents of his mind. Later he would deliberately lift the idea again into clear focus, doing this repeatedly until a solution would burst, sometimes suddenly, upon his mind. The schoolboy who is at all studious knows that after an evening's prolonged wrestle with a problem he may awake in the morning with the mystery or the perplexity solved. He might easily make the mistake of thinking that the best way to deal with problems would be to sleep over them, without the evening's mental wrestling. Let him try this, however, and he soon learns that he does not find any solution by illumination in the morning.

Now, all this is so thoroughly understood today that it is commonplace in intellectual method. Graham Wallas calls this period of unsettled, rather formless mental effort the stage of incubation, which phrasing certainly links the mind's processes with the fundamental processes of physical organisms. The idea, or the sentiment, or the determination, goes through a ripening toward full fruitage. Just what may bring the swift enlightenment at the end is not important. William James speaks of some events, or expressions, or impressions as "trigger-pullers" in human consciousness. The mind becomes filled, or even clogged with content until some chance deed, or event, or feeling pulls the trigger and a sort of discharge clears the holding mind. It may be just as well to quote here James's own description of conversion: "To be converted, to be regenerated, to receive grace, to experience religion, to gain an assurance, are so many phrases which denote the process, gradual or sudden, by which a self hitherto divided, and consciously wrong, inferior, and unhappy, becomes unified and consciously right, superior, and happy, in consequence of its firmer hold on religious realities."[1]

This may seem as if we were trying to reduce religious phenomena to the plane of merely natural law, but we are assuming that we may follow Wesley himself in understanding that natural laws are divine methods. John Wesley himself was a careful observer of psychological processes in religion. He thought of God as working through these processes, though he did all in his power to observe and set down the most accurate and adequate notes of all unusual incidents and experiences which came to his attention.

With this assumption, then, that the divine works through the orderly laws of mind, let us look at one or two illustrations of swift crowning of long processes of thought by quick illumination. We have already mentioned Poincaré. We might cite even more appropriately Newton and his falling apple. Whether that incident is historically and literally true or not, it might well have been true, for such an insignificant incident is just the type of occurrence which does lead to such momentous conclusions as Newton's grasp of the principle of universal gravitation. The story goes that Newton was sitting in his garden in deep reflection. An apple fell. Newton said: "The apple falls. *The moon falls.*" Now, Newton may not have said anything, and the apple may not have suggested anything to him, and he may not have been in his garden at all when the thought of gravitation occurred to him, but the incident is true to life, nevertheless, as showing how a long, laborious process of thinking may suddenly come to a climax in the midst of, and at the hint of, something apparently insignificant. Another illustration, altogether authentic, can be found in Darwin's account of his first convincing glimpse of the importance of natural selection. After months and years of study, Darwin was one day reading casually a passage from Malthus on population, in which Malthus was discussing the peculiarity of animal forms of life to increase in number up to the limit of food possibilities. Instantly the conception of natural selection for which the scientist was searching dawned upon him.

The relevance of the Newton and Darwin illustrations here

---

[1] *The Varieties of Religious Experience,* chapter on "Conversion," p. 189.

lies partly in that the processes had gone on through so long a time, periods longer than that of the acute phase of Wesley's spiritual struggle. A difference between the two types of inner reaching for adjustment was that in the strictly intellectual spheres there was no fighting against foe, no hint of repression, while in the spiritual sphere there probably was a need of giving up ideas which had been considered nearly, if not quite, all-essential. In spite of the earnestness of Wesley's search, one wonders whether he was as receptive to ideas about the spiritual life as were Newton and Darwin about the intellectual problems. What Wesley had in the end to turn from was virtually a system of religious idea and practice in which he had been nurtured from the beginnings of consciousness. As soon as the light broke, he felt immense relief but he had held on to the Spartan, stoic notion so long that it was hard to let go. He had to change the inner attitude of his life up to 1738.

Now, what does Wesley say as to the meaning of the Aldersgate experience himself? We have already used his own words: "I felt my heart strangely warmed," etc. How did he himself interpret it? He thought of it as a passage from the state of a slave or a servant to that of a son. This is the heart of it all, and this is the heart of the gospel. We have in Saint Paul the same idea—the life of a servant to the law is like a body of death. When the heart can cry, "Abba, Father," all changes. We are not dealing with a hard-and-fast scheme of laws in whose remorselessness we find only despair, but with a Father who takes the will for the deed, who makes allowances, who makes possible new starts with the dawning of every day. There is no relief, no satisfaction in the law in itself, or in ideals in themselves, for, when we think we have kept the law or fulfilled the ideal, new laws and new ideals loom up before us, to which we cannot hope to attain.

In a way the difference here is that between thinking of law as instrument and thinking of it as end in itself. Wesley would likely not have admitted that he was seeking to follow commandments as ends on their own account; he would have said that he was using these as means of grace, but he acted as if the laws stood in their own right. Certainly, when he fully accepted the idea of communion with the Father as all-determining, the laws became in the deeper sense instrumental. The experience of Wesley is a comment on the word of Jesus that after men have done all, they are unprofitable servants. They attain whatever success they reach as sons. A son's work may be of value to a father not at all because of what it is in itself but because of the spirit of sonship it bears. A child's letter to a father is valuable not because of its qualities of penmanship and composition, but in spite of these, because it is an attempt to get into communion with the father.

The change of focus and emphasis meant everything to Wesley, yet we do badly in attempting to make the transformation unlimited and the break complete. I have laid stress on the servantlike quality of the earlier years. Let us not fancy for an instant that John Wesley was any the less industrious or systematic in his work after Aldersgate than before. His deliverance was not from work but from a slavish spirit in his work. If anything, his devotion to system increased. The Aldersgate experience was in 1738: Wesley died in 1791. The entries in his *Journal* are just as detailed and exact in the last year as in the Georgia days. Indeed, something in Wesley seems at Aldersgate to have been released for more and more activity.

Again, the experience did not lead to joy without interruption. The entries time and again in this year, 1738, reveal gloom, and doubt, and questioning. Heaviness of soul was his after Aldersgate as before, till it lightened with the years. Moreover, ideas and feelings did not clear up in Wesley's life all at once. He felt the need of getting things into true perspective, and that took time. His spiritual vision had so long been accustomed to one focus that it had to make its adjustment to the new focus. To use a too materialistic illustration we are aware that surgical operations on the human eyes for the correction of defective sight are not likely to bring true vision at once. Sight is delicate, and depends upon the myriad movements of fine nerves and muscles to an incalculable degree. To change these movements may mean the painful development of muscles almost atrophied through disuse, or the direction of muscles wrongly used to new functions. We can easily suppose, without any strain on possibilities, that a child might conceivably be born into the world with closed eyelids which could not be opened except after surgical treatment. The child might go on for years supposing himself hopelessly blind, with only faint glimmerings of light until surgery relieved him. Now, if we should imagine that as soon as the lids opened the sight would be like that of anyone else, we should make serious mistake. Even with perfect eyes after such treatment, seeing would have to be learned.

After Aldersgate, Wesley had to reorient himself. It will be recalled that even after a more striking experience, that on the Damascus road, a greater than Wesley withdrew for long months into Arabia. Paul's spiritual vision needed more than that scales fall from his eyes under the touch of Ananias.

To get his life adjusted to the new light and the new vision, Wesley determined to visit his friends, the Moravians, at Herrnhut. Here seems as good a place as any for a word about the influence of the Moravians on Wesley and, through him, on Methodism. To begin with, they took their religion seriously and went with it to the full length, or what they thought was the full length. The Moravians had accepted Oglethorpe's invitation to Georgia to find a secure place for worship of God after their own fashion, after having moved about from one persecuting community to another in Central Europe. Most of those who settled in Georgia seem to have come from Salzburg.

We have already seen how deeply impressed Wesley was at the behavior of the Moravians in the Atlantic storm in midwinter, when the waves split the mainsail and drenched the cabins. The Moravians had been inured to hardships and took them about as they came—all in the name of the Lord. We have spoken of the impression made upon Wesley by Spangenburg and Böhler. Remembering the profound communion with God which the Moravians seemed to hold at all times, Wesley sought them out in Herrnhut, where, to all intents and purposes, Count Zinzendorf was their absolute leader, not to say ruler.

In Georgia, Wesley's contacts with the Moravians ought to have opened his eyes not only to their surpassing excellences but also to their limitations. They had firm hold of some essentials but were not authorities on the finer points of anything. When Wesley was fumbling along, making blunder after blunder in his relations with Sophia Hopkey, he made the worst blunder of all in submitting to the Moravian elders the question as to whether he should marry or not. They promptly voted no. Now, the men were older than John Wesley, but there does not seem to have been among them one who could take Wesley aside and give him a little normal human counsel. The Moravians were no doubt rich toward God, but on the manward side they were somewhat poverty-stricken.

Again, the Moravians overdid the positiveness of their religious claim. They had indeed earned their convictions. Their spiritual freedom had been bought with a great price. It was theirs. If anyone like Wesley cared to accept their fellowship, he could do so on their terms. We remember the sureness and directness with which Spangenburg spoke, and the definiteness of Böhler. The latter had studied at Jena and possessed that contempt of the intellect which men often do who have accepted and profited by the training of the schools, and then by virtue of a religious experience appear almost to despise the schools. In any event, Böhler told Wesley his philosophy must be purged away and then talked with a certainty which was not just what Wesley needed. At first it looked as if Wesley's own spiritual arrogance in dealing with men might be increased by his contact with the Moravians. Just a few days before the Aldersgate crisis he wrote as follows to William Law, a leader in religious thinking, superior to Wesley in such thinking, though Law afterward went far into the vagaries of mysticism. After reproaching Law for not better instructing him in religion, Wesley wrote: "Once more, Sir, let me beg you to consider whether your extreme roughness and morose, and sour behavior, at least on many occasions, can possibly be the fruit of a living faith in Christ." Whatever Aldersgate did for Wesley, it did not make any less his positiveness, even his overbearingness in his dealings with his fellows. This may be just as well, having regard to the task ahead of him, but it causes strange suspicions as to just what Christian humility meant to Wesley. Probably humility in the sight of God.

The visit to Herrnhut was somewhat disillusioning to Wesley. There is a story that one day Wesley was working in a garden in the Moravian settlement. There is nothing incredible in this, inasmuch as Wesley was quite an outdoor man and at times during his Georgia life gave himself to the exercise and pleasure of "felling trees." The story goes on that Zinzendorf approached Wesley and asked him to leave his work and greet some worthy personage or other, and that Wesley demurred because his hands were soiled with earth, bringing down upon himself Zinzendorf's rebuke for lacking humility. Most biographers insist that this is apocryphal, but it sounds like Zinzendorf, especially since Zinzendorf did not have any way of knowing at that time what a character in the religious world Wesley was to become. It does not sound like Wesley. It is hard to picture Wesley as taking orders from anybody.

The Moravians were sure of everything about their own religious thought and practice. To the end of his life Wesley never ceased to give them credit for the good they had done him, but he soon turned from their leadership. On the whole, the credit given them for their part in shaping Methodism has probably been given full recognition. In after years Wesley openly rebuked them for the abjectness of their dependence on Zinzendorf, for their lapsing at times into disingenuousness, for their tendencies to quietism. It is hard to strike a balance here. There were aspects in which the influence of the Moravians on Methodism was not the best. The tendency to self-assurance, which came partly from Moravianism, was something which Wesley did not need.

PART III

TO APRIL 4, 1739

"I submitted to be more vile and
[preached] in the highway."—JOURNAL, APRIL, 1739

PART III

TO APRIL 4, 1739

THERE was nothing especially exciting in the actual Aldersgate experience. The psalm which Wesley read on May 24 for his morning devotions was deeply stirring, and the anthem, which Wesley heard as he strayed into Saint Paul's, was, as he looked back at it, fitted to prepare him for the spiritual relief which came at the meeting in the evening. Wesley did not feel especially drawn to that meeting—indeed, felt reluctant to go, but he did go. When he arrived at a quarter before nine, someone —oddly enough Wesley does not remember who—was reading from Luther's introduction to the Epistle to the Romans. It is not possible to say just what it was in that introduction which brought the light to Wesley. There was a strange warming of the heart and the thought that God had for Christ's sake forgiven Wesley his sins. Those who will have it that the experience must have been a tumultuous upheaval of emotion have little to build upon. The man who sat or stood next to Wesley had probably not the slightest idea of a strange warming of his neighbor's heart. What happened? Not a great deal of anything at first. For some weeks Wesley still had his periods of dismay and despair. He told his intimate circle that he was not a Christian and never had been, with such emphasis that his brother Samuel was disturbed lest John be giving himself to something bordering on fanaticism. Gradually there came a settling down of feeling and within something over a year Wesley had found himself. His eyes were turned outward instead of inward.

The Aldersgate experience was the preparation for the work of the next fifty years. Wesley could not have done what he did with his gaze fixed upon himself. All the intensity of that inward gaze had to be turned outward. He could not have done what he did and always have been considering his own spiritual state. There was too much to be done, or too much kept crowding upon him. He had to find his own way along.

I have seen best to put the intensity of Aldersgate in immediate context with the vastness of what Wesley did. One man had for a time at least to do what it ought to have been the aim of the entire

71

English Church to accomplish. That Church, with all the power it had in the eighteenth century, could not have done what Wesley did. It could not have impressed the people. It could not have gathered such crowds as came to hear Wesley. It could not have found standing room for them in the churches. There was not a massiveness or a quality about the English Church which could have produced Wesley's work without Wesley.

I turn to some considerations—the list not exhaustive—to show how widely the Wesley fervor spread of itself. Some of these may seem matter of fact and commonplace, but the enumeration of them ought to bear witness to the concept of the force that came with the realization that God was a Father and not a taskmaster.

Without trying to be strictly systematic let us look at some phases of Wesley's career after Aldersgate which show the volume and torrent of his rushing life. We must indeed never forget that in a revival such as the Methodist, the leader is quite as much follower as leader, if we mean the following of events, even if he had at the beginning thought of himself as the leader. Moreover, Wesley had literally no precedents by which to plot his course. There had never been such a revival as the Methodist. There had been mighty popular movements with something of a religious cast, but with the chief emphasis on economic or social conditions. The Wesleyan emphasis was almost wholly religious. There were immense social consequences which we shall consider later, but these did not come directly within the field of Wesley's purposive aim. Take the remark of Spangenberg to Wesley about the necessity of his knowing personally that Christ had forgiven his sins. Rightly interpreted this remark is sound enough, but when it carries the implication of some special witness, presumably of feeling, we can see how fraught with peril it is. That many, many converts to Methodism rejoiced in marked emotional uplift in turning to God cannot be doubted, but that many, many seekers pursued into virtual despair what Spangenburg and Böhler and Wesley seemed to imply is equally indubitable. It was for preaching overdefiniteness of assurance that John Wesley said late in life that he wondered that the people had not stoned himself and Charles. It was too bad that Wesley's recognition and acknowledgment of mistakes often came so long after the mistakes had been made. We are accustomed to think of the Wesleyan revival as a long spiritual triumph once it had got well agoing. We cannot know the total of those— otherwise ready for deliberate acceptance of God—who were thrown into confusion by the narrowness of the tests insisted upon as marks of genuine Christian discipleship. We say this at the outset to indicate that the Wesley preaching at the best had its limitations. It had to feel its way along.

It is a common enough mistake in dealing with the career of leaders who have worked on vast scales to assume, not purposely but unconsciously, that those leaders have in their own time been in possession of all the knowledge which we of later eras hold of their various and varying situations. A college professor today may have more knowledge of the situation at Waterloo, let us say, on the day before the battle than Bonaparte and Wellington together possessed. This, of course, was a single historical incident, but a similar consideration stands true of the knowledge of the actors in processes working through a half or a full century. Wesley was among the best-informed men of the eighteenth century, as to possible large-scale movements in the population of England. He personally came to know England better than any other man of his century, yet he could only detect as in a haze religious tendencies which are sun-clear to us today. We look upon forces at work in the eighteenth century as inevitably bound to take a particular direction. Any historical movement seems to have been inevitable when it is completed. To those in the movements themselves, the tendencies seem to be anything but inevitable. To mention stupendous historic transformations in Wesley's time—who could have foreseen the American Revolution, or the French Revolution, or the Industrial Revolution? Arthur Young traveled widely through France, especially among the peasants, just before the outbreak of the French Revolution, and evidently did not see any foretokens of the storm so soon to break. There is nothing to indicate that Wesley foresaw the extent even of the Methodist movement or the direction it was to take. The late Charles W. Eliot was once complimented on the consistent plan which his long administration at Harvard had revealed. Eliot replied that he had not at the time been aware of any plan, that his work had resembled that of an old minister whom he had once known, who when congratulated on the clearness of his sermon outlines had replied that he knew nothing of outlines, that he had written down a sentence at a time, thanking God for each sentence as it came and then setting himself to write another. This was not quite an exact statement on Eliot's part, and would not have been a true description of what Wesley did, but Eliot's statement would, in a measure, hold both for himself as the remaker of Harvard and for Wesley as the maker of Methodism.

After Wesley returned from Germany he spent much of his time among Moravian groups in London. There began to gather around him clusters of persons likeminded with himself, or like-minded enough to respond to his teaching concerning the inner nature of the Christian life. He was still Fellow of Lincoln, but his duties there did not prevent his moving freely among the groups which came more and more to be known as Methodists, a term at first derisive and finally descriptive. When Charles Wesley founded the Holy Club, he could not know that chiefly under the leadership of John similar clubs would spring up and grow, far outside of university circles, and into Methodist societies of which the first to be formally organized took shape at Moorfields in 1740, to be followed quickly by one at Bristol. At the first, however, the societies were too small to be an adequate field for the powers released in Wesley by Aldersgate.

The idea and fact of societies were nothing new in the history of the Church of England. Any important organization like the English Church, or the Roman Catholic Church, for that matter, has to leave place for the organization of groups of like-minded persons who, while loyal to the inclusive body, find in minority associations something to satisfy their more peculiar needs. Indeed, it would seem that freedom thus to make provision for more intimate cravings is one of the conditions of the continuance of the existence of the larger body. Of course, as in the human organism, if these cells get to developing too much on their own, they threaten the life of the parent social organism, but if they are loyal to the main aim of the parent organism, they are beneficial to that organism. However this may be as a general law, minority societies had been a feature of English Church life for possibly a full century before Wesley was born. At the conference on Faith and Order at Lausanne in 1927 it is noteworthy that a bishop of the Church of England, pleading for the union of religious denominations, especially in England, argued that the aim of English ecclesiastical statesmanship should be to persuade the nonconformist denominations to come into the Church of England as societies, maintaining within that Church all they had found beneficial in their independent life. Simon, in writing the five volumes which are far and away the best history of Methodism yet given the world, devotes virtually an entire volume to the societies in the English Church before Wesley.

All his life Wesley held fast to this idea of the Methodists as composing societies loyal to the Church and yet fostering in the societies their own religious life. It has to be admitted that in the leadership of the societies Wesley seldom or never troubled to counsel with bishops or other church officials. His societies were never formally sanctioned by the English Church. Formally Wesley paid honor to church officials; practically, he had almost nothing to do with them. It may or may not be a tribute to the Church of England in the eighteenth century that it allowed Wesley complete freedom. Whatever the reason for the Church's attitude—indifference, fear of making an enemy of so powerful and popular a leader as Wesley, or recognition of the genuine worth of Methodism—the fact remains that the English Church was tolerant, and that in her tolerance made possible some of the best developments in the thought and practice of Wesleyanism. It is also true that Wesley, while so much a law unto himself, remained through all his life fundamentally loyal to the Church. It was not possible to make a separate sect of the Methodists as long as Wesley lived. What, however, fed the societies in their constant growth? What but the great outside masses to whom, following Whitefield, Wesley went forth and made direct appeal?

The outstanding excellence of Methodism on the human side was its virtual discovery of a class or classes of people, whose existence was assumed but not particularly noticed by the more favored groups. It would be sheer folly to assert that the classes which were "lower," and which largely through Methodism afterward came to be "middle," were ignored in the beginning of Wesley's evangelist career. Everybody "knew they were there," but nobody reckoned them at anywhere near their true possibilities. We today make much of Kant's doctrine of a human being as an end in himself, never to be used as a tool, or instrument, or stuff by anyone but himself without his own consent. The word of Kant's did not appear till Wesley had moved far into his career, but the latter had been acting upon the idea all the time. The consideration appears obvious enough to us now, as a principle of Christian society, but even we do not wholly practice it. One of the strangest phenomena in human affairs is the extent to which men can fail to see the most obvious implication of moral principles. We are not to suppose that the so-called upper classes in England in the eighteenth century were brutal or callous toward those less favored. The higher knew the lower were there, but they simply did not think of them. Of course some moral and human regard was paid them, but they were not taken into the reckoning. The most of them did not count even as voters. By the 1830's many, many of the Methodists had, largely through following the sober and thrifty lives inculcated by Methodism, become well to do, some of them rich. These fortunate ones looked askance at the Chartist Movement, which sought to give the franchise to the groups who stood in the same position occupied by the Methodists fifty or seventy-five years earlier.

Wesley gave himself to a ministry to the less-favored groups partly because he was shut up to doing so. The rushing current dashed in vain against some barriers. The more highly placed groups would not listen to him. Explain the limitation as we will, the truth is that Wesley could not do much with the class to which he himself by birth belonged. It is interesting to observe that in spite of the barbarity, not to say savagery, with which the lower classes of England treated John Wesley and his preachers, he felt that he could better win mobs who threw clods and stones than the more cultivated social groups, and that he could carry them farther. In the latter decade of the eighteenth century Wesley died full of honors, mourned by the whole nation. The honor came to him late in life, however, and did not come to his followers in that century at all.

There are some conjectures that we may legitimately make as to an explanation here. By the time the Revival under Wesley was well afoot he had developed a keen sense of direction as to religious guidance. Out of the experience itself he came to an awareness of the possibilities of response from different groups. In spite of all their roughness the less-favored groups had elemental qualities which provided a more promising field than did the sophisticated members of so-called higher society. The class to whom and for whom Horace Walpole wrote could not make much of Wesley. Wesley could not make much of the groups like Walpole, partly because of the fact itself that they regarded themselves as higher. They felt no need and there was at the time no way of awakening that feeling. Secure in financial strength especially, they did as men of their kind always have done—they put money in a false importance. The impatience of Wesley with the rich was wholly justified. Any leader who feels the responsibility for any social betterment, knows that while no betterment can come without material instruments, on the other hand wealth is the deadly foe of such movements. There seems at times almost a personal soreness in Wesley's contempt of the rich and high-placed, but the contempt was correctly aimed.

Wesley surely understood the limitations within which his movement must expect to succeed, if we can speak of him as consciously thinking of a large-scale revival at all. If one supposes that Wesley expected the Revival which bears his name to sweep everything before it, let him ponder the passage in which he declares that at the outset he did not expect the movement to last more than thirty years, and that he regarded it as an especial mark of divine favor that at the time at which he spoke it had gone fifty years. The reason was that Wesley felt that with the practice of industry and thrift the Methodists would become well to do and yield to the temptations of the world to softness and needless self-indulgence. He felt that the only way to meet this tendency was to preach a doctrine of self-denial which would virtually mean the giving of all one's money away. We shall deal with Wesley's rules about money later; all we seek to do here is to point out that Wesley himself felt that success would bring its own limitations, and set limits to the growth of Methodism.

Again, Wesley knew the limitations set by the character of the people of the more numerous classes among whom he moved in nationwide preaching campaigns. At least at first he did not have much hope of farmers. Consider the picture of farm life in his day which Wesley drew in a few swift strokes:

See that little house, under the wood, by the riverside! There is rural life in perfection. How happy, then, is the farmer that lives there! Let us take a detail of his happiness. He rises with, or before the sun, calls his servants, looks to his swine and cows, then to his stables and barns. He sees to the plowing and sowing his ground, in winter or in spring. In summer and autumn he hurries and sweats among his mowers and reapers. And where is his happiness in the meantime? Which of these employments do we envy? Or do we envy the delicate repast that succeeds, which the poet so languishes for?—

. . . .

"Oh the happiness of eating beans well greased with fat bacon! Nay, and cabbage too!"—Was Horace in his senses when he talked thus, or the servile herd of his imitators? Our eyes and ears may convince us there is not a less happy body of men in all England than the country farmers. In general, their life is supremely dull; and it is unusually unhappy too. For, of all people in the kingdom, they are most discontented; seldom satisfied either with God or man.

It will be remembered that Wesley went out into the New World with large hopes as to the responsiveness of heathen Indians to the preaching of the gospel. It does not appear that he even cherished similar hopes of the English farm workers. The urgency of his father that he seek the parish of Epworth failed partly because John did not feel hopeful of doing much with the Epworth community, largely rural. He does not seem to have regarded them as much higher, religiously speaking, than "heathens." He considered it wonderful that his father had made the transformation in his parishioners that did actually take place, but he evidently thought of that transformation as due to years of most painstaking pastoral service. Probably it was the cities and towns and the stirrings and premonitions of change coming from the new industrial energies that offered to Wesley his best chance, whether he himself realized the letting loose of these energies or not. Probably he did not rely on much planning far ahead. He entered open doors, or, better, he understood what doors would open under knocking or pressure.

The nation-wide success of Methodism came nevertheless with the adoption of field preaching by the Wesleys. After Aldersgate there had to be some such method. If Aldersgate was the inner preparation, the breaking of the path toward field preaching by Whitefield was the outer. The two fitted themselves to each other. Wesley's yielding to Whitefield's urgency that he preach in the fields was as important a crisis as Aldersgate. This resulted from the closing of the doors of the churches to the evangelists, from the driving urgency in Wesley's soul, and from Whitefield's breaking the path. Wesley preached out of doors because he could not get indoors and because he could not get the masses of his hearers indoors. It took some time to bring him to the resolution to go outside, partly because he himself was a churchman throughout, and the soul of regularity. We may delay here an instant to notice how Wesley kept his balance between realistic recognition of what the English clergy in many instances were, and reverent, almost superstitious, regard for the Church as an institution. With the memory of his own father's godliness always fresh in his mind, he could not disparage the clergy in any wholesale fashion: and he showed a patience in dealing with that clergy which is a spiritual marvel of the first order. Time and time again Wesley found that rectors of parishes were actually on the ground inciting ruffians to break up the Methodist meetings. Many more of them let their sympathy with anti-Methodist violence be known.

This, then, was the double barrier that Wesley met, or would have met if he had been working from the start on some grand, or grandiose, scheme for the redemption of England—the sophisticated callousness of the more favored groups and the sodden insensateness of the less favored. Looking the whole field over, Wesley might justifiably have said that it was of no use. Moving along step by step, as he felt the obstacles give way before him, he finally developed a momentum which was the power of the movement. I recur to this repeatedly because, as we look back, the work of Wesley seems to proceed on a plan foreseen from the beginning. At one time Wesley thought his own death was close at hand, so close that he prepared an epitaph for his own tombstone. Wesley had indeed long views, but he acted on short ones.

Wesley's realization of the limitations within which he must work is as outstanding a mark of his greatness as any he revealed. Remember that he was a man of faith, and that his faith in the possibilities of divine grace in the soul of the individual was almost unlimited. Yet in struggling with his task he counted his human resources to the last ounce, believing that the divine could work only through the human. There is an old story that John Knox was interrupted by his wife in a midnight prayer for Scotland. The wife pleaded with her husband to seek rest from a terrible agony of intercession. Knox rebuked her with the reply that through his prayer he already had won half of Scotland and that, if she had not broken in upon him, he would have won it all by daybreak. The story may be apocryphal but it is true to Knox. Anything like it could never have been true to Wesley, as long as he remained Wesley. Intercessory agonies like this were not common to the founder of Methodism. There was, indeed, in him a faith which at times bordered on the fanatical, but in the working out of the faith into practice the most careful calculation of means and ends, within the limits of the hand-to-hand nature of the campaigning itself.

It was over the questions of means and ends that Wesley soon came into conflict with the Moravians. On his return from Georgia Wesley kept close to the Moravians until they began to preach quietism—the complete waiting on the Spirit of God without the use of any means of grace, until the spirit had first spoken to the soul in pardon and peace. All was to come from the Lord, with no reading of Scriptures, no attendance upon religious service, no meditation. It is easy to make a fine show of dependence on God by such method or lack of method and to slip farther from religious experience with the passage of every day. A merciful Providence working through John Wesley kept the Methodist Movement from falling asleep in this fashion. Why did not Wesley make more of Moravianism? Because it was not big enough. Nobody could preach quietistic Moravianism to masses of ten thousand.

In all consideration of differences in those days, we have to hold always before us that leaders and people were feeling their way along. They did not have our "knowledge after the event." To many who surrounded Wesley it did not make any difference whether there was any widespread revival of religion or not. Samuel Wesley had said to his sons, shortly before he died, that they would live to see the Lord's work revived in England, but he had scant company in this. The Moravians had fought for their type of religious thought and practice: they stubbornly held for their own way. Quietism can be put plausibly because it seems so thoroughly to honor God. Wesley fell back on his own good sense in insisting that ends imply means, and that it is a Christian duty to find the means. Quietism practically meant retreat. Wesley was not given to retreat.

As we review these difficulties we have to revise many of our judgments as to the Wesleyan Revival. A few years ago it was the fashion among historians to disparage what they called the great-man-theory of history, insisting that vast general movements and not individuals determine the course of human affairs. One writer went so far a quarter century ago as to maintain that if John Wesley had not arisen to awaken England, some other leader would have appeared. Such statements assume knowledge beyond that of the most of us. It is no doubt true that leaders arrive in response to what we call the demands of the times, and often this demand is definite, especially in the material realms. In response to conscious or half-conscious demands for larger control over nature, let us say, acute minds explore all possibilities because of the pressure behind them. Or masses of mankind begin to feel cravings that some leader almost accidentally frames a theory or a doctrine to meet. It was not quite so in the work of Wesley. The times may have demanded a religious revival, but Wesley himself had to take a large part in shaping that demand. He, at least in a degree, created the popular demand for the message he himself was to proclaim.

Here again we have an angle from which to look at Wesley's strength. He had come back from Georgia after the dubious career there. Nothing in his recollections of Georgia could have called forth the powers which we see at work within the space of a few months. As far as experience itself is responsible, we find the key in Aldersgate. Yet after a period of getting adjusted to the new life of sonship as over against that of servantship, we do not find Wesley often looking back to Aldersgate as such. What I wish to say here is that, after getting upon the new plane of religious life, Wesley was sure not only of the Divine Father but of himself as son. He did not allow past failure to dog his steps. In the brief passage of two years after the return from Georgia he was moving ahead with full power. We have here the signs of a positive assurance that he was working with God, together with a regal self-assertiveness which nothing could daunt. We have to judge John Wesley's experience of assurance not only by what he said but by what he did. In the earlier years of the evangelistic career he speaks now and then in phrases of self-questioning and, as we shall see later, some doubts came strongly upon him toward the close of his career, but he never seems to have known anything about an impulse to slow down. Even if he did have his moments of self-distrust, he had acquired such a momentum by habitual doing of what he thought to be the divine will that he kept right on without any slackening.

The Aldersgate crisis was no doubt the key to the inner assurance, after Wesley had become thoroughly adjusted to the life of a son and not that of a servant. Nevertheless, the abiding satisfaction which marks Wesley from, let us say, the third or fourth year of his evangelistic effort clear on to the end of his life, was not in any experience to which he had to look back for re-enforcement. It was in the satisfaction of the work itself, and the success which followed his adoption of field preaching. He was a man of inexhaustible energy, especially of mind. He had to have something that called for every ounce of his strength. If there was anywhere in him a power that he felt was not being used, he was not easy. Without subscribing too heartily to modern psychology, we may say that the assurance which finally came to Wesley and remained with him to the end was that of complete self-expression, or self-realization. He felt that he was getting out into utterance the best there was in him and all there was in him. Another psychological term we can safely use, heavy and cumbersome though it is—integration. Wesley's life became a unit. It had always been a unit in aim after the highest religious experience. That one line runs consistently through Wesley's life for all his more than eighty years. His assurance as to his relation to the Divine Father solidified still further the life around a center. Beyond all this was the unity of the task to which he had given himself. He found that the type of message he was preaching won enough response, after his revival was well launched, to call forth all his energies. He did not have to waste time in prolonged consideration of what he would better do next. He would do whatever the circumstances demanded in the furtherance of the work. The passage over from the slave or servant type of experience to the son type brought an easier flexibility of method. He no longer saw the old-time sacredness in rules on their own account. Everything had to be judged by the spiritual result, by which he meant the conviction of sonship. The adoption of field preaching opened the door through which the full strength of Wesley began to stride forth. Hence we put April 4, 1739, as a critical date in his career.

As to methods, the aim of Wesley was always to keep them in the minor place. Let one read through the *Minutes* of what came to be called the Conferences and one will see how thoroughly secondary were all organizational features. The *Minutes* were in the form of question and answer. Chief emphasis was placed on the various phases of religious truth which the Methodists proclaimed.

The aim at the beginning was to appear before whatever groups would receive the evangelists—at the beginning the evangelists were old members of the Holy Club—and preach the possibility of attaining assurance like that of the Wesleys, John and Charles, and George Whitefield. All these men had entered through religious crisis into like positiveness of assurance. They kept themselves to truth of which they could feel sure, which was the first, and perhaps the soundest feature of their method. I mean soundest for the purpose in hand, though, as I have said elsewhere, the positiveness became overpositiveness, not to say at times an irreverent and undignified familiarity with the Divine which has to be reckoned on the liability side of the ledger.

The converts naturally clustered together in little groups or societies which were afterward divided into "classes." These classes had at first the prosaic purpose of collecting funds. An earnest layman, when confronted with the duty of helping get together what little money was needed for the few expenses of the society of which he was a member, agreed to collect a penny a week from a specified number of other members. Wesley soon saw that this presented an almost ready-made instrument for spiritual guidance of those who yielded to the preaching. By placing proper leaders over the groups he could make them useful and finally indispensable for religious instruction. The classes became the means of testimony and of correction.

It soon appeared that the Wesleyan Revival was to be highly emotional. In the old phrase, the converts "had experiences." Any emotional movement needs to be kept in hand, for emotional fervor left to take its own course may run wild or, more likely, run through definite stages and then die, leaving the life burned out. The criticism of Wesley that he allowed emotion free play is superficial. He sought to make place for feeling in religious experience, for he saw that the people who were responding to his appeals were not likely to find much satisfaction in anything outside of religion. The aim had to be to keep the glow of joy, and the class helped toward that end. It acted at once like a dam and a canal, storing up the flood waters and paying them out into useful streams.

This on the side of advantage. There is another side, not too good. The class leader has often been called the drill-master of Methodism, and so he was. Drilling, however, has about it a suggestion of regularity, of uniformity. So it was with the Methodist class meeting. Certain terms were used descriptive of spiritual states, one being "the witness of the Spirit." Now, this term belongs to all of Christianity. It is not the peculiar property of Methodism. Methodism, however, put into it a meaning of its own. Moreover, the class meeting developed a standardized experience, or at least an experience which all alike were to seek after. To take a single instance, Wesley never seemed to learn the difference between the mind of a child and that of a man. There could not be anything more mistaken than to put a child's transgression and a man's on the same plane. Yet in the religious training of children at the Kingswood School Wesley did just that. In the latter years he came to a more humane, not to say human view, and presumably to a better method. The early leaders were many of them misleaders. This attempted standardization of experience had harmful effects on Methodism till the rise of the present-day

methods of religious education.   Every now and again a pastor
finds members under the shadow of the fear that they have never
attained to the type of religious experience taught by the old-time
class leaders.

The class meeting provided the intensiveness of the Methodist
Revival.   Open-air preaching made possible the large-scale extensive conquest.   It soon became clear that the Methodists could not
speak in the churches—John, or Charles, or George Whitefield, all
of whom were in orders.   For years after the Revival was under
full headway, it was so unusual for John Wesley to be allowed to
speak in a church that he made comments on every invitation as
remarkable.   Wesley preached outdoors because he could not
preach indoors.   Such indoor preaching was not worth while, in
any event.   There was not the ability in the English Church to nurture the Wesley converts.

In the most merely happen-so way Whitefield began to preach
to the miners around Bristol, more particularly in Kingswood.   He
began by speaking to the groups as they came out of the pits.   The
crowds grew rapidly till they reached astonishing figures.   Whitefield pointed out the success of the method to Wesley, but had quite
a struggle to get him to adopt it.

Wesley hesitated partly because of the irregularity of such
procedure.   The church was the place to preach.   Still, the churches
were closed; and if they were opened, they were not big enough.
If the people were hungry to hear, if the churches were not open,
what was one to do?   We have to think ourselves back to Wesley's
state of mind with determined effort.   Especially do those of us
who have been reared in America have to use a good deal of will,
a good deal of attentive and steady focusing of the mind to get the
Wesley angle.   The Church standing for generation after generation in the English village gathers around it a sacredness on its own
account.   The ways of accustomed worship likewise come to have
at least a sentimental tenderness of appeal.   To all such influences
Wesley was sensitive.   Moreover, it was just to say of him that he
advanced walking backward.

There may have been another reason in the background of
Wesley's mind—the contrast between himself and Whitefield as
public speakers.   There was something almost naïve in Whitefield's
assumption that another could succeed in open-air speaking in
any such measure as he himself could.   Using the term "orator" in
its ordinary indefinite meaning of power in speech over audiences,

Whitefield was one of the most effective orators in the history of
the English-speaking race. We have heard the old, old comment
of David Garrick that Whitefield could stir the soul of an audience
by the way in which he pronounced "Mesopotamia." Everything
about Whitefield, including his crossed or squint eyes, added to
the force of his speech. We shall see later something of the unusual
power produced upon hearers by Wesley—strange psychological
phenomena. We do not hear much about such phenomena in connection with Whitefield's preaching. The effects were such as one
would expect from oratory, the response to the sublimity of pictur-
ing with a big brush, the thrill at the dramatic, especially when
judgment was the theme, the sheer emotional drive of the speaker.
Hardheaded and hardfisted men would go to meetings where
Whitefield was to plead for funds for the support of the orphanage
in Georgia. They would resolve to give only coppers, and would
leave the meeting with their pockets empty of whatever they might
have contained—copper, silver, or gold. Probably as shrewd a tribute as any ever paid to Whitefield as a pleader was the remark attributed to Benjamin Franklin that when he went to hear Whitefield, he left his purse at home. The reports that have come down to
us of Whitefield lay more stress on oratorical results as such than
upon strictly religious consequences. This is not in the least to disparage the religious purpose of Whitefield, or the depth of the impression left by him. Yet the recollections of his preaching after he
had been gone for fifty years were chiefly of his oratory. Certainly,
there is not much in his sermons as published to account for the
effects he produced. The tragic gesture with which he greeted a
crash of thunder at one of his open-air services is the kind of dramatic expression for which he was most famous. His moral quality
was not as thoroughgoing as that of Wesley, as appears from his
attitude to slavery in America. He accepted slavery in Georgia, in
connection with his orphanage enterprise, without any qualms or
misgivings discernible in anything he said or did.

Wesley might well have shrunk from confronting crowds as
large as those Whitefield usually addressed. The size of the crowds
is, of course, overstated by Wesley himself. There is no ground
for saying that Whitefield or Wesley ever spoke effectively to audiences of twenty thousand, though Benjamin Franklin thinks
Whitefield possibly may have, as shown in the following excerpt
from Franklin's *Autobiography:* "He [Whitefield] had a loud and
clear voice, and articulated his words and sentences so perfectly,

that he might be heard and understood at a great distance, especially as his auditories, however numerous, observed the most exact
silence. He preached one evening from the top of the Courthouse
steps, which are in the middle of Market Street [Philadelphia], and
on the west side of Second Street, which crosses it at right angles.
Both streets were filled with his hearers to a considerable distance.
Being among the hindmost in Market Street, I had the curiosity
to learn how far he could be heard, by retiring backward down the
street toward the river; and I found his voice distinct till I came
near Front Street, when some noise in that street obscured it. Imagining then a semi-circle, of which my distance should be the radius,
and that it were filled with auditors, to each of whom I allowed two
square feet, I computed that he might well be heard by more than
thirty thousand. This reconciled me to his having preached to
twenty-five thousand people in the fields, and to the ancient histories of generals haranguing whole armies, of which I had sometimes doubted." William Jennings Bryan spoke to as great crowds
as ever came together in America to hear a speaker. To his largest
crowds he would utter his sentences—at least the important ones—
four times, moving in turn to each of the four sides of the platform.
No satisfactory preaching is possible under such conditions.

Nevertheless, the success of both Whitefield and Wesley in
open-air preaching was the success of Methodism, even after we
have cut their estimates of the numbers down to a half or a third.
Whitefield seems to have stumbled upon the open-air method
almost by accident. When Wesley adopted it, he deliberately set
himself to master even the physical requisites. He evidently asked
of hearers who had been in the audience how well they had heard
him, and, by questioning and observation, determined how to
select tones and pitch so as to make his voice carry farthest. That
he became a master of natural speech before immense crowds is
manifest from the fact that he declares again and again that such
speech did not leave him tired, even after speaking to three or four
audiences in a single day. The most of the accounts of his preaching which have been preserved to us come from those who stood
close to him while he was speaking.

Now, the difference between what is remembered of Whitefield's sermons and what is remembered of Wesley is in the content,
of which Wesley never lost sight. The only reason for Wesley's
taking up outdoor preaching was to get the message to the people,

and he got that message so effectively uttered that the people did not have eyes or ears for anything else.

To explain the unusual effects of the preaching of Wesley, we have to remember some characteristics of the times. As to the type of man whom Wesleyanism reached most deeply, we have to get firm realization that the middle of the eighteenth century was what the Hammonds call the "bleak age." A Methodist meeting in some sections of England was a more interesting occasion than anything else likely to take place, except the bull-baitings or the cockfights. The hours of work were incredibly long, the work itself back-breaking. There was not much to which to go. Now, even when the Methodist meeting was almost sure to be a scene of riot, it was at least interesting, even interest-compelling. It brought crowds together to see what might happen, and something was likely to happen.

In all his long life Wesley never resorted to anything even resembling sensationalism. He had no tricks by which to catch the crowd. Yet the fact itself that he was persistent in preaching was advertisement of drawing power. Some went out of idle curiosity, some out of hostility, some out of more or less completely concealed admiration for the pluck of the preacher. In all these groups Wesley had to create a demand for the gospel he was preaching.

The opposition of the Established Church clergy is considerable of a mystery. There were some clerics to whom the Wesleyan ministry would be an affront because it constituted a rebuke. The number of evil-minded, or even indifferent, clergy in the English Church of the eighteenth century has been exaggerated, but there were all too many of them. The granting of parishes as livings—the grant coming if not by direct royal favor at least by the favor of somebody in power—did not make for the most consecrated type of religious servant; though let us not forget that the parish of Epworth came to Samuel Wesley, Sr., by Queen Anne's favor, and it would be hard to find in the history of the English Church a more devoted parish priest than Samuel Wesley. That was the way priests found their fields in those days, all of them, and that includes the good among those not so good. Still, the system did not make for the noblest devotion.

Large numbers of the clergy sincerely opposed Wesley on the ground of the overpositiveness of his teaching of assurance of salvation. There was almost a morbid fear of anything suggestive of enthusiasm in Wesley's time. He himself shrank from a form of enthusiasm as we shall see later, the form that desires ends and neglects means. The only object for which there was enthusiasm in those days was lack of enthusiasm. The age was rationalistic and Wesley had to encounter rationalism, rationalist though he himself was by nature. Perhaps the most influential theological work of his time was the *Analogy* of Bishop Joseph Butler. Butler showed, perhaps conclusively, that probability is the guide of life, religious life as well as any other phase. One who has read the *Analogy* would not suspect the author of being a fount of enthusiasm.

Coming back to the claims of assurance of salvation on the part of the Methodists fostered by the preaching of Wesley, we must recognize that, as the Methodists taught assurance, it was virtually new. The mistake was made of laying too much stress on assurance as attained in a crisis—preferably instantaneously— and of teaching, or at least implying, that the Methodist form was necessary to salvation. Hence came the absurdity and, indeed, the scandal of proclaiming that good and devout persons who could not tell the date of their spiritual birth were possibly, if not probably, outside the kingdom of God. In my boyhood I heard an old-time Methodist extolling assurance by describing the awkward plight in which one would have to live if one did not know exactly one's birthday. This expositor did not seem to be aware that an awkward plight did not involve damnation, and that a man who is alive can manage to put up with a deal of awkwardness. Susanna Wesley for a long time was not sure of the assurance which the teaching of her son implied, though she believed her father had something of the same type. Samuel Wesley, Jr., could not make much of his brother's doctrine.

With the ordinary hearers of Wesley there was resentment against the converts who claimed to be so sure that their sins were forgiven. Some of the resentment was no doubt justified, as arising from the obvious contradiction between profession and practice. The claim to knowledge of sins forgiven for the most part, however, was unpopular because of its reproach to those who could not make such claim. Here we come upon a strange peculiarity of John Wesley—his willingness to encourage others to make claims for themselves which he was not willing to make for himself. This will appear more clearly when we come to look at the teaching of Christian perfection. If we take Wesley's own utterances about his assurance, we find it modest enough, but there must have been something in the total situation which made the converts outrun their leader in their claims.

It is possible that we have here an instance of Wesley's open-mindedness and teachableness in the presence of what seemed to him to be fact. It is too much to say that Wesley was in any sense a scientist, except that he had markedly some scientific traits, an insatiably inquiring spirit, a respect for facts and a willingness to go with the facts whithersoever they might lead, though he himself was not always a trustworthy witness as to occurrences which he had seen. We have in mind his attitude toward the nervous uproar which attended many of the Methodist meetings—men who had resisted conviction for sin falling prone upon the earth and screaming for mercy, women under religious excitement lapsing into unconsciousness. These phenomena are now intelligible enough—intelligible psychologically, I mean—to scientific students, but were not at all intelligible in psychological terms then. Wesley observed some unusual instances with the utmost closeness, but all he could do was to set down what he saw, his testimony often impaired by his belief that supernatural agencies were at work. He did not have any scientific principles by which to guide his observations. We insert here an instance showing Wesley's careful examination of those passing through supernormal experiences.

In the afternoon I talked with two who had been several times in trances. What they all agreed in was (1) that at the time they went away, as they termed it, it was always at the time when they were fullest of the love of God; (2) that it came upon them in a moment without any previous notice, and took away all their senses and strength; (3) that there were some exceptions, but in general from that moment they were in another world, knowing nothing of what was done or said by all that were normal about them.

[Same day] Mr. B. came up and told me Alice Miller (fifteen years old) was fallen into a trance. I went down immediately and found her sitting on a stool and leaning against the wall with her eyes open and fixed upward. I made a motion as if going to strike, but they continued immovable. Her face showed an unspeakable mixture of reverence and love, while silent tears stole down her cheeks. Her lips were a little open and sometimes moved, but not enough to cause any sound. I do not know whether I ever saw a human face look so beautiful. Sometimes it was covered with a smile, as from joy, mixing with love and reverence—but the tears fell still but not so fast. Her pulse was quite regular. In about half an hour I observed her countenance change into the form of fear, pity, and distress, and she burst into a flood of tears and cried out: "Dear Lord, they will all be damned. They will all be damned." But in about five minutes her smiles returned, and only love and joy appeared in her face. About half an hour after six I observed distress take place again, and soon after she wept bitterly and cried out, "Dear Lord, they will all go to hell. The world will go to hell." Soon after she said: "Cry aloud, spare not." And in a few moments her look was composed again, and spoke a mixture of reverence, joy and love. Then she said aloud: "Give God the glory." About seven her sense returned. I asked, "Where have you been?" "I have been with my Saviour." "In heaven or on earth?" "I cannot tell but I was in glory." "Why, then, did you cry?" "Not for myself but for the world; for I saw they were on the brink of hell." "Why did you desire to give the glory to God?" "Ministers that cry aloud to the world—else they will be proved—and then God will leave them and they will lose their own souls."

Now, these occurrences did not happen frequently under George Whitefield, whose hearers were more likely almost to forget who they were and where they were under the spell of the dramatic magnetism of the speaker. They did not often take place in the audiences of Charles Wesley. This is odd. Charles Wesley was a poet and John a man of affairs. Yet it was Charles who was inclined to brush all these phenomena to one side with an impatient common sense. He even, on one occasion, announced to the audience that if any persons were seized by uncontrollable impulses, they would be taken forthwith to one corner of the room to be ministered to. This meeting was very quiet.

It may be that, though in this Charles had the right of it, John was thinking further than Charles. There is a common sense which is the outcome and product of years of adjustment to ordinary experience which guesses right in the presence of new facts, and there is an inferior common sense which is impatient of any departure from the regular just because it is a departure. Where there are only two alternatives—a course being right or wrong—this so-called good sense may often take a stand which turns out to be right. On the other hand, there is the mind not always called sensible, which is more open to fresh impressions, which welcomes anything which promises to throw light, and which as a result, through a stretch of years, welcomes much which is not light at all.

Some thirty years ago William James appeared before a committee of the Massachusetts legislature to protest against repressive measures forbidding what seemed to be mistaken medical practices. James said that to himself the practice seemed to be questionable, but that he feared that the checking of practices of the kind might close the doors to the entrance of truths which might look strange and at first queer, but which nevertheless might turn out to be true.

Indeed, the temper of Wesley as to these unusual occurrences was quite like that of James in the scrutiny of the material on which he based his studies in *The Varieties of Religious Experience*. James did not turn away from any material, no matter how apparently trivial or even unseemly, which made the slightest impression upon him as significant. Commenting on the respect and care with which he treated some of this material, he once remarked that he was more of a Methodist than the Methodists themselves. If a scientist was thus willing to explore all these phenomena for their scientific significance, why blame Wesley for like openness in the search for religious possibilities?

Again, let us note that the philosophy of the time was deistic—though few of those who heard Wesley preach knew anything about deism—the universe conceived of as a closed system running by itself, much as a cosmic clock, made and wound up by an almighty clockmaker, might be supposed to run. The deists were not atheists theoretically. They were willing to accept the existence of God and to honor him after a fashion, but verily he was a God afar off. For practical purposes there was not in deism any God worth having. Now, deism was in the background of Wesley's thinking, only he thought of God as intervening in the universe which divine power and wisdom had made. It became of immense importance, then, to recognize a divine intervention, the creation of the conditions of a miracle, if one should happen. Even if most of the leads to spiritual life through these strange happenings proved to be worthless, that did not prove that all were worthless —and Wesley kept on searching.

Still, again, Wesley believed in the existence of spirits, good and bad, which were always ready to break through into human affairs. This is to us now mostly superstition of the past, and yet not so very far in the past. Here, again, we may point to the high priest of modern psychology, William James, who was always probing into psychic mysteries. Of course it is possible to say that James did this on the scientific hypothesis that he would find nothing objective, that he would prove that there was nothing "there."

This is just say-so. James was not seeking to disprove but to find out. The difference between James and Wesley was that Wesley lived in the eighteenth and James in the nineteenth century; that the temper of James was more for knowledge for its own sake and that of Wesley for knowledge for salvation's sake; that James was not concerned with what the discoveries might reveal as was Wesley. Wesley firmly believed in spirits good and bad. Nobody could have convinced him that the noises at Epworth—made, indeed, while Wesley was away from home—were not the work of an evil spirit. In the revival work Wesley was convinced for a time that some of the phenomena were signs of the unusual power of God and others the unusual power of the devil. Most of these accompaniments of the Wesley preaching, whatever else we may say about them, had most potent advertising or "drawing efficiency."

One test we cannot well brush aside, namely, the genuinely changed lives of the majority of Wesley's converts. As the movement progressed the strange accompaniments of surrender to Wesley's preaching of the divine will grew fewer and fewer and finally ceased, so that Wesley no longer put emphasis upon them. We think of them now as the working of minds under extraordinary strain of fear, or pent-up conviction of sin, or repressed emotion, all moving according to laws which we are coming more and more to understand, if not to control. The essential is the moral and spiritual result, and this the Wesleyan movement achieved.

The question inevitably recurs as to the possible harm to those who needed spiritual quickening and who could not get it or were repelled by the Wesleyan preaching. The most of the criticism at this point comes from those already in other religious groups, like Alexander Knox, a firm friend of Wesley, a critic of many of his methods, who refused to count himself among the Methodists. Many of the severest denouncers of the Revival were those members of the English Church who resented everything in Wesley which seemed to reflect on the Church. As to those who were repelled from all religion by the peculiarities of Methodism and who never had been reconciled to religion—among them perhaps the Brontës—we must remember that such persons are always to be found at every widespread spiritual upheaval—and at other times, for that matter. They are usually, probably almost always, genuinely earnest and sincere, but are not able to adjust themselves to the particular message. Human nature being what it is both in preachers and hearers, we have to say that here both sides are about equally to blame, or not to blame.

A word about "crowd contagion," since the term is so often used to explain, if not to disparage, the Wesleyan Revival. We have been gravely told that crowds are worse than individuals as arousing the primitive instincts in men, that individuals in crowds yield to impulses to which they would never think of surrendering when by themselves.

If this were strictly true, it would be socially dangerous for men ever to assemble in crowds at all. In dealing with contagion we cannot pass final judgment till we see what is caught. If a crowd by crowd-contagion catches a lynching impulse, the result is bad. If it catches a glimpse of high spiritual values, what can we say but that the result is good? Values of this order stand in their own right, whether they are seized by men singly or in groups. Anyone who has had any experience with audiences knows that not only the lower but the higher emotions are quickened in the minds of the individuals present by the fact that the individual is listening in a group. Speakers of the longest experience tell us that they themselves find the best in themselves drawn out into utterance by the audience. If this is true in the effect of audience on speakers, why may it not be similarly true of the influence of the crowd upon the individual members of the crowd? To take an illustration from a slightly different realm, think of the rendition of an oratorio like Handel's *Messiah*. Here the importance of sheer size must not be overlooked. The chorus must be large, and the audience must be large, for the best effect. If an individual were to sit alone at a rehearsal of the oratorio, himself the only hearer, he would miss something, that something being the contagion of the audience. Of course it is possible to say that an audience is different from a crowd, but the distinction is a little too fine when we are thinking of Wesley's meetings. We must recognize that there was nothing in Wesley's preaching which intentionally made appeal to the so-called primitive impulses, unless we will have it that the emotional results previously considered were of such order; and they counted for less and less as the years went by.

There were admittedly some features of the social atmosphere of the eighteenth century which created a situation lending itself to emotional explosion—though such explosion was more often in the nature of a spiritual relief than of frustration or desperation. We of today cannot realize without deliberate effort the force of the idea of hell on the minds of men two hundred years ago. Two centuries ago hell was not a figure of speech, or a picture statement of the consequences of sin. To the ordinary mind it was an actual reality. The Roman Church had through centuries taught an actual hell. Just how men could believe in a hell of a type commonly accepted in Wesley's day we do not know. We are dealing here with one of the most baffling mysteries in human thinking. It may be that after the breakup of the Roman Empire the Church found it necessary to rule the minds of men, whose ancestors had been barbarians, by emphasis on what was the equivalent of force in the sphere of daily conduct. At any rate, many of the most kindly spirits of the olden days took literally the doctrine of a literal fire as an eternal punishment for sin. Wesley seems to have accepted this teaching.

In addition there was in England much of the Puritan spirit in its sterner aspect. We shall consider Wesley's attitude toward Calvinism later, but we must remark here that the God of the popular understanding in the eighteenth century was pretty grim.

Over all—I am speaking now of the types of persons to whom Wesley most commonly preached—there was the cloud of tragedy. Life was hard, without much to soften it. Into all this came the preaching of Wesley which, with all its acceptance by inheritance of the stiff stuff of orthodoxy, was full of hope, and that too for every man. In the circumstances the gospel has never been more worthy of its title of good news than in the sermons of John Wesley. The deists of the age virtually said that there was no news from God; the sterner Calvinists made the gospel bad news, except for themselves. It was the task of Wesley to convince the masses of his time that there was at hand news from God, and that the news was good, or better than deism or Calvinism.

Here is perhaps the most fitting place for a word about the services of Charles Wesley. Charles has been honored for the hymns which he left to the universal Church. In fact, however, his service to Methodism was in opening a channel for the relief of pent-up emotion. This relief became more than relief—it was uplift, itself a converting and exalting agency. If it is true that the Revival let loose primitive traits, it is also true that in Charles Wesley's hymns those traits were forthwith lifted up into the realm of high expression. What would otherwise have expressed a loosened tension through shouting or ejaculation, or other sheer nervous outbreak, found in the hymns utterance that was at once com-

plete and worthy. Critics of Wesley's poetic productions have said
that they now and again dropped into doggerel. It may be so,
more particularly when Wesley was jibing at an ecclesiastical or
doctrinal foe, or when he was composing a jig-jog tune on horseback, but not so when he was composing hymns for the Revival.
It is true that while Wesley wrote over six thousand sets of verses
only between four and five hundred are preserved today in the
Wesleyan hymnbook, a few over fifty in the latest edition of the
hymnal of the Methodist Episcopal Church, but that is not of much
significance in estimating the importance of what Wesley did. He
made the way of escape for strained and overwrought feeling, an
escape which did not allow the feeling to run off and away, but
which saved its value by binding it to lofty conception and deepened purpose. In telling of their conversion convert after convert
could find no better medium than to repeat one of Charles Wesley's
hymns, of which the least worthy was far, far above much of the
stuff we have all heard sung in church schools of a day much later
than Wesley's.

Let us take one hymn with a stanza which was dropped from
Methodist hymnals over a century ago, presumably because it
offended poetic or religious taste. At least the stanza has been
called doggerel by a prominent writer on early Methodism. I
refer to lines which were formerly part of the hymn: "Oh, how
happy are they, Who their Saviour obey." The concluding stanza
ran:

> "Fully justified I,
> I rode in the sky
>   Nor envied Elijah his seat.
> In a chariot of fire
> My soul mounted higher,
>   And the moon, it was under my feet."

Now, admitting all that can be said against this as religious
poetry, suppose we think of it as expression of escape from the
cramping bonds of the existence from which the Methodist Revival
brought deliverance to thousands of souls. No matter where we
rank it for its poetical effectiveness, we have to put it in a high place
for its psychological effectiveness. Utterances like this must be
judged by their force in reaching the minds to whom they are addressed. They even went farther down into the consciousness of
the Methodist groups than did many of John's sermons, or they

feathered the arrows of the sermons so as to lend them more precise aim, and send them farther under the surface. They had supreme carrying and striking power.

John Wesley left behind him in print one hundred and fifty-one sermons. The volumes in which they were published have had an incredible number of readers. Most of them were published in the *Arminian Magazine* before they were gathered together in book form. Many of them are still read. There is not a Methodist preacher the world around who has not read some of them, for all branches of Wesleyanism expect their candidates for the ministry to know something about the sermons of the founder of Methodism before being received into what is called "full connection." I wonder if it would be far astray to say that more persons had read some of Wesley's sermons than those of any other single preacher in the history of Christianity before the introduction of cheap printing about the middle of the last century.

It is not easy to say offhand just what has given the sermons their lasting power. Of course it is always possible to say that John Wesley was first and foremost an organizing genius, with a mind, if we accept Macaulay's judgment, like that of Richelieu (whatever this means), and that, through the organization of Methodism itself, he sent his preaching down through the after-generations. This is only a partial explanation, for time and again the Methodist preachers have gone back to Wesley's sermons to renew their strength. Some qualities the sermons do not have. They are not in any degree what our fathers called oratorical. Wesley put himself on record as caring nothing for "fine writing," which he condemned as "French." He seemed to think he could achieve this as well as most others if he should set himself to it, but he did not care for the style. There seems to be almost a note of irritation in his word here, as if he had met criticism for the plainness and directness of his pulpit utterances.

There can be no doubt as to the extreme care with which the Wesley sermons were prepared, at least for publication. As the one hundred and fifty-one sermons have come down to us, they are the heart and substance of the teaching which made Methodism what it was, and for the most part has been. Some of their general characteristics are worth noting.

To begin with, they are true to Wesley, or to all the accounts of him that have reached us. I repeat that they have been most carefully worked out. Wesley wrote almost incessantly, this con-

stant writing being, by the way, one of the marvels of his career.
He once spoke of himself as having to do so much traveling that
he lived most of his time alone. This time by himself he used
largely in writing, writing in a coach rattling over the English roads.
No matter what the inconveniences, the writing was carefully done.
The result of all the writing and rewriting and compression is that
we have Wesley. It would not be possible to go through the sermons and find a sentence which does not have the marks and spirit
of Wesley upon it. Every sentence published must have been
under his eyes scores upon scores of times. The sermons are evidently those which Wesley thought of as best expressing Methodism, and which had accomplished the most for Methodism. They
are here just as Wesley wished the world to see them. Every one
of them is before us as he left it.

So that, if we wish to understand Wesley, we take a long step
toward that understanding by reading the sermons. There they
are, just as he taught. If there had been in the sermons any substantial departure from what Wesley proclaimed as his message,
hundreds of readers, who had previously heard the sermons, would
have risen to point out the difference. The statements of truths
which made Methodism are here. We do not need any process of
higher criticism to tell us what Wesley really preached. We need
precious little interpretation to tell us what he meant.

With this solid mass before us, we can soon see some features
of Wesley which he himself took for granted, but which are quite
significant looked at in other times and circumstances. To start
with, in spite of all its rationalism, the eighteenth century was sentimental. I do not mean that the age was emotional in that "enthusiasm" which seemed so horrible to the period, to the upper classes
especially. It was, however, an era of appeal to tears, not boisterous
outcrying but copious and profuse weeping. The pathetic was
relished as if it were a delicious morsel. Books and sermons were
often judged by their power to set people quietly weeping. It
seems paradoxical to speak of the age as at once rationalistic and
sentimental, but so it was. Of course, it is psychologically true that
often the most sentimental eras are the hardest-hearted, because the
sentiment, having wept itself out, cannot be held to any long-
working persistence. It arouses hopes which it does not fulfill.
It seems at times as if Wesley in preaching had deliberately and
determinedly guarded himself against sentiment.

There is nothing suggestive of oratory in the sermons. We

may well wonder if Wesley himself was ever much moved by oratory. It would be interesting to know what he thought of Whitefield's preaching as preaching. We know what he thought of Whitefield as a man. He never ceased to hold him in highest regard. We know only too well what he thought of the Calvinism of Whitefield's theology. What he thought of him as a preacher we have no way of telling accurately. Wesley never painted any pictures himself, never gave himself to dramatic attitudes, never even found much place for illustration. Whitefield is said, in the tradition that has come down to us, never to have felt that he could do his best with a sermon till he had preached it fifty or sixty times. We cannot imagine Wesley having any such feeling about his sermons.

It seems just to say that Wesley thought of sermons from the instrumental point of view. He thought of the sermon only to ask the question as to what it could do. There is almost no reference to sermons throughout his writings except with this question in mind.

His own style is always rigorous, direct, and plain. He seems to wish to make it into veritable bread of life. Much of the material is dry, but it never wears out the appetite. A remarkable peculiarity is that one can read on and on, if one is interested at all, without feeling as weary as is usual with sermonic productions. Here they are—straight, bare, forceful. No appeal to pathos, no touch of humor, no illustration, no long stops for pious ejaculation, yet nourishing and sustaining. Generation after generation of Methodists lived largely on this food.

While Wesley accepted the doctrines of his Church, he did not give much space, at least in the printed sermons, to doctrine as such, except as it bore directly upon life. The sermons are ethical, not as moral essays, but as Christian truth bearing upon human conduct. The moral teaching always holds to the main track. No superfine points are raised, no puzzles are played with, no dubious points are stressed. The aim seems to be to make the way plain for the most limited of the wayfaring men.

Wesley always implied much that he did not say. One cannot rise from the perusal of these sermons without feeling that Wesley paid his audiences the fine and altogether too rare compliment of assuming that they could not only understand but appreciate his puttings of the truth. It is a curious commentary on these our days of supposedly widespread public education to learn that these sermons of Wesley had an immense reading in days that, we have often been told, did not do any reading at all. We are here in something of the same curious plight in which we find ourselves when we begin to think about those to whom, let us say, the Epistles of Paul were written. We have been so long accustomed to assume that no other age has reached our level of general understanding that we do not ask at all why it is, if this is so, that ordinary men of the time of Paul understood the Epistles so much better than we do. We have been told of recent years that the Greek of the New Testament was the speech of the common people. Was the substance of Paul's Epistles to the Romans and Galatians, then, the thought of the common people? Similarly, we have heard that in the day of Wesley the people were illiterate, that they were dull and heavy. No matter how we explain it all, John Wesley must have expected his hearers and readers by the thousands to understand him. At least he assumed that they could be brought to understand. Here was respect toward an audience which itself is a tribute to the mind which showed the respect. No preacher could have thought meanly of an audience to whom he could address such phrasings of truth as those embodied in the Wesley sermons. It is verily a hard puzzle.

As something of an explanation may be the fact that, after Wesley once got well going, he knew the people of England as no other man of his century knew them. After many years of traveling he made this claim to knowledge for himself. Shortly before the outbreak of the American War he wrote to a high government official and told him point-blank that nobody was his, Wesley's, own superior in knowledge of what was going on in the mind of the people of England. It must have been out of such fullness and exactitude of understanding that he addressed his hearers as he did. If he did speak thus out of knowledge, he saw deeper than do most leaders of opinion. For most leaders think themselves best qualified to minister to those who have had the best advantages. The young minister going out to a parish today, like those which Wesley addressed, if such a parish could be found, would be dismayed and appalled.

It is only fair to remark that Wesley himself was thus both dismayed and appalled at the suggestion that he take the parish of Epworth, for example, back in those days when he was supposedly rendering such excellent service at Oxford. He himself said that he felt called especially to work in a field like Oxford, just as many another young preacher has said since his time. Now, evidently something must have taken place in the inner spirit of Wesley to make him over into a preacher who would gladly give his best to make truth understood by the lowliest intelligences within reach. We may get into confusion by overmuch reflection on the inner nature of the transformation of Wesley the Oxford recluse into Wesley the unresting preacher moving throughout all England, but the fact of the change, or contrast, itself is inescapable.

The change was not in the direction of phrase-making as such. Apart from a half dozen sentences like "The world is my parish," Wesley did not make phrases. The power of mind seems to have been one of increasing grasp on the essentials, with the ability to state and restate from differing angles the central dominating conception. The treasures of mind and heart always have this for their peculiarity, that the more determined the resolution to share them, the more genuinely they become the sharer's own. Wesley's hold of the truths which made Methodism was not due merely to prolonged and solitary study—though there was that—but to incessant labor in actually stating and restating his message. It is a commonplace among proclaimers of ideas that the easiest task is that of presentation to trained minds. The scientific treatise, with its apparatus and furnishing of technical terms, may appear to the layman in such matters to have cost immense intellectual travail. The discovery of the facts or the principles did indeed cost such incalculable labor, but not necessarily the stating of the results in language. All a writer of a scientific monograph has to do is to get his ideas together in fairly presentable shape and the understanding mind of the reader will do the rest. Far different, however, is the task of making these conceptions the property of the lay, or common, or plain man.

I linger perhaps for what may seem disproportionate length over considerations like this for what impresses me as a good reason. It has been, or it used to be, the custom to disparage the intellectual qualities of John Wesley in laying stress on his genius as an organizer. The gloomy comment of Matthew Arnold on the prospects of culture in the United States will be recalled. Arnold once expressed a misgiving as to the future of culture in this country because there were in America so many Methodists; and the Methodists could not rise high in the intellectual scale, hampered as they were by following the leadership of a third-rate mind like Wesley's. We shall have occasion for a further remark or two later as to Wesley's intellectual services to the world, but we mention here the increasing respect for the power of the Wesley mind as we come to better recognition of the intellectual qualities required of him who would be a popularizer of any truth at all worth while. Now, if we are to put democracy in the place of supreme power as the social or governmental force, then clearly the man who best reaches the mind of the masses must be given credit for an indispensable power in the service of men. We see today especially the effort to which men go to capture, through the radio and the cheap press, the thinking of the mass about, it may be, commercial ventures of uncertain value. The skill with which this is done, in its manifold forms ranging from advertising to advocacy of catchy political novelties, is one of the marvels of our day. Much of this is clearly antisocial, but the intellectual vigor here requisite cannot be wisely disparaged.

Higher in the scale is the achievement of him who gets sound scientific knowledge into the thinking of the people. This has to be done if democracy is to gain that decent respect for expert knowledge without which it may come to grief. Scientists sometimes get impatient with the people for not accepting forthwith an expert scientist's sound knowledge rather than the nostrum of the quack. The seat of the trouble is that the quack does not know science, but he does know people and how to talk to them. The remedy is to cease to disparage what we call the popularizer and to increase the honor to him who, once in possession of sound scientific principle, either himself develops the power to give it popular statement or hails as fellow worker the one who has such power. The sheer intellectual ability to perform this task is of no mean order. On the side of statement, Wesleyanism was focused in Wesley. When we reflect that the generations to whom Wesley preached not only got such hold of his truth as to make it a working force in their own lives but that they sank it deep into the lives of their children, we get some measure of Wesley's ability as a proclaimer of the gospel.

We must admit a good many mysteries in the career of Wesley as a preacher. We have difficulty in trying to fit him into our conceptions of open-air address before immense crowds. It is easier to do this with Whitefield, though even with him we come upon much that we cannot understand. Abel Stevens repeats the legend that the voice of Whitefield could be heard a mile—which may mean much, or perhaps not so much. Whitefield may have shouted out a call that could be heard a mile, with the configuration of the surrounding ground and the atmospheric conditions just right, but we cannot imagine Wesley raising his voice in any such fashion. He used with an expert's skill his vocal resources. Moreover, his material was not the sort to be communicated in shouts, or even in a very high pitch of voice. It was instruction and exposition and argument, none of which are best accomplished at the top of the voice. Probably the most important part of Wesley's preaching was not done before the vast crowds. It is estimated that during the years of his itinerancy he preached over forty thousand times, which means, of course, that the most of the speaking must have been before rather small groups. His utterance must have been of the conversational type. We note too how many times he spoke at five o'clock in the morning, which means that many of his audiences must have been composed of small bands of earnest, sympathetic inquirers. Men by the thousands are not likely to assemble at five o'clock in the morning, nor are men prone to come together at that hour, no matter what the customs of the community as to rising, unless they are seriously-minded.

Everyone who writes about Wesley has much to say about this extraordinary power over hostile mobs. His courage no one has ever doubted. The courage, however, was not merely that of a man indifferent to danger, callous as to what might happen, or the self-confidence of one of imposing stature and manifest physical strength. Just a moderate degree of animal courage, combined with obvious muscular resources, will protect a speaker from the ordinary mob's coming too close to him, until those on the outer circumference begin to push in. Now, Wesley did not possess the stature or the unusual physical might. He was five feet six inches in height and never weighed over one hundred and twenty pounds. He did not outmob mobs, for that implies something of a mob-power in himself. We do not have much to go by in trying to picture him before hostile mobs, but we have something. We know that, because of shortness of stature, he had to stand upon a chair or a box, that he used his voice most skillfully, that he never appeared except when he was the last word—not in fashion—but in neatness in dress, that the fineness and softness of his hair arrested any glance at all observant, that he gave always the impression of perfect self-control. Most open-air speaking is a formless, catch-as-catch-can, hit-or-miss affair, depending upon smartness, or quickness of tongue and readiness of wit. Wesley held his speech to his essential conceptions and, judging by his printed sermons, kept the main aim constantly before him. In full possession of his message, he knew how to say it again and again. Probably most of those who intended merely to listen for a few minutes on the outer edge of the crowd, stayed till he finished; and those who did have to move on heard enough before they left to know what it was all about.

The self-control, according to all accounts, showed itself notably in his eyes. He is himself authority for the statement that in meeting a mob he always looked directly into the faces of the leaders. This itself must have been disconcerting, especially to leaders who in blind rage did not know what they were about. We are reminded of what Sir William Ramsey says of Saint Paul in *St. Paul the Traveler and Roman Citizen*, namely, that it was the eyes of Paul which gave him his control in dealing with crowds, as suggested by recurring passages such as "He fastened his eyes upon him." Probably a wild crowd has in it so much of the animal that a born ruler of men deals with it somewhat as an animal-tamer deals with a furious untamed beast, by looking directly into the savage eyes. So marked was this power of Wesley's that Professor F. M. Davenport, in *Primitive Traits in Religious Revivals*, is of the opinion that the evangelist possessed virtually hypnotic skill. Whatever it was, the weapon of defense was inner. Anyone who has read the history of early Methodism both in England and in America has noticed a contrast between the ways in the two countries of meeting mob attack. Wesley never sought for any human help against mobs, beyond his own strange ability to control rioters, except what might come through the legal authorities, though he does speak somewhat appreciatively of the readiness of muscular Methodist men, and of an occasional Methodist woman, to defend him with fistic might. In America, on the other hand, the Methodist of the Peter Cartwright type was entirely willing, upon appropriate occasion, to use his fists.

To return to the preaching, we have from Horace Walpole one piercing ray of light thrown upon Wesley. Walpole, detached and cynical though he may have always been, has in his letters probably given us more than any other single writer about the life of the eighteenth century from the angle of the more favored classes. In October, 1776, Walpole happened upon Wesley preaching in the open air at Bath. Here is the picture that comes down to us.

"Wesley is a clean, elderly man, fresh-colored, his hair

smoothly combed, but with a little *soupcon* of curl at the ends.
Wondrous clever, but as evidently an actor as Garrick. He spoke
his sermons, but so fast and with so little accent, that I am sure he
has often uttered it, for it was like a lesson. There were facts and
eloquence in it, but toward the end he exalted his voice and acted
very highly enthusiastic, decried learning, told stories, like Latimer,
of the fool of his college, who said 'I thanks God for everything.'
Except a few from curiosity, and some honorable women the congregation was very mean."

The impression is one of complete cleanness and tidiness in
personal appearance, of extreme whiteness of hair, of one uttering
something altogether familiar as if the speaker had delivered the
same material many times before, of an actorlike quality in the
delivery. Just what it was in Wesley that made Walpole think of
acting it would be hard to say, unless it be that absolute ease of
self-possession of which we have had ample occasion to speak. Dr.
J. S. Simon, author of the monumental five-volume history of the
Wesleyan movement, went to the pains to look up the text on which
Wesley so preached as to give the impression to Walpole that the
theme was an old one. Quite likely the theme was old, for the text
was: "Thou shalt love thy neighbor as thyself."

Speaking probably out of his own experience, Wesley did not
feel that an ordinary minister, or an extraordinary one for that
matter, could with profit speak from the same pulpit through more
than a year's residence. He insisted upon the itinerant system as
indispensable for keeping the message fresh and vital. Remember
that Wesley was not thinking in terms of a Church but of a society,
and that of a predominantly, almost exclusively, evangelistic type.
He knew well enough that the English Church, from which he
never wished to depart, had to do a more inclusive work than his
societies—priestly, pastoral, administrative tasks which could not
best be done by itinerants. Methodist leadership, after Wesley was
gone, misread his emphasis on itinerant preaching. He had to
train a group of preachers who had had no chance at the discipline
of the schools. He knew that the message which they could best
proclaim was one centering in their own experiences, that the message would soon lose its force if repeated too often to the same
group. A quite ordinary preacher can, by delivering the same message to different groups, so take advantage of the selective power of
the attentive listening of the groups themselves as to produce a few
sermons of outstanding effectiveness. The preacher almost uncon-

sciously comes to see what phrasings of the truth are most compelling and, by frequent repetition, increases the effectiveness. Under the older idea of an itinerant episcopacy, where a bishop seldom preached to the same audience more than once in a long period, the bishop could create a few sermons almost certain to be oratorically dynamic. It would not be fair to mention names, but let the reader whose memory goes back to the old system recall the preaching of some of the pulpit giants of those days. How many of those preachers had more than five or six sermons in which they were outstanding? It was a realization of such possibilities and limitations that determined Wesley's emphasis on itinerancy. If it be supposed that Wesley believed only in the itinerant ministry, we would do well to read again his word about the length of time it took his father to produce any deep spiritual result at Epworth, and about the success which Samuel Wesley at last won.

Like most other preachers, Wesley had his literary or philosophic pets which he exhibited upon occasion. He did not leave these out when he came to publish the sermons. For example, there are the paragraphs which have stirred ambitious evolutionists to claim Wesley as an evolutionist—his reference to consistent sequence in the cosmic creative processes, with each stage depending on what went before and leading in strict order to what was to come after. To read Darwinian evolutionism into this is a striking instance of scientific will-to-believe. A more plausible exposition is that the paragraph is a manifestation of the confirmed orderliness of Wesley's own mind. Wesley delighted too to dwell upon his belief that God must have provided some form of immortality for animals. This causes a smile, but is really a revelation that Wesley had acutely realized the most puzzling and baffling feature of the mystery of physical evil, namely, the vast extent of apparently purposeless pain in the animal world.

PART IV

THE PECULIAR TALENT

"I know this is the peculiar talent which God has given me wherein (by his Grace,) I am not behind the very chiefest of them."—To Mrs. Hall, Newcastle-on-Tyne, November 17, 1742.

PART IV

THE PECULIAR TALENT

PASTOR

THE inner life of Wesley found another vent in what he called his peculiar talent, that of organizer. In discussing the methods by which Wesley kept Methodism going we should consider what we may call, in the broader meaning, his pastoral work—his personal attention to the condition of the individual members of the societies, the members who had been gathered in by the tremendous success of field preaching.

It may be justly said that the societies were organized around the idea of the pastoral care of individuals. Wesley's purpose was to develop the highest type of individual Christian character. To do this he made the utmost possible use of social means. It is odd to reflect that the religious leader who is so often quoted as preaching strictly an individual gospel, and as aiming at strictly individual results, should have relied so thoroughly on social instruments. Of course what this comment means is that Wesley did not aim at the transformation of the general outside social, institutional forces. This can be more adequately dealt with in a later connection. Here we note that Wesley deliberately chose social measures for the accomplishment of individual results.

We have already spoken of the classes and of their consequences, in some directions beneficial, in others harmful. In addition to the classes there were "bands," each composed of members of the same sex, for intimate, personal, mutual confession and counsel. The "bands" after full trial did not prove to be any better than other such organizations in the history of the Church. Let us recall to our minds again and again that much of Wesley's method was influenced by his experience with the Oxford Club. In that Club there was the freest baring of the life of each to the scrutiny of all the others. Such exposure, however, justifiable in a picked group of friends of long familiarity with one another, was different from the intimacies encouraged among persons brought into the Methodist societies after all varieties of spiritual histories. Societies for counsel, surely; but for free and uncontrolled mutual confession, not so surely.

109

Of course we may defend Wesley's policy in this on the principle of sharing experiences. Sometimes even today the sharing is discussed as if it were about on the same plane as the discussions of groups of scientists putting together, in round-table fashion, the results of discoveries. Such data, however, from an objective field are quite different from those of the inner life. Sharing scientific information is far other than listening to a story of evil deeds brought out into confession. There is soil and stain for many a sensitive soul even in hearing such description. Again, some evil impulses are not exorcised by being told of but are made stronger by the fact that they are put into speech.

Here again we have to remember that Wesley had to find his way along by rule of thumb. He had to learn the same lesson so painfully put to him in Georgia—that the higher the aim in seeking to guide souls, the more precise and exact must be the reckoning with the actual realities as presented by the lives of those he was trying to help. This business of the bands was found sooner or later to make trouble, as when, for example, a prominent woman in one of the societies confessed to a dawning affection for a worthy man in the same society. It was too much to expect that sensation-loving human nature would hold this revelation as a confidence for long. To speak bluntly, the good woman's confession "got out." The most surprising feature of the incident was the surprise of Wesley himself. Just how he supposed his bands could get far without such incidents, or accidents, it would be difficult to say.

Probably a key to Wesley's successes and difficulties in pastoral administration is to be found in his own nature. With all his astonishing versatility, which is suggestive of complexity in character, Wesley seems to have been of extraordinary simplicity. This may have been the ground for the remark of his brother Charles that John was made to be a prey—what the slang of the twentieth century would call "an easy mark"—for the persons who in turn seem made to take advantage of such easiness. Probably the judgment of Charles was hasty impatience. The truth seems to be that Wesley gave other people credit for purity of aim like his own, and for complete good faith similar to his own. Wesley was singularly willing to let anybody and everybody look into his mind and heart. He did not attempt to conceal anything, because he had nothing especially serious to conceal. It is customary to say that John Wesley was thoroughly an Englishman. He certainly was not English in his lack of reticence about inner experiences.

There have been those who have supposed that in the reliance on bands, and classes as well, Wesley was trying to make use of what was good in the Roman Catholic confessional. This may be true. Wesley was so impressed with many features of Romanism that his attitudes lent some color to the charge that he had leanings toward papistry. We shall have occasion to see that this accusation followed him throughout his life. Now, the confessional is founded on the idea that the priest has the power of absolution, that he can forgive sins and can free men from the penalties of sin. This is the essential relief in the confessional—the freedom from fear of hell, and hell was a fact in the belief of the Romanism of Wesley's day. The relief in the bands was psychological, thoroughly human—that of talking something through and getting it out of one's mind. The confessional is impersonal; the penitent may not know the priest into whose ears he is pouring his tale of sin. The pastoral service that Wesley had in view was that of such confidential and trustful intimacy that the confession of sin would relieve the confessor through the knowledge that some other human being knew and understood. The ideal is good enough. Here again, however, Wesley had to learn that human beings must be dealt with as they are, that confession to a skilled knower of, and sympathizer with, troubled souls is one thing and that the encouragement of confession to a group quite another. Knowledge of psychology, in which, such as it was, Wesley took an absorbing interest in his own day, has gone far beyond anything dreamed of in the eighteenth century. We know the danger of talking about our sins. The fathers who spoke so familiarly of besetting sins did not seem to realize that the more a man speaks of his besetting sin the more the sin besets him. As to confession, it is clear that if one had done a fellow human being a wrong, one ought to go to the utmost, not merely to confess the wrong, but to make amends. Sins that have to do with the inner personal life, however, should be confessed indeed, but to God alone. Wesley was quite given to self-depreciation, but not in the concrete. In the *Journal*, which was intended for the edification of the faithful, there is abundant disparagement of himself in vague general terms, but not much in concrete acknowledgment of particular acts of wrongdoing. If the confessions in the bands had been no more specific than Wesley's own admissions of evil deeds, no considerable harm would have been done.

Wesley's advice to his followers was that they should tell one another of whatever each saw wrong in the other. If this is not done, according to Wesley, the unuttered feeling will fester. The figure of speech used—"festering"—is not altogether happy. If one could think of the cleansing of a festering sore as the removal of poison by a keen, swift stroke of a surgeon's lancet, one might see an aptness in Wesley's figure of speech. That is not often the way, however, that festered misunderstandings are dealt with. There is a mussy poking and fussing about by bungling individuals, with the last state worse than the first.

Wesley had nothing in his own nature to help him in this intimate dealing with intimates. He had a bland, unruffled quality of mind which no criticism was likely to disturb. It is highly entertaining to run through the *Journal,* especially for the years when Methodism was thoroughly going, and note the openness with which Wesley himself welcomed the criticism of the preachers and the complacency with which he contemplated it. After a piece of searching criticism directed against himself, he would enter the observation that the criticism was, of course, absurd. The humorous aspect of all this was in that "of course."

I have said that Wesley had the temper of a religious scientist. That is the only consideration which lifts some of his personal inquiries up into the sphere of dignity at all. There was indeed the determination to work righteousness down into the least and last detail of conduct, as, for example, the refusal to use tea as a beverage, but there was also a remorseless closeness of scrutiny. We shall meet Sarah Ryan now and again, but we may quote here from a letter to her under date of February, 1756: "The being continually watched over for evil; the having every word I spoke, every action I did, small and great, watched with no friendly eye: the hearing a thousand little, tart, unkind reflections, in return for the kindest words I could devise,

> 'Like drops of eating water on the marble,
>   At length have worn my sinking spirits down.'

Yet I could not say, 'Take thy plague away from me'; but only, 'Let me be purified, not consumed.'" Mrs. Wesley found this letter about herself in her husband's pocket. Then he wrote again to Mrs. Ryan that he had not seen his wife in such a temper for several years. Now, this letter, under the circumstances, by which I mean the domestic difficulties which Wesley was facing at the moment, was just about the extreme limit of indiscretion, judged by any standards that human beings are accustomed to apply. Yet, from the terms which Wesley used in another connection, we may fairly conclude that he was in genuine search of religious resources which he thought Sarah Ryan possessed. She was subject to peculiar religious sensitiveness, or Wesley thought she was.

Pastoral work, in the strict sense of visiting the members of the societies, Wesley seems to have disliked. Yet he did it, and did it faithfully. As soon as he came into a community where there was a Methodist society, he secured from the leaders a list of the members and started forth to call on every one of them. His calls aimed definitely at finding out whether it was wise or not to continue to carry the names on the lists. In some places he cut off as many as half the list as he found it. In 1758 he wrote "Though a man preach like an angel, he will neither collect, nor preserve a society, which is collected, without visiting them from house to house." In 1774, at the age of seventy-one, he wrote: "I began at the east end of the town, to visit the society from house to house. . . . This [visiting] is so grievous to flesh and blood, that I can prevail on few, even of our preachers to undertake it."

One of the surprises to the reader of the *Journal* is the heavy loss from year to year of those who, of their own free choice, had joined the societies. This was partly due to the emotional stress under which many had come in, but also in part to the strictness of the Wesley scrutiny. Wesley had before him the reports of leaders as well as the results of his own questionings. Then there was the love feast—a spiritual communion of the Methodists who came together partaking of water and biscuit or wafer as the sign of their fellowship—admission to the love feast being by tickets distributed among those who had reached a prescribed number of attendances on the Methodist services.

I fear there was much that was mechanical and even wooden about all this. Objective data, of course, can be gathered, records of attendance reported, statements of religious conditions repeated, but seldom enough basis laid by such means in every case to warrant exclusion from the society. Moreover, it is doubtful if Wesley's interviews were always wise or skillful. A man who makes careful entry in his diary of every prayer he utters during a day may miss much of the subtlety of question and interpretation of answer which marks the true physician of souls. A modern physician to men's bodies knows that no matter how important the information about a patient he may learn from the nurse's chart, the chart cannot tell all, or even the most relevant facts. In spiritual culture John Wesley was, as elsewhere and everywhere, too systematic.

We are mistaken, however, if we interpret his slashing of the society records by the standards by which we should judge a like policy in the pastorate of a church. We must insist again and again that Wesley never thought of himself as a rector of churches in dealing with his societies. Much that Wesley did throughout his career is entirely misleading to us if we do not keep firm hold of the fact that he was working primarily in a society and not in a church.

Somewhat akin to this theme of Wesley's pastoral efficiency is his personal relation to men in extreme difficulty. Within the last two or three years criticism against Wesley has revived in connection with the history of the case of Doctor Dodd. Dodd was an able writer on religious themes who lost his way morally and forged Lord Chesterfield's name and thereby stole a large sum of money. The transgression was in itself a singularly crazy deed, both of the sum involved and the prominence of him whose name was dishonestly used. Detection was inevitable, and carried the death penalty. Dodd was, of course, found guilty and sentenced to be hanged. The crime seems to have been one of those queer freaks of aberration for which a deeper knowledge of the mysteries of human nature makes more allowance now than then. Dodd's services to the cause of Christian truth had been singularly valuable. Keen students are sure that Wesley leaned heavily upon Dodd in some of his religious argument. The charge is that Wesley did not show much interest in saving the convicted doctor of divinity from execution—and that he appears badly by contrast with Dr. Samuel Johnson, who exerted himself to the utmost in the doomed man's behalf. The most, however, that can be urged against Wesley is that he was slow in bestirring himself. There does not seem to have been anything that he left undone when once he started, and there does not seem to have been much more that he could have done if he had started earlier. He called on Doctor Dodd in prison twice or more times. Still, the whole affair does leave a bad taste in one's mouth. Doctor Dodd was not a criminal in the ordinary sense. The incident is revealing in that it shows the mildness of response that such events called forth from the public. The penalty was out of all reason for an offense of the kind. It may be that the commonness of the death decree itself made even a man like John Wesley seem indifferent. It is true that there were offenses much less consequential punished in the same fashion. Again, Wesley seems to have been more impressed with Doctor Dodd's penitence than with anything else, as if that were the only significant feature involved. We cannot help remarking that, in the earlier years when the members of the Oxford Club did so much pastoral work in jails, they usually seemed to assume that the prisoners were getting about what they deserved. The triumphs of grace too often delighted in were shown in the adjustment which condemned men made to their doom. It is true that in his later career John Wesley stood nobly by John Howard in his work of prison reform, but he seems to have had in mind the wretched conditions of the prisons themselves. If he had exploded now and then against the whole English system of dealing with crime, he would have been performing quite as religious a task as listening to the confessions of miserable unfortunates about to suffer the extreme penalty. Here again, however, we have to be careful not to weigh the eighteenth century in the scales of the twentieth.

I suppose it is in order to consider the helpful works of Wesley, outside of the strictly religious, under the head of pastoral services, inasmuch as these were directed to the welfare of individuals. We look, then, at the attempts of Wesley to minister to the bodies of men. In a time like Wesley's it is almost impossible for ministers not to seek to relieve the sufferings of the diseased. At the present day anyone who has traveled in mission fields in backward countries has noticed how many Christian workers are distributing simple medicinal remedies to the sick. Sometimes the remedies are not so simple, and medical practicing by church workers becomes a peril. In my work as a Methodist bishop visiting missionary fields I have now and again found native preachers distributing physical remedies, sometimes for fees, with no medical knowledge on the part of the preachers whatever. The reason is the omnipresent horror of sickness and physical injury. Now, this omnipresent distress was always under Wesley's eyes. He felt he had to do something, and he did what he could. He set himself to investigate diseases and remedies. He is himself the authority for the statement that through virtually all his working life he made the study of physical remedies his avocation. With unwearying patience he read all that he could find on the methods of curing all manner of bodily disorders.

The results of this study he published in the book called *Primitive Physic,* with its copious recommendations of strenuous

and mighty remedies, and of tar water for almost everything. Here
we have especially to take care lest we fall to gasping with astonish-
ment at manifest ignorance and credulity. Let us remember that
all this was two hundred years ago. Moreover, Wesley got the prescriptions which he brought together from the physicians of the
time. Dr. John Whitehead, who wrote the first good biography of
Wesley, was a doctor. The prescriptions which Wesley wrote down
for his people could not have been so very different from those of
the regular practitioners, or they would have aroused the protests
of Whitehead. Medical practice was not then the scientifically
equipped and socially supervised function it is today. Berkeley, a
contemporary of Wesley, was one of the profoundest philosophers
of his time—indeed, it may well be of all times—yet Berkeley was
as ardent in proclaiming the virtues of tar water as of idealism.
Indeed, some of the best phrasings of idealism—or the best sentences
about certain phases of idealism—are to be found embedded in his
discussions of tar water. *Primitive Physic* by Wesley is a revelation
not so much of Wesley's own information as of the state of medical
knowledge in England in his time. It is also a revelation of the
popular thinking about the body and its ailments. In out-of-the-
way communities today we find mothers, and more particularly
grandmothers, recommending for babies, and older persons for that
matter, the most astounding remedies, with each grandmother saying that the remedy is good because she got it from her grandmother. Now, it does not require a long line of grandmothers to
carry us back to John Wesley's day. It always seems humorous to
us to come upon queer recommendations as to remedies for human
illnesses in the writings of a man like John Wesley. Let us not
overlook the fact, then, that almost any specific for a disease would
seem queer until it began to work. The scientist proceeds here
just by trying one article after another till he finds something that
seems to succeed. There is no *a priori* reason why quinine should
relieve malaria. All we know is that it does. The only way men
found out the virtues of quinine was by experiment. Now, our
grandmothers were not skilled scientists, but in dealing with diseases they acted like scientists, at least in trying one thing after
another. I once earned the reproof of a doctor in referring jok-
ingly to the remedies applied to Francis Asbury by the Methodist
women of the early days of Methodism in America. Asbury was a
constant sufferer from inflamed throat, probably due to infected
tonsils. The good women of the day used to cast horseshoe nails

into some stewed concoction in order that the medicinal qualities of the iron might be available for the bishop's throat. The physician reminded me that modern scientific knowledge recognizes the medicinal properties of iron, and declared that the women of one hundred and fifty years ago were feeling after knowledge which later investigation has confirmed. In Wesley's day anybody could search for remedies for illness, and one man's search might prove as productive as another's.

Wesley was scientific in making place for the control of natural laws. Long after his time men looked upon cholera as a direct scourge from God and insisted that the only way to combat it was by penitence and prayer. Wesley would have admitted, and urged, the need of spiritual resources in such a situation, but he would have tried also to find the natural remedies. At least that is what he was always striving after for the relief of suffering mortals. It is interesting to read of his researches into knowledge about electricity and his tests of electric processes on himself. John Wesley took note of the electrical experiments of Benjamin Franklin while they were actually going forward, which is something of a proof that his temper was not wholly conservative.

We must not fail to see either that some of Wesley's general rules as to health were valuable for his day and for ours. Suggestions as to moderation in diet abound in his discussions of health. He knew nothing about calories, but he hit upon dietary habits that controlled them pretty well. All his life he was himself a master of his body, making it do just about what he desired of it. He did not know modern psychiatry, but in his own life and in his guidance of the life of others he was an earnest searcher after the laws of inner life, mistaken as were some of his methods. He certainly knew the value of the regularities in the control of body and mind, the importance of the earlier hours of the night for sleep, the healthful efficacy of fresh air and plenty of it, the beneficial influence of a tranquil spirit. We smile at his advice to cure colds and other minor ailments by riding on horseback half a day in the teeth of a wind that could fairly be called a gale; but if we had seen the lack of ventilation in the humbler houses of the eighteenth century, we might have welcomed a remedy that would have driven fresh air into every cell of the lungs. We must not forget either that Wesley was entitled to some measure of authority as a health adviser because of his success in pulling himself back from death more than once. In middle age he was so near death from "consumption," possibly tuberculosis, that he all but gave up in despair, going so far down as to write an epitaph for his own tombstone, though this was probably nothing more than an instance of the demand of his system-loving mind that everything be ready for any contingency. In this self-recovery, the determining force appears to have been Wesley's sheer resolve to get well. We believe today that the best treatment of such illness as Wesley seemed to have is rest, and we have difficulty in trying to imagine Wesley relying upon a rest cure. He did, however, bring himself back to strength after death had begun to draw alarmingly near.

By precept and example Wesley taught system for body and mind. We have already seen that we have to take the bad effects with the good in all this. Wesley's system at times almost seems to take charge of him and march him off at its own behests. When a man lays so much stress on getting up on time to preach at five in the morning and has so much to say about it as Wesley had, it is a fair question as to whether the system itself is not counting too much with him. On the other hand, it is likewise a fair question as to whether Wesley did not do quite as much for his followers by drilling them incessantly to religious habits as by any of his forms of stress on the value of extraordinary moments of uplift and insight. He aimed to utilize religious power, and to do that had to harness it to regularity of worship and deed. Much of the Methodist system seems mechanical as we look back at it, but the use of the mechanical means themselves did something to bring religion into daily life. What Wesley achieved in this close intimacy with his people was to put into their hands tools for the development of, and expression of, and work of the religious life. The maker of a spiritual tool is quite as important to mankind as the inventor of a material tool. One of the farthest-reaching outcomes of Wesley's work was the setting of thousands upon thousands of men and women to systematic doing of what they were profoundly convinced was the will of God.

The outreach of Wesley's authority in this guidance of men in intimate practical affairs was astonishing. For example, *Primitive Physic* brought Wesley in royalties the sum of thirty thousand pounds—$150,000 in American money—that too at a time when money was more valuable than now. Wesley used the royalties as they came in to buy further copies of the book for free distribution.

While we are on this general theme, it may be relevant to state that Wesley aimed to make himself an educational factor among groups that had not much chance at the training or informing their minds. He was indeed a man of one book—the Bible—but it would be preposterous to take this statement literally. He read and wrote incessantly, always with the welfare of the ordinary people in mind. He wrote on all ranges of themes to bring the more weighty subjects into the thinking of the Methodists, whose ideas of propriety were not always as broad as his own. We have all read of the fate which befell his notes made on a copy of the plays of Shakespeare. They were burned as useless "baggage." John Pawson, one of the preachers who afterward enjoyed something like episcopal honors, seems to have been the one responsible for this brilliant feat.

Suppose we look at a work of Wesley's which had a predominantly educational aim, and that chiefly for Methodists. I refer to Wesley's four-volume *History of England*. I pick out this book because some biographers ignore it altogether and others apologize for it, with the remark that, of course, Wesley was not a historian. Having read the work through—the edition of 1776—the present writer, who is not a historian and lays no claim to expertness of judgment as to historical writing, nevertheless can speak as an ordinary reader, and does so with admiration and gratitude. For the book seems to me abundantly worth while, when we consider the readers to whom it was addressed. A wise man once said that not to hit a mark at which one does not aim is in itself no great hardship, but that to be blamed therefor calls for much patience. Wesley was time and again blamed for not hitting targets at which he did not aim. He was not aiming at historical research. He was not working among libraries or state archives. He had before him three histories of England—those of Goldsmith, Rapin, and Smollet—and depended upon them for the facts (one of the authors, Smollet, by the way, being most hostile to Methodism). He wrote the book out on the road—in the homes of Methodists where he stayed, in inns, in his "chaise." What he did aim to do was to put before his followers a readable narrative written from the religious point of view. The result was instructive and interesting. With many of the characters Wesley wrote in the conventional fashion, accepting the conventional moral judgments upon them, but with others he dealt in such wise as to give glimpses into his own mind. The style is straightforward and clear, the feeling for religious bearings pronounced, the prejudices manifest. Oddly enough, Wesley was an intense partisan of Mary Queen of Scots and re-

garded her virtually as a martyr. In date Wesley stood near enough
to the events of which he treated in the later chapters to make his
judgment almost that of a contemporary. It is instructive to note
that he reports his own father, Samuel Wesley, as the author of the
speech, or speeches, with which the famous High Churchman,
Sacheverell, made such a stir ecclesiastically and politically in the
early years of the eighteenth century, though John Wesley's authority is not always of the best on such points. We see the War of
Jenkin's Ear so explained as to make it thoroughly intelligible,
certainly to Englishmen. We recognize too that, so far as national
policies are concerned, Wesley regards the conduct of his country
as mostly right. The book, indeed, has no lasting value as history.
The people for whom it was written are gone. They evidently
found the history to their needs, for, though it was published in
four volumes, the edition was soon sold out. Wesley received
$2,000 in one sum for the book, to state the sum in American terms,
and within a week had given it all away.

There were other books of the same aim as this *History,* books
on all varieties of themes, written with the intent of building up the
individual Methodists into intelligence and soundness of judgment
concerning the world in which they lived. The total pieces of
printed matter published under Wesley's guidance would present,
for the times, an incredible total. Take the Christian Library, a
collection of religious documents issued in fifty volumes. Wesley
edited all this. He never turned over such tasks to a secretary.
There is not a sentence in the entire fifty volumes that had not come
repeatedly under his eye. The selection itself involved reading most,
if not all, the important published religious utterances in the history of the Christian Church. I refer especially to what we call
devotional material. To be sure, the volume of such output had
been up to Wesley's day hardly a handful compared to what goes
forth from the religious press in a decade now, but that mass was
immense to be read and scrutinized and edited by one man, the
man traveling on foot, on horseback, and in his carriage forty-five
hundred or five thousand miles a year. It is probably not too much
to say that Wesley, in the half century of his leadership of the Methodists, made a wider distribution of religious writings dealing with
the inner life than had any other man in the previous history of the
Church. I have said that one element in the value of Wesley's work
was his drilling the people called Methodists to well-determined
lives. It is equally pertinent to say that he accomplished an admi-

rable result in making the Methodists, and that by the thousands, a society of readers, and that of the best books.

This division has aimed to treat of Wesley's pastoral work in the wider sense—that of shepherding lives toward the highest ideals. I have spoken of his care of men in relation to the societies and of his interest in their physical and mental welfare. It may be just as well to speak here of the spirit of Wesley in dealing with those whom he could not but regard as moral and spiritual offenders, though such a discussion may not seem to bear directly upon the theme of the section. I do this also because there has been misunderstanding of the fact that Wesley so often broke with those who had been his close friends, as if this indicated a hard temper. We shall have occasion to look at some of these instances later. Suffice it to say here that these breaks had to do with principles, or what Wesley took to be principles. Criticism as to sternness of temper certainly could not be urged against his attitude toward penitent offenders.

The most conspicuous case of kindly treatment of a wrongdoer was that of his relation to his brother-in-law, Hall. There was a twist in Hall's nature from the first. He was a clergyman of the Church of England who sought the hand of one of Wesley's sisters in marriage, then jilted that sister and married another sister. This was a poor start, though the mother Susanna insisted that the facts warranted the courses of all three. Shortly after the marriage Hall began to reveal a looseness as to marital relations. Then follows a horribly long story of infidelity, open and avowed, with Hall advocating and preaching and practicing polygamy. Now, Wesley had every reason here to take the attitude that Hall had sinned beyond redemption. He had the most serious of personal reasons especially. Mrs. Hall was a most excellent woman. It was she who appeared occasionally in the Samuel Johnson circle, as the members of that circle are set forever before the world of English in the unforgettable pictures of Boswell. Wesley had abundant occasion to treat Hall as nothing more to him than a heathen man and a publican.

Moreover, Wesley had the warrant of the opinion of his time in holding that Hall was a deliberate sinner, and that his fault was transgression of moral law. There was no need of saying anything more to any religious leader of the day than just that—that this man was a purposeful sinner. Modern psychology was not at hand then to tell men to incline a little more to leniency of judgment. Nobody can today read through the account of Hall's performances and not feel that the case was at least partly pathologic. Wesley was not thinking in terms of pathology or psychology, or what we call psychiatry. He was thinking solely of sin and repentance. He was familiar enough with Hall during Hall's closing days to pronounce a judgment that is a veritable miracle of charitableness. He gave it as his conviction that Hall had been convinced of error and of sin, and died with assurance of divine pardon.

Organizer

We come now to the quality in Wesley which practically all who have studied his life concede as pre-eminent—his effectiveness as an organizer in the stricter sense than that of the general pastoral oversight we have been considering. Wesley himself seems to have recognized his peculiar strength in this respect.

In studying Wesley from this angle, it is well for us to see, if we can, what he was aiming at. There are some who tell us that he was not aiming at anything except to spread scriptural holiness; that he was in a worthy sense an opportunist, utilizing whatever means came to hand to advance the high ideals to which he had given himself. There is much to bear this out in the Wesley career. The class meeting began as an agency for collecting money contributions and ended as an instrument for standardizing Methodist spiritual life. The Conferences began just as conferences, meetings to confer about the best ways of advancing the spread of holiness. They ended as a powerful organism for the control of property and the guidance of preaching and worship. Outdoor preaching began because the audiences could not get indoors, and ended as the instrumentality which carried the gospel to thousands upon thousands who would never otherwise have heard it. Watch-night services arose in order that, in going to the Methodist meetings, the people might have the advantage of the light of the moon. Lay preaching began just because the crowds were at hand waiting for preaching, willing to listen to anyone who would speak to them, and ended by the creation of almost a totally new method of large-scale preaching of the evangel. Other illustrations of Wesley's use of the instruments at hand will appear as we move along.

It would be in the highest degree absurd to disparage Wesley for thus utilizing means at hand instead of seeking to create new tools outright. Wesley had no pride of originality. He sought from the beginning to make popular throughout England the highest type of Christian life attainable, popular as arousing popular response. All else was secondary to this aim.

How often it happens that, when a leader acts on what may seem an impulse, the after-effect looks like the outworking of careful plan! In making use of instruments already in a measure familiar, Wesley was insuring the success of his movement. Whether they knew it or not, the converts were asked to use in a different way what they had known, or known about, all their lives. Take outdoor preaching itself. The English, in the centers where the population was at all dense, were accustomed to get together in open spaces for all sorts of matches and sports, some of them rough. A traveler through England today cannot help noticing in any open space near a population center the large number of persons in sight, especially on Sunday or a holiday. This is, of course, partly to get outdoors, but the people assemble quickly at any spot where anything seems to promise to be of interest. It is surprising that anyone should wonder that Whitefield, and after him Wesley, should take the perfectly natural step of going forth to speak to these crowds. Yet Wesley himself hesitated before taking the step, and significantly said at last, though with an air of defiance, that he was willing to make himself vile and yet more vile for the sake of the gospel—which shows how hard it was to take an entirely obvious step, and which increases also our respect for Whitefield as an innovator, to say nothing of Wesley's acceptance of the method. All of this reveals also how limited was the service the Established Church was rendering at the time. Christening, confirmation, marriage, death were, in the eighteenth century, the few occasions on which the masses of persons felt any pressing, inevitable need of the Church. The opposition, or at least the questioning, aroused against open-air preaching is an indication of how little was expected of the Church at the time. Now, this method, which arose almost inevitably out of the circumstances, assuming the crowds and assuming the orator like Whitefield, led in the end to something resembling the discovery of a new world, or at least a new continent.

Coming back to the main question, we judge Wesley's achievements by what he expected to do. Admitting that his fundamental aim was the spread of scriptural holiness, he surely must have kept in mind always what would really spread his idea of holiness.

We must therefore look at the lay preachers whom Wesley sent into the field. The first of these were John Cennick and

Thomas Maxfield. In the *Arminian Magazine* Wesley published autobiographies of laymen to the number of thirty-six which have been gathered up and preserved in seven volumes.

It is said that a distinguished English bishop used to urge upon the ministers of his diocese the reading of these autobiographies as spiritual nourishment and stimulus. Undoubtedly the narratives must have done good; certainly they have met a need or they would not have been so widely read. As means for the development of a wholesome religious life, however, they are of doubtful value. To begin with, they are too much alike. The standardization of Methodist experience nowhere appears more distinctly than in the autobiographies of these Wesleyan preachers. I do not in the least mean by this to question the sincerity of the narrators. They were all sincere, desperately sincere. They had all had the experiences which they described. That was the advantage and that was the disadvantage. Nobody can read the narratives and not feel that he is in the presence of spiritual reality as far as the experiences themselves are concerned. By standardized experiences I mean those that were alike. Methodism did just that: it gave multitudes of men experiences that were alike. William James has been criticized because in *The Varieties of Religious Experience* he did not make more use of these Wesleyan autobiographies, and mentioned only one of them, that of John Nelson. It may be that, in the mass of material which James had to go through in his studies, he did not give as much attention as he should have done to this Methodist storehouse; but it may be, on the other hand, that James passed many of them over because they were so much like one another in characteristics to which he did give ample space in his book. All run through the same stages of fearful distress, not to say agony; all come out finally into the light.

Again there is no perspective, no discrimination in the treatment of sin, or of sins. It has been claimed as a virtue for Methodism, and for all evangelical groups for that matter, that for them sin is sin, small sins and great sins. Now, anyone who has ever sought to fulfill a Christian ideal is aware that with the most earnest followers of the ideal there is the deepest sense of unworthiness. Indeed, as previously stated, one of the paradoxes of the Christian life is that the man whose life is most free from sin is the one who feels sin most profoundly, just as the scientist who knows the most feels most keenly the vastness of his ignorance, and the artist who has come the nearest to the seizure of absolute beauty feels most heavily the fact that he cannot give beauty a perfect expression. Confusion standeth at the door, however, when the seeker after the Christ-character puts all sorts of transgressions on the same plane— the heedlessness of childhood, the pursuit of comparatively innocent pleasures, the commission of trivial errors in the same class with serious violations of moral law. To the credit of these Methodist helpers of Wesley be it said that, while they all had terrible remorse over sin, none of them in actual fact seem to have been notable moral offenders. They appear to have felt a general conviction of unworthiness and to have attributed it to their having been guilty of offenses which were not especially serious. The misery over sin which some of these men suffered in early and tender years is appalling. Our knowledge of childhood today and our better attitude toward childhood are clearly revealed if we read some of these dreadful narratives.

There was John Haime, however, who stands apart as never attaining a standardized experience. Haime never seems to have come fully out into the light of inner witness. He preached faithfully and effectively, and deserves the honor which early Methodism gave him, but he did not have the typical Methodist experience. It is surely to be regretted that the Methodists did not take more to heart, or to mind, the implications of the fact that Haime worked successfully without the type of experience which much Wesleyan preaching of the day made practically indispensable for salvation.

It was on these helpers that Wesley so much relied. He did not regard them as trained spiritual leaders—they were helpers, lay helpers. He felt that they could actually preach better than many, perhaps most, of the clergy of the Established Church, but that is not saying much. The Church was not notably given to preaching, and not at all to evangelism. Charles Wesley was outspoken in his opinion of the strictly lay character of the work of these men, but Charles was likely to give them less than justice, as John to give them more than justice. Again and again we are forced to observe the hastiness of speech and deed of Charles Wesley. He would at once rule that the preachers of Wesley ought never be regarded as anything but laymen. That judgment, we fear, came out of at least a trace of superiority in the feeling of Charles himself, who could not put men who had not his social connections and his academic training in a class with himself. John took his preachers for their merit in themselves, but he recognized their limitations and kept them under strict control.

An essential in Wesley's skill as an organizing leader was his determined keeping the authority over his preachers and his societies in his own hands. Here again we have to try to get and keep Wesley's point of view. He did not take himself as the head of a church but of a society. What he did would have been despotic beyond all description if he had thought of himself as the head of a church, assuming to himself the right to say who should and who should not have the blessings of the Church, with no other reason assigned than that he chose to have it so. Likewise, his determining by his own mind and will alone how long the preachers could remain in a place, without regard to the wishes of either preachers or congregations, would have been intolerable if he had been the head of anything more than a society. It was bad enough as it was. It is refreshing to read in his *Journal* and *Letters* of an occasional Methodist preacher who balked at moving from his field, refreshing indeed to read of one brother of whom Wesley wrote that he wondered if he could ever get him out of his place.

We shall meet after a little the charge that Wesley was ambitious, but here we have to raise the question as to what would have happened, or what could have happened, or what might not have happened if Wesley had not been just about the type of despot he was, especially in the early years of Methodism. The preachers were not trained: they were valuable chiefly as witnesses to experience: their interpretations of their experiences were likely to go astray. In fact, many who were most promising and, indeed, most successful at the beginning, finally broke away from Wesley. Of course Wesley illustrates the old danger—that a dictator seldom knows to whom or when or how to surrender his power. This, however, is to anticipate. It is enough here to remark that, while much of Wesley's ability lay in his recognition of the limitations in the midst of which he must work, the limitations of the nature of his society, the limitations in the human material of his helpers, he did not recognize some of his own limitations. All things considered, it is just as well that he did not. He kept things in his own hands until in 1784 he selected the Legal Hundred, the formal body which was to take legal control after he himself should have passed away.

Sooner or later Wesley was bound to meet the property problem—the control of the buildings in which the Methodists were to carry on their services. Like most problems Wesley had to meet, this came upon him almost before he was aware of it. As Methodism grew to some degree of material strength it was only to be expected that the lay members should desire to have preaching places built for their purposes—not somebody's dwelling place, not somebody's open field, but Methodist preaching centers built for Methodist purposes. The aim that prompted this was obviously sound and generous. At first Wesley's rule was that the seats should not have backs, and that the women and the men were to be separated while in the house, the women sitting on one side of the room and the men on the other. It was not long, however, before the question began naturally to arise in the minds of the members, "Well, whose building is this anyway?" The answer here was not always so easy as one might think. Methodists in those days, like Methodists ever since, were prone to say nothing of Methodism's pleasant justification of a debt by the euphemism, "We are building for the future." Thus it became necessary for Wesley himself to take a hand in getting this or that society out of debt and, in the later period of his ministry, he found himself under the burden of raising money for chapels scattered throughout Methodism. Even so the money came from Methodists, but it would never have come if Wesley had not raised it. No one can read through the *Journal* and the *Letters* of the days when Methodism had become thoroughly established and fail to see how persistently and how self-sacrificingly Wesley worked at this problem of the debts on Methodist properties. If anyone is tempted to believe that all that is necessary for getting money is to rouse the people to spiritual devotion and then allow the money to come of itself, let him read the efforts of Wesley to put the results of one of the mightiest revivals of all time on a sound financial foundation. The sums were not large, judged by twentieth-century standards, but they involved immense personal effort in money-raising. There was nothing that could be made at all compulsory in the appeals to the Methodists. Perhaps there never had been, up to Wesley's time, any solicitation for such a purpose on so wide a scale, with nothing to re-enforce the call except Wesley's own hold on his people, nothing to which to appeal except to the voluntary willingness of the people to help. The money came hard.

The question as to the control of the chapels came to the front as soon as Methodism began to build. The first thought would be, and was, that the chapels should be put under the authority of trustees. Did trustees therefore have the right to say who should preach in the chapels? The issue became especially acute at Bristol, where the laymen insisted upon such control. The problem here was finally settled by putting the deed to the property in Wesley's hand; a course that was followed shortly by practically all chapels. Or, rather, it came to be understood that no chapel was to bear the name of Methodist unless the entire control was lodged in Wesley.

Wesley was intelligent enough to see that he must make some definite arrangement as to the control of Methodism after he should be gone, but he did not quite show the firmness of self-mastery during the days when he was maturing a plan for his successor, or successors, that he had previously revealed. One trait of leadership Wesley lacked, or possessed in lesser degree: the power to delegate authority and to hold the receiver of such power responsible for its right use. To put it in another way, he did not have the power to hold strong leaders fast to him. His relations to White-field were long strained, and after the Calvinist controversy, never cordial. He sooner or later broke with almost every strong man with whom he had ever labored, including his brother Charles, though Charles on many an occasion unwarrantably projected himself into John's affairs. Charles never possessed sure discernment as to what might be strictly his own business. It was toward the end of his active service that John admitted that the control of Methodism was despotic, a condition which he did not view with alarm as long as he himself was the despot.

At first Wesley thought that Fletcher of Madeley ought to be his successor, but Fletcher knew better, on grounds of health if on no others. It is folly to guess what Fletcher would have done if he had ever come to the supreme authority in Methodism, but he was probably too delicate an instrument to follow Wesley. Fletcher had for a long period tendencies to consumption, of which indeed he finally died. I have already remarked that Wesley's notion of the best treatment for a cold or consumption was to mount a horse and ride from thirty to fifty miles a day in the face of whatever wind might be blowing, the fiercer the wind, the better. Fletcher was of fine and high sensibilities, with power to melt congregations to tears, though what they were weeping about was not always obvious. He lived like, and was, a saint, though not of the Wesley fiber, and with now and then a streak of hardness as when he refused a plea of his mother that he visit her, presumably for the last time.

The power finally went to the Legal Hundred—a group of one hundred Methodist preachers selected as indicated by Wesley himself. If one wishes to get an impression both of the strength and

weakness of Wesley's leadership, one has only to look over the lists
of Methodist preachers at the time of Wesley's death and ask who
in all the list would have been able alone to take Wesley's place.
One might also ask what dozen or twenty could have taken his place.
Wesley was, till nearly the close of his life, the indispensable man,
but is that a tribute to his leadership? A master artist, indeed,
passes and leaves no successor, but an organizer is not an artist
except at organizing, and organizing implies the power to train
understudies.   Here again we have to fall back upon Wesley's
own aim. He was not thinking of founding a church.   Assuming
that he meant what he said when he declared that he had not expected at the beginning that the Methodist Movement would run
for more than thirty years, and that he was surprised when it continued for fifty in full vigor, he must have aimed chiefly at holding
things together till there might come a better adjustment to the
Church.   We cannot make sense of Wesley's career except by taking at about full value his own statement of Methodism as a society
and not as a Church.   This is not in contradiction with more or
less conscious adjustments to a growing demand for independence
and separation from the Church by Methodists.

Wesley was not likely to change his views as to what course
Methodism should take even if he realized the tendency to independence.   He was not much more in favor of self-determination
by his people when he was over eighty than when he was under
fifty. Probably he did take account of the tendencies of his people
in so far as those entered into his half-conscious processes, but he
was not likely to admit even to himself his doing so.   Here again
Methodism suffered from the autocracy of its founder.   Wesley
had to do everything himself.   He passed on the eligibility of virtually every member of the Methodist societies himself, when it
came to revising the lists of members, not, indeed, after the membership had reached a total of from fifty thousand to seventy-five
thousand members, but in the earlier formative and decisive decades. Moreover, the Wesley censorship was in the last degree effective. The preachers and laymen could not publish anything without Wesley's consent. He had to know practically everything that
was said and done in every Methodist chapel and community.
Now, no organization could long hold together under this leadership. So that the question arises as to whether Wesley himself did
not suspect that the organization might break after he had gone,

and wished that, if it had to break, it would be in position to carry its vitality into the English Church.

Then there was the selection of the Legal Hundred. One hundred is an arbitrary figure and arbitrary figures are dangerous when personal choices are to be made. Presumably Wesley could not have done much other than he did, but he left sore spots in Methodism through leaving out some men who had been faithful and successful workers. There was, for example, John Hampson, Sr., utterly devoted to Wesley. Hampson was not among the Legal Hundred. The ill wind, in this case, if it was an ill wind, did blow some good. John Hampson, Sr., left a son, John, who wrote a *Life* of Wesley, published in the year of Wesley's death. The son evidently resented Wesley's treatment of his father keenly enough to correct his own vision, so that he did not fall into that mood of extravagant and out-of-focus adulation of Wesley which injures nearly all friendly utterances about Methodism's founder. The author of that *Life* without being harsh, gives us a temper of approach which introduces a realistic note into the treatment of Wesley, a note Methodists have always sadly needed. Hampson's book is out of print, but it is well worth being looked up and read by anyone who cares to see Wesley in the flesh, before the period of apotheosis fully dawned.

Here it may be fitting to say a little about another life of Wesley, inasmuch as we have been discussing Wesley's leadership. I refer to the *Life* by Robert Southey, the best written biography of Wesley, from the point of view of style, with the possible exception of that of Professor Caleb T. Winchester, of Wesleyan University. As a biography—and that is what Southey's book aims to be—it is authentic, ample, friendly, and sympathetic toward Wesley's purposes, and at the same time judicial toward some aspects of his philosophy and methods, though not as excellent in these respects as Julia Wedgwood. Now, Southey possessed unbounded admiration for Wesley, but he declared in his *Life,* at what seems undue length, that Wesley was ambitious—for power, for his own supremacy over men. Thereupon all the Methodist pens of the time began to race in defense of Wesley. The question was not worth quite so much ink. It might have been said also that Wesley was avaricious, because of his persistent begging for money, if we did not know what he wanted the money for. There is no doubt that, in dealing with men, Wesley was self-assertive beyond all description, but it is well that it was so. Wesley had remarkable ability to take himself for granted. There was something charmingly naïve in his recognition of his own peculiar fitnesses. Just think what a plight the Methodist Movement would have been in if Wesley had too often passed through seasons of doubt and self-distrust! Of course some would make the test here as to whether Wesley himself enjoyed power. Probably he did. He was one of those intensely vital beings who rejoice in the full expression and play of their energies. The so-called "integration" of Wesley's life was, so far as we can see, the absorption of his whole being in the task before him. He was contented and happy. He was conscious of a fullness of inner life which could be expressed only by field preaching and what went with it. The people could not have been reached in regular church services even if they had been willing to attend them. His inner experience and his outer method fit together like hand and glove.

PART V
THE DEFENDER OF THE FAITH

PART V

THE DEFENDER OF THE FAITH

I MIGHT call this part "Defender of His Faith." It was Wesley's own faith that he had to defend practically from the start of the Methodist Movement. I repeat what I have said so many times before: that we cannot understand Wesley without keeping in mind what he was driving at. He was trying to spread scriptural holiness throughout the land, and to do it, not directly through a Church, but through a society. He was himself the head and front of that society. That means that he could not rely on official church support. Indeed, until toward the close of his career, he got from the Church not support but indifference and even hostility. The questions about the interpretations of doctrine raised by Methodists were addressed to him. The questions were taken up in Conference sessions, but the answers came chiefly from Wesley. To be sure, Wesley pronounced his judgments within the framework of the doctrines of the English Church, but he had to pass on problems that were virtually new. English Churchmen, for example, were opposed to and even scandalized by the emotional uproar of the Wesleyan meetings. They were offended by the positiveness of the professions of assurance of salvation which abounded in the Methodist testimony. Neither Susanna Wesley nor Samuel Wesley, Jr., had had any such definite forms of assurance as those to which the Wesleyan converts laid claim. Virtually all the problems affecting experience came at last to Wesley for decision, and he had to meet them alone. It does not take much away from the burden of the task to say that Wesley would not have shared any authority of any kind with anyone; that does not change our opinion about the weight he carried.

The conduct of the Methodist societies meant at least fifty years of controversy for Wesley, controversy which began after the return from Georgia; indeed, which started even before the departure for Georgia if we remember that, as a member of the Holy Club at Oxford, he had to defend the Club against all manner of misunderstanding and misinterpretation and calumny. The warfare of which I am thinking, however, had to do with Wesley's preaching and teaching to the societies.

135

May I say at the outset that it would have been hard to show
any more genuine faith in a democratic principle than did Wesley
in bringing forward such doctrines as those of assurance and Christian perfection for the acceptance of the masses of persons, of all
sorts and conditions, who formed the host of his followers. There
is a parallel in the publication of the English Bible for the people
of England, or for all who could read. We cannot blame the Roman
Catholic Church for feeling that it was dangerous to open the Scriptures to the peoples, except as those Scriptures were interpreted by
officials of the Church. The possibilities of misunderstanding
seemed appalling to the leaders of the Roman Church. The possibilities too became actualities in innumerable instances. To throw
the Scriptures, with all their mysteries, broadcast before multitudes
of men who could, at the best, only half read, who were full of
superstition—or at least the germs of superstition—was an act of
stupendous faith both in God and man. From the point of view of
ordinary matter-of-fact common sense, the precautions of the
Roman Church had much to commend them.

Similarly with Wesley's preaching of the various stages of
assurance, or reliance on inner experience. To go out to the cross-
roads, and the fields, and the market places with a message that had
in it the emotional possibilities which his had was from the angle
of careful prudence reckless and almost foolhardy. It meant that
Wesley had not only to overcome the hostility of the crowds, of
which we have already spoken, but the excesses produced by the
reactions of the nervously unstable. There is also around the edges
of any widespread popular movement what Theodore Roosevelt
used to call a lunatic fringe. Wesley coolly matched himself against
all this. He must have known that the excesses would appear, for
they had appeared before in popular religious excitements in England. The Wesleyan Revival was not the first in English history
to be accompanied by emotional extravagance. There is room for
holding that Wesley was probably the first leader of his type of mind
and training to scrutinize these phenomena so carefully, to see if
there might be anything of value in them. It is a question as to
whether he did not go too far in this intellectual, virtually scientific,
hospitality. Whatever response to these characteristics Wesley
made, however, was almost wholly of the mind. There is not anything to suggest that he was caught in them himself. Take the case
of Thomas Maxfield. Maxfield was one of Wesley's converts who
showed at first extraordinary ability as a lay preacher. Mrs. Susanna

Wesley had been much impressed by his preaching and had urged John to send him forth as an evangelist. All went well for a time, but Maxfield soon revealed that he had notions of his own, especially about Christian perfection. In one of the most direct letters ever written by one Christian to another, Wesley tried to show Maxfield the error of his ways. The letter is long, but I quote a few passages, with particular emphasis on Wesley's word about Maxfield's not showing much of a spirit of love, the characteristic failing of those who think they have attained to perfection in love. I am not so much concerned here with Wesley's statements themselves as with their spirit—a temper of complete mastery, mastery of himself, and assumed mastery of the man to whom he is writing. There is not a trace of petulance or irritation, certainly not an item that suggests that Wesley did not know exactly what he was about. Wesley did not resort to the common practice of "viewing with alarm." He was not affrighted, or even worried. He told Maxfield what was what in language that could not be mistaken, and yet did so without uttering a syllable at which any one acting in good faith could take offense.

Canterbury, November 2, 1762

. . . I dislike your littleness of love, to your brethren and to your own society, your want of union of heart with them . . . ; your want of meekness, gentleness, long-suffering; your counting every man your enemy that reproves or admonishes you in love; your bigotry and narrowness of spirit.

This is enough, though there are marks of kindly interest on the part of the writer. Thomas Maxfield was holy in his own mind and had become intolerable. Wesley was partly to blame for having encouraged qualities in him which were good in the green and pestiferous in the dry. Of course, humanly considered, complete mastery like that of Wesley is more maddening to the one addressed than would be a loss of temper. Wesley, however, was true to himself. He took his own leadership as not to be questioned.

I pause over this self-assurance of Wesley again and again. The longer one reads, the more the marvel grows. Let us try to keep before us, not how Wesley's situation appears to us now but how it appeared to him then. These various types of extremists, against whom it was necessary to guard the Wesleyan movement, were all claiming to receive messages from the Lord. They were bearing witness in the fashion that Wesley himself had preached and encouraged. It must have been sorely puzzling to them to have Wesley sitting in judgment on what they supposed, accepting the principles of Wesley himself, had come to them from a divine source. Think, though, of the problem for Wesley. He had stood against the wisest judgment of his time in his attitude toward extraordinary claims in the expectation that he could find in them channels for the divine. What would be the effect if he should prove widely mistaken? He believed also that some of the channels were from the devil. Over them all he kept a cool watch, insisting upon doing his own interpreting. As to the messages that came along the line of what he was teaching on the loftiest spiritual state, he was markedly critical. On his own theory a man might have achieved Christian perfection, but he placed the utterances of the perfect in about the same scales as other messages when he came to assessing their values, and he always assessed their values.

A further indication of his mastery was his patience in dealing with the aberrant, and eccentric, and extreme. He could speak definitely, as he did to Maxfield, but he would not too summarily tell any man of this type that there was not any place for him in the society. Expulsions, highhanded or otherwise, had little place in Wesley's policy. He would indeed drop names from lists until the surviving number was not more than a third of the records with which he started, but that was chiefly of those who had already dropped themselves. Read his *Journal* and his *Letters* through and, while we find concern at the lot of those who were getting off the track, we come upon no distrust of his own dealing leniently with them.

More dangerous than Thomas Maxfield was George Bell, another convert who got beyond all control in fanaticism. This was the man who announced that the world would come to an end on a given date, and had hosts of Methodists in terror until the day had passed. Wesley did everything he could to keep his people quiet, and succeeded, though at considerable effort. He adopted in all such situations the wise method of avoiding everything that would in the faintest degree suggest the persecution of the disturbing brother. Fanatics usually court persecution, but they could not get it from Wesley. His method was that of persuasion, of willingness to discuss. Here, indeed, there is somewhat of irony in the actual fact. Anybody who knew Wesley knew that the persuasion would all be on one side, if there were any.

All the extremists and fanatics apart, however, Wesley had to meet and contend with a variety of opinions and beliefs and doctrines in such wise as to make his course instructive for times other than his own, for some of the problems raised are perennially recurring.

We have seen that early in the history of Methodism Wesley had to deal with quietism like that of the Moravian brethren. Quietism meant that the soul left everything to God, despising all means, even the means of grace. This all seems absurd to us now, but it did not seem so to the seekers of grace in Wesley's day. We can say outright that the means of grace have as their sole purpose to put us into communion with God, but we have to get back to the atmosphere through which the quietists looked at these means. Incidentally, the ecclesiastical religion of the time had come to regard the means as ends in themselves, just as under some conditions men do today. Even Wesley himself looked upon the sacrament of the Lord's Supper as having an efficacy suggestive of the Roman view, though, of course, he merely implied this, and would not have stated it in so many words. Quietism can be so phrased as to seem the height of faith in God, as if it were an absolute surrender to him and waiting upon him, a waiting for him to take the initiative. We see some things more clearly now than believers did then. Quietism could not then be waved to one side as we might do today. Let us remember that in all these central problems of religion the earnest seekers did not get much help from the Established Church. They got some help but not much. Wesley had to find his way along pretty much alone.

What saved him and his cause was a peculiar, indefinable good sense: an instinct for the right path. Probably this could be called a feeling for the practical consequences, an anticipation of what the consequences would be. Where there was no opportunity for consequences to declare themselves, Wesley could, like his contemporaries, give himself to follies. Nothing could exceed the vigor with which he pronounced in favor of witchcraft. He thought that giving up witchcraft would be giving up the Bible. He became quite excited when anyone doubted the supernatural nature of the noises in his boyhood heard in the Epworth Rectory. Witchcraft, however, was not cutting any large figure in Wesley's day, and the Epworth noises lasted only a few months and then were heard no more. If his followers by hundreds had begun practically to accept witchcraft and to cultivate intercourse with ghosts, Wesley might not have been so positive on such themes; or perhaps his positiveness would have been on the other side.

Wesley was not afraid to break with groups that could not or would not abide by his teaching. He was slow to cast out from the society any who did not believe in his doctrines, but he carried his own followers away from organized connection with the Moravians, and he allowed groups that would not follow him to take their departure. It may seem distressing to note the long line of broken friendships in Wesley's life, but that line is a witness to a grim leadership that could see a course and hold to it.

A second taxing problem which confronted Wesley was that of leading his adherents over the narrow strip of theological territory between Calvinism and antinomianism. Wesley made in this connection his famous remark to the effect that Methodism is but a hairsbreadth from Calvinism on the one hand, and from antinomianism, on the other. At the present hour there is quite a noticeable effort to show that Wesley was a Calvinist, and the above remark is quoted as all but decisive. Those who thus use the quotation should quote also the antinomianism reference. What the passage meant was just what it said, but it implied also that antinomianism and Calvinism were about equally abhorrent to Wesley.

Antinomianism came out of the emphasis on faith. "Works" have no value in the sight of God, as works in themselves. A man cannot earn his way, or pay his way to salvation by what he does. In this emphasis Wesley, of course, was trying to hold fast the inner reliance on Christ as the path to the soul's life, but he could not help overstating his teaching, due in part to the obvious limitation that he could not say more than one thing in the same breath, and that he was given to making his statements so strong that, taken by themselves, they seemed to stand alone. What Wesley said and did at one instant has to be set in a wide circle of context if we would get his full idea, and even then may not altogether fit into the context. Most of the difficulty as to disparagement of good works was due to the morally empty and yet formally correct religious practices of official ecclesiasticism. Then, of course, anything that men did would seem to fall short of what God would expect. The Methodists of that day were desperately afraid that men's works might have some merit in their own right.

As a matter of fact, men's good deeds have always had merit on their own account. We all feel that the good and the true and the beautiful are meritorious just as they are. Granted that they fall short of the ideal in any particular manifestation, they are worthy as far as they go. Take Wesley's own life. Wesley would have said, indeed did say, that whatever worth his work had was due to the grace of God, the unmerited favor of God. Put just thus the human virtue is obscured altogether and confusion is at hand. When Wesley was pressed for theological opinion, he would say that the good works of any and all were filthy rags. Taking him as a man among men, he enjoyed good works as heartily as any. Wesley had a peculiarity—a most annoying one to a reader of his *Journal*—of apparently being caught up into admiration of whatever might be fine or beautiful in a landscape or a building and of almost unconsciously breaking forth into applause, and then of catching himself and asking what was the use of all this anyway, inasmuch as it all had to be burned up at the last day. It almost seems as if Wesley was determined not to enjoy anything, but that he did enjoy fineness, and then brought in, lugged in by the ears, some somber reflections about the end of all things. He did enjoy the good and the beautiful until he thought that perhaps he ought not.

Now, the antinomians were logical enough in their way. They concluded that, if good works were worthless, they did not count more effectively in any direction than evil works, and evil works therefore made no considerable difference. So, if one had enough faith in God, one could do as one pleased. The logic was correct enough. What could be more suggestive of a right heart than complete reliance upon God, to the neglect of all effort to do anything on one's own account? If one had attained to Christian perfection, one had a right to expect that anything that came into one's mind would be pure. Here again Wesley had to fall back upon his indefinable good sense. In doing this he had to take his stand, and just say so.

Perhaps it would be fair to say that almost all these extremes and aberrations came because the Methodists fell into seizing only one fragment of the truth and overworking it. The supreme quality of a genuine leader is the ability not only to see truth steadily, but to see it whole. Wesley's sanity consisted largely in just this ability to get all the factors bearing on religious experience into his field of view. He did not always have the factors in the true perspective, or right relation to one another, but he did better here than any other man of his age.

How odd it would have been if he had really disparaged good works? He himself put forth a total of energy in work which remains today, and will likely remain while men study such subjects at all, one of the most arresting of human phenomena. Here was a man working at top speed through over sixty years. Yet he had to remind his followers that there was just a shade of distance from Methodism over into antinomianism.

By the way, if we wish to see how current is the tendency to this practical heresy, we can find illustration, not indeed in the Church at the present day, but in some circles of those who are so genuinely devoted to social service, and thoroughgoing social service at that, as to justify themselves in all manner of indulgences in their own private lives. If these persons were to declare that their personal conduct is their own, and that they will take the consequences of what they do, nobody on the outside could say much; but they often speak as did the antinomians of old, avowing that they are so wholeheartedly devoted to a service, which is for them the highest religion, that they can do what they please in their own individual affairs. I am not attempting to offer critical judgment in these instances, but I am saying that, while the content of such avowed devotion to an ideal is far different from eighteenth-century antinomianism, the spirit and temper are enough akin to what Wesley had to meet to render that type at least intelligible to us. The main highways to mistake in religious thinking are much the same throughout the centuries, but grass grows over them and blurs their edges, or change of name makes them seem different, till they bring the wayfarer out into the old disaster.

As to the other side of Wesley's statement, the smallness we have to recognize in the difference between Methodism and Calvinism was at the point of freedom of human choice. Calvin had compelling influence on English religious thought at and after the Reformation. The background of Wesley's thinking was close to the main ideas of Calvinism.

For example, Wesley accepted the idea that man's life was planned by God throughout. What men had to do was to find the plan and say "Amen" to it. Wesley's idea of freedom did not mean that men could defy God and wreck the divine plans by that defiance, except to the extent of disastrous consequences to themselves. Probably the comment of a noted follower of Wesley says as well as can be said what the freedom of the Wesleyan type involves, namely, that men can recognize the plan of God and say "Amen" to it, and go along with it, or they can say "No" and be dragged along. That is to say, apart from the choices of men, God is to have his way.

As to the consequences, he will not allow them to wreck his plans for his universe.

Now, this indeed is not pure Calvinism, but it is Calvinistic, predestination, even, and can be softened down into preplanning. The late Professor B. H. Streeter showed us anew that the dignity spoken into human life by Calvinism was not the result of fatalism, or determinism. If a man feels that he is the plaything of the Fates, he can do nothing better than to act as the Mohammedan does: shrug his shoulders and take what comes. If he feels that he is the outcome of materialistic forces, he may seek to adjust those forces as far as he can to his own satisfaction, or he can adjust himself to them, or he can make a gesture of defying them if he feels that there is any reason in defying an impersonal process. Calvinistic predestination means plan. If the test of a belief is the life that it produces, Calvinism can point to justifying character-effects both in individuals taken separately and in their social relationships. It puts plan into the universe and an iron plan at that.

Wesley believed in as stern a plan for the universe as did Calvin. More than that, Wesley went a noticeable distance toward Calvinistic predestination. He was hospitably inclined to the notion that God could and possibly did now and again predestine some souls to lives of righteousness. That is to say, he was willing to entertain the possibility of predestination on the side of *foreordination* to *righteousness*. Logically, this seems to give Wesley's case away. In such predestination to moral righteousness Wesley seems to imply that the human will in these exceptional characters is quiescent, or acquiescent, so that the problem of free choice does not arise. The most that can be said is that God so fashions some lives that they always will to do right, but in strict logic this does not help us much. There is no use trying to dodge the predestination aspect of some phases of Wesley's view. On the positive side some souls are predestined to eternal bliss. The difference between Wesley and Calvin here seems to be that Calvin would hold that such foreordination was the essence of his system, while Wesley held it as only occasional and exceptional and on the side of foreordained goodness.

It was over freedom of choice that Wesley stood against Calvinism. I have spoken of the logic of Calvin's system. My remark was provisional only. If we take Calvinism strictly, and make freedom of choice impossible, there is no logic in it. For, if there is no choice in conduct, there is no choice in thinking. To be sure, this is not determinism, for Calvinism reserves to God, or grants to God outright, the power to choose. So far as Calvinists can say, God has *chosen* certain persons for eternal bliss and certain others for eternal woe—all to his own glory. There is no choice for men themselves, however. That being so, there is no power of choice among their thoughts. The Calvinist thinks Calvinism because of the divine decree, and the anti-Calvinist thinks anti-Calvinism because of a divine degree.

Wesley fought mightily for the freedom of man's will, but not primarily on logical grounds. He did not add anything substantial to anti-Calvinistic reasoning as such. He fought for the dignity of man and for the honor of God. He cared with all there was of him both for man and God. As we shall have opportunity to see later, he so stood for the worth of man as to make that worth one of the important foundation stones of modern democracy.

As to the idea of God, he wrought forcefully in making that idea profoundly moral. It is customary with theologians, especially with those in whom there lingers a heritage of prejudice against Methodism, to maintain that Wesley, and the Methodism which he founded, did not make any important contribution to theological thinking. It may be so, but Wesley pushed into the foreground some considerations of which religious teachers must take account. He played his part in making the idea of God moral. Calvinism has always had much to say about the stiffest and sternest morality, and then has left God to do as he pleased. Of course Calvinism as such came of a time which was used to the idea of absolute power in rulership. It did much, indeed, to break down the claim of absolute rule for the Pope. It would have been shocked to hear God spoken of as a pope, but it accepted the idea of kingship and was lenient toward the notion that a king could do no wrong. At any event, it welcomed the idea of absoluteness in God's rule. Moreover, actions speak louder than words. When Calvin himself got virtually absolute power over Geneva, he made a sorry exhibition of what he claimed as theocracy. The God of Calvin was not moved by any moral claims that at all suggested the humane or the human.

It was at this joint in the Calvinistic armor that Wesley aimed his shafts. To borrow the phrase of one of his nineteenth-century followers, he sought to make the old idea of God tolerable, though admittedly he did not wholly succeed. His idea as well as Calvin's partook of cruelty probably inevitable in as legally savage an age as the eighteenth century. If he had tried to preach only to those who, like himself, could not find the God of Calvin worthy of acceptance, he would never have been able to bring more than a small minority of them within sound of his voice. It is easy to point to the marked influence of a leader like Calvin, numbering adherents by the hundreds of thousands. This does not settle all the question, however. If Calvinism won its adherents and then left a field clear for systems of a different type, we should have one situation; but we have quite another when it set other hundreds of thousands against itself. It will not do, either, to say that Calvinism is not a religious system for weaklings. Weaklings are as likely as others to take to an iron system. They realize their need of its positiveness and grasp it in a frenzy of desperation. On the other hand, the strong, independent soul may be the one most likely violently to reject Calvinism. Certainly, those of richness and fullness of human qualities are likely to reject it.

John Wesley could not be called a weakling, but he would have none of the Calvinism which left out freedom of choice for men. I repeat that he was quite as much concerned for the character of God as for the dignity of man. He was willing to accept the poetry of Cowper, who at one time knew what evangelical experience meant, that God moves in a mysterious way his wonders to perform; he was, indeed, ready to adjust himself to all manner of mystery, but he would not cloak the barbarity of God's sending men to eternal doom without moral fault of their own by calling the divine decrees mysterious. To Wesley such decrees added nothing to any glory of a God worth worshiping.

All this is relevant to the present hour because of attempts which are current to bring back an emphasis on Calvinism, though it goes by another name. It may be that we cannot fairly say that much theology of the twenty years since the World War takes away the freedom of man as did Calvinism, but it does take rationality out of man's actions, so that the sole duty seems to be to find what God wants and to do that. This would indeed be the sum of duty if the moral example of God were the ideal; but if God is conceived of as dictator, setting forth his own will because it is his own will, the process of producing a moral idea of God, which we fondly hoped was moving forward, is estopped. We can have an adequate God, adequate to individual and social tasks, and at the same time a God of moral love. This it was for which Wesley contended.

There are various ways of depriving man of freedom. He may be created without the possibility of free choice, as John Calvin and later Jonathan Edwards seemed to imply; or he can be set in a realm of force where orders simply have to be obeyed.   The penalty for disobedience may become so great, so out of proportion to wrong done, that the man who disobeys may take on moral heroism.   I once knew a believer in the verbal inspiration of the Scriptures who used to admit most cheerfully that one can accept that belief, or refuse it, just as one pleases; but if one refuses, one will be damned!

Against all conceptions which would deprive men of a measure of freedom which would make the choice real, Wesley waged war. Here was no foe on the outside, but one within the camp of Methodism itself.   The fight was desperate and grim, with Whitefield supported by the Countess of Huntingdon, and Wesley with the main group of the Methodists.   Wesley showed far better temper than did his opponents.   He would not break with Whitefield personally.   When some of the supporters of Whitefield distributed at the door of the chief preaching place of Wesley in London some scurrilous attacks on Wesley's doctrines, Wesley went out, gathered up what he could, and tore them up, remarking as he did so that, if Mr. Whitefield were in Wesley's place, he would do just as he, Wesley, was doing.   No man could have watched his own lips more carefully during those days of the Calvinistic controversy than did Wesley.   The attacks on Wesley by Toplady and Rowland Hill did not disturb him much.   To be called an old fox who had been run to earth would have excited a smaller man.   Wesley was big enough practically to ignore all these outrages.   Perhaps his consciousness of his own strength helped him.   The truth is that the Calvinists were seriously put to it in order to meet, not Wesley's formal arguments, but the effectiveness of the preaching based on his doctrines.   Both Toplady and Hill resorted almost to blackguardism because they did not have any other weapons popularly effective.

A further element of weight in Wesley's position was that he realized that the Calvinistic Methodists were not, after all, giants in formal logic.   John Wesley seldom forgot what Samuel Wesley, his father, had taught him: that not many issues in this world are determined by logic.   All sorts of factors entered into the Calvinistic debate.   There was the charm of Whitefield's eloquence, and his power of ready adaptation to circumstances.   He could receive and hold slaves for his Georgia orphanage, and preach most eloquently on the dignity of man without any serious mental disturbance over the inconsistency.   He got along famously with the

Countess of Huntingdon and with those of her circle. Wesley knew his opponents.

He knew the Methodists. He knew that they were not over-much concerned with formal theological theorizing though, in spite of all the acrimony, there were discussions of predestination and divine decrees before large Methodist groups which evidently received attentive and appreciative hearing. As to Whitefield, Wesley was confident that his preaching would win lives to God in spite of the Calvinism. We have heard much of Wesley's tolerance, but have never done it full justice. For usually we are tolerant toward views that do not infringe closely upon us. It is easy, for example, here in America, to take a comfortable attitude toward Mohammedanism or Hinduism. They do not concern us except in an outside, far-away fashion. Wesley's tolerance was of a wholly different order. He was trying to turn souls to God, and saw in the midst of his own group those who were holding and teaching views which, if logically carried out, would make the gospel of no effect. He did not seek to crush this movement by banishing Calvinists from his societies. On the other hand, he did not ignore the movement. He openly argued against it. There has been among church leaders at times a species of tact—so-called—which shows itself in the ability to get along with those of opposing views by ignoring those views, or by so stating one's own conceptions as to leave the opponents with the impression that one is more or less in sympathy with them. Wesley resorted to neither of these methods. Remember, he was head of a society and not of a church. He could have laid down rules for membership in a society which would not have been permissible for a church. All he had to do was to drop the name of an offending brother from the rolls. He did repeatedly purge his societies, not for beliefs, but for conduct. He could have excused himself for keeping silent, but he wished his followers to see with wide-open eyes just what Christian discipleship meant. He might have said that the mass of his followers were not theologically trained, that they could not follow the intricacies of theological reasoning, that they might lose their way. He might have kept silent, and have laid stress on the spirit of life in his followers and upon their giving themselves to practical tasks, saying of them that they were persons of "good spirit" or that they were fine workers. Under such leadership that would have occurred in Methodism which has often come about since: the appearance of a laity practically illiterate so far as concerned religious thinking. No—

Wesley did not overload his preaching with controversial matter. He kept the immediate spiritual needs to the fore, but at the same time he did write and speak against the denial of human freedom in Calvinism.

In all the discussion he was careful to hold fast to the Christian spirit. He did not utter anything which would even offend good taste, to say nothing of his freedom from anything personally offensive to his opponents. In every way he had the better of it as to the temper of the debate.

In dealing with the arguments themselves he spoke with extreme boldness. Not only did he declare that he would not worship such a God as the Calvinistic doctrine of divine sovereignty required, but he would have nothing to do with a body of Scripture writings that would give us a Calvinistic God. If the Scriptures were rightly interpreted by the Calvinists, so much the worse for the Scriptures! Of course this did not mean that Wesley was becoming "liberal" in his treatment of the Scriptures. He did not believe the Scriptures could be so interpreted as to deny freedom to men; but, if they could, so much the worse for the Scriptures!

It is possibly worth noting that the Calvinistic group had somewhat of the same characteristics that have always appeared in Calvinistic circles: a tendency away from the main masses of believers. Calvinism by its nature is a doctrine of privilege. Calvin has been given credit by some who try to make his system democratic by its placing the individual soul alone in the presence of God, without the need of any intermediary whatever. So far so good, but the idea of election in itself carries with it the suggestion of a privileged group. To be sure, the thoroughgoing Calvinist will have it that those who attain eternal bliss attain through no merit of their own, but this will not suffice. There must be some reason for the divine election. The fact itself that some are elected and others not, makes a difference between men. Indeed, we may not know who are elected, but the old-fashioned Calvinist, to use his own phrase was "led to indulge a hope." Just how this tended to foster the growth of democracy has never been explained. Practically, those who did not indulge a hope, and never thought about indulging a hope, were on the outside. Indulging a hope was not much of a witness to salvation, but, after all, it made a difference. Who has ever met a Calvinist who was not sure that he was of the elect?

We must not trace too close a connection between religious

speculation and practical conduct; but any religious system which starts with the idea of God as a dictator, with the divine reasons for granting bliss to some and woe to others so utterly opaque as to prevent men's getting any clues to their meaning, makes for dictatorship in earthly rule, and privileges for special classes.

Of course we must not blame Wesley for not urging against Calvinism an argument about the character of God which would not have been intelligible in a day of absolute power in a ruler. Did Wesley do wisely in holding fast to Divine Omnipotence? Would he not have done better to sacrifice omnipotence to love, and teach that God submitted to limitations which genuinely limit omnipotence? Is it not even conceivable that such limitations are inherent in the Divine Nature?

Another foe which Wesley had to fight was mysticism. Mysticism is hard to define. Among many, perhaps most of us who talk of religious experience, it is a general term for the inner life, for the spirit of meditation and prayer. From this angle we do not scruple to call Wesley himself one of the noblest of mystics. Indeed, he is often so spoken of. Wesley, however, says it was mysticism on which he most nearly lost his faith. He read Fénelon, Madame Guyon, Jacob Behmen, William Law. From the manner in which he speaks of them, one would not suspect the force they had exerted upon him. Without attempting any formal definition of mysticism, let us see what it was in Wesley's mind by looking at his attitude toward it. Suffice it to say at the start that we must recognize it as one of the outstanding manifestations of power in the history of the Church, that it has developed through the ages a system of thought and a method of exercise in a search after what it calls a direct and immediate communion with the Divine.

So far as the leaders of mysticism are concerned, it seems to be Behmen who most tried the patience of Wesley, this partly because of the vagueness and haziness with which the mystic wrote. He could not make much of Behmen, and in this he shared the inability of hundreds of others. The general statements of Behmen, the framework of his conceptions—if he can be said to have a frame for his theory—the impression made upon Wesley by reading Behmen was evidently about like that made upon many of us by reading the writings of Christian Science. It seemed to Wesley to be away up in the air when it was intelligible at all.

In many respects mysticism had characteristics which could have been fitted into Wesleyan experience and interpretation. A movement which has had more or less vitality throughout the whole career of Christianity must, of course, express and gratify human needs. It is a search to get into actual union with God, fundamentally the same search as Wesley's. The mystic experiences run through somewhat the same stages as those taught by Wesley, notably the periods of the "dark night of the soul" and of final illumination.

Wesley, however, could not endure the passivity which much teaching of mysticism enforced. At bottom Christian mysticism is not passive, but active, strenuously so. The mystic seeker must indeed seek, seek as if his life depended upon the finding, and the finding upon the seeking. It seems, indeed, that there have always been non-Christian elements even in Christian mysticism, these coming chiefly from the Orient. Hinduism, for example, is passively mystic—whatever the soul seeks tends toward stupefying it into unconsciousness. There are passages in the Christian mystics which seem to preach a sinking into a form of absorption into the Divine. The Hindu experience, however, is poles removed from that of the normal Christian experience, one being a veritable lapse toward unconsciousness, and the other an ineffable exaltation and ecstasy.

Now, Wesley never had the slightest doubt of the reality of direct divine action upon the minds of men, but he did object to the mysticism of his day, the type he saw presented to his followers, on several counts. As we learn more of what he was, we cannot see how he could have taken any attitude other than the one he did take.

One count was the disregard of means, the expectation of ends without the use of the instruments appropriate to secure the ends. Another was the tendency to a false waiting upon God, a quietism which cost nothing in exertion. Though he preached the spiritual gifts of the Lord as free, Wesley did feel that all good gifts have to be nevertheless gained by the effort of all the spiritual energies.

So long as the mystics merely referred to their uplifts as ineffable, or inexpressible, Wesley could not say much; but, as soon as they began to translate them into speech, he insisted that there were manifold tests by which the worth of the messages could be judged. He demanded something more than the testimony that the mystic felt thus and so before he would accept the message as authentic. He declared that the utterances should square with Scripture and that they should be in line with the Christian con-

sciousness, at least should be acceptable to the body of believers.
I say "in line with." Wesley certainly did not mean to submit
revelations to individual souls to a vote of the believers. What
he meant was that the mystic experience should fit into the outline
worked out by experience in the history of the Church, and not be
merely peculiar, or aberrant, or eccentric. Surely, centuries of
experience with mystics have shown the wisdom of Wesley's insistence here. As I have said more than once, Wesley believed and
said that religion must be social. He made it clear that he meant
by this more than merely social as manifesting itself in the Christian
spirit toward one's neighbors, society being for him not only a field
for Christian practice, but also a corrective and re-enforcement of
individual experience. This corrective aim was partly the reason
for the class meeting.

It does not do for the saints to live too much in solitude. Nor
does it do for them to act too exclusively as their own interpreters of
Scripture. The late Josiah Royce, Hegelian as he was in philosophy,
once deplored that there was not in his day more of the type of
Behmen's preaching. What he referred to was a mystic treatment
into which the Hegelian philosophy might have been read. Royce's
use of Behmen was suggestive and helpful, but it was far removed
from what the Scriptures meant. Wesley felt that the Scriptures
should be read to find what they meant, though it is permissible
always for an interpreter to tell us that his exegesis is what the Book
suggests to him. One difficulty with mysticism always has been
that, when the mystics have relied upon the Scriptures, they have
interpreted the Scriptures in a fashion that the divine authors never
could have recognized.

Wesley believed that professed experiences of revelation
should be submitted to all available tests. In some cases he went
to the limit of accepting such revelations as genuine, but only after
he had asked all relevant questions. I think I can hint at his attitude by telling of a character of whom I knew in my boyhood. An
engineer of a locomotive of a passenger train used to say that for
the most part he could tell whether all was right with his locomotive without looking at steam gauges, or watercocks, or watches, or
timetables. He could tell whether his train was on time or not
by the "swing of the engine." A preacher, hearing of this power,
made it a theme for an illustration of the Christian's feeling at home
in the universe, "by the swing of things"—the Christian's life being
in such adjustment that it did not need to rely upon artificial aids,

So far as the engineer and the Christian were concerned, they were alike in superiority to all mechanical devices, discerning the rightness and soundness of their relation, one to his engine and the other to the universe, by inner awareness.

This illustration is suggestive for its inadequacy and its adequacy. It does put us on the path of the realization that there is possible an awareness to truth which is above and to a degree independent of reasons that can be formally stated. Any artisan, or artist, or scientist, or philosopher knows that out of experience comes discernment which bears witness to itself as to nearness to the truth.

In all these realms, however, the awareness arises out of the long practice in life. The judgment of the scientist comes of years of use of all the instruments available for the discovery of truth. The expert can drive at truth, as we say, directly, because he has been so faithful in the use of the scientific knowledge and skill which has come to him as a social heritage, and because he has so consummately mastered the use of the instruments which are veritable embodiments of the skill of scientists who have labored that others might enter into their labors. So, for illustration, the scientist becomes aware that a hitherto undiscovered planet is making a disturbance in the distant skies.

Now notice: The suspected star is not hailed as a fact till it has met the tests supplied by the instruments. To go back to the more commonplace illustration, the engineer could not be permitted to go for long depending on the "swing of the engine." One mistake might mean disaster. He might not be at the top of his physical, especially nervous, fitness. He might be advancing into years without being aware of the subtlety of the approach of old age. If he depended on the swing of the engine, he might become a social menace.

There are men who have a rare sense of direction. In a dense forest, or upon a plain on which there is no landmark, they seem to be able to tell about where they are. Yet, skillful as they may be, they are reckless beyond everything permissible if they neglect the maps and compasses and any other aids within reach. The skill to do without these helps in emergency arises from the faithful use of them in daily practice. A "general" sense of direction, which now and again appears as a "gift" in an individual, amounts to just about as much in the achievement of the explorer as does a fine voice, which has no training, in the revelation of beauty in song.

Returning for the moment to the realm of science, we often read in the biographies of scientists that this or that genius suspected a fact long before he could prove it. He knew that what he sought was there as he sought for it. This, by the way, explains the reticence of many a scientific mind about making statements of religious belief. In a review of a book on physics by a fellow scientist, Bertrand Russell once admitted that most, if not all, scientists cherish "secret beliefs." From the context this seemed to mean beliefs for which they could not give satisfactory proofs to themselves, presumably scientific reasons. It is to be regretted that more seekers after revelations from God have not been careful to bring their professions to the tests, not only of Scriptures and the church teaching, but to the check and corrective of the larger knowledge of life and mind which we must, more and more, regard as possessing increasing significance for our apprehension of the divine. Scientific procedure is an extension of the ordinary faculties of the mind. It seeks, so to speak, to bring more facts within the reach even of the senses and to make it possible to watch them more closely. While, of course, we cannot put the discernment of spiritual realities on the same plane as experimentations with scientific tools, yet both the tools and the spiritual procedures are the outcome of living. The instrument in the hands of the physician is the result of careful and sustained effort by those who would make the human touch upon sick flesh more revealing, more efficient, more kindly, more healing. A poetically-minded student of the life of farmers once said that every least detail of a most ordinary-looking plow is the product of age after age of effort of the human will to get better mastery of the earth, till the plow itself is more the expression of human contrivance, and experiment, and struggle than it is of the actual material of which it is fashioned. So likewise with the forms of prayer, which to Wesley meant so much, with times and seasons of worship and meditation, with the reading of such devotional works as are gathered together in the fifty volumes of the Christian Library. So also with Wesley's careful study of all religious states which seemed to hint at anything unusual in the ability of men to find God.

Wesley was fundamentally in line with the efforts of all who would utilize advancing knowledge of the human to learn more about the divine. In a day which did not have much but rule of thumb in psychology Wesley had to find his way along the best he could.

We are confronted in the attitude of Wesley toward mysticism by something of the same condition as confronts us in his stand on Christian perfection. The background has to be kept in mind. It seemed a simpler matter to make up one's mind on such problems then than today. Wesley lived in a smaller universe than we do. It gives us something of a shock to read that he did not fully accept the Copernican theory. The evolutionary hypothesis did not appear till more than a hundred years after the mid-period of his ministry. The idea of original sin to a world that accepted an earthly history for man of only about four thousand years was altogether different from that which makes the nature of the individual man the result of forces—physical and psychological—which have been at work for hundreds of thousands of years. The present condition is one in which words like "guilt" and "sin" lose the significance they had for the eighteenth century—outside of the range of personal choices—and even there they do not always mean what they then did. The consequence is that to understand much of what Wesley taught we have to think ourselves back into a thought-frame which has ceased to be. It may be remarked in passing that the spiritual gains for our own later time include a healthier feeling for reality, a more charitable attitude toward the frailties of men, a more hopeful assessment of genuine spiritual possibilities.

For Wesley himself the path to communion with God was in doing the divine will. The contrast between the Wesley of Oxford and the Wesley of all-over-England was not in fundamental purpose. In the Holy Club he had the same purpose as ever after: the search after God, after communion with God, after the highest form of communion possible. The difference was that in the earlier days he directly sought for such communion through specific exercises. In the later years he became absorbed in the work of bringing God to his fellow men. Woodrow Wilson used to say that character is a by-product, that we win character, at least of the highest type, not by deliberately seeking for it, but by losing ourselves in noble tasks. It would be easy to misuse this wisdom, but it is wisdom nevertheless. Students of Wesley's *Journal* and *Letters* have noted that, as the years went by, the writer spoke less and less of his own spiritual states and more and more of the work that was demanding every ounce of his strength. This is not to be explained by the increase of practical activities, as if Wesley became so busy that he did not any longer have time for meditation and prayer. Wesley said of himself that he had more time on his hands than

any other man in England, because of the hours he had to devote
to solitary travel.   It was not that he was too busy to seek spiritual
graces as would a monk in a cloister; his life was absorbed in the
redemption of his fellow men, using the word "redemption" to
include all of a man's nature and activities.

This outward gaze in the search for communion with God is not
a mere trick by which, after having failed to seize a prize by direct
approach, we come upon it from the flank.   We are dealing here
with one of the fundamentals of the Christian life.   No one realized and taught more persistently than did Wesley that Christianity
is a religion of the will.   It is not thinking, as such, or feeling, as
such; but these as based upon a will set to do righteousness.   This
being true, communion with God, even the most mystic vision, has
to come from doing the will of God.   Let us assume that one could
press on in religious experience till one might behold the face of
God, if we may be allowed a grotesque imagining.   Assuming the
vision to be true to Christianity, toward what would the gaze of
God himself be directed?   Not to the ninety and nine lives already
in safety, but to the one still lost.   Not to pleased contemplation of
him who had found his way to the secret of the Divine Presence,
but to the outer circle of those still to be reached.   If God is a seeking God—and what else is there in the New Testament if he is not?
—we see God by looking at the objects toward which he is looking.
The deepest communion with him comes from working together
with him.

Now, the sureness of Wesley's religious insight and grasp
came out of his labors for men.   His thought and feeling and deeds
were for them.   He kept his feet on the ground.   He did not know
anything about a philosophy which did not appear till a century
after he had died—the pragmatic system.   If one wished an illustration, however, of the soundness of the pragmatic method, one could
not do better than to read the *Journals* of Wesley.   Every insight to
which he attained come directly out of purposeful set of his will.
If Wesley had ever had any doubt about the witness of the Divine
Spirit, he never had any reason to doubt the witness of his own
spirit.   If anyone, looking on his life from the outside, ever had
any doubt about the divineness of the quality of his life, such an
onlooker still had to account for the drive of an energy which, in itself, was a unique human phenomenon.   One shrewd commentator
on early Methodism remarks that John Fletcher had a reputation
among the early Methodists for surpassing piety, but that the piety

necessary to the soul of a Fletcher living in quiet, far from the incessant distraction of administrative duties, did not guarantee the re-enforcement required by Wesley's continuous and complete putting forth of energies.

The indefinable good sense of which I have again and again spoken served Wesley throughout his leadership. He believed in "guidance," by which he meant the discernment of spiritual direction which came out of the adjustment of his total life to God's will. In the instances where he seems to us to have relied upon virtual miracle, as his praying that the cloud might shield his face from the sun while he preached in the open, or that the rain might cease till after the preaching, he seems always careful to ask this help where the issue was of no important consequence. He could have preached if the sun had been in his face, and he could have ceased preaching during the rain. Moreover, he could not easily be persuaded to accept a guidance vouched to anyone but himself.

In the main, he kept close to the ideal of religious life and conduct set forth by Jesus. The mystic experiences of Jesus are not recorded for us, at least not so as to make them like the experiences of which the professed mystics tell. Still, there is the immortal summary: we are to love God with all there is of us, heart, mind, soul and strength, and our neighbors as ourselves. If we look at what seem to be inner experiences of Jesus, we always find that they have to do with the tasks of his career. Even the temptations of Jesus must have involved deep soul-stirrings out of which came plans for men. There is not any way by which we can make the experiences of Jesus just visions on their own account. There are indeed those who tell us, after the old-fashioned interpretation which made all religious experience strictly personal, that the impulse to turn stones into bread was the pressure of the physical appetite, that the call to bow down and worship Satan in return for the kingdoms of this world and the glory of them was the tendency to ambition, that the suggestion to leap from the pinnacle of the Temple was craving to show the favor which Jesus held with his Father. Where is there in the Gospels any hint that such appeals would have meant anything to Jesus? Judged by his character, what made these feelings temptations at all was their attractiveness as methods for the redemption of Israel.

Wesley found a way which made his leadership compelling. He threw himself with complete abandonment into his work. The driving motive was love for God and man. This does not at all mean that he reminded himself through all his waking hours that he must show love to God and man. It did mean that, having given himself to a course which was the best he knew to set forth the highest type of devotion to God and man, he lost himself in the task. When men thus lose themselves, the multitudes soon find them.

To sum up, the three foes within Christianity itself which Wesley feared most were Calvinism, Antinomianism, and Mysticism. Now, each of these three produces a distinct quality of life. Each quality was resistant to the appeals of Methodism. Here, however, were limitations which made for the strength of Methodism.

The terms just mentioned have today but little of their eighteenth-century meaning. Wesley had no quarrel with Calvinism except at the point of predestination. Calvinism stood for a planned life, but Wesley would not accept a plan which left out choice by the lives planned, and left some of the lives outside any plan in the universe, and left no freedom even for the elect. With Wesley the choices of men had to count. He did not worry overmuch about the future consequences after the honest choice had been made. A discerning student once said that the present-day commonplaceness of Wesley's teaching came out of Wesley's power to make it commonplace by driving it into the mind of his society. Calvinism has immortal merits, but in its strict logical frame, it would have fastened the iron system of John Calvin upon any widespread growth of the idea of the worth of the individual. When we have said our last word about the despotic sway of Wesley, about his arrogance, and his impatience of those who stood in his way, we have to remember that his coming squarely up against Calvinism so forced the inhuman features of Calvinism out into the light as to make Methodism a power for democracy. Of course Calvinism in its predestination aspect could not have kept any hold on men at all if it had carried any implications that Calvinists themselves were not among the elect. This inevitably tended toward making a religious belief a buttress of privilege. The English Church all through the eighteenth century courted privilege, reckoned its officials as belonging to the privileged, and naturally enough leaned toward Calvinism. The predestination debate lasted in force, in America at least, till far into the nineteenth century. It repeatedly comes to renewed force, but in sixty years Wesley saw it settle into a presumably permanent place in Christian thinking, without decisive power of universal appeal.

The second foe was antinomianism, a notion so absurd that it has all but dropped out of religious thinking: the claim that he who is saved by the merits of Christ does not need to do anything on his own account; that all the good works of men are as nothing in the sight of the Lord anyhow. So the Christian is free from the law. Today the man who desires to be free from law does not trouble his head much about religion. In Wesley's day the stiff Wesleyan standards of moral conduct screened off the morally loosely knit, to say nothing of swarms of fanatics. This could hardly be called a limitation, but this moral rigor marked a field or a path out of which Wesleyanism would not stray. Those who have ever had anything to do with the emotional types of religion will realize how closely Wesley had to watch against the depreciation of moral conduct by those who maintained that their redemption was due to a work of Christ like the payment of a price. The debate has faded now from the interest of men, but at one time it brought Methodism into peril. Wesley through sixty years saw it sink into insignificance as a doctrine.

We have already spoken at length of mysticism. Here, again, was a danger which, Wesley said, might at one period have wrecked his own religious life. Mysticism at the present time can be so described as to apply to almost anything religious. It can mean everything or nothing. Probably the one point of resemblance in which all shades of mysticism more or less agree is in the belief of direct, unmediated communion of the soul with God. What this means there is no telling, except as one is dealing with a particular mystic, and then there may be no telling. For a human soul to lose its own individuality and become merged in the Divine Soul is an absurdity. The human soul might repeat within itself divine experiences, but that is not merging.

The mysticism which seemed dangerous to Wesley was that which put stress on reaching for ends without means. This also was Wesley's definition of "enthusiasm"—the search for ends without the use of means.

Now, this also shut Methodism off from some religious groups who might have found place in a Church. Methodism, according to Wesley, had to be system and plan, or nothing. He was not striving to make Methodism all-inclusive. Throughout his life he was dominated by the idea of a society within a Church. The three foes I have mentioned—Calvinism, Antinomianism, Mysticism—were points through which a confining circle was drawn.

Within that circle, developing by its own laws, was Methodism.

One of the enigmas about the times in which Wesley labored was the horror which those of the "upper" classes felt about what they called "enthusiasm." So far as we can see from looking at contexts in which the term was used, "enthusiasm" referred to anything calculated to arouse the feelings of men at all. Religion became a careful, prudential course of life without appeal to the emotions.

The most plausible explanation of this antipathy to "enthusiasm" is that the eighteenth century had been preceded by the seventeenth. With even the most superficial acquaintance with England in the seventeenth century we know the uproar of the nation from the time of Charles I on to the coming of William and Mary. The economists tell us that all the fearful struggles of that distressed century were at bottom economic. This may be. The discussion, however, had to do with political and religious issues, or with anything which drew the line sharply between those for the established order and those for change. Whatever economic forces were at work increased the bitterness. The execution of Charles I released emotional forces in England which have hardly become quiet to this day. The horrible events in Ireland, on the responsibility now of papists and now of Protestants, engendered a rage of which we can form but slight understanding. Questions like bishops or no bishops, Church or no Church, sacraments or no sacraments, led not merely to fierce debates but to murderous physical fighting. After the terrors of the seventeenth century England desired above all things internal peace. Men were sick of strife, so that the quiet of the eighteenth century came like a blessed boon after the uproar of the seventeenth. I have already said that Augustine Birrell has reminded us that there were four "purges" of the Church of England by political authority in the two centuries just preceding Wesley, each depriving the Church of many of its finest elements. At the very mention of religious excitement those who feared most the recurrence of strife became almost beside themselves. All the power of the established order went to the discouragement of "enthusiasm," which meant anything emotionally upsetting. The conflicts of the seventeenth century had been carried through with tremendous passion and conviction both by Roundheads and Cavaliers. The sincerity on both sides was but little short of desperate. This conviction and the expressions of it by the men of the seventeenth century seemed to the eighteenth to be "enthusiasm" of an extreme degree. Now, it is easy to see that the enthusiasm of the Wesleyan Movement was not of this brand. As we look back to the seventeenth century we see reasons why Wesley did not want the enthusiasm of the Methodists to take political direction. The path of safety for Methodism was in its attending strictly to the salvation of the souls of individuals. The most serious danger from public opinion that Wesley had to meet was the suspicion that he was a papist. This became so widespread that once, when in a moment of public excitement against papists all papists were told by the authorities to leave London within the next five days, Wesley gave up important engagements outside London during that period for fear that leaving the city under the circumstances would be widely construed into an admission that he was a papist.

Like Paul of old, Wesley sought to get into the English courts when mobs attacked him and his followers, so that he might not merely stand upon his legal rights, but that he might prove that he was not starting any "enthusiasm" which would lead to civil disturbance. When John Nelson, one of Wesley's best preachers, was seized by a press gang taking men for His Majesty's navy, it required all Wesley's skill and energy to get him released—a procedure which would have been of no great difficulty if it had not seemed to the authorities a good chance to get a leading Methodist out of the country. The English Church sought to be known as a supporter of the Government, an agency to keep the peace. The denunciation of "enthusiasm," then, seemed to be a key to the favor of the ruling powers.

This, then, was the background of the eighteenth century's opposition to enthusiasm; the only enthusiasm of that century was the enthusiasm against enthusiasm. The temper dated far back. It is to be remembered that Wesley was born just a little after the close of the tensions of the seventeenth century, in a home in which regularity was the watchword and practice. He took care to see that the excitement of the Methodist meetings did not arise from or reach to political causes. So much was this true that careful students of religious movements have pronounced Methodism so distinctly religious as to make it a definite manifestation of spiritual power on its own account, without interest, except incidentally, in any social problems. Some have seen in this one of those special seasons of divine favor to men for which all ought to be thankful; others have called it a hindrance and a slowing down of social progress.   In any event, this limitation of "enthusiasm" to religious aims has led to a tradition in some Methodist circles that intensively inner religion is the only concern worth becoming enthusiastic over.

We must next note that Wesley also denounced enthusiasm, giving it a definition with a twist of his own. He defined enthusiasm as a seeking the ends without using the means that would lead to the ends.   It is somewhat baffling to try to make much of this definition until we look at the religious beliefs and practices with which Wesley had to deal, most of which we have already at least glanced at.   Some of these are no longer living issues, as for example, quietism, which did not rely on what we call the "means of grace." God would meet the soul in his own way. Therefore wait for him and do not trifle by reading the Scriptures, or paying attention to church ordinances. We can see at once just about how well all this would sit in the mind of a man who all his life had been trying to find means to apprehend the holiness of God, and means to spread that holiness over the earth.

We can at once see that in our time "enthusiasm," as Wesley defined it, would be in some varieties of mysticism—those that incline toward a direct union with God beyond the aid of all instrumentalities whatever. Historically speaking, mysticism has depended quite as much upon means as any religious practice the Church has ever known. The approach to the mystic vision has been up the hard, steep steps of prayer and fasting and extreme self-denial. Yet the vision, once reached, has been so ineffable that it could not be communicated or described. The objection Wesley had to the mystics as enthusiasts was that they did not make enough place for the distinctly Christian means—the study of the Scriptures and the classic utterances of the Church. This, together with his opinion that the mystics talked much rank nonsense, made him so fierce against that highly regarded mystic, Jacob Behmen. If we are likely to think that Wesley was alone in his attitude toward Behmen, suppose we listen to Richard Baxter, writing a century earlier than Wesley. "Their doctrine [that of the Behmenists] is to be seen in Jacob Behmen's books, by him that hath nothing else to do than to bestow a great deal of time to understand him that was not willing to be easily understood, and to know that his bombasted words do signify nothing more than before was easily known by common familiar terms."

Wesley's definition of "enthusiasm" seems today to be unusual, but becomes more apt and pertinent the longer we look at it. What is wilder, or crazier than the attempt to bring things to pass without appropriate means? Benjamin Franklin used to refer to man as the tool-using animal. Human, material progress has come from man's ability to make and use tools. The similar truth holds in the realm of thought, as, let us say, in mathematics. It has been said of old that God geometrizes and that, in the high reaches of mathematics, we think God's thoughts after him, though it is only within the last ten years that a scientist has informed us that God is a mathematician. If, however, God is a mathematician, we cannot read his mathematics until we have mastered the mathematical tools with which we can bring him within our reach. If a seeker after mathematical truth should say that he was weary of equations and formulae and should insist upon gazing directly upon the truth, what could we say of him but that he was an "enthusiast" in Wesley's definition? We should probably put our judgment in stronger phrases still.

In the social realm we have to advance by social instruments. Take the threat of war, so omnipresent and so nearly omnipotent today. What is the trouble? Can we say that wars come because the nations hate one another? Not altogether. Certainly, personal hatred of the soldiers toward their enemies is not the chief cause. Fear of one another in the hearts of the various nations counts for more than hate, or greed, for that matter. Nationalistic impulses count, but a portentous lack counts also, the lack of any social machinery by which the disputes between nations can be adjusted, or prevented from arising. It is an ironic comment on the so-called progress of civilization that, while the nations of the earth are racing furiously to get deadlier material instruments of war, they go at a laggard pace in the invention of the social instruments to prevent war. For men seem to think that peace can come and stay just by the development of a peace sentiment. Peace sentiment has to be more than sentimental. It has to be more than a wish for peace. It has to be the will for peace, the will which will deliberately seek agencies by which peace can be made. According to Wesley's definition, "enthusiasm" for peace would mean shouting for peace without the willingness to seek peace and pursue it. This is just about the next door to mental and moral aberration, to put it gently.

There are those in Christian churches today to whom Wesley's conception of "enthusiasm" is definitely applicable. I refer to the good people who break out now and again in protest against all methods and means and agencies for the discovery and application of Christian truth, declaring that they are sick and tired of all these things; that, if we would only get directly to God, we could push all these devices to one side. I once attended a most important Methodist meeting where the duty was that of the wisest and most equitable distribution of missionary funds. The plans were necessarily intricate. One had to listen carefully in order to vote justly. In the midst of the session one brother raised this protest that we ought to get close to God. When asked how, he moved that we set aside the prepared program and devote the session to telling of our experiences in evangelism. Which we did. For three hours we told of evangelistic conquests that we had known here in America. That our problem was foreign missions did not seem to occur to any of the speakers. The events described were all of a bygone day. Nothing that was said bore directly on the tasks before us. After we finished, we had but a short time left to do the work for which the Church had sent us to the meeting. That work was jammed through hit-or-miss. The "spirit" of the meeting was good; we "had a good time"; and missions and missionaries paid for it all in the bungling results of a session that had become "enthusiastic" in the Wesleyan meaning.

Anyone who has read through the *Larger Minutes,* the minutes of the "conversations" in the early Methodist Conferences as revised by Wesley himself, will recall how careful Wesley was in urging smaller meetings where converts could be followed up for planned instruction as better than the large meetings where results could not be garnered. The competence of Wesley is in nothing more manifest than in his finding means for his religious ends, and means too that came out of the life of his followers and lay close to hand. It is often said that the highest inventive intellect is not that which can invent something outright of raw material, but that which can take the commonest material, or that which in largest quantity and closest access can be utilized for the desired purpose. Wesley did just this. It has been urged against him that he did not create anything outright. This ought not to be discount but praise. He could not have left a Methodism with any lasting power whatever, if he had depended upon strange or totally new contrivances. He was a popularizer of religion even in the means available to people.

PART VI

TOWARD METHODISM'S INDEPENDENCE

PART VI

TOWARD METHODISM'S INDEPENDENCE

A LITTLE over thirty years after the Aldersgate uplift Wesley wrote: "Being alone in the coach I was considering several points of importance. And thus much appeared as clear as the day—that a man may be saved who cannot express himself properly concerning imputed righteousness. Therefore to do this is not necessary to salvation. That a man may be saved who has not clear conceptions of it, yea, that never heard the phrase. Therefore, clear conceptions of it are not necessary to salvation. Yea, it is not necessary to salvation to use the phrase at all. That a pious churchman who has not clear conceptions even of justification by faith may be saved. Therefore clear conceptions even of this are not necessary to salvation. That a mystic who denies justification by faith (Mr. Law, for instance) may be saved. But, if so, what becomes of the *articulus stantis vel cadentis ecclesiae?* If so, is it not high time for us *Projicere ampullas et sesquipedalia verba,* and to return to the plain word, 'He that feareth God, and worketh righteousness, is accepted with him'?"

Now, this was written when Wesley was sixty-six years old. It is quite the custom to look for Wesley's wisdom in the utterances of his early years and to slur over the utterances of the later times as due perhaps to a lessening of vigor or to what Coleridge in a note on a margin of Southey's *Life of Wesley* called "the poison of the easy chair." Sixty-six was not for Wesley old age, however. He was then at the height of his power and Methodism at the full tide of success. The judgment just quoted was mature. It is notably different from that of thirty years before, just as positive in its conclusion as the harshness of the early period, but, if anything, simpler and more direct, certainly more reasonable and scriptural. He that feareth God and doeth righteousness is accepted of him. Wesley still had his own standards as to what "fearing God" meant and what constituted doing righteousness, but he spoke in a vastly different temper from that of the opening years of his ministry.

The author of the article which deals with Wesley in the *Cambridge History of the Eighteenth Century,* quotes Lord Acton as saying that the crucial date in the relation of Wesley to the

Church of England was December 1, 1767, on which date Wesley entered in his *Journal* the conclusion quoted above that we must get rid of long words and simply fall back on the truth that he that feareth God and doeth righteousness is accepted of him. Lord Acton says that this date rather than 1784 marks the separation of Methodism from the Church of England. If the entry of Wesley has this significance, it has more, for, taken in its full implication, it means the secondary nature of any church organization whatsoever.

This leads us to what is possibly the most important of all Wesley's legacies to the world: his emphasis on the right of way of the primary spiritual demands over all organizational factors whatsoever. When Wesley penned the words to which Lord Acton referred, he was sixty-six years old. The idea there expressed had been germinating in his mind through many years, possibly without his realizing what was taking place in him or to him.

First, a word as to the channel through which the conception came to him, namely, his actual practical experience in seeking to save men. The notion of salvation as dependent upon connection with a church, or the Church, once it takes hold of a life is almost impossible to shake off. Of course Wesley was not trying to minimize the Church, but to put it in its rightful place: that of an instrument of righteousness. Here was a man who had for forty years been seeking to save men. He had seen them saved; he had talked to them intimately about what salvation meant. He had seen transformed lives. And in what had he seen these transformations result? In lives fearing God and working righteousness.

It is understood all along that we are thinking of the Church on its organizational, doctrinal, ritualistic side. The Church is fundamentally the people who compose it. It was this that Wesley had before him when he spoke of salvation as social, and as coming to little apart from social relationships. He believed in organizations as bringing people together, but the organizations must be taken as instruments and not as ends in themselves. It has been said that the logic of the Protestant Reformation is complete individualism; which, indeed, it may be, but individualism is not opposed to companionship with one's fellows. The logic is not superior to the needs of life. There has never been complete individualism. There has never been an individual living absolutely alone. The historical and social fact is persons living together, living together at least in the beginning of the history of the race in such close union that it was only late and slowly that the idea of distinctiveness of individuality arose. All this Wesley knew and taught and acted upon. He made the social relationships significant for the salvation of the individuals.

The belief in a Church as an instrument, of course, has to meet the objection that we come out at the same place as when we think of the organization as an end in itself, for, if the Church is indispensable as an instrument, the indispensability is all-important. To which the reply is that, if an instrument is indispensable, it is a means to an end, and is subordinate to the purposes for which it is intended. An instrument is sacred for what it can do. An instrument which can do better work than another instrument is more sacred than that other. An instrument can be modified, or changed completely, or put aside, if some other and better tool can be discovered or invented.

To apply this conception to the matter in hand: Take the rites of the Church—baptism and the Lord's Supper. At the beginning of his ministry Wesley held views which made these rites more than instruments. They had a sacredness on their own account. Something happened to a man in baptism due to the rite itself. Wesley said that the power of cleansing in his early baptism had not been wholly lost at Charterhouse. It was not merely an instrument, or symbol of dedication of the life to righteousness, or a sign of the spiritual cleansing of the heart by the Divine. The cleansing efficacy was in the rite, with inevitable emphasis upon the significance and power of a redemptive force in the rite as a rite. Now, move over to the other position and think of the rite as ceremony marking the determination of a human will to do the will of God, and of the redemptive cleansing by spiritual—not material—power. If a particular baptism is necessary for salvation, that means either that a peculiar virtue is lodged in the water itself, or that God so cares for one material method that he will not redeem through any other. One notion is just as worthy as the other. How man could believe this or anything like it is not our task to consider. Suffice it to say that for a time Wesley believed this, though he would never have put the belief in such stark terms as these.

So with the spiritual results of partaking of the sacrament of the Lord's Supper. In college Wesley used to "communicate," as it was called, two or three times a week. It is not easy to suppose that he would have done this if he had not believed there was saving

efficacy in the sacrament itself.   No belief in the history of the
Church is more persistent than that of supernatural power in this
sacrament.   The present writer once served on a committee to see
if by various Protestant denominations, including one important
group in Europe, any theory as to the sacraments could be worked
out which would draw these denominations into closer unity.   One
of the committee, a distinguished theological professor from
Europe, kept laying stress on the supernatural efficacy of the Lord's
Supper.   I finally asked if the will of the participant, his determination to lead a new life, had any importance in the spiritual benefit
to the communicants.   The reply was "No," that we had to keep the
emphasis on the divine element.   I then asked if a participant who
partook of the sacrament unwittingly, or even unwillingly, would
be benefited.   The reply was "Yes," which came very near to saying that a man could be made good in spite of himself or whether
he wished to be made good or not.   Now, the entry to which Acton
referred may not have meant that on December 1, 1767, Wesley
was thinking specifically of the Lord's Supper, but the implication
was unmistakable enough.   If he who fears God and worketh
righteousness is acceptable to God, and if that is the main requisite,
then the sacrament is instrumental, unless we are ready to say that
partaking of the sacrament is indispensable in fearing God and
doing righteousness.

Wesley just had to see, working as he was, that no sacrament
could be the fundamental in the salvation of men.   Chiefly for
the sake of not breaking with the Church of England, Wesley would
not allow his lay preachers to conduct the sacrament.   Inasmuch,
however, as he beheld men converted from sin to righteousness by
the preaching of his laymen, and their lives marked by the fear of
God, he could not, as a sensible being, put that preaching in a place
inferior to the sacraments.

Then as to regularity of the ministry: Wesley was brought up
in the belief of the sacredness of ordination.   There is no use trying
to blink the fact that he took ordination with high seriousness.
It was in the earlier years important to him that he had been
ordained by one who stood in a line making possible not, indeed, a
belief in apostolic succession, but in ecclesiastical continuity.   Himself a regular by nature, Wesley easily and naturally fitted into the
belief in an especial sacredness in the regular ministry.   Two things,
however, must have sunk deeper and deeper into his mind as he
traveled up and down England—indeed, he repeatedly talked of

them. First was that in the actual persuasion of men to quit sin and turn to righteousness his lay preachers were more effective than many, if not most, of those of the Established Church. Wesley did not cherish any illusions about his lay preachers. He did not think of them as of any other training than that of practically leading men into new life. If one were as good a Hebrew scholar as any he had ever known, he said so in terms of highest appreciation; but he did not look to his lay helpers for technical scholarship. He himself guided their study, always with the increase of religious effectiveness in mind. He gave all credit to the ministers of the Church of England for the good they could do, but he did not think of these ministers as to be put into the same class with his preachers for evangelistic effectiveness. Now, let a man like Wesley have, day after day, chance to think this over, away from all church influences, about the sacredness of the ministry as based on correctness of ordination, or other formal organizational requirement as such, and he can come to only one conclusion, namely, that such requirement is secondary. We wonder that it would take a man of ordinary eyesight, to say nothing of insight, any considerable period of attention to see this, though many, very many, do not see it to this day.

The second consideration was the worldly conduct of many of the clergy of the Established Church. This argument has probably been overworked. There were many clergymen in the Church of England who were thoroughly devoted to their tasks. They lived in a barren time, religiously, and could not find any way out of the spiritual desert. Still, there were secularly-minded clergymen, some of whom were loose in their lives. Now, when Wesley heard as often as he did that it was not the character of the minister that counted but official connection, as something sacred in itself, it was more than he could stand. He was himself working night and day, all the days in the year, to bring men to the kingdom of God. When he saw others utterly idle, it could not but undermine his confidence in the efficacy of a sacredness which was professedly official.

Moreover, Wesley had the witness of his own consciousness as to something of the secret of his own power. In some respects Wesley had the strength which comes from profound self-knowledge. He knew how he had obtained the new life. He knew how little mere official connection with a church had to do with that life. Just what relation there was between his ordination and the experiences to which he attained again and again would become more and more of a mystery to him whom the Church was opposing just because he taught the experiences.

Not only could Wesley not help seeing the absurdity of the claim that ordination by a bishop gave a minister a sacredness, when the bishop was not himself sacred in character, but he became most realistic in his attitude toward bishops themselves. He had become convinced, he said, by his studies of the primitive Church, that a presbyter was a bishop, and that, therefore, he was himself on the same level as a bishop. This has often been taken as a theme for prolonged argument. It has been assumed by some church historians that they have disposed of Wesley's attitude toward bishops when they have pointed out the limping weaknesses of his historical argument. This is not taking Wesley by quite the right hold. Wesley was not overanxious to put himself on the same level as bishops. What he was doing was to show that he did not take them with especial seriousness. The actual encounters he had had with them were not of the happiest. Joseph Butler he admired profoundly, as we have already seen; but it was from Butler that he received the order to get out of the Bristol diocese, where a host of Methodist converts had been won. With other bishops he had sharp passages. Once, when asked whether he did not intend to obey the bishops, he replied that he would do so if they were worthy. This was to put his own judgment above that of the Church which had created the bishops. It was the essence of rebellion against regular ecclesiastical authority. This meant, at least in implication, that while Wesley never let go his loyalty to the Church, he had come to rank it as an organization altogether in a minor place, its sacredness to be determined by its efficiency in producing spiritual results. What happened to those whom the Church touched?

All this now seems commonplace, though there is here and there something of a revival of the older notion. It was innovation at the time it was first uttered. Tell anyone today that both Wesley and Whitefield deemed it necessary to preach that a preacher himself ought to be a man of religious life, of new birth, conversion— whatever term one pleases—or that the life of the preacher ought itself to set forth the truth proclaimed; and one is likely to be met with a stare of bewilderment at such utterance of the obvious. Yet the Church organization and its ordinances, as sacred in themselves, had such hold on the eighteenth-century religious thinking that the importance of Church regularity overshadowed the necessity of right living in the ministry.

Or think of the regard with which in America the sacraments were held after Methodism began to spread. There was no bishop in America—bishop of the English Church, I mean—who could ordain ministers here. After Methodism began to win converts, there were not enough priests of the English Church to administer the sacraments. The heaviest pressure for the ordination of ministers in America came from this demand for the sacraments; the stiffest opposition from the feeling of the sacredness of the ordinances of the Church. It was almost impossible for a time to make headway with the idea that sacraments were instrumental. If a miracle was wrought in a sacrament, of course the utmost scrupulousness would have to mark the observance of the conditions which would lead to the miracle. If a sacrament is an instrument, it can be dealt with more freely. In a word, Wesley believed in means of grace. The ordinances of the Church were means, but means of grace. The grace made sacred the means, and the means helped to the attainment of the grace.

If one fancies all this is to be taken as a matter of course, one will never gain any appreciation of Wesley as an innovator. Wesley was not an innovator by choice or by inclination. He never made any departure from the ordinary path except as he was virtually compelled to do so. The labor of seeking to save the souls of men forced him to the emphasis that the all-essential was to get men to fearing God and to doing righteousness. At this point the rift between him and the English Church was indicated by the entry on December 1, 1767, but the seed sown there did not bear fruit till far later. Unless one does have the cue given by this entry, one will have to pronounce Wesley insubordinate and rebellious. On the assumptions of the "regular" clergy of the time the case against Wesley is fairly complete. The ordinances of the Church were sacred to Wesley, in the instrumental sense. He was devoted to the Church, and never ceased saying so. How to reconcile his devotion with his attitude toward the bishops the orthodox churchmen could not tell.

There is always difficulty about understanding a middle way. To the regular churchman of the eighteenth century the Church as an institution had to be all or nothing. Either it was a sacred object of divine power, or just nothing at all. When, therefore, Wesley insisted upon saying for himself when the Church was to be obeyed, he seemed virtually to be putting himself outside the Church.

It sometimes happens that an observer on the outside can see a meaning in what a historic leader does which the leader may not himself suspect.   Lord Acton called to our attention that Döllinger, the Catholic historian, considered Richard Baxter and John Wesley the most significant Protestant figures since the Reformation.   Acton affirmed that Döllinger was thinking of Wesley as he was after December, 1767.   Lord Acton, as well as Döllinger, was a Catholic.   The reason why Acton spoke thus was that he saw at the above date a complete break by Wesley from the English Church.   The discernment of these two as to what Wesley was really doing may be sound enough, but if they had any notion that Wesley would under any circumstances have felt differently toward the Roman Church, they would have done well to point out something other than Wesley's emphasis on a religious experience that was altogether above the reach of religious organizations as he knew them.   Lord Acton too did not take sufficient account of the Wesleyan psychology, which allowed room for at least as much contradiction in his life as in the experience of other human beings.   Men accept principles without realizing their implications.   Sometimes the implications play havoc in a mind's life through the stress they set up, but oftener they lie dormant until they break forth with unforeseen explosion in a crisis.   Oftener still they do not come into clear light until the followers bring them forth.   Wesley's theory of the Church did indeed change, but he did not relax in his insistence that his followers remain in the Church of England.

All this may seem like carrying out a commonplace observance to intolerable length, but will the reader please have patience a moment longer?   Here is involved the essence of every form of High-Churchism.   If a Church has organizational values which are necessary to men's salvation, then, though there may be possible exceptions like those provided for by the Roman Church in the doctrine of invincible ignorance, there is no salvation outside the reach of the sacred ordinances.   Here we are on the path to the terrible battles between religious groups, which so often end in persecution of one type and another.

No matter how absolute some of the claims of a Church may be, this emphasis on virtual High-Churchism often does have an instrumental basis, in spite of the declarations of the Church to the contrary. Take the doctrine of papal infallibility: the claim that when the Pope is speaking *ex cathedra* his is the veritable voice of God. As such there is but one course for the faithful. They have only to obey. They do not have room for debate or question. Now, approach a Roman Catholic about papal infallibility and you often find him quite willing to talk. This willingness itself is significant; for, if the Pope actually speaks for God, there does not seem to be much reason for talk by men. The Roman Catholic, however, makes the same appeal to results as does the pragmatic holder of the position that any church belief has to be justified by the practical consequences. From the outside, from the assumption of the non-Catholic, the papal infallibility is instrumental. It is a device of expediency, a court of last resort like the United States Supreme Court. In all institutional doings someone has to say the last word. The insistence that the Pope speaks as God's voice necessarily makes his word the last. Those of us who are not Catholics are sure that the Pope is not infallible. If the Roman Church could see how much difficulty it would escape by taking the instrumental position, and would act upon that understanding, it would be better off in every way. Churches are always prone to claim more than is necessary. A good Catholic would go wild to hear the Pope compared to an umpire, but he ought to see that umpires are among the most useful agents in modern life. Their decisive word closes cases and helps the game go on.

Even if Wesley's word on December 1, 1767, were only a seed dropped, it will not do to take it lightly. Wesley's after development was an unfolding of the principle there stated. Moreover, the statement itself went far. Wesley said that it was clear to him that a man might be saved even if he did not know anything about imputed righteousness. Inasmuch as that was one of the doctrines taught by the Church, Wesley's remark was equivalent to saying that, at least on one important doctrine, it was not necessary to salvation to be taught by the Church. This was, under all the circumstances, the opening of a wide gate.

As to the instrumental nature of church doctrines, we have no right to claim Wesley for modern pragmatism, though his words look in that direction. Any doctrine formulated, let us say, in the twentieth century, if it has any appreciable degree of truth at all, has been anticipated in utterances of acute thinkers and observers decades and even centuries before. Any doctrine is at bottom an attempt to bring out into clear system what has already been implicit in ordinary human experience. Pragmatism of the extreme type holds that truth and usefulness are one and the same, that the only measure of the truth of an idea is the extent to which it can be used. Wesley can be claimed only for pragmatism as a method. He would judge doctrines by what came out of them. The method would help to the seizure of the truth, and be an indication of the soundness of the truth, but that would be all. The awareness of Divine Presence—God is with us—was to Wesley the spiritual state above all others to be sought. We may be confident that Wesley would regard a formal theology of a Church as a means to help on to self-evidencing life. The theology itself he would not at most have regarded as more than a tool, and that an imperfect tool.

I have repeatedly said that we must always try to keep ourselves at Wesley's center of view. If we do this, shifting of emphasis from the Church ordinances to the instrumental relationship will appear to be one of Wesley's most valuable bequests to the world. After all, it is not so self-evident today that the instrumental idea has won a complete triumph. At the death of Wesley in 1791 a strain was set up in the Methodist groups over the question of the sacrament of the Lord's Supper, which promised to wreck the movement itself. We now and again read that, as soon as the hand of Wesley fell from the helm of Methodism, the ship steered itself straight away from the Church of England. Methodism did indeed soon begin its existence as a separate Church, but not quite as inevitably and as speedily as we sometimes fancy. Moreover, it was not merely the influence of Methodism which was holding the society back, but this feeling about the sacraments. Many who had the most complete devotion to Wesleyan principles stopped stockstill when they were asked to receive the Lord's Supper at the hands of the preachers of Methodism who had not been ordained at the hands of bishops of the English Church. These secondary features of a Church have a power that has to be felt to be understood. Abraham Lincoln was reported to have said that, when he found a Church that would set up as its sole requirement that men should love God with all their hearts, soul, mind, strength, and their neighbors as themselves, he would be glad to join it. There has never been any such Church of large numerical proportions, and it is not likely that there soon will be. In every denomination the secondary features get up, sooner or later, into the primary importance.

The theme is admittedly difficult. Wesley insisted that salvation was social, and that it had to be so from the nature of man himself. Inasmuch as the Church is a group of men who are ends in themselves, sacred on their own account, the Church as this group is a veritable body of Christ. There are, however, impersonal features about a Church which serve the personal. Practically, these impersonal factors are for the most of us indispensable. Yet even here the Wesley principle opened the door to those outside the Church. Moreover, do we ourselves not seldom speak of an invisible body of Christ—the body of true believers whose religious life may or may not be drawn from church connections? This doctrine of the invisible body implies that there may be in the Church those who have not the Spirit of Christ. Likewise there may be those outside the Church who have the Spirit of Christ. Wesley was most careful here. He was convinced that the heathen who never had heard of Christ were to be tested by their living up to what light they had in their own consciences. Here, again, is an open door. For heathenism cannot be called an affair of geography. What about the heathen who live in Christian lands? Have these all heard Christ preached? It is easy to say that all who live within sound of a church bell have had opportunity to hear Christ preached. Would John Wesley have admitted this? We can be quite sure that he would not. Was the service in the Church of England in Wesley's day the preaching of Christ? Not always. If much that I have been saying in the last few paragraphs seems to deal with far-off forgotten things and battles long ago, let us remember that we cannot understand Wesley unless we understand the battles which were real in his day. The same battles are more real in our day than we always care to concede.

The whole problem is complicated to us of today, and it was even more complicated in Wesley's day. All sorts of practical expediences crowd in to obscure the essentials. I once heard Bishop Gore addressing a group of some hundreds of churchmen who were trying to define the Church in such fashion as to win the approval of representatives of a score of different denominations. Bishop Gore reminded his hearers that none of the proposed definitions had included one most vital consideration, namely, that there were large numbers of persons, some of whom he knew intimately— skeptics, agnostics, or atheists—whose spirit was that of Christ and who must be brought, at least in our regard, into the membership of the invisible Church. Whereupon a sturdy denominationalist arose and declared that he did not doubt the truth of what the

Bishop had said, but that he was sorry such words had been spoken, inasmuch as they tended to weaken the authority of the Church. It seemed that the authority of the Church would be weakened if the full glory of the Church should be revealed. It will be noted that this objecting brother virtually admitted that he was moved by a practical consideration.

It is none of our task to discuss the Roman Catholic theory of the Church beyond saying that the notion of the sacredness in itself of the Church of England was an inheritance from Rome, from which, except politically, the English Church did not break. Not two centuries before Wesley was born the Church of England broke from the Pope to take Henry VIII as its head. The dissenters were the determined foes of Rome. Though Wesley's ancestors on both sides had been dissenters, he was solidly opposed to dissent. His mother had been born into a dissenting family and had turned again to the Church, and his father had deliberately rejected dissent. Wesley called himself a High Churchman from the beginning. All the more remarkable, then, his acceptance of the idea of the Church as instrumental.

We have come to a day when church union is a current theme. We may just as well note, then, that the Wesleyan doctrine of church organization as instrumental may deepen the movement toward union, or it may do just the reverse. The emphasis on the Church as the means of the development of religious life may make the choice of means so indifferent that it will not seem worth while to those most earnest in the search for higher life to trouble themselves overmuch about organization. That the seekers for the best are brought into a larger fellowship may seem so important as to warrant any surrender of organizational forms. On the other hand, the denominational forms may seem to others to be important as making a rallying point for the smaller groups, the minorities in whose association the seekers after life may find a more intense, although narrower type of experience.

The attitude of Wesley toward the Church, as might have been expected when he made the uniting bond of the Church only a common interest in spiritual concerns, sent his followers in different directions. There were those who remained in the English Church, and probably after the death of Wesley had less and less to do with the Methodist societies. This was all more possible because, after the persecution of the Methodists ceased, let us say about 1760, the Evangelical Movement in the Church of England began to take on power, and had become a force to be reck-oned with by the end of the century.   To Wesley himself we may give a generous share of the credit for the evangelical impulse in the Church, though there were other men making their contribu-tions besides Wesley, and other influences besides Wesleyan.   The Church, awakened by the evangelical spirit, began to think of Wes-ley as a leader and saint, and has continued to think of him thus to this day.

A second direction taken by other followers of Wesley was that of membership in the Methodist Church as an ecclesiastical body, independent and ecclesiastically self-sufficient.   This was not what Wesley intended.   Some students think that Wesley's course with his societies made separation inevitable.   Perhaps. Nevertheless, a number not at all negligible refused to follow the societies out of the Church.

The separation, if it had been inevitable and foreseen, would have led Wesley to a different course in training his followers.   He did not think of Methodism as a Church.   If he had foreseen that it was not possible to prevent its being a Church, he in all likelihood would have sought to make it, in many respects, a different instru-ment than it was when he left it.   The Legal Hundred was the nucleus of what afterward became a Church.

By the way, Wesley's choosing a hundred to be the legal body raises interesting questions which we do not have time to consider. The number was, of course, arbitrary, and left out some good men. This brought a quite unnecessary tinge of bitterness into the beginnings of the formal body.   Wesley avowedly had no sympathy with republicanism, which to him meant actual rule by the people. One hundred made up a considerable number, though not the "people" by any means.   Wesley took his lay preachers as the heart of the Methodist system, but he had no place for laymen as such in the government of Methodism.   He met the problem of lay control when the laymen sought to be trustees of the preaching places which they had paid for, since he did not care to have lay trustees passing on the virtual choice of ministers, by himself deciding who should or should not preach in this or that preaching place.   There are signs, however, that the favor of laymen counted in the choice of preachers even in the old days.

The Legal Hundred group went ahead finally to the organiza-tion of a new denomination, following what might be called the conservatism of Wesley, conservatism in ministerial control and in

attitudes toward social questions. Other Methodist groups broke
away and proceeded along more democratic roads. It required
over a hundred years of church experience and of the general
world-progress of social understanding and practice to get Methodism together again into a unified body.

In this emphasis on the instrumental aspect of a Church, Wesley opened the door to splits and secessions. If the stress is thus put
on religious results of the inner type, naturally an individual, feeling that he may choose the instrument which will best suit his
religious purpose, will move about among church organizations
more or less at his own will. He will not pay much heed to many
features of a long-established Church which tend to hold the
members in one body—the venerable impressiveness of the town
cathedral, the continuity of the liturgy through centuries of use,
all the emotions which are aroused by the teaching that the creed
has been believed always in the Church, by everybody, everywhere.
This latter consideration weighed heavily with Wesley himself in
his earlier years.

Now, this emphasis on the Church as an instrument for the
development of the inner personal life can be balanced by the
realization of the value of the Church as an instrument for what
might be called collective or corporate prophecy on social questions.
This realization, however, was a long time in coming to Methodism. It is indeed a recent arrival, and has arrived only when the
united sentiment of the Church has been aroused over questions
which are chiefly personal, like Hugh Price Hughes's attack on the
leadership of Charles Stewart Parnell because of the irregularities
of Parnell's personal conduct.

Wesley's difficulty in holding the Methodist group together was
owing somewhat to the fact that the new population of which I have
already so often spoken had never known any church but Methodism. This is a point which we must insist on even with wearisome
repetition. The gains of Methodism were not made in chief degree
among those united with the Church of England. One reads the
diary of Parson Woodforde, for example, who served a country
parish for nearly half a century, and wonders why there is hardly
any reference to Methodism. Woodforde was a close enough observer to have seen what was going on. If the Methodists had been
making any deep impression in his neighborhood, he would have
written at least a few entries about them. In the five large volumes,
however, there is almost nothing of the sort. This was because

Woodforde did not live in an industrial center, but among people whose needs the Church appeared to satisfy. The dwellers in the new industrial centers knew Methodism, and could not make much of Wesley's insistence that they ally themselves with the Church of England.

I have aready spoken of the Hammonds—J. L. and Barbara. No one has understood better the labor situations and developments in the England following the Industrial Revolution than the Hammonds. These tell us that the important social movement in England of the latter part of the eighteenth century was toward trade-unionism, which concerned the same class as that which Wesley touched; that Wesleyanism split the interests of the labor class and diverted to other-worldly interests energies which should have gone to the organization of the unions. The Hammonds argue their case with cogency, but at times they become absurd, almost to the verge of silliness. For example, they speak of the money raised for the Wesleyan chapels as if it ought to have gone to trade-union movements; indeed, the implication is that the contributions of laborers to Wesleyanism were a diversion of funds from their true, natural purpose, and that to this extent the churchmanship of Wesley, or his devotion to his societies, was a mistake. All of which is quite a tribute to Wesley's making his societies successful. We cannot make much of the career of Wesley up to the years near the close unless we think of him as loyal to the Established Church and as aiming to make Methodism a society in that Church. It may be that we get astray through not taking adequate account of the part played by societies in the churches which have had a history of centuries. We in America are not likely to have much basis for the judgment of the worth of a society in a church. We are likely to think of it as a Ladies' Aid group, or a Men's Club, or a Christian Endeavor organization. In fact, we have to look to the important orders of the Roman Catholic Church, or to the many societies in the career of the English Church, to understand what Methodism on the organizational side meant to Wesley.

In any considerable Church which aspires to be at all catholic, there must be room for groups of like-minded members who give themselves specifically to the development of particular phases of the truth or forms of practice. Such groups must, of course, be loyal to the main organization, but they can often best show that loyalty by developing and maintaining what might appropriately be called their own specialties. It is about as clear as anything of the sort can be that it is only by the existence of such smaller units in a larger body that the main body can accomplish anything especially worth while. Principal A. D. Lindsay, Master of Balliol, in his *Essentials of Democracy*, has shown that in nationwide democracies like England and the United States the large bodies are safe only as they contain within themselves smaller organs of like-minded persons, such as trade-unions and professional organizations which have massiveness enough to hold guiding ideas before the democracy. If this is true in a democracy, it is perhaps more true of a Church that reaches throughout a nation or through many nations.

This does not quite mean federation, for federation has about it, in view of the federal principle of the United States Government, a suggestion of states territorially separate. A society in a Church is not likely to be organized territorially, but may be composed of members throughout the whole connection. Nor does this mean the recognition of minority groups as ordinarily understood, for, when we speak of a minority, we usually carry a hint of a party in opposition, and a society in a Church may not be in opposition. Wesley's aim was to spread scriptural holiness, speaking in the name of the Church to those whom the Church could not reach, or was not reaching.

It may be that at the beginning Wesley did not even think of any special form of society, but he could not have gone far without asking himself whither his movement was tending. There cannot be any doubt that he did not countenance the notion of his group's becoming a body of dissenters or nonconformists. There cannot be any doubt either that he thought of himself as a High-Churchman, for that is what he called himself. Understand, we are trying to find the ideas in Wesley's mind during the active days of his leadership, for those ideas must have colored all his work. Unless we are prepared to concede that Wesley was not sincere in what he urged upon his followers, we must hold fast to his meaning what he said, which was that he would not countenance any secession of Methodists from the Church of England.

This means that Wesley's greatness as a leader had as one of its qualities a willingness to work with a limited aim. We have quoted in Part IV his remark that, when he started out upon his wider campaigning, he did not expect the Methodist Movement to last more than thirty years, and that one of its most astonishing achievements was that, at the time of the remark, it had gone fifty. Now, when a man lays plans for thirty years, he is surely working with a different set of ideas from those he keeps before him when he is planning for an indefinite future. Wesley certainly expected the English Church to last more than fifty years. Moreover, he sought to prevent the Methodists from holding services at such hours as to conflict with the services of the Established Church. This can be interpreted as an attempt to prevent any friction between the Methodist meetings and the regular exercises of the Church, but such interpretation would not be enough of an explanation of a rule to be followed for half a century. The more satisfactory explanation is that Wesley desired his followers to get something from the services of the Church. This meant that there were, in Wesley's judgment, some religious values to be found by Methodists in the Church which they could not find in their own meetings.

It will be urged against all this that Wesley did give himself to courses that made the establishment of Methodism as a Church virtually inevitable. We are not, however, just now so much concerned with the outcome of Wesley's attitude toward ecclesiastical problems as with his intentions, and with the limitations he set upon himself. These limitations reveal Wesley's understanding of the human material with which he worked, and of the conditions under which any revivalistic movement must be carried on. We must remember that Wesley conceived of his task as revival. His father had told him that he would one day see the work of the Lord revived in England, and he had lived in that expectation. With all Wesley's disparagement of the Church, he does not ever seem to have questioned either its perpetuity or its place in the divine plan for the redemption of the world. Now, a Church which exists solely for revival can hardly be called a Church: it is an agency for performing one of the functions of a Church. Revival work, in the nature of things, is preliminary. Of course the analogies are not happy, but the revival efforts of a Church and the recruiting efforts of an army and the promotional activities of a business are alike in that the main task is to be attacked after the recruiting and promoting are accomplished. Promotion of any variety demands an order of ability peculiarly itself, a high and rare ability indeed when the promotion takes the form of evangelization for Christianity. Yet such ability is not the final Christian grace. We refer again to the remark of William James that certain types of mind are trigger-pullers for human consciousness—those that have the power of so suggestively stating truth, or so compellingly phrasing it, that their utterances are of a crisis-making order that discharges, so to speak, the stored-up mass of the content of their hearers' minds into resolution or insight which might never have been possible if it had not been for the trigger-puller. The difficulty here is that the evangelistic trigger-puller so often thinks that he can store the mind with the "load," let us say, that is to be released. That load may be the teaching and reflection and dreams of many previous years, released into life-changing power by the trigger-puller, but the trigger-puller may be himself the last man fitted to do the loading of the mind. Wesley knew all this perfectly. He did not, at least until age had made inroads on his mental vitality, have the slightest illusion as to the nature and characteristics of the Methodism he had founded and led.

What men mean when they say that Wesley made the separation from the Church inevitable is his consenting to ordain ministers for the administration of the sacraments. This happened, it will be remembered, in the closing years of his life, when the springs of his strength had begun to run low. The oft-quoted word charged against Wesley's conduct is "Ordination is separation." Of course it is, if the leaders of a Church are bound to have it so. In an age when some special ordaining sanctity is supposed to be lodged in the hands of the ordaining officiary, it is possible to utter wise saws like this. Then, of course, it is possible further to talk of apostolic succession and other such nonsense, in which Wesley himself did not believe, and in which some of the strictest adherents of the English Church themselves do not today believe.

The nub of the talk of Wesley's countenancing separation is the ordination of some men to be virtually bishops—Thomas Coke in particular, inasmuch as Coke was the first of the few to be so ordained. Coke was thinking of the American situation, and more than a little of Coke. The American situation was in a word this: that from 1766, or from 1770 on, the Methodists in America had grown in numbers to several thousand. They had to do without the benefit of the sacraments unless a minister of the English Church happened to be near at hand. There is no other instance in ecclesiastical history to compare with the loyalty of the American Methodists of those early days to the Established Church, a loyalty which is about equally pathetic and ridiculous. Methodists were converted, brought into a society, and led devout lives for ten or a dozen years without even having been baptized or having partaken of the sacrament of the Lord's Supper. The strange feature is that the Methodists did not draw the conclusion early in this stage of affairs, especially after the English Church had refused to send a bishop or to ordain Methodist preachers in America, that the sacraments were of no value anyhow. The Methodists in America were three thousand miles away from England, a six or eight weeks' sail across the dangerous Atlantic—as far in time as today the borders of Tibet are from New York. Few historians today will say that the Declaration of Independence of America from England was a mistake, historically speaking. The separation was inevitable. The separation of the American Methodists from all English ecclesiastical connections was likewise inevitable, and likewise the severing of all official connections between American and English Methodism. As to America's becoming independent, Wesley could not help that. The situation in America was totally different from that in England. The Methodists in America, persistently loyal to Wesley, waited for some advice from him, but finally they acted on their own. Asbury would not accept the ordination, or the setting apart, for supervision of Methodism, till he had been elected superintendent by the Methodist preachers in Conference. The Conference took matters in its own hands and made itself the organ of a separate Church. Whether Wesley had a right to lay hands on Coke's head, or Coke to lay hands on Asbury, has no significance. A gleam of light as to Wesley's feeling on the whole matter, however, can be found from that famous letter of his to Asbury—the "Dear Franky" letter. It is refreshing to read that Wesley was so upset by Asbury's calling himself a bishop. Asbury did do just that, but American Methodism acquiesced. Wesley is content to be called plain Mr. Wesley, as dictators usually have been. There is considerable point in the old remark that, if a leader of a mass of men wishes dictatorial powers, he would better not allow himself to be called by any title that itself suggests such powers. He would do well to accept no title but plain "Mr." For titles like "king" in the political sphere and "bishop" in the ecclesiastical put the doubtful on their guard at once. At any rate, Wesley's control over the Methodists had been all but papal. It is delightful, therefore, to hear him reproach Asbury for assuming the title of bishop.

London, September 20, 1788.

There is indeed a wide difference between the relation wherein you stand to the Americans and the relation wherein I stand to all the

Methodists. You are the elder brother of the American Methodists: I am under God the father of the whole family. . . .

But in one point, my dear brother, I am a little afraid both the Doctor [Coke] and you differ from me. I study to be little: you study to be great. I creep: you strut along. . . .

One instance of this, of your greatness, has given me great concern. How can you, how dare you suffer yourself to be called Bishop? I shudder, I start at the very thought! Men may call me a knave or a fool, a rascal, a scoundrel, and I am content; but they shall never by my consent call me Bishop!

Thus, my dear Franky, I have told you all that is in my heart.
          Your affectionate friend and brother,

                                        JOHN WESLEY.

Asbury referred to this letter, the last he received from Wesley, as a "bitter pill." One cannot help wondering how Wesley would have felt if Asbury, in replying, had addressed him as "My dear Johnny."

All this from the chiefly personal side, but this is not all. The "Franky" note reveals something of Wesley's feeling on the main issue. The truth appears to be that in the last half dozen years of his life, or in the period when he had passed eighty, Wesley had lost something of the old sureness of his grasp. He was against separation from the Church of England, but he had to deal with men who were pushing him in that direction, among them Thomas Coke. Coke's ability and devotion were beyond question. He was a man of thorough educational training, made possible through what was in those days reckoned large wealth. He had as high a degree as Oxford could give. Coke had more than any other early Methodist a true missionary spirit. First and last he made nine journeys to America, and boasted that he could travel on horse-back ten thousand miles a year in America, though he never did it. Asbury averaged five thousand miles a year, and Wesley from forty-five hundred to five thousand. Coke was distressingly full of the desire to be a bishop and finally prevailed on Wesley to lay hands on him in ordination to a position which Wesley thought of in terms chiefly of superintendency and which Coke soon called bishopric. When Coke tried to exercise episcopal functions in England, the preachers protested. When he planned to go to India as a mission-ary, he wrote to an influential lord of the English realm to see if he could not be made a bishop of the English Church—and failed. Nobody knows just what passed between Wesley and Coke, but

Coke got from Wesley something that he felt warranted him taking the title bishop, though he finally agreed to use the title only in America.

Now, it was evidently with much of this in mind that Wesley wrote to Asbury. He had misgivings as to what he had done, and perhaps unconsciously revealed those misgivings when he reproached Asbury for using the Episcopal title.

It is a tangled story. Some things, however, are clear. Wesley did not want separation from the English Church, yet he could not but be aware of the tendencies toward separation. The Church was not willing to make any concessions which would help the Methodists as to baptism and the Lord's Supper. That was an ugly fact, of which more in a moment. Over all was the idea of some sort of sanctity in the ordination of the so-called "regular" way, a notion of which Wesley was not himself free. Charles Wesley was scandalized when he heard of Wesley's laying hands on Coke, for, if there was any especially sacred virtue in Wesley's thus ordaining Coke, there would have been just as much virtue in Coke's laying hands on Wesley, technically speaking. John wrote back to Charles stating that, if Charles had been at hand to lend advice, he, John, might have done differently. This surely was going far for John Wesley.

Underneath all this wretched suggestiveness which clings to the laying-on of hands, the suggestion of a mystic and magic impartation of at least ecclesiastical power, there are two firm strands of fact. After all allowance has been made for John Wesley's almost superstitious regard for some features of ecclesiastical procedure, he was possessed of a sound instinct in standing for Methodism as a body within the English Church. He knew the shortcomings of the Church; but he knew also that, in spite of those shortcomings, the Church had continuity of history, a reach over all England, a body of doctrines substantially agreed upon, a priesthood which could at least be trained into effectiveness. He knew that there was a living body there, no matter how weak and debilitated it might for the moment be. He knew also that separation is the path to anarchy. There was a regularity about John Wesley which was more than conventionality. He knew the worth of ecclesiastical results achieved through centuries; he knew that, if these were lightly left behind in separation, it would take centuries for the new body to develop them anew. With all due respect to Methodism since Wesley's day, we have to concede the soundness of this

instinct. Methodism's methods of worship for the last century and
a half have certainly not been barren, but it has just as certainly
been what can too often justly be called bare.

Now for the other side. The pressure on Wesley for consent
to separation became almost irresistible. Methodism, conscious
of a conquering force, did not think of its own limitations—indeed,
did not know them. On the other hand, the larger part of the
blame for the separation must go to the Church of England. One
of the profoundest tributes ever paid that Church was Wesley's
stand against the Methodists' leaving it. We have heard the charge
against Wesley that he was at best a rebellious son of the Church,
that he virtually defied it all his life. One of the most devoted of
Methodists writing in the *Contemporary Review,* July, 1887, marvels at the leniency of the Anglican bishops in not bringing Wesley
to book, and seems to think that this was due to the tolerant spirit
of the English episcopacy.

Tolerant spirit indeed, but it seems more like lethargy, sleepi-
ness. The Church had lost from its leadership almost all trace of
venturesomeness except that which was revealing itself in Wesley.
It might have, if it had been awake, done immense service for itself,
and for Methodism, and for Christianity, and for the world. About
as far as any bishop ever went was to say, as one did, that the
Methodist doctrine of assurance was essentially the same as that
of the Church, and to ordain, as another did, a minister to help
John Wesley, that he might prevent that good man's working himself to death. On the other side there were arguments against
Methodist enthusiasm, and protests against Wesley's not confining
himself to this or that particular diocese. Admittedly, there was
not serious attempt to block the campaigning of Wesley. To that
degree the English Church is entitled to credit for the evangelical
awakening, to that and to the fact that Wesley was born and lived
and died a son of the Church.

After all, historically speaking, this question is rather futile,
for the reason that even if the Church had been well disposed toward
Wesley, it could not have given him the chance he found outside.
More than that, we must remember that the Church had been bled
white four times in two centuries.

PART VII

THE SEEKER AFTER PERFECTION AND WHAT HE FOUND

"And yet I dare not preach otherwise than I do, either concerning faith, or love, or justification, or perfection."

PART VII

THE SEEKER AFTER PERFECTION AND WHAT HE FOUND

IN the opening pages of this book I said that Wesley's earliest experiences were a search after the best in religious life, and that search for the best determined all that he did. There was something almost desperate in his quest for the highest, the first years of his ministry being largely given over to mistaken methods, or to a learning of the means by which he must work toward the ideal through imperfections in the world around him, in others, and in himself. Jeremy Taylor had, with the interpretations of Susanna Wesley, given him some sound guidance as to holy living, and William Law had sharply and definitely set before him the ideal of Christian perfection.

If this ideal, whose content we shall soon proceed to discuss, had been an affair of the closet or of the cloister, it might soon have been pushed to one side in Wesley's thinking. The ideal was with Wesley to be made a reality and that in the multitudinous details of his daily evangelism. When Wesley got away from the notion that he was preaching and working to save his own soul—though, as we have already said, it was possible grievously to misunderstand this utterance—and began to carry in his mind night and day the salvation of the souls of others, the ideal of the best came to be more and more a practical concern with him, a necessity in his work of laboring for the conversion of men. The ideal of Christian perfection took on the form of a practical expedient: the most idealistic phase of his teaching had to be used for the most practical of purposes.

What I mean is that Wesley had no sooner begun his evangelistic work than he realized that the preaching of conversion, as the term is ordinarily understood, was not enough. Conversion was a beginning, but a beginning only. There had to be something beyond. The life of the people to whom Wesley preached was simple in content, somewhat impoverished, in fact. They had to have something continuing, something to strive after, an ideal which would call forth all their energies. Religious experience had to be kept interesting or it would die out. As it was, there was a terrible loss in the lists of Wesleyan converts. At Newcastle in 1743 he "purged" two for swearing, two for Sabbath-breaking, seventeen for drunkenness, two for retailing spirituous liquors, three for quarreling, one for wife beating, three for willful lying, one for laziness, twenty-nine for lightness and carelessness—total one hundred and forty. Eight hundred remained. Seventeen years later at Cornwall he had lost five hundred members out of seventeen hundred. In 1777 he wrote that about a third of his converts endured. "Two thirds of those grown rich are greatly degenerated."

Now I am not saying that Wesley put Christian perfection to the forefront just for expediential and instrumental purposes. Nevertheless he says repeatedly in the *Letters* that he is convinced Methodism will go to pieces without the preaching of the experience of Christian perfection. Wesley believed in the experience interpreted in his own terms, and believed in the communicability of the experience, and believed that in any event the Christian stood in dire peril of losing all he had if he did not keep pressing forward to the highest ideal.

Whether we accept Wesley's teaching on perfection or not, we must admit the loftiness of mind and soul which could preach that the highest conceivable ideal should be made the aim of every Christian. There is, indeed, a sense in which the highest religious experiences are not everybody's affair, just as the highest philosophy, and science, and art are not everybody's affair. It was the intent of Wesley, however, to get the highest in religion down within reach of the lowliest Christian. Here is the contrast between the Wesley of the earlier and the Wesley of the later days. The experiences of the Oxford Club at Oxford almost necessarily made the highest in religion the ideal of the few. Wesley definitely said to his father, when the question of the son's succeeding the father at Epworth was up, that he could best look for the nurture of his own soul at Oxford—this when John was in reading, and study, and prayer, and in good works striving for the highest and best in religious attainment. Now the distance between that life and the years when he went up and down England preaching the doctrine of Christian perfection to anybody and everybody cannot be measured. No matter whether we today follow Wesley in his teaching on perfection or not, his willingness to cast the best he had before men everywhere is one of the fine things in the history of our religion.

Again we must often recur to the point of view that Wesley

had, the point of view to which he was limited, and not try to think of him as acting in the light of experiences reached through nearly two centuries of effort since his time. In every phase of his work as a revivalist Wesley was pioneering. He had no precedents. Since his day revival methods are the commonplaces of religious effort, too commonplace if anything. Where, before Wesley, were there methods like his?

The preaching of perfection was beset with no end of difficulties. It was a relative and not an absolute perfection, whatever that means, unless it means the highest attainable under a given set of circumstances. There has not been any doctrine in the history of Methodism which has been hedged about with more troubles and trials than this. To begin with, it is the manifest duty of the Christian to aim at being a perfect Christian, just as it is the duty of a scientist to strive after perfect knowledge, or the duty of an artist to seek the perfect expression of beauty. The words of Jesus cannot be interpreted away which tell us to be perfect as the Father in heaven is perfect. Even if the words were to be explained away, the command would be binding from the nature of moral insight itself.

In the next place, nobody can fulfill the ideal of perfection perfectly. Wesley used to say that Christian perfection meant that we should have all the mind which was in Christ. Who can do that? Here we may as well accept the judgment of James that the facts of human experience and observation do not warrant such claim. There was not enough difference between the life of those who made such claim and those who had not to justify such exalted claim.

Again, when a Christian proposes that he is perfect, the proposition is itself a sign that he is not. A man who says that he is perfect as a Christian, in the saying-so reveals that he is not. The insistence of Wesley that the Christian must push on to perfection was altogether sound, but Wesley had not gone far in the preaching before he had to make so many qualifications to fit the teaching into actual life that it became a fountainhead of confusion. There is not much spiritual edification to be found in most Methodist exposition of perfection.

The perfectionist is likely, especially, to resent any criticism of the use of the word "perfection." If the teachers of what is apparently meant by perfection could have contented themselves with some other word, a deal of unprofitable controversy could have been avoided. To be sure, we are at liberty to use words according to our own definitions, if we keep the definition clearly out before us, but this is hard to do when we are handling words which have a fairly well-agreed-upon meaning in ordinary usage. It might be permissible for me to use the word "circle" as if it meant "square," but it would not be an especially rational performance to attempt to do so, even if I repeated my definition every time I used the word; and if I did this, I should probably find myself saying "circle" as if it meant "circle," and that would make trouble enough. I have never known any professed perfectionist to use the word "perfection," no matter with what announced qualifications, without every now and again seeming to mean just what the ordinary person would mean by it. For illustration, one of the most elaborate treatises on perfection published in the last quarter century makes the essential in its definition of perfection "unbroken communion with God." This is, however, just one item in a full definition, and a somewhat dubious item at that. It is at least conceivable that an imperfect moral character might have unbroken communion through an imperfect medium. If one of the glories of human life is power to speak through the imperfect, that glory must belong to God in supreme measure.

Wesley no sooner began to preach perfection than he found it necessary to explain what he meant. He always somewhat elaborately explained what he did not mean. First of all, he said, he did not mean sinlessness. Whitefield thought he did, which meant that Whitefield was not satisfied with Wesley's statement. Wesley said he meant by perfection freedom from intentional sin. This does not seem to be enough to warrant all the controversial uproar. We make the assumption of freedom from intentional sin concerning ourselves and concerning our neighbors and friends and even our casual acquaintances daily, for in our own normal dealings with our fellow men we assume good faith all around. There is abundant falling from good faith every day, but there is nevertheless this universal assumption of good faith. Any of us would feel insulted to learn that he was suspected of intentionally doing wrong in his daily contact, or of lacking good faith in his dealing with his fellows. If that is all perfection means, why all the discussion?

Wesley said that by perfection he did not mean freedom from liability to mistake through faultiness of judgment. Here, again, we wonder what the agelong debate is about. This assumption is so common again that in all discussion, for example, we are to make a distinction between the personal and the impersonal, and to consider questions impersonally on their merits without any hint of reflection on the holder of the opinions, no matter how mistaken they may be. This distinction, by the way, has been and is one of the most fruitful agreements as to discussion in a democracy. It takes much of the bitterness out of debate, through relieving the debaters of question as to their personal demerit in case of fallacious reasoning.

This, however, is not the whole story, suggestive and helpful as it may be as far as it goes. It does not go far enough. For there are situations in which we must hold the makers of mistakes blamable for the mistakes. One of the most urgent and insistent needs of this present automobile world is that upon the highways travelers shall not make mistake. It is not a question of merely holding blunderers responsible for their blunders, but of keeping men from making blunders!—for if a blunderer so blunders as to cause the death of one of his fellow men, there is no way that holding the blunderer responsible can bring the dead man back to life. In other words, seekers after the highest Christian ideal can never in any convincing degree talk of perfection so long as they make mistakes harmful to their fellows. A man might conceivably persuade himself of the complete uprightness of his own intention and yet be a positive menace to the community in which he lives. He is responsible, not merely for the point of departure of his act in his own intention, but for the point at which the act arrives in outer consequence.

The moral life, which is, of course, the center of Christian effort, has several different angles from which we can view it, and judge it. There is the moral purpose, the spirit of good will, to speak in the New Testament meaning. This is the absolute feature, without which there is no reason in talking of moral character. A moral man aims to do right in all forms of his activity. He must do right with all that there is of him.

A second factor is the aim to determine by all the light available what should be done in a given set of circumstances. This demands the pursuit of all the truth within reach. This introduces difficulties beyond that of intention. A man may have a full intention to do right, but he may not have exerted himself to the utmost to determine what is right at a given time and place. If the will to do right is called absolute, this content of what the right actually is must be called relative. It demands a firmer and finer moral quality to deal with the relative here than with the absolute.

Back of all this, and around it, is the growing ideal of the Christ-life as the guide for human life. Wesley called this "all the mind of Christ." In the nature of Christianity, this "all" must be all the time growing. It means far, far more for us today than it could possibly have meant for Wesley himself.

Again, we have come to see that living according to the mind in Christ means making Christian those deep and hidden springs of our natures out of which impulses and stirrings of will arise. It is this last phase of the problem which makes the struggle for Christian character today more hopeful and yet at the same time more serious. The more penetrating of the teachers of perfection have always been aware that the heart of the difficulty has been with what has been called original or inborn sin. Wesley himself recognized this, but he never seemed to clear up, if not his thinking, at least his speech about this aspect of the difficulty. That difficulty is that —and who can improve the words of Saint Paul?—when we would do good, evil is present with us.

Much of the confusion has come from our getting the ideas of guilt and inborn evil, or tendencies to evil, tied up together. If sin is inborn, we are no more responsible for it than we are to blame for physical deformities with which we are born. Wesley was, of course, right in insisting that guilt has to do with our own wills. In the next breath, however, we have to admit that acquiescence in our admitted imperfection is itself a choice of will, and an evil choice.

The problem in Christian character, so far as concerns the individual, is to carry the Christian ideal down into what modern psychology calls the subconscious realm. This term is not at all satisfactory, but we know what it means. Of course there are those who tell us that our responsibility for this realm is owing to the fact that what comes up to us from below consciousness has been previously in full consciousness, and has gone down into the subconscious by our allowing it to do so. Thence it comes back up into clear consciousness fully matured, none of which would have happened if we had not, at least to a degree, been hospitable to the suggestion in the first place. That there is truth here it would be impossible to gainsay, but not the whole truth. Suggestions come upon us without our realizing their presence till we think of them afterward.

What I wish to insist upon, however, is that, no matter how this phase of our nature came to be what it is, we may be in one sense not responsible for it at all, and in another, responsible for the attitude we take toward it. It is the acquiescent adjustment to what we are which is a contradiction to the ideal.

Let us refer again to an illustration which may at first seem somewhat apart from a predominantly moral struggle, namely, that of Sir Isaac Newton's remark about the limitations of his own knowledge. He said that he felt like a child picking up a few pebbles beside the shore of the ocean of knowledge while the vast deep, the unknown, stretched out before him. Now, this did not mean that Newton did not recognize the genuineness of the pebbles of truth that he possessed. Among those pebbles were the binomial theorem, the universality of gravitation, and certain principles of optics. Newton's admission of ignorance in the expression quoted did not prevent his fighting most valiantly for the truth he had already gained, or prevent his determined search for as much more of the truth of the ocean of knowledge as he could explore. Newton worked on the assumption, commonplace in science, that every item of the ocean of truth, every drop of it, so to speak, was in itself intelligible, beyond the range of any one human intelligence indeed and yet fundamentally intelligible. As a scientist, Newton gave himself to unending exploration of the sea of knowledge.

The illustration falls short, but it does have value. It seems at times as if, to use the phrase of William James, the dam between the human consciousness and the sea of life around the human were by some agency so lowered that the "Mother Sea" presses in, revealing some of its infinite vastness. James thought of this "Mother Sea" in terms that would make it essentially divine. If we were to think of it thus, we should say that Christian duty consisted in welcome to it and surrender to it. At times, however, this psychical sea seems to be of a different order. It was James himself who told us that the impressions from the world around us storm upon us in one big buzzing confusion. It is the duty of the rational mind to meet this confusion on the threshold of consciousness and to rule it into order, compelling it to yield its secrets and to make sense. Similarly, it is the duty of the Christian will to meet all the storm of moral stimulus and rule it in the name of Christ. The problem is so to handle the nature of ourselves that our bringing the Christ-spirit to bear upon our impulses becomes what we call second nature. The work of redemption is not complete till all there is of our lives and characters acts according to the spirit of Christ.

The task has to be handled with wisdom. Just to show how in discussing we almost inevitably fall into contradiction, may I recall what I have said about the moral fault of acquiescing in our admitted imperfection. I do not withdraw my remark, but I have to qualify it with another which seems contradictory. There are imperfections which are beyond our reach, as there are bodily infirmities which we cannot change. Take the problem of body itself. What a tangled realm we get into when we think of the influence of the body on the mind, and upon the moral life! There are moral peculiarities which come out of a subtle influence of the body. The body may not be strong enough to furnish the basis for anything like a normal moral experience. The body, on the other hand, may be too strong, too wild in itself, too riotous for a moral career at all ideal. How far shall a man acquiesce in bodily conditions which he cannot control? The ordinary, steady life does not have the data for judgment here. By the way, we who have sound physical organisms may be indebted to the organisms themselves for what seems to be moral steadiness.

Now, Wesley defined perfection as perfection in love, love to God and to one's neighbor. For the most part, after the emphasis on perfection had come to be central in his religious teaching, he kept himself to this most important phase of the teaching of Jesus, that we are to love God with all there is of us—mind, heart, soul, and strength, and our neighbors as ourselves. A nobler, more genuinely Christian ideal could not be found. Who could aim at anything higher than perfection in such love?

The difficulties and divisions and confusions began when Wesley started to preach perfection as an attainable experience here and now. It is, of course, entirely conceivable that a Christian might love God and man with all his powers, but it is questionable whether one doing so might not be taking too little a view of the ideal. When the Wesleyans began to define perfection, they usually limited it so that they might just as well have used some other name. I repeat that the perfectionists always seem irritated, in spite of their perfection, when one tries to expound their doctrine from the point of view of the customary meaning of perfection. We are thinking, however, of the practical outworking of this preaching in the days of Wesley, and we cannot help seeing that the ordinary hearers put into the term meanings suggested by the customary use. Look back at the marks of the moral life on which we can agree—the central will to do right which is absolutely binding in every life; the obligation to find the solution, relative to every situation; the expanding ideal of the Christ revelation. Wesley complained to Edward Perronet in 1750 that he had not six men who had their wills broken enough to serve him as sons in the gospel. Assuming that we do love God with all there is of us in the central intent of our lives, the old, old question as to the neighbor recurs, not merely as to who the neighbor is but as to what we shall do to show love for him.

When the perfection movement spread pretty well throughout the Methodist societies, increasing numbers of members began to claim that they had received this power, or blessing, of Christian perfection, and many of them averred that they had received it instantaneously. A rough-and-ready common sense might have protested against such claims, but Wesley was too open-minded for that. As I have said time and again, he did not close the door of his mind against anything which claimed to come from God. His openmindedness did not preclude the most careful questioning on his part, but he did not close the questioning against the claim till he had heard all the evidence he could.

Naturally, then, Wesley listened to these witnesses who claimed that they enjoyed the experience of perfection in love. He had to handle forthwith many knotty puzzles. The scheme of any moral life which I outlined above, and which Wesley accepted, had to make room for growth. If life has to be thought of as always growing, if the will can become stronger, if the devotion to God can become deeper, if love for men can become more of a ruling passion, then life can become absolutely perfect only as to fixity of direction. That would be enough, it would seem, but I am not sure that Wesley himself did not mean more than that.

As in all these matters, we have to get back to Wesley's own times and to the ideas which he could not help breathing out of the thought-atmosphere in which he lived. Wesley had as a background the deistic philosophy of the eighteenth century, though he was the unyielding foe of deism as such. For the deist, God had created the universe and had then left it to care for itself, a machine virtually self-running. On the other hand, Wesley felt that God was always at hand to intervene, if need be. Nobody, of Wesley's intellectual standing I mean, ever made freer use of the idea of divine intervention—so free use that, indeed, he nearly cheapened that idea. He was once about to open a service in the open air and rain began to fall. A word of prayer, and the rain stopped. On another occasion, while he was preaching, the sun smote heavily upon his bared head. He prayed, and a cloud covered the sky. Wesley would not in this have seen a miracle—with miracle defined as a setting aside of law—for he always insisted that only "enthusiasm" could hold that ends could be achieved without the appropriate means, but he conceived of God as using the laws of the universe for any special providence for which a believer might pray. There did not seem to be any difficulty in Wesley's mind with the notion that, if the believer prayed for Christian perfection, the petition might be forthwith granted. The possibility of receiving this blessing in the twinkling of an eye appealed to him most powerfully.

Just to show how his general theological system played into his interpretation of Christian perfection, we note that Wesley maintained that, if perfection were not reached in this special experience, it would have to be arrived at in the hour of death, when, according to Wesley, it was granted to most, if not all, Christians. We see here that the notion of the eternal life, or conditions in paradise or heaven, were working in Wesley's mind to determine the interpretation of psychological experience. It would not do for Christians to enter heaven without having attained to perfection, taking Wesley's definition of perfection as loving God with all the heart and one's neighbor as oneself. Just how such an experience of Christian perfection was to be achieved at death would be utterly beyond any experimental test. The dying man could not tell it: observation from outside would be impossible. I give this point an importance altogether beyond any inherent worth in it just for the sake of the glimpse it grants us of the activity of Wesley's mind on one of its stranger sides; perhaps we would better say a glimpse of the extent to which Wesley would allow a speculative consideration to influence his construction of what would have to be an actual psychological experience. The requirements of the Christian heaven had to be considered in deciding what was possible to souls here on earth. It must be admitted, however, that Wesley believed that divine power could deal with freedom with earthly factors, including the factors of man's actual constitution as a man. It can be doubted whether, with all his seriousness, Wesley took the problem of perfection seriously enough. This seems an odd thing to say of a life whose every breath was for the uplift of his fellow men, who paid himself out in service of those fellow men; but the judgment is warranted, especially when we think of what such an experience would call for in acceptance of responsibility for the welfare of all men within reach. Wesley never taught that all inbred sin was to be removed, all tendency to evil taken away, every taint of "corruption" washed out merely that the soul thus perfected could enjoy such a spiritual luxury, but he did not consider sufficiently enough the effects of such a life in the human relationships. How lives transformed by the perfection of love toward their fellow men ever could continue to be adjusted to a world like that of the eighteenth century without constantly crying out against it is one of the mysteries. Wesley was too easily content with triumphing over this world by turning the back upon it. When we look at the astonishing work of grace necessary to render a Christian free from all tendencies to evil, we may well wonder if such grace, received under a feeling of Christian trusteeship, could lead to a soul's turning inward upon itself and not outward upon the needs of a distressed world. (It is possible here to use the old, old fallacy that it is better to be than to do, a fallacy to which so many pleaders for character as such are fond of resorting. The adage is a comfortable one indeed to all who turn away from the needs of the world.)

Returning to the feature of the instantaneous, which was so notable in Wesley's teaching about perfection, we must remark that this emphasis had pronounced effect upon Methodism's search for religious experience. Anything which resembled or suggested a sharp crisis, anything, in a word, happening suddenly, came to be regarded as especially divine in its origin. Here we must concede that this notion came from the deistic tendencies of the time, but, if so, it was re-enforced by Wesley's positive stress on instantaneousness. Wesley had to admit that there was a gradual work preceding this instantaneous operation of grace, and that there was a growth following it; and he had a hard time giving the pre-eminence to the instantaneous. A lot of the exposition here, especially that in correspondence with Charles Wesley, has an air of unreality, even of pious and unintentional frivolity.

There has been some criticism of Wesley for encouraging over-introspection and absorption in spiritual exercises looking to the development of one's own soul. Here again we have to make discriminations which are taxing to ourselves and probably not convincing to readers. That the result of Wesley's teaching was over-introspection there can be little doubt, but Wesley did not aim at

self-scrutiny for the sake of the soul itself. Much that he said
sounds as if this were his intent, but that intent was fundamentally
redemptive, evangelistic. The men whom he selected to preach
his teaching were put on months of trial, not to see just what inner
grace they could develop, but to train them in leading men to
accept Christ. It is fair to use here an illustration from the realm
of art. A violinist or pianist gives himself to anxious self-scrutiny
in the most arduous, even the most painful training, not for any
delight of his own but for the sake of learning to make a channel
for his music out to the world.

Here, again, so intricate is this realm, we come upon the re-
minder that, if a man does too much of this introspection, even
for the purpose of helping others, he spoils his instrumental effectiveness. Too much sharpening of the sword harms the edge.
Moreover, the constant introspection, for which I will not say
that Wesley has the sole responsibility, led the Methodist to take
himself too seriously. Unless this whole exercise of introspection
is held easily, and at times even with considerable humor, it throws
the believer altogether out of perspective and focus concerning
himself. In 1762 Wesley wrote: "To set perfection too high is the
quickest way of driving it out of the world."

Now we come to the most controverted part of the Methodist
attitude toward Christian perfection, namely, the testimony of
some to having attained the experience. Wesley received such
testimonies in all good faith and genuine hospitality; though, as he
went on in his career, he found it necessary to speak positively,
almost sharply, to some of the claimants. The logic of the claim
seemed sure enough, namely, that if a Christian could have the
assurance that he was Christian, why could he not also have assurance that he was wholly, or perfectly Christian? A little consideration of the implications of this reasoning might have indicated how
far it fell short of being convincing. To know that one is perfect
in any definition of perfection, one would need to possess virtually
perfection of knowledge—perfect perspective, perfect familiarity
with all that might be in consciousness at any instant, and with all
that might be below the threshold at the same moment; perfect
poise. Wesley had said that Christian perfection did not imply
perfection of knowledge or understanding or insight. It is not,
however, just a playing with words to ask how an admittedly imperfect mind could pass on the perfection of a soul when that soul
might be uttering judgment on itself. Remember, revelation here

would have to come along the channel of a perfectly sound judgment. The situation would not be like that of flashing a picture upon a screen to be seen by an onlooker. It would be more like a message to be read off, implying the power to read.

In an earlier paragraph I said that, if a man professed to be altogether perfect, in the Wesleyan meaning, we could be pretty sure he was not perfect. The reason for this judgment is that the assertion of such attainment is likely to manifest a spiritual self-sufficiency which is altogether out of keeping with Christian humility. / Phillips Brooks once preached a searching sermon on the text, "Is It I?" the passage being the question which the disciples asked of Jesus when he told them, on the night of the Last Supper, that one of them would betray him. The theme of Brooks was that the closer the disciple gets to Christ, the more vividly he realizes the possibility of not being fully loyal to him. This did not imply that Brooks meant that the possibilities of evil in a believer's heart are so overwhelming as to keep him in terror, but that only the pursuer of the ideal sees how far short of the ideal he falls, / and the possibilities that come out of that distance between ideal and attainment. With the true disciple, who understands what discipleship really involves, the query is relevant as to how any disciple could actually raise the question as to whether he had already reached perfection or not. To ask some questions is to make a significant revelation of one's own limitations. Suppose we look at the problem for a moment through an illustration from the sphere of art. Here is a painter or a sculptor who has practiced all his life to put into expression his conception of beauty. Suppose he should ask himself, "Have I attained perfection?" Such a question might naturally leap into the mind of an artist, or, indeed, it might have haunted his consciousness through the years. The question might, indeed, be a statement of the artist's ideal, for what would an artist amount to if he did not strive for the ideal? Can we imagine an artist of the first order, by which we would mean one who had gone highest in the judgment of those qualified to have an opinion, entertaining for an instant the fancy that he had attained perfection? He might say to himself that he had done the best he could, and that he therefore could not go any higher. Was it not Thorwaldsen who, when he felt that he had at last done the best he could, fell into despair, avowing that the feeling of satisfaction was a sentence of doom? The best critics might, indeed, say that the work of a particular artist was final; nothing could surpass it. Indeed, we know that some types of statues, like the Venus of Milo, or some types of building, like the more significant cathedrals, seem to exhaust the possibilities in given directions. In this meaning, an achievement may be perfect as having exhausted the possibilities in a given direction. Likewise, a Christian may achieve a perfect result in a particular deed. Whether that is Christian perfection, however, in the fulfillment of the moral ideal, is possibly another matter.

I am quite sure that some readers have long since become weary with what may seem to be the repetitious nature of this chapter, with its qualifications and tangles and apparent contradictions. I bespeak the reader's patience. The teaching of Christian perfection has, on the side of religious experience, been looked upon as the original contribution of Wesley to the world. It is well, then, that we look at it, not only from the angle of his own teaching but, from our larger knowledge of the workings of the human soul which science possesses today, that we may see better the aims and achievements and limitations of the Wesleyan teaching.

We say, therefore, that, in the next place, those who taught that the experience of perfection could be recognized by its witness to itself and that it was a duty to testify to it as an achieved result, did not take enough into their account the temptations which come with the growth into higher life. To take a simple illustration: there are temptations which arise out of sheer selfishness, or the grosser impulses. The Methodist thought of sin in rather restricted fashion so far as actual transgressions were concerned. Lapses into bodily evils of the more sensual type were above all others serious. There are temptations, however, coming out of unselfishness, out of desire to please others. All the temptations of Jesus seem to have been of this order, like those in the wilderness when his whole aim was to find the method by which he could best do the redemptive work for his people; like that where Peter virtually told him to put aside the cross, the temptation taking on renewed force because it came on the lips of a dear friend and loved disciple. Moreover, the ascent into the higher reaches of spiritual life calls for a finer balance. The loftier the height, the more dangerous the slip. A Christian might reach a plane on which the grosser impulses meant nothing to him at all, and yet be exposed to subtle appeals to evil which the man battling with the lower impulses might, on the other hand, not understand. This latter might not know of the possibility of the higher perils, or what they would be like if they were possible.

Aside from this finer aspect, Wesley laid too much stress on asceticism, or upon a near-asceticism, as the sum and substance of Christian duty to be entitled to be accepted as a teacher of a sound doctrine of perfection. The content was not large enough. It was too negative. A leader who repeatedly enjoins women not to wear ribbons or who takes time to write a voluminous denunciation of tea drinking has his perspective askew. A searcher after the perfect life ought to be sure that his purposes are not only sure enough, but big enough. They ought to be chiefly positive. It is true that, in spite of his asceticism, Wesley himself did live a marvelously full life. It is even said, on what seems to be unquestionable authority, that he left among his papers notes on Shakespeare's plays, or some of them. John Pawson, as we have previously said, a sturdy Methodist, found them and destroyed them as "useless baggage." The notes were quite possibly not of high value except for the light they might have thrown on Wesley's own mind. There is something amusing, though, in Pawson's throwing out the notes. There is not much in Pawson's record to suggest that he would know whether they were baggage or not. He was a rough, vigorous preacher whom Wesley, in later years, "ordained" to work in Scotland; who rejoiced in his power and dignities until he had to return to England, where Wesley would apparently not recognize the ordination which had professedly been valid in Scotland. Pawson showed some human and natural peevishness in giving up the "gowns" and "bands" and the title of "Reverend," which he seems to have enjoyed while they lasted.

Wesley never ceased to think of the Christian life as a field for at least a mild form of asceticism and this conception colored the search for the perfect experience. For Wesley himself, disciplined as he was, asceticism came naturally. For many of the Wesley followers asceticism was of the ordinary lot. They did not have much of this world's goods. The entire emphasis, however, tended to an other-worldliness which is not a mark of perfection. Much of Methodism was an inheritance from Puritanism, and Puritanism of those days, important and necessary as it was, was too solemn to suggest the perfect life. The Puritan ideal has to be supplemented with something else if it is to be held as a Christian aim throughout a lifetime. Wesley's frowning upon pleasantry in speech, to say nothing of his displeasure at wit or humor, did not make for the soundest life. Too much was thus left out. Moreover, when a man will not allow himself to be even for an instant a conscious humorist, he is likely to end by being an unconscious one—which may be calamitous. If Wesley had been a little more definitely and purposely open to the funny side of things, we might have been spared that oft-quoted remark in his *Journal* which tells us that, in an attack upon his coach by a mob, he was providentially kept from harm from flying stones by the fact that a fat woman sat upon his lap. That was in 1752, when Wesley was about fifty.

Did Wesley ever claim to have attained to perfection? We have said he never did. This has been a sore puzzle to many claimants of perfection and to many students of Wesley's life. One writer, the late Professor O. A. Curtis, declares that a certain experience described in the *Journal* must have been that of the arrival at perfection. The passage is as follows: December 24, 1744—"I saw every thought, as well as every action or word, just as it was rising in my heart; and whether it was right before God, or tainted with pride and selfishness." Tuesday, 25th—"I waked, by the grace of God, in the same spirit; and about eight . . . I felt such an awe and tender sense of the presence of God . . . that God was before me all the day long. I sought and found Him in every place." This is interesting, but not at all convincing, inasmuch as the experience there set forth does not bear out what Wesley states perfection to be. He has, by the way, suffered much from those who have sought to classify his experiences for him. If, in all these matters, we stick to the facts as he described them, we shall be better off.

In everything he says we note the workings of a realistic temper. Here is his word in 1765: "When I was young I was sure of everything. In a few years, having been mistaken a thousand times, I was not half as sure of most things as I was before: at present I am hardly sure of anything but what God has revealed to man." Wesley was clearly open to any religious claims that were genuinely and sincerely put forward, but he would not make any claim for himself of which he did not feel sure. We have here a most noteworthy instance of his poise. No leader in the history of the Church ever acted as if he were more sure of himself. There was always the assumption of his own leadership, without any question whatever. At first thought we might have said that Wesley would be just the one to claim that he had attained to Christian perfection. He did not, however, make any such claim. It is a strange situation

we confront here—a man preaching through half a century an experience as the heart of the Methodist belief and practice, and yet
never claiming to have received the grace himself. At one time he encouraged his followers to bear witness to this blessing, and at others
he urged virtual silence about it. There must have been pressure
put upon him to make a statement concerning his own search for
the experience, but there is no hint of such pressure either in the
Journal or *Letters*. Did the followers of Wesley assume that he
himself had the type of religious life which he so vigorously urged
upon them? Or were they content to let Wesley be what he might
be, and say what he might say, and ask no questions?

There is no way of answering these queries. Probably in some
aspects of his life Wesley thoroughly understood himself. There
is at least not much suggestion of uncertainty about himself. Even
in the days when he says that he was walking in darkness—and we
have to remember that in those days he declares that he did not
have sleepless nights—he held to his purposes with complacent
fixity. In the midst of his self-depreciations he never reveals any
trace of impulse to give up in despair, so far as his central purposes
are concerned. His close relatives, like his sister and his brother
Samuel, might be shocked when he said, as he did even after
Aldersgate, that he was not a Christian and had not been; but
he did not give the least sign of giving up his strivings. He went
ahead living a Christian life. Wesley knew of his devotion to the
Christian ideal. At Aldersgate one feature of the experience was
an assurance that he did trust Christ. He knew that, but he may
have felt unwilling to make claims for himself that he encouraged
others to make if they could do so in good faith. Tyerman avows
that in May, 1738, after Aldersgate, Wesley "was much buffeted
with temptations which returned again and again."

Of course it is possible to ask insistently and repeatedly if one
cannot have an assurance of perfection inasmuch as one can have
an assured conviction of one's salvation. There is a world of difference between such phases of assurance. It would be the height
of absurdity to say that we, who sincerely accept Christ as the guide
of our lives, could not be warranted in that acceptance. Consciousness of devotion to the Christ ideal is far different, though,
from arrival at a final goal. The one testimony means everything:
the other may raise so much question as practically to mean nothing
at all. A foremost exponent of Wesleyan perfection in this country
used to profess that he knew he was entirely sanctified up to the

measure of his self-knowledge. This came from a most worthy man who, however, was not as fully informed as to his own qualities as were those who looked upon his life from the outside. Taken by itself, the testimony is about of the same value as if a man should say that he was in perfect physical health up to the measure of his self-knowledge. This is a realm in which personal assurance about oneself does not count for much.

It is perhaps interesting for those who like to argue everything out to the last inch that Wesley was once asked by a philosophically-minded follower if Christian perfection meant the elimination of all inbred evil. Wesley said yes. The inquirer then asked if a child born to parents from whom all trace of inbred sin had been removed by the grace of Christian perfection, would have any trace of inbred sin. Wesley did not answer.

If we wish to sum up what can safely be said about Wesley and Christian perfection, we can put it down that this perfection was the chief aim of Wesley's teaching and work; that it was the highest ideal which he held before himself. We see also that he paid human nature the immense compliment of assuming that it could be made perfect—an enormous assumption even with all the qualifications which Wesley insisted upon. It may be worth while to note here the doctrine of Karl Marx as to human perfectibility. Marx, who wrote about half a century after Wesley had disappeared from the scene, taught that the so-called evil of human nature was due to the environment of men. There is no record that Marx ever paid the slightest attention to Wesley, but the contrast of his teaching as over against that of Wesley at least catches the attention. Marx taught that, with environment changed, man's nature would change as a matter of course. Wesley assumed that environment counted for little or nothing in the change of human nature, that this change was wholly from within by the grace of God. The Marxian point of view would probably not have been intelligible to Wesley. His whole mind was absorbed in the approach from the opposite direction.

Continuing the summary, we may say that, along with this high idealism and high expectancy as to human nature, Wesley was in an extraordinary degree realistic. This worked in two ways in his dealing with people: it made him open to whatever they might testify to, and open in caution and rebuke also when the "witnesses" to exalted experiences were showing signs of any temper which did not fit in with their claims. As to himself, Wesley's realistic temper it was which probably prevented his making any final claim. Some oddly thinking persons have sought to make out that Wesley was not quite sincere in holding up to his followers an ideal to which he did not profess to have reached.   If a man, however, believes that an ideal can be attained by men, and believes from the testimony of men that they have thus attained, the charge against him that he is not sincere in advocating the belief is wrongly drawn. The most that can fairly be alleged is that he is mistaken. After long years of experience with those professing the experience, Wesley seriously modified his way of speaking of it, as appears from the following quotation: March 15, 1770: "Many hundreds in London were made partakers of it, within sixteen or eighteen months; but I doubt whether twenty of them are now as holy and happy as they were."

It is evident that the difficulties about the teaching arose from the nature and degree of its realization in actual human life. These difficulties clung like a blight upon Methodism for a hundred and fifty years. Various groups of interpreters of the doctrine were continually falling afoul of one another. Methodism brought peace to thousands upon thousands in their relation to the Divine; but, paradoxically enough, not so much peace in the relation of these Christians one to another. In congregation after congregation the scandal arose that those who professed perfection in love, quarreled and fought with one another. Wesley himself once raised the question as to whether he should not altogether drop the preaching of Christian perfection. Certainly, in 1768 in another context he declared that "perfection is not joy."

Yet the ideal itself has been the glory of Methodism. It would have been in extreme degree questionable and tragic if a forward movement in religion like Methodism had made no mention of perfection. When one picks up a book on political obligations by such a writer on abstract philosophy as Thomas Hill Green, for example, and finds him telling about the quest for perfection as influencing the development of States, and when one notes how often the idea of perfection appears as a driving force among those who labor in the artistic realm, one can only feel grateful for a religious leadership that definitely placed the ideal of perfection in Christian life on high before the people called Methodists. The definition may have been faulty, and the methods askew, and the outcome anything but ideal; but all these shortcomings could be corrected. Anything but let the ideal fall! Wesley kept it from falling.

Wesley finally got his idea of perfection into the scriptural terms of loving God with all the life—mind, heart, soul, and strength and the neighbor as oneself. If one could do that, one would certainly have met all Christian requirements. When we get away from the metaphysical refinements about the difference between inbred sin and guilt, and all the rest of such futile material, and look at what Wesley did, we see just about as adequate a commentary on what perfection would mean as any we can find in the history of the Church. The love of God and the love of man were certainly held together. The witness to Wesley himself of any attainment of perfection in an "experience" would have been, in any event, negligible as compared with the satisfaction which he found in pouring himself to the utmost in love to God and service to men. How strange it is that it was only when those detached from religious connections altogether began to praise Wesley's emphasis on perfection in ideal and work that the respectably good began to see the greatness of the Methodist leader! There is something ironical in that the skeptically inclined, like John Richard Green and W. H. Lecky and Leslie Stephen, were among the first to assess Wesley's achievements at their true value.

The parts in parentheses in the following letter are in cipher, presumably so that only his brother Charles could read them. Under date of June 27, 1766, he wrote to Charles:

I do not feel the wrath of God abiding on me, nor can I believe it does. And yet (this is the mystery) (I do not love God. I never did.) Therefore (I never) believed in the Christian sense of the word. Therefore (I am only an honest heathen, a proselyte of the Temple, one of the φοβούμενοι τὸν θεόν (God fearers). And yet to be so employed of God! and so hedged in that I can get neither forward nor backward! Surely there never was such an instance before from the beginning of the world! (If I ever have had) that *faith* it would not be so strange. But (I never have had any) other ἔλεγχος of the eternal or invisible world than (I have) now; and that is (none at all), unless such as fairly shines from reason's glimmering ray! (I have no) direct witness, I do not say that (I am a child of God) but of anything invisible or eternal.

And yet I dare not preach otherwise than I do, either concerning faith, or love, or justification, or perfection. And yet I find rather an increase than a decrease of zeal for the whole work of God and every part of it. I am φερόμενος (borne along), I know not how that I can't stand still. I want all the world to come to ὅν οὐκ οἶδα (What I do not know). Neither am I impelled to do this by fears of any kind. I have no more fear than love. Or if I have (any fear, it is not that of falling) into hell but of falling into nothing. . . . Press the *instantaneous* blessing.

Now, this presents us with an important problem, far beyond the personal in its significance, namely, the relation between Wesley's own religious experience and what he preached himself and called on his preachers to preach.

First of all, there can be no doubt of Wesley's entire good faith in this letter to Charles. I mean that he is speaking the truth about himself as far as he knows it. He is evidently keeping nothing back. The *Journal* of Wesley is one of the world's outstanding religious documents, but it has one shortcoming for religious effect. It was purposely written for the edification of the Wesleyans. The most self-revealing diary in the English language is that of Samuel Pepys. Pepys was not writing for any eye except his own, at least not for any that would read the diary till long after he should be gone. With moral self-revelation such as that of Pepys, we do not wonder that he did not care to have anyone who had ever personally known him see what his pages contained. Now, there are profound revelations of religious experiences in the eight big volumes of Wesley's *Journal,* but all were elaborations of notes made in the diary, with the spiritual help of the Methodists in mind.

With the utmost honesty and candor and sincerity in the world, a document written with a purpose of such edification has its serious limitations. The language used has to be intelligible to the readers. Moreover, it has to be such as will suggest a given type of experience. Now, Wesley was always talking about assurance, and the need of it—assurance as to conversion and the presence of God in the life, and even the assurance of having attained perfection. Social scientists, in talking about the service of Wesley in individualism, say that, of course, Wesley overdid the emphasis on assurance, but we should always remember the services to democracy. Of course we should, but we are now trying to form some estimate of the services distinctively religious. We have to ask whether the preaching and teaching of Wesley tended to hold out expectations to seeking souls which, in the nature of men's minds, could not always, or for the most part, be realized.

It is all but self-evident that this letter of John to Charles came out of depression. The physical resources of one who never rests finally run low. When the tides of bodily strength are out, the mind is like a stretch of barren sand. Wesley ought to have admitted more often his moods of depression. Many, many men have such moods but not all of them are preaching a doctrine of assurance that does not seem to make place for depression. There is no doubt that, in his remarks about many of his own peculiarities, Wesley has to be discounted. A student of his life, Rev. F. F. Bretherton, has tabulated over sixty entries in the *Journal* which have to do with the illnesses of Wesley, serious illnesses too, so serious that Wesley himself on several occasions concluded that death was at hand. How to fit these entries into that famous utterance about never having lost a quarter of an hour's sleep is a puzzle. It is easy to say that we ought to remember the limitations of human speech and not make ordinary language as hard and fast as a legal statute, or a scientific law. All this we heartily admit, but Wesleyanism worked toward a standardized set of religious experiences, and these resulted partly from the definiteness of the speech of Wesley himself. Anybody who has ever had much to do with Methodists who have taken their religion earnestly knows the spiritual distress into which many of them have been plunged by the oversharpness of Methodist testimony as to the presence of God. Bishop Butler once said to John Wesley that the claim to receiving special revelations from God was a "very horrid thing, sir, a very horrid thing." Taking the words just as they stand, generation after generation of Methodists have been fond of treating these words of Butler's as spiritual obtuseness. Taken as they were intended, and under the circumstances in which Bishop Butler spoke, they were what Wesley needed to hear. The pathetic, bewildered search of some men, and women and children—especially children—after an assurance encouraged by Wesley's preaching has been not a "very horrid thing," indeed, but a very distressing thing.

Suppose now that, instead of writing the above in a confidential cipher to Charles, Wesley had frankly said the same thing publicly. He would have forestalled harm. He could have admitted the testimony of many, many Methodists to experiences more striking than anything he himself had ever felt. Wesley was most careful in his claims as to direct, personal crises. Most of his claims to divine guidance were in the field of interpretation, which could be questioned or doubted without any reflection upon himself. For example, Wesley's avowal that a rainstorm which changed its course so as not to interfere with his open-air service was a direct divine interposition, could be accepted or not as a hearer might decide for himself. Preaching a positiveness of assurance of salvation, which might or might not be possible to a majority of persons in a congregation, was quite different.

Here we come upon a peculiarity of Wesley's leadership which must have been more or less deliberate. While Wesley was kindness itself in dealing with individuals who sought his personal counsel, he did not seem to concern himself to hold fast to his societies those who could not fit themselves into the Methodist frame. He appeared to feel that, if men could not adjust themselves to the Methodist ways, they would better go elsewhere. Not that he asked them to go elsewhere. Again it must be remembered always that Wesley took himself as the founder of a society and not of a Church. A Church cannot properly give itself to the exclusive development of any one religious doctrine, or feeling, or method.

There cannot be any doubt that Wesley believed that the assurance he preached was attainable. He believed that it was taught by the Scriptures and that it was witnessed to by countless Methodists. Yet, if his letter to his brother meant anything, it meant that the experience which he had all but demanded of the Methodists was certainly not always his own.

Wesley carried his craving for practical results pretty far into his preaching. He was not by any means a Jesuit, but he judged virtually every means by the end it attained. He preached what came to be known as the Methodist experience because he felt such preaching would produce the most decided and positive effects. He was not a truthseeker as following truth whithersoever it might lead, though he has few superiors for open-mindedness. If he saw that what he supposed to be the truth was leading him in what he took to be the wrong direction, he did not, indeed, declare false what he had taken to be true: he simply changed direction. In this same letter to Charles he urged Charles to preach the instantaneous work of grace that he himself might have more time to preach the gradual work. Here we have the administrator judging his messages almost wholly by their practical efficiency.

This policy was sound enough if Wesley was thinking of the spread of Methodism. It was no more untrue than for a military general to train a section of his army as his shock troops. Yet it was not truth-seeking in any definition except that of the pragmatic philosophy: that truth is what you make out of it in an instrumental use. Truth is what works, according to this theory. Works how? Wesley's influence was in making the truth work in the practical concerns of life. Religious truth, however, in some of its higher reaches, may not have any considerable direct bearing on workaday duties.

Something of the same administrative impulse appears in a letter written to Charles from Edinburgh a few months after the one just quoted: "I am at my wits' end regarding Christian perfection. Shall we go on asserting perfection against all the world: or shall we quietly let it drop?" Wesley is asking whether the Methodists should continue to preach perfection or quietly let the theme drop. The reason was that the preaching of perfection was causing schisms and rancor in the societies. It is curious and interesting to note that this Methodist preaching of perfection has so often made for the manifestations of imperfection among the professors and claimers of the experience. Wesley held fast to the doctrine, which is something of a mystery because, according to the Wesleyan pragmatic principles, the preaching ought to have ceased on account of the dubious results. Here, however, while admitting the doubtful outcomes, Wesley determined to continue the preaching. His hard, good sense prevented his making any profession for himself; he saw the divisive results of the doctrine; and yet, after confessing time and again that the fruit of the emphasis was far from satisfactory, he went on insisting upon teaching perfection. The only explanation of this is that, self-sufficient though he for the most part was, Wesley would not put his own experience over against what seemed to him to be the teaching of the Scriptures, when that teaching was re-enforced by the positive testimony of Christians in whom he had confidence.

Returning once more to the letter to Charles: In spite of the perplexities it arouses, it is a noble testimony. Here is an unquenchable zeal for the kingdom of God, an unresting desire to be always at the task, a consciousness of being borne along by the divine will. When he says that he does not fear God, or love God, that only means that there was a dying down of emotional glow. Just what chance there was for such emotional glow in the life of a man working as was Wesley is itself a mystery. Yet there was glow, the glow of white-hot iron though not of blaze. Here was the highest and best witness that Wesley could have: the satisfaction in the work itself. He is not carried on by emotional love or kept back by emotional fear. His only concern is about falling into nothingness, that is to say, of having the work cease. We have here the best of Calvinism—the conviction that it is God carrying the life along. We have here the best of Arminianism—the constant ratification of the Divine Will by the human choice of Wesley's own free will.

It is to be regretted and deplored that this letter to Charles Wesley was not made public as soon as it was written. It shows how ideas and their expressions can catch men as truly as can machines which, though the creation of men, sometimes get beyond the control of men. By his instruction and encouragement Wesley had built up standardized religious expectations for the Methodists, and now found himself, as he thought, falling short of the standard. The pathos, however, is not here, but in his failure to tell the world —perhaps his failure himself to see—that in the letter to Charles he had expressed a higher experience than anything he had taught his followers. Here was a witness better than any mystic voice: the witness of life itself pressing irresistibly for outlet in word and deed. This is the spiritual treasure the Methodists should have seized upon, rather even than Aldersgate, important though that was, though Wesley himself never said as much about Aldersgate as did the Methodists. Aldersgate lent itself to interpretations Wesley never intended, and helped raise in many a Methodist mind expectations of strange warmings in themselves destined never to be realized.

The doctrine of assured salvation was sometimes so taught by early Methodism as to carry with it a claim of absolute certainty about gaining heaven and avoiding hell that all but robbed belief of any moral worth. One could conceivably become so sure of the bliss of the saved and the woe of the lost as to choose the righteous path from prudential and not from moral motives. If a kingdom of heaven is to be conceived of as worth while at all, it must be as a realm of venture where the good life is chosen for the sake of the good life itself, and for no other reason. This letter of John's to Charles is the noblest statement of such choice in Methodist history. It is the life itself which is bearing Wesley on. It is the fear of the cessation of the life which is the supreme terror.

In an earlier passage I referred to an overweighting of the scales in some old-time evangelistic appeals, such appeals as: "Here is salvation before you. You can take it or not, but you will be damned if you don't take it." With so fixed an outcome, especially with the outcome phrased in predominantly material figures of speech, there was not room for much moral worth in the choice it-self. To seek a life, however, because of the life itself, to follow it whithersoever it leads, to ask no heaven better than the life itself, to fear no hell more than the loss of the life—this lifts all up into a genuinely moral realm and appeals to the highest and best in human nature. If we seek an utterance of experience in which the purely Christian fiber of the life of Wesley shows unmistakably, we come to this letter as the end of the quest. Moreover, the ex-perience, being so largely of the will, is supreme as a Christian ideal.

Here, then, was a seeker after Christian perfection. Did he find it? In the form he first sought it, the form of a witness to a complete inner transformation? No. In the form of a possibility of self-emptying in Christian activity, and a satisfaction so deep that he ceased to ask whether he was satisfied or not? All we can say is that we should not know how to go about searching for a closer approach to the ideal.

PART VIII

"WESLEY AND WOMEN"

"The Wesleys are snares to young women. . . . All fall in love with them."—JAMES HUTTON TO COUNT ZINZENDORF, 1740.

PART VIII

"WESLEY AND WOMEN"

WE come now to the vexed and vexing question of John Wesley's relation with women. Early in Wesley's career James Hutton wrote to Zinzendorf that the Wesleys were snares to young women. "All fall in love with them." If the question were merely a personal one, there would be no need of doing much more than mentioning it, but it has to do somewhat with his standing and efficiency as a religious leader, and with his general reputation through the centuries.

It is doubtful if Wesley, outside of his mother and sisters, ever knew any strong women in the higher meaning of the word "strong." The Countess of Huntingdon was of superior endowment and attainments, but there is no indication that she was to any marked degree even a close acquaintance of Wesley's. A sister of one of John Wesley's college mates, with whom he corresponded under Latinized classical names, declared that she loved Wesley more than all mankind, except her God and king; but she finally broke off with him completely. Again, let us remember that, after he began his evangelistic work, Wesley's opportunities of meeting women at all above the ordinary in endowment or training were not many. The correspondence that passed between him and his women friends indicates that they were persons of sound judgment, mental alertness, and of eagerness to learn; but the extraordinary opportunities which are today within the reach of almost anyone, woman or man, were not available to them. It would be easy to overstress this, however, for there is nothing to indicate that Wesley cared to have around him what we used to hear called the "educated woman."

All the women in Wesley's Epworth home were extraordinary, with intellects of more than usual ability and of manifest strength of will. It may be that some of Wesley's difficulties with women arose from his judging them after the pattern of his mother, which would have led only to blunders, for Susanna Wesley was the only one of her kind. Wesley's sisters too were all strong, with traits of distinction which showed itself in the protests of more than one of them against the hardness of their lot at Epworth. The eighteenth

219

century offered little enough to young women of the Wesley type. Samuel Wesley thought only in the conventional terms of getting his daughters suitably married.

John had some correspondence at Oxford with young women: sisters of college friends of his. Each correspondent used a classical pen name, as I have already noted. The letters seem to us of today stilted and lifeless, but that is no proof that they seemed so to the persons who wrote and read them. The overtones, the shades of meaning, the suggestions and half-suggestions in letters, are almost impossible to grasp after an interval of two centuries. We find in Wesley's college letters one characteristic true enough to life: his anxiety to improve the spiritual condition of the young woman to whom he wrote. Of course, under the circumstances, that may have meant anything or nothing at all. Nothing came of the correspondence, not even a continuing friendship. There is now some doubt as to the identity of the one who seemed most attractive to Wesley, but the question is of no consequence.

Of the affair with Sophia Hopkey in Georgia we have already spoken. I have quoted the cynic who said that any man can fall in love with any woman, provided he be near her long enough. Wesley told his father in 1735 that he went to Georgia to keep away from attractive women. This gives a little too much importance to spatial propinquity, but such nearness did have something to do with Wesley's affectionate interest in Sophia Hopkey. She was eighteen; he was in the early thirties. Certainly, she had never known much of the world before she met Wesley, and, no matter how much she had known of the world in Georgia, which boasted a population of a thousand, she never could have met a man like Wesley for the sufficient reason that there was no other like him. Wesley's main concern at the time was the pursuit of spiritual perfection, which was not wholly that of Miss Hopkey, estimable young woman as she no doubt was. The affair ended awkwardly, as we have already seen, with Miss Hopkey commanding more of our respect than Wesley.

The next love affair was with Grace Murray, widow of a sailor who had been lost at sea. Mrs. Murray appears to have been a sensible, efficient person, notable for the care of one of the Methodist houses, or homes, or hostelries, which Wesley established as Methodism came to increasing success. Probably Wesley admired Grace Murray first for her neatness, and orderliness, and dispatch of business at the Newcastle house. Wesley was death on women whom he called "sluts." He avowed that he would not have any "sluts" around any Methodist establishment. He declared in a letter what today would have brought upon him a court sentence for libel or slander—that one good Methodist sister of whom he was writing was a "consummate slut." Wesley did not mean by this term just what it connotes today, but it does suggest, by contrast, some of the excellence of Grace Murray.

Wesley and Mrs. Murray were thrown together a good deal. It appears that she traveled with him on some of his tours. She evidently knew how to get along with him, and is probably entitled to the unique distinction of being the only woman that Wesley ever met who did possess that extraordinary ability. After a long acquaintance and working together, Wesley told her that he wished to make her his wife. She declared that the honor was too great for her, which is what anyone would have known she would have said under the circumstances, and accepted the proposal. Wesley does not seem to have suspected that there was the slightest difficulty ahead, or likely to be, and went on without any misgiving, expecting, after a tour of the societies which would take him for a time away from Mrs. Murray, to marry her.

There was, however, something in the way. Mrs. Murray had had an acquaintance with John Bennet, one of Wesley's preachers, which had, it is to be supposed, ripened somewhat beyond the limits of friendship. Moreover, Charles Wesley was in the way. For one reason or another Charles did not wish John to marry. Charles never had a high estimate of John's ability to select intimates. He once made the not overbrotherly remark that John had been created for the benefit of fools and impostors. Evidently, he thought of himself as the spring of wisdom created to supply all John's lack of wisdom. As soon as Charles heard of the possibility of his brother's marrying Grace Murray, he took to horse, dashed off the miles to where Grace was at the moment, and said something to her which caused her forthwith to marry John Bennet. What Charles actually said is not known, but he left the impression on Grace Murray that everything was off—that John would not marry her. The uncertainty is whether Charles acted in good faith. Whether he did or not is not especially important. He did not apparently know what he was about. Yet he may have acted with a sound instinct, though he was dealing in affairs which were not strictly any of his business. The most charitable judgment upon his course is that he was convinced that John could not meet the duties of the leadership of Methodism and be married. Probably he knew too that John would neglect a wife rather than neglect the work—not a happy prospect—though Charles did not act as if he were troubling himself overmuch about Grace Murray.

It has been often alleged that Charles Wesley blocked the marriage of John and Grace because Grace had been a "serving woman." Possibly there is something in this, though, if true, it was not so serious a fault in Charles as we of the present are prone to think. The English valued social status highly in those days, as they do today. Methodists of the Charles Wesley type—I mean those who thought strictly in terms of the Church of England, with all that that implied as to the social standing of a priest—feared a loss of social prestige if John married Grace. Indeed, that would have been the effect if Methodism had had any prestige, or if the Methodists had been hoping to rise in the social scale out of the rank in which Methodism had found them. It goes altogether without saying that this consideration could not have had a feather's weight with John. It is worth while to remember, however, that, social rank counting as it did in England and with the Methodists aspiring to rise in the world, Charles Wesley had, what was to many of his contemporaries, a valid point against the marriage of his brother with Mrs. Murray. Still Charles's getting into this sorry business was not to his credit. His upset state of mind appears in his remark to John, as he met him on the morning after John Bennet's marriage to Grace Murray, that he intended to treat John henceforth as a heathen and a publican. All this was soon set to rights between the two brothers, but it was bad enough while it lasted.

What about the part of Grace Murray? There is no telling, except that remarks like that of Tyerman that she was a jilt—whatever that is—are utterly unjust. I have said that she knew how to get along with Wesley, but, with Charles at hand talking as he was doing, and with John Bennet at hand also, she solved the problem in one quick stroke. Looking at the whole situation, she probably knew, or felt, what she was about. She felt and said that the marriage to Wesley was a happiness of which she did not feel worthy; but that did not necessarily mean much, with another man at hand with whom she had been in love. Taking the incident as like hundreds of others of the kind, it is probable that she had for Wesley a deep reverence, but that a crisis forced by the meddlesome Charles helped her in an instant to know her true feeling better than she had ever done before, and to choose accordingly. We may well guess that the realization that taking John as a husband meant also taking Charles as a brother-in-law meant something to Mrs. Murray.

The victim in all this was John Wesley. He does not seem to have had the least inkling about what was going on till all was over. He had a right to feel that he had been badly treated throughout. Mrs. Murray does not seem to have told him enough of her feeling for John Bennet. Wesley himself was altogether open about any matters he was willing to discuss at all. It never appears to have entered his head that there was the slightest question about marriage with Mrs. Murray, once the determination had been reached between them.

His account of the experience was set forth in a manuscript, now in the British Museum and repeatedly published—a straightforward putting of the case which commands our respect and admiration quite as much as anything Wesley wrote. There is thorough genuineness of feeling, no weak sentimentalism, deep disappointment. As soon as the crisis was over, Wesley considered the case closed and said no more about it. There was a tensely dramatic scene when John and Charles, John Bennet and his new wife met together, with sharp recrimination from Charles, then tears in the eyes of everybody, then as much reconciliation as was possible under the circumstances. Whitefield was, after a fashion, hanging around on the edge of the crisis; but, inasmuch as he was the suitor who informed his own bride-to-be that he had none of that foolish enthusiasm which the world calls love, it is not likely that he could help much.

What became of Grace Murray? She kept up her relation to the Methodist societies throughout a life which lasted into the nineteenth century. It is recorded that in the after years she met Wesley once, in an interview that seems to have been altogether formal and commonplace. Her husband, John Bennet, broke with Wesley in the later period of Wesley's life, which, all things considered, was not surprising. He might, however, have been a bit more respectful in the remarks which he thereafter made about Wesley. Mrs. Bennet died in 1803, and her funeral services were in charge of Jabez Bunting.

It is an interesting though futile question to ask if John Wesley's career would have been much different if he had married Grace Murray. Possibly the wisest word here has been spoken by

Doctor Leger in *Wesley's Last Love,* to the effect that it would have made no particular difference as to the final outcome whom Wesley married, that he was wedded to his work and that he would have acted the same with Mrs. Murray, as his wife, as he did with Mrs. Vazeille. Probably Mrs. Murray might have been more submissive than Mrs. Vazeille, but that would likely have been the only difference. If we keep our consideration of this whole sorry matter down close to what we know of human nature, we may surmise that Grace Murray had all along a half-conscious realization of where John Wesley's chief interest lay, and of what the future with him would be like, and that the overpowering opposition of Charles Wesley, which broke off the engagement with John Wesley, may have forced her to a decision in line with innate good sense. Moreover, she was no doubt aware that Wesley, though deeply grieved, would not be rendered hopeless or paralyzed by her decision. More than one biographer has noted that, after the night of the harrowing meeting of all the parties to the climax, Wesley preached the next morning at the same hour as usual.

We come now to the marriage which did take place—that with Mrs. Vazeille, after a courtship, according to Tyerman, of fifteen or sixteen days. The best introduction to this is in the famous passage in the *Journal* which tells us, just after the time of his own marriage, that he called the single young men to remain single for the kingdom of heaven's sake, unless where there might be reason for exception. This is one of the most bewildering and illuminating utterances which a reader of diaries is likely to come upon in a lifetime. How any human being, of ordinary good sense, could ever have brought himself to enter that passage in a *Journal* which he himself intended to be published for the guidance of his followers, is a mystery of the first order. Yet it is a revelation of John Wesley; of his singular openness; of his complete lack of reticence as to what most men consider strictly their own business; or his innocence of any questioning as to how an entry like the above might affect the party of the second part—if one could call Mrs. Wesley a party of the second part. One wonders what he thought marriage was anyway. This consulting with the brethren; this view of marriage as aiding him in his work; this incredible entry about the advice to the young men who were unmarried to remain in the single state—where in all literature can we find anything to match this, under at all similar cricumstances?

Mrs. Wesley had been the wife of a fairly well-to-do business

man, who left her a considerable competency. Money could not
have been in Wesley's mind in contracting the marriage, for it is
on record that he never took a penny of his wife's money. He was
a careful handler of money and gave his wife at times good advice as
to what to do with her resources, but he would not receive anything
of her income for himself: the most he ever did was to borrow small
sums to be repaid in a month's time.

The marriage started off well enough, except for an outburst
from the officious Charles, who was grievously hurt at John's marrying without consulting him. It did not seem to occur to Charles
that, after the Grace Murray episode, John could be excused from
not letting Charles know of his plan until it had been carried out.
Mrs. Wesley evidently sought to adjust herself to her companion's
nature and manner of life in good faith and with an earnest purpose. She traveled with him over England for two years continuously, when travel itself was a stern hardship.

The first breach between the two seems to have opened over
the inconveniences of this same traveling. Wesley wrote a passage,
August 31, 1755, which has been often quoted, that to have one
complaining about hardships of travel was like tearing the flesh off
his bones—the reference being to his wife's querulous faultfinding.
To adopt an old adage, Wesley did not seem to realize that a complaint against a complainer is just as much a complaint as any complaint. Mrs. Wesley did not like the riding on horseback, and the
dirty roads, and the rainy weather, and the poor beds, and the ill-
dressed food at the inns; and Wesley did not like her finding fault
about such matters. In a letter which has recently come to light
Wesley said that he had had the itch more than a hundred times—
an item of record which may explain Mrs. Wesley's feeling about
the hardships of travel.

There is not much ground for supposing that the Wesleys,
man and wife, were very companionable with each other. Wesley
had been drawn to Mrs. Vazeille when he was sick and she was nurs-
ing him. He does not seem to have had much acquaintance with
her before this experience of being cared for by her. A marriage
contracted on the basis of the relation of nurse and sick man is
always of doubtful worth. The situation is too much out of the
ordinary. A man like Wesley would show during illness a milder
temperament than when he was in normal daily activity. The task
of merely keeping up with Wesley, as he moved about at his work,
would have been a strain even to a woman of livelier type, or fewer

years, than Mrs. Wesley. She had attained to mature age, had grown children of her own, and naturally desired a more fixed abiding place than she saw, after some months of trial, that she was ever likely to get with John Wesley. He had said that, if marriage ever meant that he had to preach one sermon "less" by being married, he would never marry. He had always had good words to say about a celibate ministry—words that hinted that, as to marriage, he inclined to the ascetic for asceticism's own sake. Now, asceticism, to appear lovely at all, must be assumed and undergone by the ascetic's own free will. Not much of spiritual good can come of one's asking another to join in an ascetic course—to say nothing of the positive harm done—when one forces one's self-denials on another. Mrs. Wesley, however, did try to keep up the Wesley pace till she broke down under it. For a woman well into middle age, accustomed to a more placid order of living, she did wonderfully well.

It is not easy to imagine what they found to talk about together. Mrs. Wesley, probably to Charles' horror when he heard about it, had, like Grace Murray, been a "serving woman." No doubt her lifelong interests had been household and domestic. No word of any kind has come down to us directly from her—which is always to be borne in mind when we are thinking of the Wesley domestic tragedy. It is not likely that she met Wesley's discourses on religious themes with overpatient understanding. Grace Murray impresses us as a woman willing to listen to John Wesley, but Mrs. Wesley does not leave just that impression. It must be said, though, that, if Wesley ever became bored by the type of conversation which dealt with the range of affairs in which Mrs. Wesley took interest, the feeling of boredom on the other side must have been equally distressing. Aside from this, it is probable that Wesley liked to be alone on the long trips. He spoke of himself as the loneliest man in England, but that did not mean lonesomeness. It was on the long trips that he found time for his omnivorous reading and the incalculable output in writing.

Judged by all the standards we can get, Mrs. Wesley was in love with her husband—at least until she at last became insanely jealous. With her outlook on life there was enough to make her jealous. Wesley was a constant letter-writer and many of his letters were to women. The letters dealt, for the most part, with religious experience, but such letters tend more than others to become intimate. Without the deepest sympathy with her husband's work, and without the most thorough understanding of his nature, Mrs. Wesley could put constructions on some of the correspondence that passed between her husband and women that made her unhappy. How much she saw of what her husband wrote in such letters, and how the women wrote to Wesley, we do not know; but Mrs. Wesley knew enough to sow the seeds of trouble in plenty. One of Wesley's complaints—as affairs finally got bad—was that his wife interfered with his mail. She had reason for so doing.

There is no need of dwelling long on the tragedy. It lasted for years, and differed from other tragedies of the kind only in the peculiarities of the details. The judgment of most Wesley biographers puts most of the blame on Mrs. Wesley; but the biographers write so exclusively out of desire to glorify Wesley that they can only with difficulty be fair to Mrs. Wesley. If she acted in an incredible manner, so also did Wesley. During the Calvinistic-Arminian controversy she sought to betray him outright into the hands of his foes. John Hampson, Sr., declared that he once entered Wesley's house without knocking and found Mrs. Wesley standing over her husband, who had evidently fallen or been pushed to the floor, with some locks of Wesley's hair in her fingers. Some have attempted to discount this story on the ground that Hampson had a grievance against Wesley for being left out of the Legal Hundred when Wesley made the selection. This attempt at discounting is altogether extreme. Hampson was not that stamp of man, even though he was disappointed in failing of selection for the Legal Hundred. John Hampson, Jr., was convinced that Wesley had treated his father unfairly but nevertheless wrote a careful and discriminating biography of Wesley. It must be admitted that Mrs. Wesley's feeling against her husband was fierce enough to make Hampson's testimony all too credible. If her conduct seems beyond belief, however, think of the letter of Wesley to her in which he tells her how obscure she had been when he married her, how she should be content to be obscure and to be ruled by him alone as he was ruled by Christ. One could pick out two or three letters from Wesley to his wife which, taken by themselves, would be capable of accounting for any extreme of frenzy on Mrs. Wesley's part. Think of writing a jealous wife to be content to be a private, insignificant person, "ruled by her husband as he was ruled by Christ." Rather a high place assumed by the husband, one would think! Of course the letters cannot be thus taken out of their context, inasmuch as they are in their turn products and results of the wife's attitude toward the husband. It can be said that both sides were to blame; but we must be careful not to weight the scales against the distracted wife.

There was, to look at a single instance, Wesley's interest and regard for Sarah Ryan. Sarah Ryan was a woman of that peculiar nervous constitution which made her susceptible to religious impressions we now and again call distinctly "spiritual." Her life had been irregular. She had three husbands living at one time, from no one of whom had she taken steps to become legally free. From the character of Wesley's references to this woman, it appears that he was more interested in her as open to what he conceived of as divine impressions than in any other wise; but he was guilty of the folly of writing to her about his domestic tragedy. Even though Sarah Ryan may have been especially responsive to spiritual influences, to say nothing of her being herself an authority on domestic tragedy, she was the last human being to whom Wesley should have written about his troubles with his wife. Affairs reached a climax, as far as Sarah Ryan was concerned, when at a dinner at London at which possibly twoscore guests were present—Sarah Ryan and Mrs. Wesley among the number—Wesley referred to the gracious influence of Sarah Ryan on his own religious life. He thought of her, it seemed, as an efficacious channel of divine influence upon himself. Here is how he had written to Mrs. Ryan in 1758: "The conversing with you, either by writing or speaking, is an unspeakable blessing to me. I cannot think of you without thinking of God. . . . You bring me straight into his presence." To Wesley she was a "jewel." After Mrs. Wesley had heard enough of this she arose and pointed out to the dinner party the matrimonial career of Mrs. Ryan.

It is to be admitted that Mrs. Wesley committed all manner of dreadful wrongs against her husband, for which the most intelligible explanation is that she was at least half-crazy. She told about Wesley falsehoods of the most preposterous order; she broke open letters that he had written, and interpolated in them remarks calculated to make him direst trouble.

The justification for giving so much space to this matter, here and in other books about Wesley, is that, inasmuch as Wesley's followers have claimed for him a Christian experience which made his life flawless, it is well, if we are interested in experience which is to be a lesson to others, to keep close to facts in thinking of Wesley. There is here too the question as to whether the extraordinary religious life, which Wesley's was, can be fitted into the ordinary routine, or whether the ability of such a life to get along in some natural human contacts does not of itself call for extraordinary spiritual resources. Wesley remarked in his closing years that perhaps God had overruled this terrible experience for good, because he might not have achieved so much if he had been happy at home. Mrs. Wesley might have turned this the other end around and have replied that she could have been happy if her husband had not tried to achieve so much.

Tyerman wrote as if to pass judgment on the whole wretched business: "Wesley was a dupe; Grace Murray a flirt; John Bennet a cheat, Charles Wesley officious." There is slight warrant for any of this judgment except that about Charles Wesley.

Interest in Wesley's love affairs—the entire sweep of them—has been for the moment revived by a book entitled *Son to Susanna,* by Mrs. G. Elsie Harrison, daughter of the John S. Simon who was the best authority on Wesley who has yet appeared. Mrs. Harrison has read much in modern psychology, has had as close access to the facts as anyone, possesses an imagination for which "vivid" would be a mild term. In interpreting the events of one hundred and fifty to two hundred years Mrs. Harrison needs but the bare statement of the fact. She can put a body upon a mere skeleton of fact with incredible speed, but she creates the body. For example, she finds the clue to about everything John Wesley did in a "curtain of fire" his mother threw around him dating from the date of the plucking of the brand from the burning. In the opening of *Son to Susanna* the fire might have been started by Samuel's roaming around with a torch in his hand—after there had been brewing through the day—with his mind filled with the victories of Marlborough. On the next page but one after that Samuel did set the house afire—and Susanna despised him for it. Mrs. Harrison's imagination is not deep but fast. Again, when Samuel appeared on the scene after the alarm of fire, he had his "pantaloons" in his hands, probably because he wanted to put them on. A house on fire, however, is not the best place to put on "pantaloons." A little later Mrs. Harrison has Samuel waving the "pantaloons" over his head, to the scorn of Susanna, who detested the "old man"—aged forty-two. Just how the fire-curtain, even after such a start as this, determines all John Wesley's love affairs, the reader may decide for himself.

Another instance: Grace Murray was the widow of Alexander

Murray, a sea captain drowned at sea.   There appears to have been some disagreement between Grace and Alexander because of Grace's increasing interest in Methodism.   Alexander was lost overboard on his next voyage—"for," asks Mrs. Harrison, "why should he return?"   Mrs. Harrison, in her patient search for facts as starting grounds for her imagination, might have done well to steady herself with a little examination of the traditions of British salts, especially of sea captains who, no matter what else is sacred, keep the devotion to their ships in the first place.   Alexander was lost overboard—that we know.   That he willingly allowed himself to be washed overboard is a supposition which shows what an imagination can do when it is working with ample sea-room.

Wrestling Jacob, by Marjorie Bowen, is another psychological interpretation of Wesley's life.   There is a deal of insight in the book and a cool, rational temper, together with no small amount of skepticism.   It is a helpful handling of the life of one who with all his faith—and credulity—was himself much more of a rationalistic and skeptic than some of us have been willing to allow.

PART IX

SPREADING SOCIAL RIGHTEOUSNESS

PART IX

SPREADING SOCIAL RIGHTEOUSNESS

THERE are two shades of opinion today as to Wesley's social achievements. On the one hand are those who will have it that Wesley was not interested in what we call the social results of Wesleyanism; and on the other, are those who tell us that the broad human outcome of his work was what concerned him; that he was so interested in this that, if he were living today, he would utilize even the agnostic, perhaps the atheistic notions of our time, using them as he did the theological conceptions of his day as instruments for bettering human life. One interesting biography of Wesley has been written from this latter assumption.

Wesley was chiefly concerned with a personal, individualistic message and practices. There is no need of our trying to prove anything else. He would help by giving men jobs if he could. In 1787, "he took a view (presumably admiring) of Mr. Ryle's silk mill, which keeps two hundred children in perpetual employment." He was not primarily dealing with social agencies. The study of his career as a social force reveals both the strength and weakness of such a purpose, and shows how the social atmosphere was a cause and effect of many of the most important phases of the movement.

The geographers tell us that England owes her geographical importance in large part to the Gulf Stream, which, starting from West Indian waters, carries warmth from the tropics to the British Isles, the tides lapping around the Isles on all sides. A shift in the Stream would utterly transform the range and quality of life in England. In the eighteenth century a new stream of life began to play upon England, and by spiritually climatic processes transformed the life there. Some of these forces came to sweeping expression. The effects of the Revolution, especially in its anti-feudalistic phase of 1688, were beginning to make themselves decisively felt by the time of Wesley's birth. During the eighty-eight years of his life there came the American Revolution, the French Revolution, the Industrial Revolution. The result was the release of new forces, some of them through the creation of new physical tools, some through new governmental procedures, some through

233

new social customs, some through new ways of looking at the world. Out of the material, ponderable facts came imponderables—spiritual currents and atmospheres which actually swept around the world. Probably few if any of the seers of the century knew what was going on around them, but the whole world was on the march nevertheless. It was in such world in transition that John Wesley played his part. The part has of late probably been overestimated, but it was important enough to demand the attention of historians as long as history is studied. The truth seems to be that the work of Wesley came to its mature power just at about the dawn of modern capitalism, if we may accept without holding too seriously the judgment of the Webbs that capitalism is about a century and a half old. There have always been the rich and the poor, the haves and the have-nots, but modern capitalism means everything industrial on the large scale—large accumulations of money, large aggregations of men, large tools worked by those who do not own them, large, indeed, world-wide markets. If we wish to set a beginning for this type of capitalism, we may say that it coincides with the independence of Methodism, conceded by Wesley's deed of declaration in 1784.

I do not mean that Wesley at all detected or appreciated the lineaments of the capitalism coming on the stage just as he was going off Those who read through this book, however, will see that it does hold that Wesley kept two values—that of men and that of money, or material things—in such relation to one another that he influenced markedly the capitalistic movement which he never saw nor foresaw. Just as a single item we note that in 1790 there were twice as many country laborers in England as town; fifty years later there were twice as many town laborers as country. When Wesley died, therefore, his teaching was to get a setting the like of which he had himself not seen.

One element in the strength of Wesleyanism as a social power lay in that it took any account at all of what we call the masses. It does not make much difference whether or no Wesley deliberately turned to what we call the plain people because the higher classes would not hear him. He did turn to them virtually from the first, and that he did so had a social significance. He could not carry on his spreading method without attempt to reach the largest numbers, and in doing so he inevitably "spread" his truth into the large social relationship, even if he did not intend to do so.

It is not necessary to paint the eighteenth century in total blackness to enforce the social significance of Wesley's ministry. We have only to look at the people to whom he spoke. Could there be any surer sign of Wesley's belief in the inherent responsiveness of men to goodness than his willingness to preach to crowds in the open air? One of the mysteries to us of today is why the mobs rose against Wesley's attempt to bring to them the gospel. We shall have occasion to note later that there were attempts to make Wesley out a papist, and thus to arouse patriotic feeling against him, but this was an afterthought. Probably we have to take the mob excesses as owing in part to the fact that the magistrates could not enforce the laws outside the cities because there was virtually no police. The brutality of the crowds in their treatment of the Wesleyan preachers would have been enough to tell us what the century was like, even if we did not know of the cockfighting and the bullbaiting and the bearbaiting.

As far as possible the leaders of the nation ignored the masses. The franchise was limited; the ordinary man had little chance. We need only glance at what we should call the lower courts of law to see that the boasted English justice, so far as the masses were concerned, amounted to little or nothing. How many times, at least in the early days, was Wesley refused even the elementary rights which today would be supposed to belong to the humblest citizen! In this insistence upon preaching to the crowds, Wesley fulfilled the essential requirements of the later nineteenth-century liberalism—free speech, free assembly, and elementary human rights. Of course the list of these primary rights became broader in the course of a century, but Wesley stood in the path that led to the enlargement. If Wesley had not done anything else than to stand upon his right to speak, he would have rendered England notable service. He has to be reckoned among the champions of free speech—one of his best contributions to his time and to all time.

In insisting upon this right he acted in legal fashion. There is little evidence to show that in their mob-threatened and mob-attacked meetings the Methodists struck back—physically, that is. There were not among them in England any who could outmob mobs and outbully bullies by fist power. Wesley depended upon seeking to get redress against mobs from the law, though it does not appear that he ever got what we should call police protection. There might have been an occasional stalwart, a leader of a mob, overcome by Wesley's calmness and persuasiveness; and once in a while even a woman of Amazon proportions, who literally struck out in Wesley's behalf, but Wesley did not countenance use of force.

To get back to the point from which we started: the assumption in Wesley's appeals to the crowds. A crowd, even in a bullying temper, is quite proud of itself because of the sheer weight of its numbers. Wesley had the high strategy of ability to break the crowd up into units by appealing directly to the conscience of the individuals that composed it. We have heard about the crowd contagion of Wesley's meetings, and we have to recognize the place and power of such contagion, as, indeed, Wesley himself did, but we must not miss Wesley's ability to speak so directly to hundreds of men as to make each individual feel that the soul-searching words were aimed directly at himself alone.

In spite of all the rage which Wesley had to face, it did not take forever for the ordinary people to see that here was a leader of men, of fine appearance, of evident knowledge and wisdom, who cared for them as if they were of inherent worth. Nobody could go to one of Wesley's meetings and leave, if he listened at all, without gaining the impression that the least and wickedest in the crowd had a soul worth saving. Men always ask, when a religious leader appears, what the leader is getting out of it himself. There was nothing that the crowd could see that Wesley was getting out of his work itself except the consciousness of doing all possible for his fellow men. Wesley met the masses to whom he spoke on the level. He certainly did not look up to the crowds as if they were at all his superior, even in physical might; he as certainly did not look down upon them with any trace of superiority. He never threatened, he never cajoled, he never flattered. He could make men thoroughly ashamed of themselves and yet not leave them in any groveling self-contempt. It was no slight social service, no small contribution to the forces which would one day create the public opinion of England, to have Wesley going up and down the land for sixty years on the assumption that the people to whom he spoke were worthy of the best he could give them.

The connection between Wesley's thought of God and his attitude toward men was immediate and complete. He sought to view men from the divine revelation. Let it not be supposed, however, that we are to picture Wesley as traveling through life with his eyes fixed on the stars, occasionally glancing at men with regard for them because of the divine love for them. He valued men as Jesus did—on their own account. It is not possible to get any impression from reading hundreds upon hundreds of pages of Wesley other than that of interest in and care for men because of themselves. This is, indeed, just another way of stating that he saw in them the souls for whom the Lord Christ died, but he saw them as Christ did. He treated them with supreme regard to their personal worth and dignity.

Again, an important social influence in Wesley's attitude toward men was his making his societies agencies which recognized and made use of the excellences of men, of any men who showed the excellences. Here was an organization built up of men just as Wesley found them—all sorts and conditions of men. There had to be leadership among the societies. Wesley used any talent for such leadership that he could find, wherever he could find it. In its way the Methodist society in a community opened a door upward into a service, which, no matter how apparently insignificant it might be, was a door open to a position which gave importance to the man who held it. This may not seem to be worth much attention, but anyone who has had to deal with the problem of leadership in a church will know what I mean. It is common in religious circles to hail the merger of smaller into larger church groups as wise economy, and so it is in these days of costly expenditures in ecclesiastical enterprises. But it is not always so when we are dealing with the development of religious leadership. The small Methodist societies all over England were instruments and fields for the development of leaders. Even a class leader, entrusted with the financial and spiritual guidance of a group of not more than a dozen persons, was a figure of consequence in the Methodist community. The Methodist societies were training grounds in a leadership which might, without Methodism, have been totally lost, or never realized or heard of. The leaders trained among the Methodists could use their powers and skills in wider fields than the specifically religious. When lay preaching became customary, the training in public speech of scores of Methodists became a social service of incalculable worth. Wearmouth has recently shown us in *Methodism and the Working Class Movements of England* the force which such Methodist training revealed in the industrial activities, especially trade-unions, in the first half of the nineteenth century in England.

Years ago, just after Lenin arose to such power in Russia, I came upon a Communist—then called Bolshevist—at work in China. I asked how he could hope, under the obstacles which confronted him, to make headway toward converting any considerable mass of Chinese. His reply was that he was giving himself only to the preliminaries, of teaching the Chinese how they could work together in discussion groups, and put motions, and take actions in a parliamentary fashion. When they had learned how to do this, he said, it would be time enough to put content into the actions. The laymen of Methodism, likewise, soon learned some of the secrets of control of one's fellow men by speech and by organized group activity.

This should be kept in mind, when we think, as we must, of the dictatorial rule of John Wesley over his societies. Wesley was by talent and choice and training a despot. No matter how complete his impulse toward despotism, however, it was practically limited. Fifty miles a day was fast traveling for Wesley, though he occasionally, as in 1759, rode ninety miles in one day. The intervals between the visits to a particular society had to be long, and in those intervals the Methodists had to handle their affairs as best they could, even though when Wesley came a second time he remarked to the members of one society "in plain terms that they were the most ignorant, self-conceited, self-willed, fickle, intractable, disorderly, disjointed society that I know in the three kingdoms." Wesley might rebuke his lieutenants, but he usually had to let stay done what they had done. He told one of his preachers that he talked too long and another that he talked too loud. We speak of his close supervision of the societies—and it was close when he was at hand, but he was not often at hand. A despot is not so terrible where are not railroads, or telegraphs, or telephones, or fast mails, or newspapers, or the radio. Wesley's followers had to do what he said, but he could not say much about all detailed situations. By the time the followers found out what he had said, the urgency, or crisis, of a threatening situation had passed. It will be recalled that Wesley wrote sharply to the American Methodists about their taking things in their own hands. While the Americans wrote back with renewed avowals of esteem for their spiritual father, they went on doing what seemed best to them. So it was in lesser degree all over England.

It may seem like forcing a point to speak of the Methodist meetings as training grounds for leadership. The Methodists, however, took all these opportunities seriously. Life did not then have the distractions that it has now. In many a community after dark there was no place to which to go but to the Methodist meeting place. Except the day's work, which was terribly heavy, the experiences at that meeting place were the most absorbing in the life of the Methodists.

The captain of one of the world's mightiest ocean steamships some time ago declared that, in his judgment, the best training for a youth who might aspire to rise to a position like his own is on the old-fashioned sailing ship. At first this seemed like a half-sentimental praise of a phase of sea life now almost wholly gone. Not so, however, after the seaman gave his reasons. On the old-fashioned ship, it appears, the sailor does not, indeed, learn the mechanism of the modern steamer, which is a triumph of scientific genius. One knowledge he does acquire, however—knowledge of the sea. He is down close to it. There is so little of distraction on the deck of the sailing ship that the sailor has nothing to look at except the sea. As the popular song has it, when he goes to sea, he sees the sea. A wave looks different when it washes across a deck from the way it appears when it breaks harmlessly against the steel sides of a liner, yet the skillful handling of the liner depends upon intimate knowledge of how waves and tides and currents act. Similarly, the intimate knowledge of human nature, as it acts ordinarily and in crisis, was learned by the leaders of the units of Methodism until many of them became veritable experts. The expertness was gained down close to the waves of elementary human experience, where, without much chance at the artificialities of life, men had to act about as they were.

There have been critics of Wesley who have at least implied that he gave himself to the humbler classes because they would make the most devoted followers; that those who had had no chances at advantages of birth and training felt honored, not to say flattered, at the attentions paid them by a son of the Established Church who had become a Fellow of Oxford. If this is urged to support the contention of a Southey, already referred to, that Wesley was a human being actuated by the human quality of personal ambition, it is not worth long consideration. If a man is acted on by personal ambition, in its selfish forms, he is not likely to drive along under such a power for over sixty years. When we speak of ambition, we think of that inner realm where the inner cannot be seized by direct inspection but only by outer effects. Making allowance for all the alloy in human nature, we are not so blind to the limitations of selfish ambition as to fancy that such ambition can force a leader

up and down the England of the eighteenth century through nearly
three quarters of that century.

All this is entirely compatible with the belief that Wesley did
see and did take account of the fact that he knew that he could do
more with the humbler than with the higher classes. The higher
classes—using higher here in the accepted meaning—would not have
listened to Wesley and would not have heeded him if they had
listened. So he went elsewhere.

Here let us remark that Wesley committed that offense which
members of privileged classes so often find unpardonable—he would
not remain true to the attitudes and expectations of his own class.
It would not be fair to say that Wesley to any degree betrayed the
class into which he had been born, but he certainly would not conform to it. He was himself a High Churchman and a Tory, by his
own avowal, but he certainly spoke his whole mind on High-
Churchmen and Tories.

It must have been manifest from the outset that the Methodist
Movement would not have more than the slightest effect in the
narrower "social" sense. It would not open the doors to the ranks
of nobility or bring titles of social distinction. It is conceivable
that, if Wesley were now on earth in this year of our Lord 1939,
completing sixty years of such service as he rendered in the eighteenth century, he might receive some token of honor from the
English court. He might even be granted a seat in the House of
Lords, though that requires a strain on the imagination. It would
be a strain too on the loyalty of a world-wide Methodism. Any
social honor of this kind for a leader of Methodism in Wesley's day
would have been unthinkable.

I have just said that Wesley rendered a service by opening a
door upward for the larger usefulness of men who might become
leaders in Methodist circles. I now say that he did everything he
could to develop among those groups from whom the Methodists
came a proper class consciousness, at least a legitimate pride in their
own circles. To Wesley salvation was social. Making salvation
social, however, meant the development of a minority group of
deeply intense cohesiveness which had large social possibilities and
results. It is worth noting that social students today hold that the
line of progress is in the direction of recognizing the importance of
such groups.

This class consciousness did have at times a tendency toward developing spiritual pride. A man as conscious of his own salvation as were some of the early Methodists can be a good deal of a nuisance. Indeed, a measure of the disfavor of the early Methodists came from this source. Nevertheless, it was socially important that the class of people to whom Methodism came attain to a proper self-respect. There was no chance of their getting into the so-called higher classes. All the more reason, therefore, why they should develop the spirit of their own class. Wesley was an admirable social force in this regard, for he knew what was in the so-called higher society, especially how little was there when it came to genuine moral and human value. He knew how to beget in his followers a satisfaction with their own fellows without any subserviency toward those who are called the more privileged.

Wesley knew, however, just how powerful was this social prestige, or feeling of superiority, or whatever we choose to call it. He feared the shadow of respectability. He knew that nothing likely to happen in his own lifetime would break the self-defenses of social prestige, and he did not think it worth his while to try. This is the last fortress of privilege to be broken anyhow. You can take away from a class all political and financial control and leave it the power of decreeing social standing and you have left in its hand a surpassing resource, human nature being what it is. The genuine remedy is the development of high ideals of human worth within the so-called less-privileged classes. Methodism did not arise even among the so-called middle classes of England. It began farther down than that. In nothing is what we call the statesmanship of Wesley more manifest than in his acceptance of the limitations which sent him to work among the lowly. If one is to start a fire of new interest in religion, it is well to apply the torch at the bottom of the social heap.

I stay on this point probably to the weariness of my readers. It is charged, too often with justice, that when a leader of conspicuous ability arises among the less-favored groups, the more favored to a degree make him one of themselves, for their own purposes. If the favored realm is that of material wealth, the accusation is that, as soon as a mind of high technical promise appears, or even of evident leadership among the laboring class, the favored "higher-ups" immediately proceed to "pick his brains" for the advantage of themselves. This can be done in many ways—by financial rewards, by social attention, by any one of a score of subtle flatteries.

In this connection we may be pardoned for pointing again to
the contrast between Wesley and Whitefield. The Countess of
Huntingdon acted in all good faith in creating opportunities for
Whitefield to preach before members of her social circle. Her own
experience of conversion had evidently been deep and genuine.
Still, we cannot see much evidence that in his preaching to the
Countess of Huntingdon's guests Whitefield got far. They were
astonished, indeed, at his oratorical ability, but that was about all.
It is esteemed an honor to Whitefield that Lord Chesterfield was
impressed by his gifts of speech and commented that he talked
ably on the "divine attributes." As Sam Weller would say, "This
is rayther rich." But it would be hard to find the faintest trace of
moral or spiritual effect of Whitefield on Chesterfield. Whitefield
rejoiced in the "tip-top nobility" that he met at the home of the
Countess, which is somewhat of a self-revealing utterance. There
is more moral worth in Wesley's contemptuous references to Chesterfield than in any oratorical spells that the magic eloquence of
Whitefield wove around the cynical lord.

It is charged against Wesley that, in his preaching to the less
favored, he dwelt on an other-worldliness which made them acquiescent in the evils of this present world. If this means that he did
not preach revolt, it is true; but it is not true if it means that he
preached submission to ills which could be remedied. Everywhere
he went he gave his attentions to the conditions under which men
actually lived.

There are those who are fond—perhaps overfond—of quoting
from Lecky that, if it had not been for John Wesley, scenes like
the wholesale guillotine slaughters of the French Revolution might
have been common in England; that Wesley forestalled a revolution like that of France from reaching the shores of England. This
striking tribute to the significance of Wesley is sound enough
rhetorically, but it requires qualification. It is more an outburst
than an insight. Some interpret Lecky's word as meaning that
Wesley so gave himself to the inner life of men that he made men
too good to rebel at evil institutions; and they claim him for conservatism, while others condemn him for a conservatism that prevented in England changes like those brought to France by the
Revolution. All agree on the conservatism.

There is no doubt about the conservatism, as far as Wesley's
intent and temper were concerned. Nevertheless, Wesley worked
deliberately to make better the physical condition of the people.

We have seen his interest in their physical state, as shown in his own remark that, outside the studies which bore directly on his evangelistic tasks, he gave most of his time to the investigation of human diseases and their cure.   We know what he did with the royalties which came from the sale of *Primitive Physic*.   We know too his interest in education and in the spread of cheaply printed books throughout England.

Now, the path to successful social change does not altogether lie in the notion that at last, after unspeakable woes, the people will rise against their woes; that the worm will at last turn; that the worse social conditions become, the closer we are to revolution. The truer philosophy is in the other adage, so often used as complaint against reformers who seek for advantages for their fellow men: Give unprivileged groups an inch and they will take an ell. There is an oppression that succeeds, succeeds in stamping out all initiative and all hope.   Conditions can be so bad that there is no chance. Wesley did not find anything of this desperate nature. He found enough moral and spiritual responsiveness to call forth all his energies in optimistic effort.   Without any sympathy for the social revolutionary doctrines current in his time, especially in his later years, he nevertheless put in the hands of his followers the instruments which would in the end bring about changes which, if he could have foreseen them, he would have regarded with horror. That is, if he could have seen only part and not all.   There was nothing though in what he taught or did which would lead to any swift uprising.

Those who praise Wesley and those who blame him for standing in the way of movement toward anything like a French Revolution, moreover, forget that there is not any one simple pattern of revolution which can be applied to all peoples alike. The ideas released by any revolution do indeed spread pretty well through the earth, but they do not make revolutions everywhere.   Lenin, in our own day, certainly knew something about setting a revolution going, and he has told us, speaking with authority, that a revolution to succeed in a given social situation must be exactly fitted to that condition, called forth by particular needs, adjusted to the mood and temper of the particular people, supplied with instruments native to and usable by the particular people.   If the revolutionary ideas spread from one land to another, they must in that other land take on forms which express the mind and mood of that land.   This, of course, before they become popularly effective in that land. I am not speaking of the little knots of sympathizers in every land with any and all revolutions in every other land.

Even if Wesley had given himself to preaching the doctrines like those of the French Revolution, it is doubtful if he could have started a revolution in England like that which near the close of his life came in France. Nobody has ever surpassed Walter Bagehot in the understanding of the English mind and temper. Bagehot long, long ago pointed out that there is a type of logic which appeals to and manifests itself in the French mind in utter contrast to anything on the English side of the Channel, a logic which seizes an idea quickly, gives it a speed of movement which travels from Paris out to the remotest frontiers as swiftly as the fastest vehicles can carry it and pushes it at once to extreme action —to racing to the full length. If it be replied to this that the French are much steadier now than they were in the middle of the nineteenth century when Bagehot wrote, we must remember that Bagehot was nearly a century closer to the French Revolution than we are today, and it is conditions then of which we speak. On the other hand, Bagehot laid stress on the socially conservative side of the English character as expressed, not in stupidity, indeed, but in slowness of mental movement. It was in this connection that he, an Englishman, told of that oft-quoted interview which he had with an English farmer at the time of the Crimean War. The farmer was sure that England and her allies could never win, because they could never catch "he Czar." No amount of explanation availed to make the farmer see that it was not necessary, in order to defeat Russia, to catch "he Czar." Bagehot declared that this stolidity of the farmers of England made for social stability. The French peasant can be just as stolid as anything in England, however, but Bagehot might have replied that this also proved his point as to social steadiness, though what he was trying to say was that the French mind, of his day at least, moved faster and went further than the English. In any case, the revolutionary violence of the French did not fit into the English scheme of things. The English were brutal enough, and they suffered abuses, but as a mass they did not readily take fire. Their outbreaks were sporadic. The Church depended, for example, in large part upon the tithe system, which the farmers of Wesley's day accepted as in the regular order. When Samuel Wesley found one of the farmers from whom he received rents making away with some of the tithe crops due him —Wesley—he was about as shocked as he was over the attempts of the Epworth villagers to burn the Rectory, and at least thought that he had terribly humiliated the thief by exposing him to the neighbors.   The ordinary dweller in England too had to suffer from grievous laws.

The press gang seized John Nelson, one of Wesley's best lay preachers, chiefly because he was a Methodist.   Still, the feeling of grievance was not so deep or keen in England as in France.   The Established Church in England was not to be mentioned in the same day with the Church in France, when it came to oppressiveness.   The excoriations of Voltaire, if directed against the Established Church in England, would have had some point, but not much.   The worst that could have been said against the English Church was that it was remiss as a servant of the people.   Likewise with the nobility.   The charge against them could have been social uselessness, but not cruelty.   Both Church and nobility were socially expensive, but they did not then have to meet the question as to who paid for them.   Indeed, that particular question has never been raised in England with any insistence at all searching, not to say desperate.

John Wesley no doubt did something to make an England proof against a revolution like that of France; but if he did, he did not deserve any noteworthy credit.   What finally prevented any considerable sympathy in England toward French Revolutionaries were the gains already won in the Revolution of 1688, which struck the mortal blow at Feudalism and the excesses of the Revolution itself.   I have referred to Bagehot's opinion of the logic of the social thinking of the French.   It was just a step beyond French logicalness, so to speak, to social lunacy.   The career of Robespierre, to take the conspicuous instance, is that of a leader of clear vision, of complete sincerity, who in his devotion to the abstract gets clean away from the concrete.   What abstract logic called for abstract logic must have, under Robespierre's leadership, even if that meant heads in the baskets at the foot of the guillotines.   Moreover, could even a Robespierre have persuaded the English to behead George III?—scant as was George III's popularity.

There have been three leaders of world-wide importance in the past two centuries, who have believed in human perfectibility. One was Karl Marx, who felt that the evils in man's nature were due to a bad environment, and that, if society could get the bad out of the environment, it would at the same time get the bad out of human nature.   A second was Robespierre, who, though he came to power after the life of Wesley had ended, was training himself for leadership while Wesley was still preaching in England. Robespierre believed with all his soul that absolute devotion to the ideal was all that was necessary to introduce a virtually perfect society—perfection to be achieved by putting evildoers out of the way. Facts, realities of the actual order, counted with him not at all. The ironic outcome has been that the man who in modern history was totally devoted to an ideal of a perfect social creation has thus far been regarded as one of the blackest villains in the annals of time. Certainly, his deeds objectively considered were black enough.

Now, John Wesley taught perfection, not clearly, not consistently, but definitely, nevertheless—the perfectibility of the individual life. He was as much devoted to the ideal of helping men on perfection as any idealist who ever lived. He was as uncompromising in principle as any one-ideaed doctrinaire, but he put in his whole life trying to adjust his ideals to actual circumstances, and making circumstances over, as far as it could be done, to bring about an earthly setting for the ideal.

It is only just to say that many of the propositions for social betterment in Wesley's time virtually lay outside the sphere of his thinking. We live in a day when the social opportunities of the Church are urged upon the Church in scores of ways. It was not quite so two centuries ago, at least the social obligations were not so definitely preached. No one could have spoken more definitely about matters like the *Just Price,* for example, than did Richard Baxter, a century before Wesley, but Baxter was an exception, a pathbreaker, and was urging upon individual Christians their duties as individuals. Moreover, it is lamentably true that social evils are not always as apparent to men actually facing them as to those looking back upon them a century or two later. "How could have human beings put up with such conditions?" we ask in horrified tones, as we glance back after a century or even a half-century. How indeed? The students of the twenty-first century will ask the same question about us, and in the same shocked accents. A foremost leader of our Civil War was once asked why his army had not better followed up a particular victory. He replied that, after three days of terrible struggle, nobody thought of following up anything. The illustration is inadequate, but it does hint at the shortness of view of those in an actual struggle. Life is under such stress that to get through one crisis and on to the next is the sole idea

of many a worthy leader.   Wesley's life was passed under such stress.
In addition, his primary interests were not social except indirectly.
Much of the criticism against him was of the order that blames
men for not hitting targets at which they do not aim.

The first thing that Wesley used to notice about the Methodists
as he traveled up and down the land was the conditions in which
they lived—their material resources.   Those who tell us that Methodism suffered from the otherworldliness that helped them to put
up with hardships here for the sake of happiness hereafter ought
to give a little heed to the efforts of Wesley to improve the lot of
his followers here and now.   He held to the hereafter, not as something to be dreamed about, but as something to be worked for by
the right use of material goods here.   He conceived of men as stewards of wealth—and stewards are not to be idle.   In his volumes
of standard sermons there was no sermon on hell or heaven.

So we have that famous sermon on the use of money—with the
oft-quoted advice: "Gain all you can, save all you can, give all
you can." There has seldom been any such utterance worse handled.
Gain all you can has been taken to mean by any way you can,
whereas, if one were to read Wesley's limitations on methods of
getting, one would find an outline of business ethics to which the
world has not yet attained.   In the section: "Gain all you can,"
there are eight divisions: (1) We are not to seek to gain at the
expense of our bodies, (2) of our minds, of our souls.   We are not
to gain (3) by hurting our neighbor in his substance, (4) or in his
body, (5) even as physicians delay to cure illness for prolonged
gain, (6) or in the neighbor's soul.   We are to get (7) by honesty
in every form of work, (8) by progressively making the best of all
that comes to our hands, constantly learning to do better work.

The other main divisions have likewise many subdivisions.
Saving does not mean hoarding, but the avoidance of waste.   Much
of Wesley's oft-discussed asceticism was due, not to a Romish desire
to "mortify the flesh" but to avoid useless expenditure.   The
legitimate desire to make the most of one's appearance in dress
meant nothing to Wesley, hence his denunciation even of ribbons
as waste, although actually Wesley was scrupulously careful in his
own dress.   One cannot resist the feeling that Wesley was as
anxious about the impression his appearance was making as any
leader of his time.   This, however, is aside from the point.   Saving,
in Wesley's meaning, was absence from expenditure for display.

All of which, of course, revealed a lack in the Wesley understanding of human nature. Most of us live our lives in the gaze of our fellows, and do not feel that there is anything wasteful in producing as pleasant an impression as may be upon the mind of our fellows. Here, again, Wesley did not have the teachings of our psychology as to the inevitability and legitimacy of many normal human impulses. Wesley himself did not do so badly as to impressive appearance "with his cassock, his black silk stockings, his large silver buckles." To Wesley, wasteful expenditure was a sin, as, indeed, we think today, the difference between our day and his being as to what expenditure is wasteful. By saving, Wesley did not mean hoarding.

We come next to the most important injunction of all: "Give all you can." By this Wesley meant give practically all. The only reservations were that the care of dependents was not to be neglected, and that money for the actual carrying on of a business could be held in one's hands for that purpose. This was, indeed, a counsel of perfection.

It is particularly notable that in the days when Methodism made so much of Christian perfection there were not more who saw that Wesley's doctrine of giving all was, for the time, a major feature of that doctrine. The chief test of Methodist regard for the neighbor had to be the use of money, mostly for the relief of distress. Wesley was consistent in teaching that, if a man was to be perfect, he must bring all his money under the ideal of perfection—as indeed he must at any time. The one path to perfect service of the neighbor that Wesley could see was in the actual relief of poverty by giving. Extensive emphasis on legislative and social measures came after he had gone. At least the one duty which lay most out in Wesley's full view was that of the giving of one's substance, for the relief of men. Wesley had hardly got well into action—this was in 1740—when he set collections going among the Methodists, which fed each day about one hundred and fifty who were out of work. The Wesley contribution here is in bringing "all" under Christian principle. There has always been a tendency in the Church to compromise on this problem of the Christian use of money. Compromise is indeed inevitable, and that without necessarily involving moral fault in the compromiser, for the field is not always definitely marked out, and in many cases there is no moral guidance in the facts themselves. The result is that, with a loosening of the determination to bring "all" under the law of perfection, inner strictness begins to relax. The outcome is the double standard, or a division of loyalties between the religious life and the pursuit of gain. Religion becomes religion and business business. The only safety is the tight grasp on the ideal of the whole activity as subject to Christian purpose whether one can see clearly what to do with a specific problem or not. It cannot be claimed that Methodists ever followed Wesley's injunction about giving all. It can be maintained that he himself was as nearly perfect in consistency here as any mortal could well be. He earned before his death large returns from his books. He gave away altogether about thirty thousand pounds. He did not spend anything upon himself beyond what most of us would call the bare necessities. He did leave an annuity for Sally, the daughter of his brother Charles, but that was all. When the grave closed over him and the "poor men" who carried him to that grave had been paid the pound apiece that he had ordered, and his library had been set aside for his preachers, that was the end so far as his own personal wealth was concerned.

Wesley's thought of the redemption of society by economic means was conceived in terms of the individual's use of money to help his fellow men, either by direct gift or preferably by giving them work. In 1740 he found a way to get places for twelve of his followers, carding and spinning cotton. Still, Wesley could not travel five thousand miles a year throughout England without seeing the play of causes of distress which were not due to the activities of individuals taken separately. At least some evils were owing to the fact that "everyone was doing it." Wesley's suggestions as to what would remedy bad economic conditions were not worked out with any scientific thoroughness by himself or by anyone else, for that matter, so that we have to regard Wesley's utterances, therefore, as lay observations of a traveler of keen vision but of no extensive familiarity with economic discussion. The prevalent economy of the century was mercantilism, which is not taken seriously now, but which was the only economics to which England paid much attention until Adam Smith appeared. Adam Smith's *Wealth of Nations* did not arrest the attention of the English thinkers till 1776, by which date Wesley was seventy-three years old—too far along to try to revise whatever economic notions he had picked up. In a word, mercantilism taught that a nation's material prosperity depended on a favorable balance of trade—more exports than imports—the balance owed on the exports being paid to the exporting

nation in gold. It was inevitable after the abandonment of the
personal services, demanded by feudalism, and the substitution of
payment in money made possible by the increase of coinage after
the conquest of the Americas, men should think in money terms as
never before. Scholars say that mercantilism has not been given
full credit for the services it rendered to the mercantilist nations
in its maturity. It is easy to see now the effect of all this balance
paid in gold on the prices of the receiving country; and the preven-
tion of a nation's developing the resources in which it is best fitted
and importing from other nations the goods which they are better
able to produce. In so far as Wesley thought of economics at all,
it was in a mercantile framework. He accepted outright the mercantile principle that colonies exist for the sake of the mother
country.

He was most at home in the sections of this field that presented
discernible moral issues. He was stiff with anything resembling
financial delinquency. Bankruptcy was abhorrent to him, probably because of the possibility of chicanery in bankruptcy proceedings.

Under date of December 9, 1772, Wesley wrote a letter to the
editor of *Lloyd's Evening Post,* which is as nearly as anything a
statement of his economic views. Look for a moment at the salient
points in this letter:

He calls attention to the fact that thousands of people are
starving in all parts of England. He had seen one woman picking
up sprats from a dunghill and carrying them home for herself and
children "and another gathering bones which the dogs had left in
the street, to make broth." This was because of unemployment.
Many who once employed fifty men were employing only ten.
Food was so high that the "generality of people" were hardly able
to buy anything else. Corn was dear because so much was used for
distilling. Oats were dear because there were too many horses
kept for display. Sheep and oxen were not raised because the
breeders were raising horses. Pork, poultry, and eggs were dear
because of the monopolizing of the farms by enclosures. "The land
which was formerly divided among ten or twenty little farmers
and enabled them comfortably to provide for their families is now
generally engrossed by one great farmer." The dearness of victuals
too is caused by luxury. "A person of quality will boil down three
dozen of neat's tongues to make two or three quarts of soup"—amazing waste. "Land is dear because gentlemen cannot live as they

have been accustomed to do without increasing their income, which most of them cannot do but by raising their rents. The farmer paying a higher rent for his land, must have a higher price for the produce of it. This tends again to raise the price of land. And so the wheel goes round."

Everything is dear because of the enormous taxes. Why the taxes? Because of the national debt. Where is the remedy? Give the people work. Cut out the distilling. Reduce the price of oats by cutting down the number of horses. In fact, stop all luxury. Discharge half the national debt—and so on.

There are live nerves here. I think the boldest step, socially speaking, Wesley ever took was his denunciation of enclosure. Almost from time immemorial English land had been farmed by distributing strips of cultivable ground among groups of farmers, each strip of three in turn lying fallow every third year. In addition, was the waste land and the common land from which the farmer could cut his firewood and get pasture for his cattle. The farmers regarded waste and common land as their own. Long before Wesley appeared great landowners were under one pretext or another enclosing this common land for their purposes—sheep runs, for example. The result was that thousands of small farmers were ruined. It was consummate social heroism for Wesley to criticize enclosure.

Much of this, perhaps all of it, causes the present-day technical economist to smile. He asks how England would have successfully coped with the demand for distilling. He sees in Wesley's letter an illustration of fallacies which economists love to denounce. He especially likes to remind us that rent of land—economic rent of land, that is—does not enter into the price of land produce. All of which is conclusive enough to himself, with his familiarity with Ricardo. Practically the control of England by the landowners till the passage of the Corn Laws was the most anti-social feature of England's history.

Nevertheless, it will not do to brush Wesley aside with a smile at his inadequate economics any more than it would do to smile at Christopher Columbus for not having better maps of the world. Men like Ricardo and Malthus and Adam Smith were indeed at work on economic problems in the eighteenth century, and a little later Jeremy Bentham, but they had not yet so systematized their work, or even stated it, as to make it generally understood. After it was published it was wrongly used.

Apart from all this, we note the closeness of observation of Wesley, the genuineness of his common sense in fields where common sense could form an opinion, his sympathy with the have-nots or the have-littles, his passion against the inequalities in the distribution of wealth. He stated, as well as anyone in his day certainly, the contrast between the condition of the rich and the poor. In the letter above quoted he tells that, while the poor women are gathering up the bones left by the dogs in the streets, the rich are living in more than lavish plenty. We have heard altogether too much about Wesley as teaching the poor to be contented with their lot. To Jane Hilton he wrote in 1768, "When poverty comes in at the door, love flies out the window." There was a time when the song that the poor are to "live on hay" here, in the confidence that by and by "they'll eat pie in the sky," was urged as having especial reference to the preaching of the Methodists. Wesley was fearless and unsparing in bringing to the public the distresses of the poor and insistent in his urgency for their relief. That letter to Lloyd's was a fearless bit of utterance. The rich—especially the titled rich—did not like better than now having their extravagances pointed out. Nobody in the Church today is any bolder than was Wesley in his pleas for the poor.

Then as to the limitations of his economic knowledge. We surely have not advanced much beyond Wesley in realization of the wastefulness of useless expenditure. The prohibition of luxuries, such as gentleman's horses, for example, might not have helped the prosperity of the country as much as Wesley fancied, but he was putting his finger on a weak spot in the social organization of his day nevertheless when he talked about expenditure for display as waste. Thorstein Veblen and Wesley are not far apart in this.

There are some aspects of English life which an American, especially one studying the eighteenth century, finds it almost impossible to understand. Or, to put it more exactly, an American does not know the existence of some problems. I mention again something to which I have already alluded: the stratification of English society—the difficulty of a man's rising out of the class into which he was born, into a higher class, though under strip-farming a worker did get a chance to buy portions of arable land. The American tradition has been that of climbing. It is the boasted tradition of Americans that, starting at the bottom, one can rise to the top. Abraham Lincoln once spoke of this possibility as a peculiar glory of American conditions. Of course in some realms of activity this was possible in England, but the possibility was not part of English tradition or expectation. The American did not often think of those who failed to get up. The adage itself, which reminded American youth that there was always room at the top, bore witness to the fact that not many got up, else there would not have been so much room at the top. Now, it was just as well, under the circumstances, to have one who could earn money, and did earn it, and who could speak out of first-hand knowledge without bitterness, informing his constituents that riches should be an entirely secondary aim. This was not otherworldliness of the paralyzing order, but hard common sense.

Looking back for the moment, Wesley's opposition to bankruptcy and to making money by handling "bills" and notes was a protest against making money, or getting money, by plans which seemed to be merely manipulative without productive effort. We have to consider that Wesley moved among groups which saw little actual cash, and who estimated money as veritable life's blood. In 1756 he wrote: I have "never put out six pence to interest since I was born."

A traveler in lands where the ordinary people do not see much "cash" is impressed and depressed by what seems to him the stinginess and meanness of the people in money affairs. This is not due to niggardliness, inherent or acquired, but to the preciousness of money. We all know that the more money we have, the less value any particular piece possesses. The "marginal" value of the money is less, the more we have. On the other hand, the less we have, the higher the value of each separate piece. Now, Wesley's converts were mostly among those to whom money was as valuable as the air they breathed. This did not mean avarice or anything like it. If it was materialism, it was the materialism of the poor. The rich are materialistic in thinking too much of money: the poor, likewise, can be materialistic in thinking too much of money. They have so little of it that they must give too much attention to what they have. This renders intelligible the temper in which Wesley would regard men who made money by discounting notes and bills—"shaving" notes, to use the old expression. These men seemed to him dishonest. Even if they did not yield to opportunities to cheat, they seemed to be getting money by something like sleight of hand. It was this realization of what money meant to the people that blinded the eyes of Wesley to any social service rendered even by those whom we might look upon as speculators. Dr. E. D. Bebb states in *Non-conformity and Social and Economic Life* that the Methodists in London in ten years contributed fifteen thousand pounds to their own poor. This would be seventy-five thousand dollars in our American money and would probably be worth, to the people who gave it, three times as much as it would be to us of today.

In all the emphasis on keeping the balance between poverty and riches Wesley succeeded in getting his movement well launched without dependence upon the well to do. He said (in 1779) that "the rich make good scaffolding but bad materials for building a church." We have seen that, as soon as the Methodists became well enough off in this world's goods to be able to pay for chapels, they began to insist that the chapels were their own. Wesley saw the peril here at once. He knew how unpopular his own teaching had been and how unpopular Methodist preaching must upon occasion be, if it were loyal to itself. How likely would a congregation of those increasing in wealth be to listen to any minister, except Wesley himself, on the perils of wealth? His aim in keeping control of the chapels in his own hands was due somewhat to his own autocratic temperament, no doubt, but more to his desire to make it possible for the preachers to preach according to the spirit and aims of Methodism. Here again we must hold before us the understanding that Methodism was a society and not a church. The purpose was to spread scriptural holiness throughout the land. The center of the Movement must be kept sound in order to do this. Much that would have been intolerable in a church was tolerable enough, indeed inevitable, in a society set on the one resolution, determined not to compromise.

Wesley was a wide reader in church history, especially of the early Church, if not a profound student. He said repeatedly in various connections that the Christian Church suffered by becoming the official Church of Rome, which he called the greatest blow that Christianity ever received because of the flood of riches, honors and power it conferred especially on the clergy. We can see his wholesome fear of similar connections in this judgment, a judgment that has been repeated by practically all church historians. It is admittedly easy to make sweeping generalizations to the effect that the Christianization of the Roman Empire was the Romanization of the Church, much easier than to make any valuable suggestion as to what the Church could have done other than it did. The barbarians had come upon Rome like a flood. The result was somewhat like the choking effect when a mass of fuel, some of it slowly combustible and some of it not combustible at all, is thrown upon a fire burning brightly. The first three centuries of the career of the Church had been glorious in the profusion and variety and courage of Christian thought and practice, probably, as Bishop Gore said, because the possibility that a Christian might at any moment be thrown into prison just because he was a Christian kept in the Church only those of high moral vitality. It is a wretched story, that of the alliance of the Church and Rome. Now, Wesley never seemed to feel the same critical spirit toward the Church of England, itself an Established Church. He called himself a Tory and a High-Churchman, and he knew that the Church of England had been left by the Reformation more Catholic than some of the Churches on the Continent. The lofty ideal of the Church was always before him. Nobody can read what he wrote and said to his followers without feeling that Wesley believed he could serve his Church best by keeping Methodism loyal to the ideals which had controlled it from the start. Indeed, from his reading of church history, he must have known the part played in the history of the Roman Church by the powerful societies within that Church, and he had before him also the history of the societies within the Church of England.

A society within a larger body can succeed only as it refuses to compromise in preaching its ideal. It has a right to exclude from its lists those who refuse or fail to live up to its ideals. Much of the success of the Roman Church has been due to its willingness to let the societies go as far as they would so long as they remained loyal to the Church itself. If a group of Romanists have at any time desired to be ascetics, the Church has favored them. If another group has sought to establish friendly relations with centers of financial strength, well and good. In relation to the Church of England, Wesley felt that it was worth while to have within that Church a society which could avoid asceticism, on the one hand, and too considerate regard for wealth on the other. Thus it was that he insisted on keeping the assignment of preachers in his own hand.

Wesley fought a battle for free speech, as an Englishman. It cannot be said that he allowed much freedom of speech within Methodism itself. He was altogether outspoken himself as to the perils of wealth, but it is doubtful if he would have allowed his preachers the same freedom that he took. Their work was soul-saving. He himself would do the speaking for the society when it came to the attitude of the society toward the problems of this world's goods. As to politics, the Methodists were free to speak on politics from the pulpit, if they praised the king.

Here, again, we must get back to Wesley's point of view. He had seen religious movements go to pieces when they became economic. The danger was not so much that such religio-economic movements would upset or do harm to the established order as that they would lead to wholesale attack upon themselves by privileged forces. If the Methodists had acted as did the peasants at the time of the Peasants' Revolt in Germany, they would probably have met a fate like that of the German peasants, though it is inconceivable that Wesley ever could have in such a crisis advocated ruthless killing of rebels as did Luther.

Here is as good a place as any to look at Wesley's Toryism, for Tory he was by his own profession. If we strike out of Toryism the power which money gives, we have robbed it of considerable of its evil. Wesley was a Tory in that he had been well born, that he had been reared in the home of a rector of the Church of England, that he had been educated at Oxford. He inherited the notion of authority as vested in superior character rather than in superior position. He may not have thought of *noblesse oblige,* but he certainly acted on the obligations implied in the phrase.

In his regard for the inherent dignity of humanity he was a democrat. It has been urged against him that he was not a republican. He was not. He had almost an abhorrence for the notion. Just who, however, would have expected him to be a republican? Here again we have to keep our dates in mind. During the years when Methodism was coming to its strength, there was no such thing as republicanism actually at work on any scale which led to favorable reflections at all decisive. England was not republican, and not even democratic. The House of Commons was too small, elected by too narrow a voting constituency to be representative of much more than the members who composed it. It is probably not wide of the mark to say that an orator like Pitt, Burke or Fox had, during the later days of Wesley's life, only to sway convincingly a group of two hundred and fifty members in the House of Commons to shape fatefully the destinies of England and the British Empire—a handful of persons easily to be brought within range of an orator speaking in conversational tones.   It was in Wesley's time that a notable continuance of the old battle over the personal authority of the king raged: George III making a stubborn fight to restore the power of the monarchy of the old days before Charles I. As we look back at the conflict now we assume that George made a perfect score in doing the wrong things.   Yet Wesley stood by him through thick and thin and with much reason, for George was honest and thoroughly patriotic.   He could not see how any country could desire a better king than George III.   Yet his fundamental feeling as to the artificiality of kingship shows in a sentence or two written in 1756.   He stood close when the king put on his robes, "a blanket of ermine around his shoulders, so heavy and cumbersome he can scarcely move under it, and a huge heap of bonny hair."

It is not necessary or wise to take seriously Wesley's views on popular rule.   The doctrine of exemplary man in a state before civilization, with civilization as an agency which bound men with chains—the doctrine of Rousseau, in a word—could not have been expected to mean anything to Wesley.   Wesley knew too much about men without civilization for that.   We have seen his opinion of the American Indians.   If Wesley had not gone to Georgia he, at one stage of his career, might have been captivated by Rousseau's pictures of man in his natural state.   Not, however, after the experiences in Georgia.

Wesley held that the people could not govern themselves at all.   He declared early in 1736 that "the majority of people are not the wisest or best part."   An aristocracy was better than popular rule, and a limited monarchy better than an aristocracy.   Remember, this was nearly two centuries ago.   The French Revolution had not yet arrived; the American republic was yet to come, and was not much of a republic when it did come.   The American State was for a generation or two an oligarchy.   There were limits in America beyond which the statesmen of the day could not go in dealing with the people, but that is true almost anywhere.   Wesley told one of his preachers that he must not do something or other.   "The people will not stand it," he said.   "They will not take that from you, and they will not take it from me."

Here, again, let us not hold Wesley to blame for what he was not trying to do.   He was not trying to train his followers in political method.   He was trying to spread scriptural holiness.

We get a little light here too by remembering that in those days of bad roads, or no roads, where in some places the roads were just the open commons, communities lived more to themselves than after the means of traveling had become better. If these little groups had got started to debating all sorts of problems, Wesley's main point would have been lost. The question here is not as to what Wesley ought to have striven for, but as to what he was striving for. He was seeking to develop a group of likeminded Christians. He himself was almost the only bond of union among the different societies. He did not care to see his purpose thwarted by republican experiments in a world in which there was practically no republicanism. The preachers were not to preach on political themes, except as they praised the king. All such utterances would come from Wesley himself. The formation of the Methodist societies did help on the democratic movement by training men to think and speak on social themes, but not in the Methodist preaching places.

It has been remarked, and that with considerable justice, that in dealing with historical and social questions Wesley judged almost entirely from the personal character of the leaders. It is not hard to believe that Wesley's admiration for George III was largely due to George's being a man of prayer, to that and the royal favor repeatedly shown the Methodists. Wesley never could appreciate the worth of Charles James Fox—Fox happened to be a gambler. That made it impossible for Wesley ever to realize that Fox was one of the most significant Parliamentary leaders, especially of a minority, that England has ever known. Diverse as were their spheres, it would be an interesting question—academic I admit—as to whether Wesley or Fox did the more for freedom of speech in the eighteenth century. For "that rascal Wilkes," Wesley had such wrath that he approved an outrageous denial of Wilkes's rights by the House of Commons. Wilkes's personal dissoluteness was too much for Wesley. The private evil more than overbalanced, in Wesley's mind, the public services Wilkes was rendering to democracy. Americans should not forget that Wilkes made one of the most forceful pro-American speeches ever made in the House of Commons. In 1770 Rousseau was to Wesley a "consummate coxcomb"; in 1773 David Hume was "the most insolent despiser of truth and virtue that has appeared in the world"; Jonathan Swift was "trash." Wesley had even a sneer for *Laputa,* one of the keenest bits of satire in English. So along the line. Wesley pronounced Machiavelli's *Prince* just about the wickedest book ever written; Machiavelli, "the first-born of hell." It would have been better, instead of taking out his righteous rage on Machiavelli, if Wesley had recognized and pointed out that the *Prince* was a formulation of the principles by which, in Wesley's time, kingdoms conducted their policies. The wickedness was in policies which kingdoms were actually following, just as they are doing in some respects today. Wesley took the book as a personal offense committed by a very bad man indeed.

Another character whom Wesley evidently abhorred was Tom Paine—this, again, because of Paine's religious utterances. This abhorrence was shared by thousands in England and America, and the feeling lasted more than half a century after Wesley's death. Yet Paine was, as we see him now, one of the benefactors of his day, fighting for liberty in America, England, and France. The oft-quoted reference, by the late Theodore Roosevelt, to Paine as "a dirty little atheist" has led to the equally oft-quoted reply that Paine was neither dirty, nor little, nor an atheist. Yet it is not enough to say what Paine was not. A survival of orthodoxy and Puritanism prevented Wesley from seeing the services of Paine. Even the deism of Paine was in its day a liberating influence.

Again, there was Wesley's hostility toward Voltaire. Voltaire's statement to one whose right to freedom of speech had been attacked that he would defend to the utmost the right to state such views, while he himself detested them, had quite an effect toward the same type of freedom for which Wesley was toiling. If Voltaire had lived in England during the days when mobs were trying to break up the Methodist meetings, he would have defended the Methodists. If Wesley had lived in France when Voltaire was being persecuted for his criticisms of the Roman Church, it is doubtful if Wesley would have forgotten the irregularities of Voltaire's private life long enough to have helped him in the battle for liberty.

I once heard a leading Methodist draw a contrast between the old age of Wesley and that of Voltaire. It appears that Voltaire, along toward the close of his life, was approaching Paris where he was to be given a public reception because of his continual battling against social abuses. As the coach halted at a customs post near the city, the revenue officer inquired, as he looked into the face of Voltaire, "Anything contraband in here?" To which Voltaire answered, "Nothing contraband in here except myself." The Methodist orator waxed eloquent over this as the utterance of a tired and wornout cynic in despairing disgust with life, and pictured the radiant hopefulness of Wesley at the same period of age. It is regrettable but true that this is the type of stuff that was supposed properly to honor Wesley a half century ago, and it is further regrettable that the contrast was somewhat appropriate to the temper of Wesley himself. The words of Voltaire were anything but cynical or despairing. They were intended to be witty, reminding the officer that he, Voltaire, was usually called contraband and expressing a joy of living and of preaching a defiant social righteousness quite as keen and full as that of Wesley.

It is surprising to see how far Wesley's admiration for a leader of blameless personal character would take him in a praise which simply would not see public faults. Wesley had no patience with Cromwell or his achievements. He declared that Charles I had been put to death because he had acted too much like a Christian. It will be noted that the death of Charles I was an event likely to arouse all the horror of one so regular in all his social attitudes as Wesley, and that Charles's way of meeting death would stir Wesley deeply. For there can be no doubt that, using the word "Christian" in its ordinary personal implications, the manner of the end of Charles was nobly Christian. The dignity, the self-control, the calm confidence that he was about to exchange a corruptible for an incorruptible crown, cast a genuine spiritual glory over his meeting the execution. It would be too much to expect to think that, in view of this Christian bearing, Wesley would not take the side of the king against Cromwell. We read in a book written a little later than the reign of Charles I the following:

"Then the King, turning to Dr. Juxon, said, 'I have a good cause and a gracious God on my side.' Dr. Juxon: 'There is but one stage more; this stage is turbulent and troublesome: it is a short one, but you may consider it will sure carry you a very great way, it will carry you from earth to heaven, and there you shall find a great deal of cordial joy and comfort.' King: 'I go from a corruptible to an incorruptible crown, where no disturbance can be.' Dr. Juxon: 'You are exchanged from a temporal to an eternal crown, a good exchange.' "

Another instance of Wesley's taking a prejudiced attitude was in relation to the American question. When the difficulties with the American colonies began, Wesley tried to make it clear to the English government that it would not do to wage war against the Americans. As days went by, however, Wesley took a distinctively Tory stand. In *A Calm Address to the American Colonies* he seconded Doctor Johnson in "Taxation No Tyranny" so strongly as to lay himself open to the charge of having borrowed from the Doctor

a little too freely; but Johnson himself approved Wesley's statement, paying Wesley the fulsome compliment that he, Johnson, was
satisfied to speak as long as Plato listened.   There is no way of making Wesley's course in this crisis anything but Tory.   To be sure,
it may be said that Wesley, like so many other religious leaders
before and since, was caught by the war fever, but that explanation
does not amount to much.   There were many in England who were
ardently on the side of the Americans.   Wesley was, if anything,
caught in a Tory fever, and gave way to expressions of fierce impatience.   Nevertheless, he had more right on his side than we
Americans are disposed to admit.   Taxation without representation had practically come to mean more to Americans than to the
English, who had very little to say about taxation.   The British
taxes asked of Americans amounted to almost nothing.   The Bos-
ton Tea Party was little else than vandalism.   George III was a
much stronger and better man and king than Americans ever have
admitted.   Wesley himself had to pay taxes without being represented in their assessment, and he could not see why the Americans
had to declaim against taxation without representation.   Which
shows how loosely Wesley got hold of the American idea that
Americans had become different from Englishmen, and how
thoroughly he had absorbed, probably all unconsciously to himself,
the view of the English ruling classes that the Americans were a
bumptious set of Englishmen to be taught to behave properly.   The
English view was mercantilism, a view in which colonies existed
wholly for the benefit of the mother country, though in 1776 he
referred to the merciless cruelty of the English despoilers of Hindu-
stan.   If Wesley had been asked if he were a mercantilist, he would
probably have avowed that he was not interested in names; but he
would probably have taken—indeed, did take—a position substantially like that of the government, at least after the Americans had
begun to fight.   In 1775 he wrote that he was in danger of losing his
love for the Americans because of their miserable leaders.   Again,
he showed that he could not think of the Americans as other than
sinners in need of repentance.   He could not endure the notion,
and especially the fact, of insubordination, though he himself, as we
have had occasion to see, always took it on himself to say how far he
would obey his superiors, the bishops.   He obeyed the bishops, in
so far as he thought they were godly, which usually meant in so far
as they approved the views of John Wesley.   No; Wesley's own
character, his training, his career, what he knew and what he did

not know, put him out of the class of Englishmen who could be
trusted to look upon the Americans with understanding. There
were Englishmen who could do this, but Wesley was not one of
them. The most that can be said is that, after the Americans had
won their independence, Wesley, like so many of his class, accepted
the accomplished fact, though calling it a strange fact. Even while
giving the Methodists their independence of Wesleyanism in England and bestowing his blessing on them as they went their way,
Wesley had to speak of their independence as brought about by a
strange providence. He adjusted himself to the American victory
without understanding it. He accepted misstatements of fact as to
the cause of the struggle. He wrote "a compassionate address to the
inhabitants of Ireland," in which he said that the army of "General Washington" was fast melting away. He gave as authority for
this that he had met some one from Philadelphia who had told him
so!

The question arises as to how well Wesley understood the currents toward a different England—socially and economically considered—beginning to flow in his time. The Industrial Revolution
was well on its way, though perhaps in an underground way, before
Wesley died. With that Revolution came, we all concede, a material improvement in England, at heavy social costs. Wesley notes
the beginning of improvement. He traveled his forty-five hundred
or five thousand miles a year and declared, after fifty years of travel,
that he knew England better than any other living man. Travelers
assure us that the best speed for traveling through a country, if one
wishes to learn a country, is three miles an hour, the rate of one
leisurely walking. Even though he traveled first on horseback and
later in a coach—"chaise" he called it—Wesley walked thousands of
miles—usually, twenty-five a day, twelve of which he spent in reading—and saw the life of the lowest classes in England at the closest
possible range. In his pastoral visits he went up into the attics and
down into the cellars to visit the poorer members of his societies.
The roads, he declared, were continually getting better, gravel
taking the place of earth trampled into mud. This was no doubt
true, but Wesley's tendency to disregard minor inconveniences
probably kept him from being the best of judges on such matters.
One of his complaints against his wife was that she would not put up
with the inconveniences of travel!
It is doubtful too if Wesley fully appreciated the bleakness of

the age, to speak in the phrase of the Hammonds. Wesley was so fed from within by the strength he needed and had such zest in life itself that he could appreciate the barrenness of the common life only in a scant degree. The long hours of work, the squalid conditions of living, the dearness of the necessities of life—these simply could not get hold of him as they got hold of the people who had to endure them. Wesley was a vital person, running over with life. As long as that stream was not thwarted or dammed up, his joy was complete, no matter what the inconveniences for the moment might be. Like others, he did not think much about some of the hardships, which, after all, come into men's lives without their taking much notice of them. We do not know that some phases of life are hardships till after we have experienced something better.

All I am trying to do is not to make the times too dark. When we hear of the long working hours in Wesley's day, we have to remember that the laborer of that day labored a good deal in spurts, working four or five days at terrible hours and then taking two or three days off. Nevertheless, the times were dark enough. There was admittedly an increase of material goods at the disposal of the working groups, in the later years of Wesley's life, but all such increase is at first an increase of distress. Old economic habits have to be broken up. There is friction and at times industrial warfare, when new machines displace old tools, especially the tools of handi-craftsmen. Food prices rise. In the long run there is gain, but a particular generation may not get much of a chance at the long run. It is not of exceeding comfort to one generation to tell it that, because of the changes, the next generation will have an easier lot. The question as to conditions here and now is most vital for each generation. English workers are indeed remarkable for the degree to which they take the future of their children into the account; but, after all, when workers are struggling for their daily bread, when they are worrying about the loss of their jobs, they are not more open than others to consideration about the good time coming. Wesley saw the workers at close range, but he did not get as far into their minds as one would have supposed.

At least three factors had to be at hand to make the Industrial Revolution a success, not that anyone deliberately planned to make a revolution. There had to be large sums of money for investment. As soon as the mills began to pay, the money was forthcoming. Some economists have thought that since the reign of Henry VIII there had been heaped up sums in England waiting for profitable investment, and the most conclusive evidence of this is that the money did come forth. A second factor—probably it ought to be called the first—was the application first of water power and then of steam power in factories, the machines being capable of relatively large-scale manufacture. This made mill centers on the banks of streams, displacing the former homework conditions in which the worker labored with his own tools, with his own hands, in his own home. Thirdly, the factory age was possible because workers were available to flock in increasing numbers to the new manufacturing centers, to work at machines which they did not themselves own, under conditions over which they did not have control. The germs of about all the labor troubles since were planted in those latter days of the eighteenth century.

Wesley saw the population movements quite distinctly and noted them in his *Journal*. In 1776 he declared that the population of England was greatly increasing. He saw also the new demand for foodstuffs created by the growth of population around the factories. He recognized the extent to which his followers were taking advantage of the new conditions and, by their industry and thrift, were "getting ahead." As we have had repeated occasion to remark, he regarded this as a peril to the Methodist society.

Methodism flourished most in the new industrial centers. It was in the new centers that men could take hold of a preaching and teaching ready to adjust itself to the new conditions. Agricultural conditions in England in the eighteenth century were desperately conservative, though in the latter half of the century measurably scientific methods brought about almost revolutionary improvement in agriculture. There was not much chance for a larger farm population than the land was supporting, let us say, at the middle of the century. The people in the villages settled down around the parish church and attended services or not, as they felt inclined. At the new industrial centers, however, there was stir and bustle, and the people responded to Methodism in part because it too was stir and bustle. After its fashion, the Industrial Revolution gave Methodism a chance. As a preacher of honest labor for wages, of industry and thrift, Wesley helped supply the Revolution with a quality of labor as important as the quantity.

As we look at the latter years of the eighteenth century when events were hastening on to the fulfillment of the Industrial Revolution, we have almost a feeling of awe or dread. The vastness of the forces at work begin to show themselves and the outlines of the coming events seem to be taking shape. England appeared to be settling itself around a new center, or at least around a center, for the England of the earlier centuries seems, economically speaking, not to be especially centralized. The agricultural conditions did not lend themselves readily to centralization. The farms were self-sufficient units without much immediate prospect of a raising of the standard of living. The enclosure proceedings had deprived many, many holders of small properties of their fields and had set them to roving about as landless wanderers. The rise of the big industrial centers was attracting these landless, and the surplus workers on the farms. There was the movement of new life, of a definite stamp. Goods were being made more to standard, markets were opening up overseas, ships were carrying larger cargoes.

This new life seems at first to have come along of itself, or to be the expression of forces beyond human control. The promise in some material inventions is at first so slight that only a few catch their significance. After careful reading of all of Wesley's *Journal* and *Letters,* I do not now recall any reference to the possibilities in steam power. There are comments on Benjamin Franklin's discoveries in electricity and some little experimentation with an electrical machine by Wesley himself, but this only with curative properties in mind. Till the close of the century, nobody seemed to realize the portentousness of the social changes that were almost at hand.

Of the larger social possibilities Wesley seems to have been as oblivious as anybody else. I say "seems" because Wesley must have observed much that he does not mention. The *Journal* is not the handbook of general information it is sometimes represented to be. It is full of close observation of what Wesley thought to lie along his own line; aside from that it is notably barren. For example, historians of the eighteenth century have a deal to say about the lawlessness of England in that century, especially in London and upon the highways. Wesley has almost nothing to say of this lawlessness except as it took the form of disturbing Methodist meetings. He did once remark that he had traveled the English roads "without interruption." If the plight was as bad as the historians declare—and likely it was—on that evening of May 24, 1738, as Wesley went to the meeting in Aldersgate at a little after eight at night, he was lucky in not being set upon by highway robbers, not that Wesley would have been diverted from his purpose by such assault. There must have been robbers all along the roads of England, but in traveling distances almost totaling, through his lifetime, the distance from the earth to the moon, Wesley did not see enough of them to make it worth his attention to mention them. No doubt the lawlessness was rife enough, but it apparently did not impress Wesley. Now, this is objective and presumably visible to the naked eye. The less visible characteristics of the time Wesley did not see, or did not care to discuss. One cannot help wondering where Wesley kept his eyes, when the Poor Law was operating as it was in his day. He probably felt that he was doing all that he could, when he sought to make Christian character or characters to meet the new day. Wesley held to the notion that, if we could get all men converted to God in an inner individual experience, all other difficulties—social, political, and all other problems—would offer no considerable obstacles. This hoary fallacy never met more complete demolition than in the relation of evangelical England to the Industrial Revolution. As hoary as the fallacy itself, is the old, old inability of the Church itself to take the disproof seriously.

The reason for all this is plain enough on a little inspection. Men acting in groups reveal tendencies that they may not show when acting as individuals separately. Let the mass of the workers of a country, who have been struggling along at a poor dying rate, find new doors open to them and they enter the doors with no thought of the social consequences to themselves or anyone else. That they do not longer work with tools of their own, but with machines that others own, that as individuals they do not especially count and that they would better do just as their fellows do, transforms them for the time into a herd, with the herd instincts, especially of self-preservation, controlling them. The employing classes, caught in a fiercely competitive scheme, are at a longer distance from their individual workmen than in the old days when they hired only five or ten, and act impersonally. They think now, not of men working for them, but of labor markets and "hands." This goes on from bad to worse.

In a way the social experience gained in the Methodist fellowship did have noteworthy results. Characteristically enough Wesley thought only of those affecting the specifically religious interests. He feared that the Methodists would become well to do and thus lose their religious zeal. Whether this was lost or not, it is clear that the increase of material wealth must have added to the total of human welfare. The Methodists, no doubt, had to meet a different type of temptation as they got along better in the world.

There is no doubt too that it is possible to exaggerate the rigors of working conditions in the industrial age. Men had worked long hours in the preindustrial age. Hardships of a particular time cannot always be judged by themselves. They have to be looked at in comparison with what went before. Men worked long hours before the Industrial Revolution was ever dreamed of. To be sure, they worked chiefly under their own direction, but it must have been a relief to some to have responsibility taken off their shoulders by mill conditions. It has always been the "English way" to leave workers to do as they please outside of working hours. There was not much time for themselves in the workers' lives in the eighteenth century, but what there was could be used as the workers thought best. It is a proof that the workers were not utterly exhausted by working conditions that they rose at five in the morning to attend the Wesleyan meetings. That was a regular and not an occasional hour. It would have been difficult to convince Wesley that there was hardship in any working conditions that got men out of bed at four or four-thirty in the morning, for he preached early rising as a religious duty for the good of one's soul. In Georgia he exercised by swimming at daybreak, according to his *Journal;* this, however, because it was cooler then and it was easier to keep out of the way of alligators at four or five in the morning!

It is probable too that the emphasis on the quality of the work when the worker labored by himself in his own home has been overdone. Sidney and Beatrice Webb have told us that work done at home always tended to bad conditions in the home. Of course a man's being away all day in a factory had its disadvantages, but his being at home, with almost everything about the house under the necessity of adjustment to his work, did not make the home attractive to him or to the other members of the family. Then all the talk about the artistic quality of products made when the worker controlled the whole process from start to finish must be heavily discounted. As to this, many of us need no other authority than our own recollections. The clothes made by the village tailors of the old days may have gratified the artistic impulses of the tailor, but did not add to the aesthetic delight of those who had to wear the clothes or of those who had to look at them. There was occasionally an artist among the workers, but only occasionally. The excellence of the products was usually in solidity, in lasting quali-

ties, which meant weight and coarseness. Anything fine like lace
was manufactured at extreme human cost.

No matter about any of this, though. The machines came to
stay. They have stayed and have brought all manner of social
changes with them. Religious organizations never anticipate such
changes. They seldom see the changes actually going forward before their eyes. They always lag behind while the first generation
of workers, under the changed conditions, pay the penalties. It
would seem, however, that Methodism could at least have had more
to say about the human values involved and wasted in those beginning years of the Industrial Revolution. The older historians used
to contrast the French and the Industrial Revolutions at the point
of their constructiveness, the palm being usually given to the Industrial Revolution as surpassing in construction, as against the
destruction wrought by the French Revolution. The French Revolution was out more in the open, where its guillotine horrors were
in view of the public. The horrors of the Industrial Revolution
were under cover, many of them underground.

Methodism, though its avowed adherents numbered only
about seventy-five thousand at the time of Wesley's death, ought to
have been powerful enough to have created a social atmosphere
which would have at least softened the horrors of the labors of
women and children—especially in the coal mines. We concede
that the slightest familiarity with the significant dates of English
history in the eighteenth century shows that the worst of these
horrors appeared after Wesley himself had passed from the earthly
scene, but our caution here does not quite face the issue. There
must have been a low estimate of the worth of women and children
—of human beings, indeed—in a society where such conditions were
possible. The Methodist leaders worked more intimately with
the laborers than did any other religious leaders. There ought to
have been something in their view of humanity which would have
made a difference from what actually came about. If it be urged
that the horrors of mill and mine conditions did not reach their
peak till after Wesley had gone, we are not much relieved, for the
tendencies were present from the outset. The use of women for
virtual draft animals to draw coal cars in mines would not have
been possible if there had been any genuinely sincere thought of
carrying out Wesley's estimate of the worth of either women or
children.

Forthwith, however, we have to admit that, as to children,

Wesley's own teaching must have been, if not to blame, at least a contributory force in the outrages by the industry of the time. Wesley put children on the same plane as adults, except in actual years of age. At the Kingswood School he made them get out of bed and go to work at five in the morning. It was there that he published that crazy notion that he who plays as a child will play as a man. He was blind to the need of the eighteenth-century man for more play. One of the wrongs perpetrated on the mature men of the time, as well as on the youth, by the enclosure of common lands was that the playing grounds for the English games were done away. It is a comfort to read that the Kingswood School boys had enough raw humanity left in them, in spite of Wesley, to get out of bounds and not only play but fight with the children of the miners, to Wesley's horror. We must not forget though, that in his later years Wesley looked at a group of children at play and had to admit that it was hard for him to believe that they were under divine wrath. One of the unfathomable mysteries in nineteen centuries of Christianity has been the attitude of Christians toward children. Perhaps it would be better to limit the remark to the centuries since the Reformation, for the old Church treated children better than did the Protestants. The Calvinists doomed children to hell by the millions by divine decree; the Protestants of the Industrial Revolution sent children into an actual hell on earth, or under it.

Recurring, for the moment, to Wesley, we note here again his teaching that children must always obey their parents, obey as long as the parents lived. It never seemed to dawn on Wesley that children are not in this world by their own choice, and that, therefore, the heaviest obligation on any generation is to the new generation which the older produces. In nothing has the presence of the Divine Spirit in human life been more manifest than in the sheer inability of the older generation, in a period like the eighteenth century, to stamp all impulse to progress to better things out of the younger.

It may be said that, in all periods like that of the Industrial Revolution, men are at the mercy of blind forces which it is not possible to control. This doctrine itself is one of the instruments by which at such times the more favored groups seek to keep the less favored in their place. In this utilization of a theory for practical purposes, the ruling classes in England of one hundred and fifty years ago showed consummate skill. I am thinking, for instance, of the purpose to which they put the teaching of Malthus about population. Thomas Malthus was a clergyman of the Church of England who, in the early days of the nineteenth century, announced a theory of population to the effect that, if left to themselves, all forms of animal life, man included, will increase until they press on the food supplies till something strikes a balance; that man increases in geometrical progression and food supplies in arithmetical progression; that when men become too numerous for the food supplies, war, famine, disease, infanticide cut down the numbers till mankind starts to progress again to a new adjustment. This theory has in its main outline stood the scientific discussions and attacks of at least a century and a quarter. The relation arithmetical and geometrical between the "progressions" has not been sustained, and in many details the law has been corrected and supplemented. Malthus did not mean that mankind is to be forever at the mercy of impersonal inevitabilities. He even insisted that, by late marriages and self-control, the numbers of mankind could be kept to the subsistence resources without being periodically invaded by horrible catastrophes.

Those making the most of the wealth-producing powers of the Industrial Revolution seized upon the Malthusian theory to maintain that men would produce offspring up to the limit of the food possibilities in any case and that, therefore, work for the lower classes at any wage was a mercy. If, now, the privileged class could use a theory like this, was Wesleyanism living up to its duty in not matching such a doctrine with something more humane? Bearing in mind always that the full force of the Industrial Revolution did not strike England till after the death of Wesley, was there not something that could have been set before Wesleyanism that would have sooner purged the Revolution at least of its worst horrors? If the dominant economic theory came to be a perverted Malthusianism, could there not have been an emphasis on loving one's neighbor as oneself that would have made at least some headway against the false doctrine? Or, conceding all the merit possible to Jeremy Bentham's "greatest good of the greatest number," was there no church group that could see that at one time the "greatest number" will ride the minority nearly to extinction, and, that worse still, the "least number" may tyrannize the "greatest number" into degradation?

The truth is that after Wesley, Methodism took an unforeseen direction. It is not worth while to ask if the Movement might not have better gone in another direction. The Movement released forces which had to run about as they did. With Wesley being as much of a Tory as he was, it probably was not to be expected that the Movement would remain a stirring of what we call, just for designation, the lower classes. As far as it was related to economic issues, the Movement was upward. One could probably find considerable evidence in the early history of Methodism to sustain the charge that in a class at all depressed there are lost fine talents, economic as well as other forms. The Industrial Revolution gave sphere for abilities that without it would have gone to cattle- and sheep-tending. Napoleon said of the French army after the French Revolution that the strength of the army lay in that the knapsack of any, or every, private soldier carried essentially a marshal's baton. With some allowance for rhetoric, it might likewise have been said that in the Industrial Revolution every worker carried somewhere about himself the possibility of rising to industrial captaincy. In fact, however, Napoleon regarded the French soldiers as so much cannon fodder; and, in fact also, the industrial leaders regarded the workers as so much stuff to be used up in labor for profits for the employers.

To a degree the principles for which Wesley stood, and those for which the Revolution stood, were alike individualistic. Wesley taught the worth of the individual soul, and the Revolution, the right of the individual to get what he could out of the industrial order. Methodism said that God is for every man; the Revolution declared, "Every man for himself, and the devil take the hindmost."

There was not much individualism for the ordinary worker, except that if he did not succeed, he was left to himself. Workers were looked at in the mass by the employers, but if they tried to act in the mass, they soon found out what employers as individuals could do. Adam Smith helped all this forward by his doctrine that an "invisible hand" guides all individualistic effort to the common good—another philosophy which employers as individuals used and degraded to the utmost.

The influence of Wesley may have counted in developing a group consciousness among the workers. Tory though he was, Wesley had much to say about the uselessness of those highly placed in the social scale. The English workers never have been much impressed by the nobility. They have been loyal to the king, but likewise loyal to their own groups—that is, after the Revolution revealed the limitations within which it must run, and showed that individualism was mostly for the employers. When the Labor Party came to power a few years ago, R. H. Tawney, in an article in the *Political Quarterly,* 1932, remarked as a Laborite that if one of the party had to be made a Lord for the good of the party, one should be drafted on the understanding that the choice was not to be regarded as an honor. This attitude comes down from the early days of the Industrial Revolution, and is far removed from that of the farm laborers dependent on landowners.

The Industrial Revolution benefited the classes which Methodism served. As Wesley feared, the qualities which made the converts good Methodists also fitted them snugly into the demands of the Revolution: industry, sobriety, honesty, thrift. Wesley died thinking that his followers had so well learned the lesson of benevolent giving that they could be trusted not to lose their spiritual power as they became well to do. The lesson of individual giving had indeed been pretty well learned; but the lesson of a larger social redemption, through the care of the masses of the less privileged groups, had not. The winning party in Methodism, in the years of social change in the first third of the nineteenth century, was on the side of conservatism and privilege. There is not much to the credit of Wesleyanism in the story of the Chartist struggles—of Wesleyanism, that is, as an ecclesiastical organization, especially that controlled by the Legal Hundred. The body called Primitive Methodists is entitled, according to the Webbs in the *Story of the Durham Miners,* to lasting honor.

Still, we must be careful not to try too strenuously to assess praise and blame. There had not been anything quite like the Industrial Revolution since time began. It meant the emergence of a titanic force, blind perhaps, but leading on, no one knew just whither. No one yet knew its final influence on civilization. Wordsworth sang of the French Revolution days, when to be alive at all was bliss and to be young was heaven. Anyone thinking of the new mastery of nature as typified by the Industrial Revolution might at first have felt a similar thrill. It was hard, however, to think of being young as like heaven after the guillotine got to working in Paris; and it was not calculated to give one a holy thrill after the Industrial Revolution got to making human beings old at twenty. If one is willing to enter a chamber of horrors for a little, let him read a summary of Sadler's Report as given in the *Life of*

Lord Shaftesbury, by the Hammonds. Joseph Hebergam, at the age of seven, was working as a spinner from five in the morning to eight at night, with a half hour off for lunch. He had become deformed after six months of such work. Samuel Coulson testified that his daughter, not yet eight years old, worked from three in the morning till ten at night. An overseer at Bradford testified that he had a list of two hundred families; that "all have deformed children," all of whom had been made crooked by the process of "piecening," which involved a "throwing up of the left shoulder and bending the right knee." Sadler's fight was fought in 1831, just about the date when Methodism ceased generally to follow Wesley's advice to "give all you can" for the help of needy causes, and began to give a tenth, or less. In face of this, with men like Macaulay, after the manner of their kind, professing sympathy with Sadler's aims and objecting to his concrete proposals, about all that Methodism could do was to praise the businessmen who tried to be a little better than most businessmen. It is to be regretted that those who trace the influences of Wesley after he was gone, as so powerful that it prevented the "procession of tumbrils" to places of execution in London, do not discuss the failure, or inability, or indifference of Methodism in the presence of the outrage upon child-life in England in the years almost immediately following Wesley's death. It is estimated that about twenty thousand persons were put to death in France during the French Revolution. How does it happen that floods of tears have been shed over these deaths in France, and so little grief shown over the lot of children during England's Revolution? There is altogether too much reason to believe that, in addition to the fact that the French Revolution was more dramatic and spectacular than the English, there was the other fact that the French victims came from a higher class than those of England to account for some of the tears shed over the victims of the guillotine.

One of the famous books in Methodist circles in England during the nineteenth century was *The Successful Merchant,* by William Arthur. Arthur was a recognized expositor among Methodists of the higher spiritual life. He wrote the *Tongue of Flame,* which was studied by successive generations of Methodist preachers for its teaching on the work of the Divine Spirit in the human heart. According to the biography—for *The Successful Merchant* is admittedly an actual biography—the hero made Christian principle bear, with marvelous effectiveness, on the problem of personal material success. The virtues which he stood for and exemplified were those of uprightness, honesty, industry, thrift, frugality. These virtues in the employed not only helped the employed along but the employer as well. The "Merchant" of the book was a benevolent despot. He would not tolerate any deviation from his rules; claimed to have the power by looking at a man to discern whether he was "straight" or not; was quick in discharging the unworthy. He looked upon those who pleased him with a kindly eye, gave them gifts, and won from them a subservient deference.

The significance of this "Successful Merchant" was not that the Methodist Movement produced a man of this type merely, but that he was the ideal businessman of the Methodist brotherhood. The book sold through a quarter of a century and ran into over forty editions, the last published as late as 1885.

This successful merchant came nearest of anybody in Methodist circles to adopting what is nowadays described as the doctrine of daily work as a calling. Max Weber, in Germany, and after him R. H. Tawney, in England, have taught that Calvin helped the building up of modern capitalism by making the pursuit of one's daily work the heeding of a divine calling, and by transforming the sacrifice necessary for worldly success into an asceticism secular, but sanctioned by the divine plan. The truth here is clear on a little reflection, as is also the overemphasis. Calvinism did not found capitalism. It may, however, be that in the idea of the "calling" we have a rationalization most acceptable to those anxious to make, at one and the same time, the best possible of two worlds—that which is and that which is to come. The capitalism of today did not take its start in a religious motive. Money-making assumes its forms in each generation without much regard to religious ideals. Most of the money-makers under the capitalistic system have never heard of a religious motive. The ordinary worker of the world, as soon as he is on his own, starts out to make a living in whatever lies best to hand, which is at all available to him. Those who religiously guide him may seek to a larger or lesser degree to make religion count in his daily work. The main drive is the pressure for daily bread; which is the drive of hunger; which is the drive for self-preservation. A leader like Calvin may seek to hold this drive in check, or to increase it, or to control it; but the drive is there, even if there are no Calvins about. This does not mean that the material forces are beyond human control, or that they are necessarily beyond religious control. They belong to that natural, which is first, and which is afterward to be made spiritual. This emphasis on the function of the "calling" in the development of capitalism has not received elaboration till within the last twenty-five years. Whatever importance the "calling" may have had must have been in the realm of adjustment and ease of mind, of the wealth-winner. It is fine to talk about making our work, worship; but much depends on what the work is and on the notion of worship. We cannot help noting that Wesley wrote, in 1778, "For riches, the Calvinists beat us altogether."

To get back to the "Successful Merchant." No matter whether Calvin introduced the idea of "calling" or not, this merchant is set before us and that by a religious leader of the Methodists, as finding God in daily work. The merchant seems to have had comfortable existence; and his life seems to teach that, if one will follow God in his daily business, God will bless him in that business. *The Successful Merchant* must have offered aid and comfort to many a Methodist mind, the mind of the Methodist whose career was taking the course Wesley had predicted: arriving at wealth because of the cultivation of the virtues that, on the whole, tended to yield a money return. Arthur's "Successful Merchant" was not a Calvinist, but he did illustrate Calvin's doctrine. He was one of the men to whom the business situation, which came about in connection with the Industrial Revolution, gave their chance. He would probably have succeeded if he had not been particularly interested in Calvinism, or Methodism, or any other religious belief; but he did make probably the best religious use possible of the conditions of the period and so is entitled to credit. He must not be judged too closely by the later standards when men sought to assess the good and ill of the Revolution as a whole. There were not enough Methodists who actually succeeded to make the experiences of the book typical. "Calling" is one thing to the employer and another to the employee. Yet the fact of the enormous circulation indicates that the "Merchant" was the ideal to whom thousands of Methodists looked.

We have no sooner said that Methodism was not especially influential in checking the abominations of the Industrial Revolution than we have to pull ourselves up with the reflection that we are dealing with Methodism as an organized group, and especially with Legal Hundred Methodism. The evils of the Revolution, of the more outrageous stamp, were attacked and put out of the way through the leadership of one man—Lord Shaftesbury, an evangelical of the strictest order.   Shaftesbury is the man who said that Seeley's *Ecce Homo* was the worst book ever vomited forth from hell, whereas the book is a classic statement of that Christian humanitarianism to which Shaftesbury devoted his life.   It was through Shaftesbury that factory children and chimney sweepers got any human chance.   The religion of Shaftesbury was the last word in intolerance.   He held it as a matter of life and death for Christianity to take literally the Genesis story of the creation of the world, the flood and Noah's ark.   He considered that secular education without definite Biblical instruction meant the undermining of the State.   He had no use for democracy.   Yet he was the instrument, so far as any one person could be, through which the savagery of the British industrial interests was tamed.   Shaftesbury was the incarnation, not of Wesleyanism, indeed, but of evangelicalism. He had in him traces of fanaticism which would have worried Wesley, yet he had a furious passion for human welfare which he shared with no other evangelical, Methodist or otherwise.   As we think of his terrible rage at the manufacturers, we wish that Wesley, who lived long enough to see what the manufacturers were to do to the child life of the poorer classes of England, might have shared the rage.   It might have been better if Shaftesbury had had some of the broader, kindlier outlook on life which Wesley possessed, but not if it had slowed him down.   It required decades after the death of Wesley to get into Parliamentary effect the evangelical estimate of the worth of man as man in the abolition of the gross wrongs brought about by the Industrial Revolution.

Lest we put too exclusive a burden upon the Industrial Revolution, as if it alone were responsible for the evils of childhood exploitation, let us glance at another horror which it required decade after decade of strained effort on Shaftesbury's part to do away with, namely, the employment of boys as chimney sweeps. The Hammonds point out that as early as 1773 the evils in chimney sweeping were denounced by a public-spirited leader in England. Wesley must have known about evils like this, but he does not say anything of them.   It was customary to send children of from four and a half or five years of age to seven years, through the chimneys to clear them of soot, the chimneys seldom being more than twelve inches in diameter.   The elbows and knees of the sweeper had to be hardened in brine.   The soot was terrible in the respiratory passages; the chimneys were often filled with smoke and now and

again were hot.   Occasionally a boy fell into the fire and was burned
to death.   It is estimated that when Shaftesbury began his fight on
this barbarity there were four thousand chimney sweeps in England.   There was something peculiarly diabolical in this abuse of
childhood which reveals the low regard for human values in the
social atmosphere in which Wesley worked.   When we turn away
disgusted from the accounts of the pupils' experiences at the Kingswood School, at the frightful regulations of the place, let us remember that Wesley's regard for child life was far above the ordinary
sentiment of the age.   In a period which saw little value in childhood, just on childhood's own account, Wesley did think of children as capable of spiritual salvation.   In that wretched story of
frenzied, nervous excitement at the school, which Wesley pronounced a glorious revival, Wesley was at least investing the lives
of the children with the same worth in the sight of God as those of
adults—and that was something, even though Wesley did not seem
to see much of chimney sweeps.

We pass to mention a few specific social evils to which Wesley
gave heed.   There was smuggling, of which Wesley had much to
say.   By the way, it is to be noted that in his efforts for social betterment Wesley always did best against offenses where the wrongs
were done by individuals acting as individuals and where the transgressions were of a rough order.   Historians have avowed that Wesleyanism was of definite benefit to Cornwall, some even going so far
as to say that Wesley helped purge Cornwall of the awful crime of
displaying false lights to ships at sea so as to wreck and plunder
them.   Wesley himself seems to think he did good in this direction.
There is not much evidence, however, that this wickedness was
actually going on in Wesley's time.   Very good men have maintained that, in speaking of such alleged wrecking which was really
plundering of ships already wrecked, Wesley unintentionally
helped propagate a cruel slander.   Cornwall, however, was rough
enough, and Wesley helped in its social salvation.

About smuggling: It is curious to observe that Wesley spoke
of smuggling as robbery of the king, as if it were a personal injury
to the king.   That would give the evil deed point in Wesley's
opinion.   Again, the goods were often gin and rum.   In a naïve
and human journal of the eighteenth century, Parson Woodforde,
a rector of the Church of England, records that he himself used
constantly smuggled spirituous liquor.   Indeed, he seems to have

had his own smuggler. Since the smugglers smuggled gin, that
would add to the heinousness of the evil in Wesley's view. He
forbade the Methodists to drin spirituous liquors, tolerating only
ales and wines. I mention sm gling at such length because it
shows Wesley's propensity to a ck evils without paying much
attention to the demand out of w h they arise. He would have
the smugglers cease smuggling, wh would, of course, have disposed of the evil; but he did not pa uch attention to that force
of demand which kept the industry ving. Smuggling was bad
enough, but was not as important as e other evils of Wesley's
day. It is not surprising to see him pa much attention to it,
but so much attention as compared with her evils. In a crime
like this, however, there was something t t Wesley's objective
and scientific mind could positively take ho of. A man was a
smuggler or he was not. He bought smuggled goods or he did not.

Wesley's attitude on slavery was consistent throughout. He
had from the outset of his public career called slavery the sum of all
villainies and American slavery the vilest under the sun. We are
fond of quoting his letter to Wilberforce, a noble letter indeed,
but written when Wesley was near the end of his life. Years before
Wesley had denounced slavery, that of England and especially that
of America. He wanted the system abolished by definite social action. On this problem, he was wholly on the right side, as were many
outstanding evangelicals of the time. I cannot forbear quoting here
verses from one whom the evangelicals are always pleased to honor
—William Cowper. Cowper had a distressingly melancholy history, with stretches of bright mental sunshine darkened at fearful
crises with half madness, perhaps madness outright. We think
of Cowper in his happier spiritual moments, writing as fine spiritual poetry as the evangelical movement knew:

> "For thou, within no walls confined,
>   Dost dwell with those of humble mind;
>   Such ever bring thee where they come,
>   And, going, take thee to their home."

This bespeaks a quiet, meditative mind, in tranquil communion
with the Divine. Here are verses of another order, which I quote
to show the presence of the same factors working in behalf of the
slave trade, as work in behalf of even the most monstrous evils
in all generations, the poem being long but perennially up to date.

"PITY FOR POOR AFRICANS"

"Video meliora proboque,
Deteriora sequor.

"I own I am shocked at the purchase of slaves,
And fear those who buy them and sell them are knaves;
What I hear of their hardships, their tortures, and groans,
Is almost enough to draw pity from stones.

"I pity them greatly, but I must be mum,
For how could we do without sugar and rum?
Especially sugar, so needful we see;
What, give up our desserts, our coffee and tea!

"Besides, if we do the French, Dutch, and Danes
Will heartily thank us, no doubt, for our pains;
If we do not buy the poor creatures, they will;
And tortures and groans will be multiplied still.

"A youngster at school, more sedate than the rest,
Had once his integrity put to the test;
His comrades had plotted an orchard to rob,
And asked him to go and assist in the job.

"He was shocked, sir, like you, and answered: 'Oh no!
What! rob our good neighbor? I pray you don't go!
Besides, the man's poor, his orchard's his bread;
Then think of his children, for they must be fed.'

" 'You speak very fine, and you look very grave,
But apples we want, and apples we'll have;
If you will go with us, you shall have a share,
If not, you shall have neither apple nor pear.'

"They spoke, and Tom pondered—'I see they will go;
Poor man! what a pity to injure him so!
Poor man! I would save him his fruit if I could,
But staying behind will do him no good.

" 'If the matter depended alone upon me,
His apples might hang till they dropped from the tree;
But since they will take them, I think I'll go too;
He will lose none by me, though I get a few.'

"His scruples thus silenced, Tom felt more at ease,
And went with his comrades the apples to seize;
He blamed and protested, but joined in the plan;
He shared in the plunder, but pitied the man."

Wesley, I repeat, was sound on his attitude toward slavery, sounder than Whitefield, for example. Wesley's mind was singularly free from illusions on questions like slavery. Perhaps one reason was that he did not allow himself to get tangled up in a material or financial way with the evils. Whitefield had the Georgia Orphanage to look after. He accepted slaves for the work there, and then added to the number by his own purchases. There is no record of Wesley's being compromised in any similar fashion. His followers in America became tied up with slavery to an extent which rendered American Methodism, both North and South, a poor, halting thing on the larger social issues for nearly a century. Francis Asbury was sure of the wickedness of slavery, but did not see what he could do about it, administratively. There did not appear to be any other way of developing the resources of the South than through slavery. When Thomas Coke traveled with Asbury through America he was critical, even impatient, of Asbury for a lenient acquiescence toward the buying and selling of human beings. It is impossible to say what attitude Wesley would have taken on the traffic in men, if he had accepted the invitation of the American Methodists to visit America in the years just after the Revolutionary War.

It is perhaps worth while to think of the straightness of Wesley's record on slavery, because slavery was capable of the most plausible arguments in its defense of any of the historic social evils. Of course there it stands in itself as the flat denial of the most fundamental of human ideals: the worth of a man as an end in himself. Look, however, at the arguments, with the caution always in mind that the present writer is not making a defense of slavery but is seeking to show reasoning which went in Wesley's day. This has more than historic or biographical relevancy. In essence it bears on the relation of Methodism and of Christianity, for that matter, to the spread of the kingdom of God in social contacts in all ages.

The first argument was that slavery was not to be taken as a thing in itself; that it was better than what it supplanted: the killing of prisoners in war. Just how that bore on the slavery of Wesley's day was never made evident. The argument changed into the form that slavery had been here as long as the mind of man could remember and that civilizations like that of England in the West Indies and of America in its Southern territories could not get on without it. It was pronounced an evil, but an inevitable evil. Las Casas, the apostle to the Indies, one of the noblest fighters for humanity the world has ever seen, encouraged the importation of slaves from Africa into Spanish America to save the Indians, who were being exterminated by slavery. In his last years Las Casas regretted and repented of this advice, but the repentance was altogether too late to undo the harm. Wesley met this argument by denying that conquerors ever had any right to kill prisoners taken in war; and by insisting, rather academically, that men are not to yield to evil, however inevitable it may seem.

The other effective argument was that Negro slavery gave the Negro a chance which he would not otherwise have had. This was, of course, a rationalization, but so sincere that it could not always be called such. Take the case of the Indians again. Nobody who reads the history of the conquest of Spanish America, can for an instant doubt that the conquerors were in part moved by a genuine desire to convert the Indians. Gold and souls made the double motive. Religion was more consciously present in the minds of the men of those days than now. One dubious result of the Protestant Reformation was that that Reformation brought about such a division between secular and sacred that men did not definitely think as much about religion afterward as before.

We read that old story about the peace of mind of the pious sea-captain Newton, as he sailed from Africa to America, with a cargo of Negroes captured to be sold as slaves. What a hypocrite he must have been! Not consciously. His experience of peace, of communion with the Divine may have been genuine. Men in all ages have done wrong ignorantly and in unbelief. There were thousands of slaveholders in the British colonies and in America who maintained that slavery gave the Negro his chance; that at least he was better off in slavery in America than in liberty in Africa. The defenders of slavery in the United States have always insisted that, comparing slavery with the conditions of the Negroes in Africa, slavery was an advantage to the Negro. On the material side it is yet to be proved that those who advance this argument are not right. Even with the white man in Africa, perpetrating today outrageous wrongs upon the Negroes through such institutions as forced labor, the white man will prevent killings by the witch doctors if he can. To be sure, there is merit in the native customs and institutions of peoples, but in these institutions the native peoples practice cruelties on one another. Within the memory of men now living the populations of African villages have been summoned by drumbeat to hear the sentence of doom passed upon a poor Negro by a witch doctor, to see his head cut from his body, the witnessing natives shouting hysterically as the head fell, the hysteria being that of the relief of every uncondemned native that the death decree had not fallen on himself. The slaveowners in the British colonies never did anything like that. They were not as bad as witch doctors. British control of slaves in Jamaica, for example, was just enough —if there can be justice under slavery—to lay a foundation of knowledge of what justice is, strong enough to make, when freedom came, a society of free Negroes which calls forth the admiration of all students of such problems. When Wesley was denouncing slavery, he was denouncing a situation in defense of which much could be said; and much was said. Moreover, in all such public problems men are inclined to be specialists. They are interested in one benefit to men rather than another. Wesley met this argument of good to the slave through slavery by condemning it as insincere. He would listen to none of it.

Now, I have drawn all this out at length to illustrate the directness of Wesley's moral insight when the violation of human rights was involved. Wesley heard all these proslavery arguments. He knew what Whitefield thought and did. He knew the practical considerations which made slavery seem so inevitable to so many. Yet to him slavery was the sum of villainies, and he said so. Moreover, he saw the denial of the higher rights involved in slavery. He knew American slavery, which he called the vilest under the sun, back in the days when the colonies were part of Great Britain. Yet, when he wrote to Wilberforce, he talked of such matters as the law's refusal to take the word of a slave as evidence in a court. This is to put the whole question on a high plane. In that letter Wesley referred to a tract on slavery, written by an ex-slave—and most excellent writing, if the present author is any judge. The book tells of the physical horror of slavery—and of much more. It is interesting to note that Wesley seized not upon horrors as the chief wrongs, but upon the denial of a slave's right to have his word taken as that of a man.

Another reason for stressing slavery at such length is that slavery, in one form or another, is perennial. It is one of the old foes with a new face in every generation. Peonage is virtual slavery. It is no longer possible to buy outright a human being from another human being, but it is possible to buy human beings from themselves, driving such terms with them for their labor that the man who has been forced to sell himself is not free. Of course a man's sale of his labor may be a glorious manifestation of an individual's right to dispose of his services as he sees fit; and to enter into co-operation with him who pays him. This is not the situation of which I speak, however. Much of the eloquence today in behalf of the freedom of the laborer to bargain means merely his right to take or leave what is offered him. If he acts by himself, there is but little chance for him for freedom worth having. To be free there must be fair remuneration, some leisure, some power of self-direction. It may be that the latter-day slave is not lashed by the whip of an overseer, but he may be virtually chained to the machine. All this is characteristic of modern industrial life, and all this is in direct line with the slavery which Wesley so openly and flatly denounced.

There is no freedom where one of the alternatives, from which a man is to choose, is heavily overweighted, so heavily overweighted that the other alternatives do not count. If the choice is between a particularly evil course and starvation, the choice is likely to swing to evil, and is not in itself to be called immoral. A hero may say that he will starve rather than to do wrong, but he does not leave an imitable example for the ordinary man. We have practically to assume that, if the choice is between life with evil and good with starvation, it will take the evil. The whole system under which men live has to be filled with that assumption of the worth of man as man, which Wesley declared in the attack on slavery. This, after the criticism of enclosure, was Wesley's boldest assault on a social evil of his time.

Wesley was opposed to the distilling of spirituous liquors. His rules forbade the use of such liquors, though the rules did not succeed in making the early Methodists into total abstainers. It is usually objected to Prohibitionists, using the term as referring to those who would do away with the use of alcoholic liquors as beverages, that their main moral effort seems to be interference with the personal habits of people other than themselves for the sake of the moral improvement of those persons. Wesley did not have any noticeable scruples against inquiring into the private affairs of his followers, but he did not put his objections to distilled liquors on the effect of liquor drinking on the character of the drinker. That aspect he urged on the drinkers indeed, but he objected to the distillation of liquor on broad social grounds, as that in one year of his lifetime England distilled eleven million gallons of spirits. Such distillation pushed the price of grain up so that it could not be used for food. Here, again, he had to meet those who sought the largest possible return for their grains. These were a perennial foe. Still we swing around here on the same old circle, or the circle which has proved itself new with every generation. If the demand of the drinker could be cut down, more grain could be used for food. So the personal interest in the reformation of drinkers applied after all. Yet the economists can smile all they please at Wesley's economics of the liquor traffic. The drink problem was one of most serious questions in the England of Wesley's day.

In this field we again run into Wesley's extremism. An extremist is seldom discriminating. It is always easier to be extreme than discriminating. Usually a reformer is a specialist. He thinks if he can get his one reform through, that his victory will carry everything else with it; or, if this does not happen, his measure is the most important anyhow. There are moral leaders though who develop the extremist habit of mind in everything. Wesley was firm and unyielding as to fiery liquors, but at one stage of his crusading interest he carried his passion against drink over into an opposition to tea drinking. He wrote a long tract against tea, useful as showing what he could do to make out a case on trivial grounds. One phase of progress in moral custom Wesley did not seem to master. He did not see that sometimes better customs take the place of worse; that an increase of tea drinking may mean the decrease of drinking something stronger. There was enough of the ascetic in Wesley to prejudice him against any victory over evil by substitution. He enjoyed his moral struggles. He would have rejoiced more in the struggle of a will in the agony of a terrible appetite than in victory won by the use of a substitute, however innocent. After Wesley had gone, England did, purposely or not, substitute beer for spirits. To read through the arguments of those days one would think one was listening to the speeches for the repeal of our Eighteenth Amendment. Nothing was said in those speeches that had not been said in England a hundred years before. In that day the greater use of beer left the social situation about as bad as ever.

A curious glimpse of the peculiarity of Wesley's mind can be seen in his feeling about suicide. He could not endure the thought of one's taking one's own life, and sought to prevent suicide by urging a law that would hang in chains the bodies of all those who killed themselves. This was a strange twist of thinking. Just what difference it would make to a suicide to have his body exposed in chains after his death does not appear. Hardly anything more futile could have been suggested. Moreover, it is significant of a queer callousness prevalent in the times. The only conceivable deterrent in such cases would have been the notion of public disgrace. What can be said, however, of the effect of such spectacles on the public? Probably the truth is that Wesley, like most others of his time, had become used to such horrible spectacles. If this be so, it is a fearful commentary on the finer feelings in England in the eighteenth century.

We have looked at several of the specific measures and attitudes through which the influence of Wesley worked to make England better socially. Perhaps, when all is said, this influence cannot be measured or estimated. We are dealing with those imponderable forces which go to making social atmosphere. Imponderables come out of all sorts of general conditions—sometimes out of what may be called the general working together, or focusing, of powers which may not seem to bear directly upon a given problem.

As we now look back at Wesley's day, we see that his life worked, all unconsciously to himself, to fit into a situation hastening toward three of the greatest revolutions of our modern age: the French, the American, and the Industrial. Each of these was the outcome of factors that had been working through generations. In addition to these there were the political and ecclesiastical changes in England itself which, after the "glorious Revolution of 1688," cleared the path for Protestantism. The religious indifference in which Wesley began his work was really a prophecy of something better than the strict control for which the old Church had always stood. We hear much about the cool rationalism of the eighteenth century. Some of it was just the mind of the age coming to its own power, taking advantage of a freedom which refused to be hurried into anything which did not have the sanction of the mind itself. Through long processes in England there had been a gain in intellectual and moral freedom. It has been said that one reason why there was no French Revolution in England was because the middle class in England already had enough of what the middle classes in France were striving for to deprive a revolution of the French type of decisive appeal. The French Revolution in a degree brought the bourgeoisie as a social force out into view. Neither the English Revolution of 1688, nor the French Revolution a century later, was proletarian in any strict meaning. Both Revolutions meant that both the English and French Revolutions had put a new spirit into the mind of the middle classes. The American Revolution meant that the English civilization was, in a manner, getting a new start free from some of the useless baggage it had to carry in England. It was a revelation to England itself, and to the world, of what English ideas could do when stripped of their nonessentials, or when stripped of features which did not seem essential anywhere but in England. When thus stripped, they helped develop an Americanism quite un-English. Puritanism in the Church and the political relief in England from Catholicism, had set the world toward a genuinely new individual and social life. It remained for the American Revolution to show what this type could mean both for good and ill where it had a chance on a frontier free from those class divisions that amounted almost to caste, and where it gave a man opportunity to see and show what he could do on his own. Nothing could be more significant in its way than the horrified surprise of the English, even of the type of John Wesley, when America began to "talk up" to England as she did. In 1789 Wesley wrote that Asbury "refused flatly to accept Mr. Richard Whatcoat in the character I sent him. He told George Shadford: 'Mr. Wesley and I are like Caesar and Pompey. He will bear no equal and I will have no superior.' " On the political and, speaking generally, the social side, Wesley had taken the Americans as inferiors. His utterances after the war broke out had revealed this all too clearly. In England this revelation of independence by English colonists brought a new something into the atmosphere. It is the custom of some who talk of unity among nations to deplore the American Revolution as breaking a unity which by our day might have given the world the greatest manifestation of social and political oneness that mankind has ever seen. When we realize the unconscious and involuntary attitude of men like Wesley toward the Americans though, we find it easy to adjust ourselves to American independence. The dwellers at the central nation of an empire have always found it hard to think of the dwellers in colonial territories as equal to themselves. So far as we can see, it would have been a calamity for the Methodists in America to have remained in any measure subordinate to the English. They had ceased to be English. American political independence also did much for England. It was through the attitude of the American leaders that an idea dear to Wesley, the necessity of an actually ruling monarchy, received some of its stiffest blows. Let us not forget, however, that after pouring out the vials of his wrath on America, Wesley made his adjustment to American independence, especially as concerns Methodists, within a year after peace was signed between England and America; and called the separation providential, though strangely so.

Of the Industrial Revolution, we have spoken enough, but a sort of line brings us back to it. Methodism reached down into the classes that the Revolution was to touch as workers. It made over some of the lower classes by helping them to take advantage of the chance to rise, materially speaking, in the world. It was probably too acquiescent in the face of the evils. Here we have to be very careful. Thinkers like Harold J. Laski insist that Wesleyanism hindered the advance of the workers by making them too acquiescent. Probably it was just as well that the ideas of the worth of men for which the whole evangelical movement stood had time to take deep root in the mind of the workers before the actual battle for better conditions began. This is speaking generally. Nothing can excuse the savagery of the earlier factory owners, or of the later ones. Nevertheless, part of the fullness of the time to which Wesley attained was that his teaching as to the worth of men to themselves and to one another and to God had been going forward long enough to impress the public mind, or to make possible the creation of a sentiment which Shaftesbury could use for human rights in the factories. Moreover, the difficulties of Shaftesbury's fight reveal, as not much else can, the desperate state of that England in which Wesley had wrought: the willingness of masses of men to work under inhuman conditions; the low regard in which the women and children were held in industry, together with what was conceived of as the absolute necessity of the services of women and children; the slowness, even the deadness, of the social interest of the ruling classes in England—I refer especially to Parliament— in giving heed to human values. It is the old story of the paralyzing power of desire for gain over the more humane instincts—one of the manifestations of this power being the unwillingness of those in control of an industry to set themselves seriously to the task of working out improvements. The Wesleyan Movement is an illustration of the time it requires, or did require, for a new consciousness of human worth to find expression in actual industrial changes. Sometimes the consciousness simply does not connect itself with the economic realm at all, either in the purpose of employers or employed. Men are prone to take things as they find them and to adjust themselves to actual situations.

Here was the service rendered by the trade-unions, which, however, did not begin to make themselves thoroughly felt till fully half a century after Wesley had gone. They were not only instruments of power in action but of the communication of feeling. I do not mean to be frivolous when I say that they roused workers to the consciousness of hardship and injustice. It used to be said that the workers would have been all right if the unions had left them alone; that they were not conscious that they were having a hard time till the unions told them so. No greater praise could be given the unions of those days than just this: that they roused workers to a consciousness of their own needs. Here, again, may have been at work a force that was generated, or whose possibilities were revealed by, the Methodist meetings.

If I seem chary of giving unstinted praise to the preaching of the Methodists as lending that dignity to men's attitude toward themselves which finally found expression in better laws as to working conditions, may I say that I am not stinting the praise, but that I am trying to indicate the length of time it takes for such realization to get to work in the world where men are busy with earning their daily bread. Wesley did not see, perhaps did not think of, the economic implications of his teaching as to the worth of a man's soul. Probably he would have opposed trade-unions if they had begun to show force in his day. Shaftesbury hated them. Most probably Wesley would have seen in them rivals to his societies. Moreover, Wesley was so much of an autocrat himself that he would not have had much sympathy for the limitation of autocracy in industry. All forward movements depend for their final success on what we today are fond of calling "implementation." An actual method, or technique, must be found to carry out the moral insight into legal or other practical expression. When the proposals for such implementation become serious, the opposition becomes serious, not to say furious. We cannot blame the leader of a movement for not being himself able to suggest means of implementation. There is, however, something wrong if there is not vitality enough in the movement to keep up an insistent and persistent demand for the actual working out of the change.

Before we leave this theme of Wesley and his century we look at the criticism of men like G. D. H. Cole, who insist that, allowing as we must for the greatness of Wesley's work, his influence on the mind of the classes among whom he worked was not always of the best. Cole seems to imply that Wesley allowed his followers to hold fast to ideas which were socially harmful.

It is difficult to deal with this criticism because of the complexity of Wesley's own character. There is a temptation, as we look at Wesley's sharp statements of religious duty, to think of his power as arising from a straightforward directness—until we see that the simplicity lay only in one direction. We have here something of the difficulty we have when we read Wesley's avowal that he was a man of one book, the Bible. We know today what Wesley meant, but in the mind of the readers to whom the remark was first addressed it called for explanation. So Wesley appears at times so clear and logical and direct that he seems a child of the eighteenth century itself, abhorring anything without a sharp edge. Even in studying the influence of the divine on the human, he is as careful and systematic as a thoroughgoing rationalist. He contemplates ecstatic states as a scientist would. Yet we no sooner say this than we have to think of belated superstitions which he was among the last to give up, superstitions which lingered among the minds of the lower classes especially, and which he ought to have denounced or ought to at least have been in a position to denounce. For example, there was witchcraft. Trevelyan, in his *Age of Queen Anne,* has remarked that in England the deliverance of the lower classes from witchcraft was a gift of the higher classes to the lower. The respect of the lower classes for the higher was so deep that, when the humbler people saw what they called their "betters" casting witchcraft aside, with something like amused scorn, they too began to let go the belief. If this is true, Wesley was remiss in his leadership of his followers. It is easy to smile at Wesley's notions of witchcraft as a whim, but the fault is too serious for that. It was in Wesley's own lifetime that hanging for alleged witchcraft was done away. The belief in witchcraft might have done immense harm if, at a moment of crisis or public excitement over some queer old woman, Wesley had come out with one of his dogmatic statements of belief in witchcraft. On matters of this kind he was dogmatic. It was only in his latest years that he said that he had become less certain of almost everything as time had gone by. In 1768 he had not given up the belief in witchcraft. When Wesley became dogmatic he was stubborn. The only reason he had for accepting witchcraft was that, if he did not, he felt he would have to give up the Bible. He did not feel quite thus when he was denouncing Calvinists who claimed to have the Bible on their side. What he then said was practically that, if the Bible meant Calvinism, so much the worse for the Bible. Wesley could be firm in most unpleasant fashion when he was exercising his will-to-believe, especially when he had nothing but the will-to-believe. We cannot blame critics who suspect that, in all this standing for popular superstition, Wesley was perhaps unconsciously to himself keeping hold of that popular fear which he knew how to arouse for religious purposes. If this seems harsh, we feel justified in reminding our readers that, in that morbidly frenzied excitement among the Kingswood School boys which Wesley pronounced a work of divine grace, he permitted the taking of the boys to see a corpse in order to increase their terror. In all of this dark side of his mind probably Wesley was sincere enough, but that does not relieve the notions of their character as a social menace. It is only fair to say of Wesley that he held fast to such superstitions as beliefs in witches and ghosts long after other leaders of intelligence had given them up; and, when he had to face something of mild ridicule for his support of such things, Wesley would not stand it to hear the famous noises in the Epworth Rectory spoken of skeptically. As already remarked, Wesley was not at home during the disturbances by "Old Jeffery," yet he was the most partisan defender of the supernatural character of the disturbances. It is hard to resist the impression of mild amusement at Wesley's acceptance of the genuineness of spirit appearance which both Johnson and Boswell give us in one of their references to Wesley. Johnson gave to Boswell a letter of introduction to Wesley, that he (Boswell) might get from Wesley the grounds for belief in a ghost reported to have appeared at Newcastle-upon-Tyne. Boswell got a very polite reception but no satisfactory evidence about the ghost.

Looking over the whole eighteenth-century drama, we see now that Wesley was himself a giant walking among giants. Whether there is or not something in the social atmosphere of particular eras which calls forth clusters of geniuses the world around, the historic fact remains that the geniuses do come in clusters, and did in the eighteenth century. We think of Goethe and Kant in Germany; of all the actors in the French Revolution, beginning with Rousseau and ending with Napoleon; of George

Washington and the founders of the American republic, to say nothing of the Pitts, of Burke and Fox; of James Watt, of Swift and Addison and Pope, as all contemporaries of Wesley. It would be folly to try to compare these characters with one another as to the quality of their lives. For sheer continuous putting forth of energy, however, especially when we reckon years of activity, Wesley stands at the head. Moreover, he lodged in his teaching a carrying power which sent it pretty well over all parts of the world where the English had gone or were soon to go. For one effect of the Industrial Revolution was to provide a world-wide increase of England's foreign trade. Cheaper goods in the end meant larger markets. The nineteenth century saw the beginning of the making of ships that could carry immense cargoes. All this meant the expansion of world trade. Where trade went the Methodists went. In dealing with historic characters we usually speak as if they foresaw what was to come in the days ahead and give them credit for that vision. They are entitled to the credit, but not for the vision. Wesley did not foresee such a wide spread of Methodism. It was only in his last years that he or anyone else got any glimpse of what was at all likely to happen in America, for example. The credit is his for being ready to enter any open door without necessarily being able to see what was beyond the door. More than that, if the door did not open easily, he pushed it open. The old jibe against him was that he was like a man rowing a boat—that he never saw anything until he had passed it. To which the answer is that this is the way men row boats, and the way leaders travel to revolutionary changes. They know that they are on a navigable stream and that they are moving; but all they can see unmistakably is in the past. Leadership in any crisis is more an indescribable feeling of direction than an open vision. It is an awareness that the right road is in one quarter rather than in another. Leaders cannot at the moment of choice tell why they take one path rather than another. When they try to tell, they cannot always give the reasons.

It has been noted that Wesleyanism in the main followed the course leading to the Industrial Revolution. The most responsive centers to Methodism were industrial. We might almost say that the Revolution created a new class in England, and all over the world, for that matter wherever the Revolution reached. Wesleyanism chiefly served what may be designated as the lower middle and the lower classes. At least, this is the judgment of careful historians, though Overton, most sympathetic of all Church of England students to Wesleyanism, may be slightly influenced by the consciousness of what in England cannot help thinking of itself as a superior class. The English workers came to the factories off the farms and out of the lower groups of the cities. They came without tools and would not have been skilled enough to use tools if they had had them. They had to tend machines which they could not themselves expect to own; to adjust their activities to the machines through an incredibly long day; to become almost slaves to their employers and to the machines. With some this lot, unspeakable as it was, was better than the life they had left. Anyone who has paid any attention to the Parliamentary debates made necessary by Shaftesbury's agitation is aware that the millowners retorted with force upon the reformers that working conditions on the farms, including the estates of Shaftesbury's own family, were no better than in the mill towns. However this may be, the proletarian class came to be not merely by influx from the farms and cities, but by increased birth rate in the class itself. It seems terrible to say so, but in that class children were an economic asset, though one shudders at what this meant for the children. Wesleyanism was adapted to the degree of religious receptiveness of this class. Its manner of evangelism had in it enough of what Davenport has called the primitive traits to wake a response in souls that had never had a chance to rise much above the primitive; though the extreme features of nervous uproar had mostly ceased at the Methodist meetings, before the larger industrial changes set in.

Looking at the social effects of Methodism in the large, we sum up by saying that the effect on the industrial situation was threefold. First, it ministered to the hard lot of the workers, helping them discover themselves, by lifting them above the sordidness of their condition and opening to them doors to a higher spiritual world. After the more cruel features of the Revolution had been done away, or at least softened, multitudes of Methodists settled down into the industrial condition and became measurably content, though without much chance to get a surplus which would enable them to give their children a better start in the world than their parents had known.

Second, it fulfilled Wesley's prediction as to the outcome of the thrift and frugality and industry encouraged by the Wesleyan ideal and helped some workers to industrial leadership, which usually landed them in conservatism. Adam Smith was, after 1776, preaching individualism with might and main and was being interpreted to mean that government should not interfere in economic processes at all; and Malthus was soon to be held up, mistakenly indeed, as the prophet of pessimism to the poor who had to increase in number up to the last attained pound of food, and of optimism to the employers who worked the poor to the last penny of profits they could make from them. Many Methodists got into the class of the successful merchant or industrial leader.

The third effect was in arousing minds of the Shaftesbury type to the wrongs possible and actual under the new industrial order, though Shaftesbury would have to be accredited to the evangelical temper as a whole rather than to the Methodist branch. Shaftesbury is the outstanding refutation of the old easygoing notion that, if a religious group will but preach the truth, the evil will disappear of itself. There is sound judgment here, if this refers to the creation of a general social atmosphere in which evils find it hard to thrive. Evils, however, once established are put away only as some one puts them away. Suppose Shaftesbury had himself heeded the doctrine that the gospel itself causes evils to disappear "of themselves." The world would have lost Shaftesbury, and the workers would have suffered on till some hater of industrial evil arose with a different theory and a more sensitive conscience and a more militant will than this easy notion of the gospel provides.

The century after Wesley brought out to the full light not the contradictions but the differences that for long existed side by side in the Wesleyan implications. In the nineteenth century Methodism split into three branches: the main body, with its nucleus the "Legal Hundred," tending socially to a stolid conservatism, professing to be impartial between progressive and conservative but leaning to conservative; the others moving to a democracy of an extreme type. In the social struggles centering around Chartism, Legal-Hundred Methodism did not acquit itself with any especial credit, though individual members wrought valiantly.

There have always been Methodists, themselves interested in social advance, who have felt that Methodism as an organization should keep out of the social warfare, especially out of politics, its pulpit limiting itself to the proclamation of gospel ideals and leaving to other agencies, and to individuals, the grappling with specific

and detailed situations.   This attitude is in itself sound enough,
except that it is suspiciously welcome to the privileged classes.
Moreover, a Church as an organization has in itself a possibility
of what may be called collective or corporate prophecy, owing
to the fact that the body, which we may loosely call a social organism, can attain to an insight as its members work together which
they may not attain as separate individuals.   This advice to Methodists to abstain from social discussions, especially from political
debates, is today fruitless.   The Methodists indeed do not often
enough show themselves, in the mass, as advocating social advances
which would bring larger social opportunity to men, preferring
to range themselves on the side of causes which would limit the
possibilities of the individuals going wrong in personal vices such
as the drink and gambling habits.   It would be a hardship, however,
to Methodist bodies to ask them to refrain from expressing opinion
in politics, as the term is ordinarily used.

Jabez Bunting was the outstanding leader of Methodism after
John Wesley, with all Wesley's autocratic spirit and without his
range of interests and graces of character.   If Bunting, however, had
desired to defend his indifference, if not hostility, to democratic
processes he could have said that he was but following in Wesley's
footsteps.

Wesley never said or did anything undemocratic, in violating
or ignoring the interests and welfare of the people.   He knew that
his society, if it was to be worth while at all, must keep close to the
popular needs.   In studying the fundamental good of the masses
Wesley was democratic.   It may be objected that he was too democratic in giving so much weight to the significance of what I have
already referred to as the "primitive traits" in men in times of
religious excitement.   Whatever power he sought for and kept for
himself, he sought and kept with the welfare of his followers in
mind.   Even though in state affairs he was a monarchist, he thought
of and honored Parliament as the embodiment of the popular will.
He never stated his theory of monarchy consistently.

He was sure he knew what was best both for the preachers and
for the people.   To use the oft-quoted word of his, he admitted
that Methodism was a despotism, but he saw no harm in that as
long as he was the despot.   Some apologists for Wesley have sought
to make out that the class of people from whom the Methodists
were drawn were not able to govern themselves.   A defender of the
American Methodist Episcopal system has told us that that system

got its start and took unshakable hold because the American Methodists like to be governed. In England Wesley was really heeding the people in not surrendering his power because they preferred having an authority tell them what to do, somewhat, I suppose, as Roman Catholics are said to want a pope to govern them. On this supposition Wesley surely cannot be regarded as having taught much self-government to his people in fifty years of control over them. One test of leadership is the leader's ability to train his people to get along without his guidance. In the local societies the Methodists gained that skill, because Wesley was away on incessant journeys. The training in those small units was what counted, for Methodism and for the political and industrial democracy of the nineteenth century, though there are not many indications that Wesley gave much time to the consideration of such training and what would come out of it. It is said that the strength of Methodism was in the class meeting. The strength of Chartist Clubs and of trade-unions was in the appropriation of the class meeting as a tool of a democracy that reached that ordinary man in whose power to rule Wesley did not have much confidence. It is, however, quite a tribute to Wesley that he was at last willing to leave his authority to the Legal Hundred, of course on the understanding that he was to select the hundred.

It is usually assumed that, when men become deeply religious, especially with an inner experience, their relations with their fellows are peace and concord. It has not been so in Methodism, though the Methodist Movement has held together singularly well. Wesley stamped something upon the soul of his followers that gave them a loyalty to their society at the same time that it left open the possibilities of disagreement. It has amusing features—this picture of a society preaching perfect love and yet bristling with differences that do not suggest such love at all. Here, again, we have to reflect that we are dealing with a social organism thoroughly alive. We may wonder a little that Wesley did not see more clearly that for perfect individual experience we need a perfect environment. Wesley would, no doubt, have met an objection like this with the avowal that the most important environment for human beings is other human beings, and that in our struggles to make other human beings better we ourselves travel along the path to perfection. The sound and not so sound in this position are alike obvious.

Before we leave this section, we enter an expression of deep gratitude at Wesley's freedom from anything like place-seeking. This may seem to the reader like a strange remark. Why should Wesley have sought place? Well, place-seeking was an ugly fact in the life of hosts upon hosts of the English clergy in Wesley's day. The rector called on all of his friends, and pulled all of the wires within reach, and put himself under obligation to bishops and squires and court officials to get a parish better than the one he might have. The custom was universal. Of course this obligation to those who made possible the advancement of a rector, tied that rector's tongue against any socially prophetic speech, and is to this day measurably to blame for the notion that the preacher is to let social themes alone. We may say that Wesley did not want a parish—and, of course, he did not—but in an age when it was the natural custom for priests of the Church of England to seek for favors, he sought none. We read with pain and shock of the persistency with which so sincere and honest a priest of the Church of England as Jonathan Swift—and Swift was sincere and honestly devoted to the Church of England, whatever else he may have been—sought for place in the Church. There is not a thing suggestive of any of this in Wesley's *Letters* or *Journal*. His father wrote a letter in a perfectly legitimate way, when the Fellowship of Lincoln College was open, and that was all. If Wesley ever asked anything at the hands of those who had favors to bestow, there is no trace of the request.

From this point of view Macaulay's comparison of Wesley to Richelieu is not fortunate. Richelieu, no matter what the aims, always worked by appeal to desire for place, for his followers and himself. He moved upon men from a knowledge of their weak spots. Wesley did not seek for himself, and he appealed to them from the angle of the highest and best in them.

Wesley has been blamed for not encouraging his followers to see the importance of trade-union channels. This blaming a leader for not following some other course than the one he took, and for not aiming at some other goal than he did, is among the most futile of historical procedures. The Hammonds, of course, concede that religion can exert much influence in the cultural life of any society. They have done something to make vivid to us the state of the English Church at the time of Wesley. They admit that, with noble exceptions here and there, that Church was doing incredibly little. Now, would the Hammonds themselves judge that Wesley, reared and trained as he was, would have done better to abandon religious effort and throw himself into something like the trade-union effort? Strictly speaking, there was not any such effort in his lifetime. From the tendency in the Church of England when Wesley came to the front, it could have been judged that by the end of the century there would have been no religious culture in the country whatever, if the country had only the English Church on which to depend. There probably never has been a time since the beginning of the Church when the question was more definitely whether there was to be any future for Christian religion at all or not than that when Wesley began his work.

As to that emphasis on otherworldliness of which the Hammonds complain: that was somewhat due to reaction. The Church of England was paying enough attention to this present world. It was not considered in good form in that Church to speak of any other world than this. Wesley preached an otherworldliness that arrived at an effect here and now. Without any question the Hammonds believe in other worlds, other kingdoms than those of the daily round of the livelihood—the kingdoms of truth and beauty, for example. Wesley's preaching of the good was quite as important for laborers, for the fullness of their lives, as anything else that could be brought within their reach. All of which we have elaborated in earlier sections of this book.

It may be as well to remind those who complain about Wesley's draining off resources that should have ultimately gone to the labor-union movement, that perhaps there was a middle ground between the English Church culture, and the religionless culture that England would have had, if the industrial population had been left to trade-unionism. It was substantially the middle way that Wesley found—a religious idealism and practice that frankly faced the tragic in human life, that saw and proclaimed the surpassing dignity of men in an age when anybody who had any power over men forgot that those whom he was controlling were men. There is another reason for the success of Wesley besides his power to draw men away from the feeling that they were an exploited class, something besides an unworthy indifference among Methodists to the sufferings of their fellows. Dealing with the laboring classes in such fashion as to describe them in two groups—those with a vision of the possibilities before themselves and their fellows, if they would but stand together in union, and those lured by the excitement of the Wesleyan Revival into visions of the other world into which they were to come, preferably by sudden, almost catastrophic conversion—is much too simple. I think it is the Hammonds themselves who have said that the Wesleyan preaching drew with especial power upon the coal miners who worked alone and in peril, with tragedy always imminent. It is possible that the Wesleyan preaching was meeting a need of the miners that membership in a labor organization might not touch. Is it not significant that from the beginning of trade-unionism Methodists have been among the most forceful trade-unionists?

What I started to say was that the Christianity preached by Wesley came finally to make a middle way between the formal deadness of the Established Church and the lack of emphasis on religion in the labor movements of the time. As we look at the experience of some of the more favored Englishmen—in the nineteenth century, highly endowed and trained—who gave up all religious belief because of their disgust with the Church, we cannot help feeling that the laborers were more fortunate than they. Of course these more favored rebels against the Church would not have been at home in the Wesleyan preaching places but, if they had only known it, they could have found there something of what they needed.

The Hammonds speak as if the wilder emotional outbursts were characteristic of Methodism all through the period when trade-unionism was coming to its power. By the time that movement was at all well developed the Methodist Revival had become very orderly indeed. It does not make much difference as to the degree of emotional intensity with which a movement starts. It has to settle into regular channels if it is to continue to count with social effectiveness. Wesley himself seemed satisfied with the progress his societies were making in the later years of his life. There was probably not more excitement in the Methodist meetings of the last decade of the eighteenth century than in the meetings of labor groups.

It is almost impossible to come to a satisfactory judgment in dealing with a problem like that now before us. Looking back after all the years we see that what measure of actual deliverance from intolerable conditions the laboring men won they won chiefly by their own efforts. The Hammonds are right in classing the Methodist organization as such among the conservative forces in the early labor struggles; Methodism did not make an enviable record in those strenuous beginning days. It is not fair, though, to hold Wesley himself responsible for all the shortcomings of the institution which he left behind him. He was naturally conservative—never gave himself to a new method till he had to. Trade-unionism had not gone far enough in Wesley's day to be intelligible to a mind like his. He was a surpassing organizer himself, but he did not have much place for any organization except his own. Inasmuch as we are now treating of the continuing influence of Wesleyanism, we must admit that, so far as alignment went, Methodism for the half century following Wesley's death was on the side hostile or indifferent to labor. This is true, however, chiefly of the organization based on the Legal Hundred. It is not true of what was known as Primitive Methodism.

All such judgments must be set in the context of the times. The historian gives credit to the Evangelical Movement for the enthusiasm of certain outstanding leaders for humanitarian enterprises. If one is tempted to suppose that Methodist leaders were alone in standing aloof from the organized efforts of the laboring men themselves, one should read some passages from the lips of evangelicals, who have been regarded as great friends of humanity, in the later days of the eighteenth and the earlier days of the nineteenth centuries. There was Hannah More, intent on the salvation of the souls of the poor, but so filled with class consciousness that it is a wonder that any self-respecting human being of any class but her own would listen to her for ten minutes. She was strong for the piety that made for devotion to the established order. Shaftesbury was far and away the ablest and sincerest friend the laboring group had, but he looked on trade-unions with detestation. Hammond has written a biography of Shaftesbury—and a noble biography it is—but, if Hammond is to condemn Wesley and his followers for drawing off strength from the organized effort of laborers to help themselves, why not condemn Shaftesbury for efforts so exclusively legislative?

Students like the Hammonds are willing to concede that those who gave themselves to the Wesleyan meetings got something besides the direct teachings of the Wesleyans. In their later writings the Hammonds make generous concessions to what came of Wesleyanism. Methodists got skill in conducting meetings and in addressing them. Moreover, Wesley always laid stress on the need of reading. Many of the Methodists learned to read from their fellow Methodists, especially from the leaders of the societies. Now once put the power to read within reach of a mind and there is no putting limits on what the reader may read, though Wesley tried hard enough to set such limits.

We have already remarked on these by-products of association in the Methodist societies—important by-products, and by-products are never to be despised. There are times when they are much more important than the main products.

It would be scant honor to the Wesleyan Movement, however, to limit its social significance to the by-products. The most powerful single force in directly curbing the inhumanities of the Industrial Revolution was Shaftesbury, and Shaftesbury thought of his power as arising from his evangelical experience. It would be interesting to see an attempt to fit Shaftesbury into the religious system of the English Church as it was before the Evangelical Revival aroused it, involving, as that system did, the least possible reference to God and to a righteousness beyond the merely proper and conventional morality. Shaftesbury believed thoroughly in the Christianity of the Evangelical Movement. It was not any by-product which aroused his deep interest in the distresses of factory workers and chimney sweeps, but the Christian view of God and man.

So also with Wesleyanism. The founder had a sense of perspective. What Wesley taught was the worth of a man in the eyes of God. The man might be corrupt and degraded but he had an immeasurable value. Of course there are those who always miss the manward reference in Christianity and speak as if anything which has to do with man at all, rather than with God, is not inherently Christian; but there are Christians who know the teaching and example of Christ. In that teaching half of the all-inclusive commandment has to do with the neighbor. Who is the neighbor? The man who happens to be at hand, whoever he may be. Anyone who misses this may be religious, but not after the Christian manner.

When men talk of the by-products of Christianity, they may have something in mind which is not by-product at all but direct resultant. For example, a particular church may speak glibly about the brotherhood of man and make scant attempt to act upon that brotherhood. A casual attendant upon its service, however, may get a vision, or at least a glimpse of what brotherhood implies and go forth to set it to work. That is not by-product but direct effect. There are today powerful leaders outside the Church who got their basic conceptions inside the Church, or at least from the Church. Their quarrel has been with the Church as an organization. Now, in Wesley's day his followers kept close to the main highways. They got these essentials to the attention of men. They gave the fundamentals of the gospel a chance at classes who had never heard of the gospel.

Professor L. T. Hobhouse, in an article on Christianity in the *Encyclopedia of the Social Sciences,* has held that there is no system which has given nobler expression to the worth of man than has Christianity, when that statement is stripped of the theological terminology in which Hobhouse himself had little or no interest. Hobhouse seems to mean too that it does not rob Christianity's expression of its force to charge that organized Christianity itself has not lived up to its own teachings about mankind, for Christianity is a religion of ideas and spirit; that, whatever its own shortcomings, its handling of its ideas at all, gets them into men's minds.   The criticism of Christianity in history has not been so much with its ideals as with its practices. The treasure has been carried, sometimes kept, in an altogether earthen vessel. What Wesley did was to make real to thousands upon thousands of men the Christian belief in God and man.   His influence is not confined to those who were his professed followers, or to the incidental by-products of his organization, but reaches outward also to those who have sought to carry the idea of God and man into relations which the Church has ignored.

As I have already said, Lord Acton seemed to regard Wesley as one of the most significant figures in the history of the Church since the Reformation.   Acton wrote a standard work on the *History of Freedom.*   Now, Acton was too sincere, too devout, for anyone to make him appear anything but Christian.   Yet during the American Civil War he was against the North because he supported human slavery.   He believed also in social classes and in the inferiority, if not the subjection, of the lower classes to their "betters." There is not any method of satisfactorily explaining such personal phenomena.   We may remark in passing that half the American Methodists, without ceasing their loyalty to Wesley, broke away from the other half because of the difference about slavery.   When a leader announces a conception or a policy, there is no telling what those who call themselves by his name in the after years will do with what the leader bequeathed to them.   As long as the master is at hand the practical implications of his teaching may not be drawn; but after he is gone what seems like an inherent and inevitable logic tends to work itself out.   One camp of followers may say that this is what our leader meant; that if he were living now in our places, this is what he would do; and another camp may take exactly an opposite view.   It would be a great mistake to imagine that Christianity is at any one period the final interpreter of what it is handing down to the oncoming generations. It sometimes serves merely by passing an idea along, without having itself any adequate notion of its meaning. Take the conception of God. The transmission of the conception itself has been an incalculable service, though the interpretation of a particular time may have no lasting value after that time has passed. So with the doctrine of man. Wesley left an idea of the Christian man's life capable of indefinite expansion. It has been said that the glory of man himself is that he is capable of being indefinitely improved. Likewise, it is the glory of the idea of man that it can be indefinitely expanded.

Here again we fall afoul of the Hammonds. I mention them so often because they are undeniably important for the study of the eighteenth century, and because they do see shortcomings of the Wesleyan Movement which are real enough to demand the attention of anyone trying to understand Methodism. The Hammonds speak as if the convert to Methodism entered by his experience, no matter how intense that experience might be, into a narrow world. The same criticism continues to the present day in the judgment that Wesleyanism has been a restricting and confining agency, giving a new lease of life to a Puritanism which ought to have been allowed to fall into atrophy, and that it has encouraged a foolish asceticism.

There is not a little validity in this charge. Wesley did encourage an insistence upon trifles as a mark and test of Christian character. Some of this insistence, if Wesley had made it merely a rule for his own life, would have been regarded as only a personal idiosyncrasy, a peculiarity more than offset by his own wholehearted absorption in his tasks. He did, however, encourage his followers to courses which seemed to him like worthy self-denial, but which tended to loss by them of a wholesome perspective. Wesley sought to make abstinence from all games a sign of righteousness, though he did except card-playing on the frankly affirmed reason that his mother played cards—a refreshing bit of information which makes Susanna Wesley more human than any other single little stroke, and which gives us some slight feeling of satisfaction that any light relief was available in the dreadfully heavy tasks of the Wesley household. Wesley's condemnation, however, extended to all feminine adornment, including ribbons.

This all had a serious side for Wesleyanism. It was of no consequence that Wesley gave himself to little odds and ends of self-denying exactness. This was not a trial to him anyhow, for he enjoyed this treatment of himself, which was never serious enough to distract him from a central purpose which demanded the last ounce of his strength. Not so, however, with scores of his followers, who needed anything rather than to have a narrowing influence set at work in their lives. Wesley was traveling from end to end of England. It would have been a psychological miracle if his own mind had become narrow, but the Methodists' lives were narrow to start with. Under wrong examples they narrowed fast, demanding of themselves conduct which concerned itself with items always smaller and ever smaller. This is a danger the more real, the more sincere the person involved, for the sincere conscience keeps asking itself if it has carried righteousness as far as it could. "Have I done all I can?" is a maddening question, likely to get a good honest soul into direst confusion. One tendency with the Wesleyan Revival was to permit the attention to get away from, or not to see, the wide social duties, and to fasten itself on insignificant pettinesses. There is no need of trying to explain this away. It was a tendency in Methodism which, first and last, did much harm.

Perhaps an explanation of all this is that such questions were not so likely to be divisive, as some of a larger order. Wesley resembled most leaders at one point—he did not like trouble which would make divisions among his followers. He entered into controversy with extreme reluctance, refusing even to get into the Calvinistic battle until he had to. There is chance enough to land in controversy over questions having to do with the inner experiences, but they are not so divisive—except in debates over so-called perfection—as the more objective issues of social life. In the actual direction which Methodism took in its emphasis on problems affecting the personal life, we must admit that it tended to a narrowing result.

At the risk of appearing over apologetic, may we insist again that judgment here should take account of the times in which Methodism arose. The social questions lay outside the reach of the ordinary intelligence. If Wesley had been asked why he did not call the attention of his followers to social problems which ought to have filled all the horizon of the public mind, he might have replied that he had never thought of doing so. One of the immense surprises in reading his life are the vast stretches of useless or evil custom which he did not seem to notice. We are dealing here with the futile question to which I have so often referred: why did not this outstanding historic character do something other than what he did? There were many evils in Wesley's day, especially at the beginning of his career, which he did not see or which appeared as chiefly personal, the task being to turn individuals away from them: the grossness of the sports, such as bullbaiting and cockfighting; gambling and drunkenness. Every historian of the period concedes the seriousness of the situation created by what can only be called popular bestiality. Wesley appears to have encouraged the experience which would, preferably by sudden crisis, break out of this life into another. So when the Hammonds refer to the intensity of the Methodist experience of conversion, and concede its worth, but declare that the experience was narrowing, the criticism has to be balanced by the remembrance of the conditions out of which the converts were "narrowed," a point on which the Hammonds and the Methodists do not agree. How "narrowing" is it to pass out of drunkenness into sobriety?

Again, assuming that the Methodists did have much to say about a world other than this, what was there "narrowing" about such speech? Underneath all the crudeness of the utterances about heaven—and they were crude enough—such discussions supplied material in two directions: they brought dignity into the meaning of human life and they quickened the imagination. This last contribution of the Methodist Revival has not received its fair share of recognition. Granted that the imaginative deliverances of the early Methodist preachers were fantastic and grotesque, they did, nevertheless, open a door into an imaginative realm which ministered vitally to worthy human cravings. The imaginative scene-painting of the early Methodists was not so raw as much present-day fiction and poetry which are pronounced powerful works of imagination. It is odd that this should have taken place under the leadership of as practical a mind as Wesley, but take place it did.

As an extreme instance of the degree to which imaginative power can be developed in an illiterate mind, may I recall to the memory of some of my readers the sermons of John Jasper, a noted Negro preacher of a half century and more ago. "Brother Jasper," as he was called, was famous for his proof that the sun moves. The proof was laconic and direct enough: "There he is in the morning and there he is in the afternoon." Yet Jasper, on the imaginative side, was little short of genius. Some of his word pictures, as of the Egyptian plagues, had an emotional appeal beyond description. Or, if we wish to look at something nearer our own times, think of the scenes and sentences of surpassing beauty in the play, *Green Pastures.*

It may be objected that the illustrations are not relevant because the Negro race is singularly rich in imaginative vigor; nevertheless, the Negro's imagination came to flower under preaching very similar to that of the early Methodists. To be sure, the old-fashioned Methodist oratory is out of the mode now. There are many of us still living, however, who can remember the flights of genuine eloquence of preachers who in turn got their inspiration from those who had actually worked under Wesley.

Moreover, it will not do to talk as if all the narrowness of the eighteenth century came from Methodists. Almost everything that called itself breadth was then tied up with an easy and complacent attitude toward life which pronounced it bad taste to look tragedy squarely in the face. There is also good ground for believing that much of this talk about Methodist narrowness came out of a class consciousness. The possessing groups in England, whose instinct in such matters can be taken as a reasonably certain index to the truth, regarded the Methodists as potential if not actual disturbers of things as they were. Upper-class arrogance had more than a little to do with spreading the opinion in England that the Methodists were a narrow-minded, indeed, an evil-minded, lot—an opinion which, in the same circles, has here and there persisted to the present hour. The continuance of such opinions long after the conditions that originally produced them have ceased, is one of the curious and neglected puzzles in human history. Just glance over the following bit from Horace Walpole, written after Wesley had come to a nationwide fame.

Whitefield, A Rogue.

To the Rev. William Cole,
Strawberry Hill, April 16, 1768.

. . . I hope the Methodist, your neighbor, does not, like his patriarch, Whitefield, encourage the people to forge, murder, etc., in order to have the benefit of being converted at the gallows. That arch-rogue preached lately a funeral sermon on one Gibson, hanged for forgery, and told his audience, that he could assure them Gibson was now in heaven, and that another fellow, executed at the same time, had the happiness of touching Gibson's coat as he was turned off. As little as you and I agree about a hundred years ago, I don't desire a reign of fanatics. Oxford has begun with these rascals and I hope Cambridge will wake. I don't mean that I would have them persecuted, which is what they wish; but I would have the clergy fight them and ridicule them. Adieu, dear Sir.

Yours ever.

No wonder that Wesley said in 1764, "I do not desire any intercourse with any person of quality in England."

Once more it must be remembered that Wesley held that the Methodists formed a society and not a Church. This accounts for much that is otherwise unintelligible. There were some phases of Christian service which he was not thinking of at all. He was the head of a society which men could take or leave as they pleased. He could ask them to leave if he did not like their deeds or their words or their lives. They too could leave if they did not like him. The organization had been created for the specific purpose of spreading scriptural holiness throughout the land, and for that alone. Other tasks came along necessarily, but apart from the main purpose. The massing of the opinion of the society against grave social evils might have seemed to Wesley a more serious obligation, if he had been founding a Church. No, he was in his own mind set to found a society to cleanse the Church, and the nation indeed, but to do so by spreading scriptural holiness throughout the land.

Wesley definitely declared that he was not attempting even to give his followers a full religious service. As late as 1789, he published in the famous *Minutes:* "But some may say: 'Our own service is public worship.' Yes; but not such as supersedes the Church service: it presupposes public prayer like the sermons at the University. If it were designed to be instead of the Church service, it would be essentially defective. For it seldom has the four grand parts of public prayer; deprecation, petition, intercession, and thanksgiving."

The above is an expression of Wesley's attitude throughout his career. If Methodism was to be taken as a Church, then its work was narrowing at least to the extent of taking a part as if it were a whole.

The question as to whether Wesleyanism was narrowing or not takes a somewhat different shape as we look at Wesley himself. He was broad in his charitable attitude toward the opinions of other men, broad in the range of his reading, and in his thinking. He is to be blamed, however, for not allowing his followers to see more of his own breadth. Much of it they could have seen for themselves: his wide knowledge of history and of what science there was. He read where he pleased, but he does not seem to have encouraged his followers to do the same. There was that chronic hankering to supervise the lives of those whom he thought of as committed to him. One can imagine what he would have said if he had found one of his preachers reading Shakespeare and making notes upon the plays. Yet he did this himself, though his references to the "heathenish" poet are few. In a letter in 1769 he spoke of Simple Master Shallow. That was the first Shakespearean reference in thirteen years. In 1756 he had alluded to Goneril and Regan in *Lear*.

The truth seems to be that Wesley, like so many men who fashion rules for other men's conduct, asked his followers to give themselves to rules which meant little to himself. Think of this, written five years before his death: "We cannot allow a baker to remain in our society if he sells bread on the Sabbath day. But if he only bakes pies, we do not exclude him." I wonder if the reason was that to taste best a pie must be eaten on the day it is cooked. He never seemed to realize how full his own life was. He found an absorbed delight in complete service to his cause. He thought of nothing else. He went from one society to another, preaching possibly ten times or more a week. When he left a society, he did not leave a group living as full lives as himself, but persons who had to go back to the humdrum and drudgery of daily work. To use the current psychological term: he was himself finding abundant means for "expressing" himself. He rode his four thousand or forty-five hundred miles a year from one end of England to the other. There was no need of talking as if this were hardship to him, for he enjoyed it. Now, when a man like this begins to declaim against the little things in other people's lives which could not possibly mean anything to him, he cannot escape the charge of acting, at least in these respects, as a narrowing force. What did "personal adornments" mean to Wesley? It was to be noted, however, that he took most scrupulous care of his personal appearance, which was altogether to the good. A man who was thus scrupulous, however, would have done better not to say so much about ribbons and ruffles as signs of sin. He was himself living a life of supreme happiness in leading the Methodists—partly because he was leading.

Perhaps we shall have to come back to praise Wesley for leaving behind him an emphasis for which both he and his followers have been blamed, or at least discounted, namely, the stress on the quantitative spread of the kingdom of God, the attempt to reach vast numbers.

It is only recently that adequate regard has been paid to the popularizer of knowledge. Democracy means government by discussion, discussion by masses of people. If the discussion is to be of any value, it must be based on sound knowledge. The sound knowledge is at least at the outset the discovery of individuals. Agassiz once said that the easiest scientific statement to make is that to scientists; the next hardest that to the laity; the hardest of all, that to children. One of the present-day movements which promise most for the welfare of democracy is the attempt to bring scientific knowledge down to the ordinary understanding. If democracy is to endure, it must be on the basis of knowing the facts; and if the people are to know the facts, they must be able to grasp the facts, which means that the facts must be put in graspable form. One of the achievements of our time has been the skill with which the results of science have been put within the reach of the plain man of the street, and shop, and field. A degree of success has been won even in popularizing mathematics. So it has been also in the appreciation of all forms of art. I repeat that this is at last coming to recognition. For a long time the higher forms of knowledge and art were supposed to be almost the sacred reserved possession of the privileged groups.

John Wesley as a popularizer of knowledge I have already discussed. It remains to add a word about his making religion a possession of the English people. This is implied in his oft-quoted plan: to spread scriptural holiness through the land.

John Wesley had a distinctively and specifically religious task to perform every day and all the day. He gave all his time to such service. Speaking of marriage, he declared that he would not think of marrying if doing so meant traveling one mile less or preaching a single sermon fewer during the year. Now, this notion itself puts Wesley's experience outside the normal. When the pursuit of perfection is stated in such terms that it involves living all the day with a conscious religious purpose, then one of two things becomes necessary. The life must be wholly given to specific religious tasks or the daily secular work must be such that it can all be done as unto the Lord, which implies an approach to perfection in the nature of the work itself. Now, the daily work of mankind has never been of this order, unless it has been of a simple farm type, or a field which has called forth the constant opposition and attack of the Christians. Daily work has not often been conceived of thus. Men have taken it as something to which to adjust themselves as best they might. To reach any numerous groups of followers under such conditions it has been necessary so to phrase and enforce religion as to make it readily intelligible and sternly arresting. This Wesley succeeded to an extraordinary degree in doing. He kept his own preaching and that of his preachers close to a center, with not much chance for deviation. As we read his *Journal* and *Letters*, we feel as if we were almost in the presence of one of the impersonal natural forces, in the days before man appeared on the earth, which kept the unfolding forms close to type and crowded out any departure from that mold. Holding up the religious experience which was characteristic of Methodism, Wesley made the experience of seekers tend toward that typical form.

It is fortunate that the scientific method has been used so fruitfully in these recent years upon the social influence of Wesley. There was general recognition of the larger influence of Wesley by the older historians like Macaulay and John Richard Green for a long time, but there has been of recent years most important work done by Miss MacArthur on the economic ethics of Wesley, by Eric M. North on early Methodist philanthropy, by Maldwyn Edwards on Wesley and the eighteenth century, by W. J. Warner on Wesley and the Industrial Revolution, and by E. R. Taylor on Methodism in politics. These authors have all worked more closely and realistically than the earlier writers, and with even deeper sympathy.

Considerable effort has been expended to show the significance of Wesley for the literary life of the latter half of the eighteenth century. Probably as important a service as any rendered in this field was to increase the size of the reading public, by making the less favored groups readers of good books, and by making the books cheap enough for their financial reach. As to the Wesley style, its simplicity, directness, and force were communicable. At least fifty of Wesley's preachers were masters of terse and idiomatic English. Yet in this rather technical sphere of style the English of the eighteenth century was the creation and tool of more than a few giants—Swift, Defoe, Richardson, Fielding, and Burke. For some of these Wesley did not seem to have any enthusiastic appreciation.

What does seem clear is that the Wesley emphasis on spiritual realities played its part in the movement of the latter eighteenth and earlier nineteenth century toward romanticism. Romanticism is proverbially hard to define. We usually attempt to describe it, or we say that we know it when we see it. Whatever our definition, we know that it deals more with the human than with the impersonal, with the idealistic than with what we vaguely call the realistic, with the imaginative rather than with the matter of fact. John Wesley was profoundly interested in human values, but he was not the only great writer of his century thus interested. Gray's "Elegy" dealt with a plowman, and Goldsmith, who was rather contemptuous of Methodism, spoke of the times in which wealth accumulated and men decayed. Wesley's thinking was personal but also institutional, realistic as well as spiritual, administrative as well as absorbed in the inner life, more deeply and highly ethical than most of the romanticists. Nevertheless it is fair to count Wesley among those vital, enkindling, enlightening forces which so changed the atmosphere of his time as to make it hospitable to Wordsworth and Burns and Dickens, when they came. It is absurd to say that these romanticist geniuses would not have come at all if it had not been for Wesley, but without Wesley they might not have come so soon, or have wrought so powerfully for the release of the higher human possibilities.

PART X

THROUGH SIXTY YEARS—AND BEYOND

"To most great men it is given to do their work in a comparatively short time. By noon or afternoon they are done and gone. Wesley lived through the morning, through the noon hours, through afternoon and evening and far into the night."—CHARLES EDWARD JEFFERSON.

PART X

THROUGH SIXTY YEARS—AND BEYOND

ONE of the most notable features of Wesley's career was that it lasted so long. If we are dealing, not with poets or seers who in a flash can open to us new worlds, but with administrative length of service, time itself counts mightily and may become in itself an overwhelming fact. To select an illustration, slight in itself: Wesley kept a daily account of his money expenditures from the first day he had anything of which to keep account until within just a few years of his death. Here are a set of account books kept by a single hand, the accounts running through seventy years. Or think of the time through which the *Journal* was kept. Dip into the *Journal* anywhere and the first impression is not especially arresting. There is a record of duties done, sermons preached, groups met, books read, miles traveled, letters written, and prayers offered. Look merely at a few entries and we find a straightforward English style, sound practical sense, deep devotion. Read on, however, through the eight large volumes, and see always the same unceasing doing of these daily tasks until finally the effect becomes massive. This goes on day in and day out, week in and week out, month in and month out, year in and year out, till we find ourselves in wonder and amazement, asking if this uniformly marching procession of deeds is never to stop or slow down.

It has been urged against the *Journal* that it was written for publication and that, therefore, Wesley always had his readers in mind. As late as 1781 he wrote: "In Georgia I wrote three journals. Afterward I extracted one from them all, for the use chiefly of the children of God, omitting abundance of things which I judged would not profit them." It is also charged that he did not lay bare his heart in his *Journal* as those have done who were communing with themselves in their diaries. There is a degree of truth here of which we may find occasion to speak again, but that truth has to be qualified by the length of years through which the entries took place. In entries running through half a century a writer could not help revealing himself; he could not keep much back through so long a stretch. The *Journal* had to be written through all ups-and-downs of moods and of feeling. No matter how

313

much reserve Wesley might have had by native temperament, he could not have helped revealing himself through so many decades. He could not have kept everything back. We cannot but conclude that something of everything in the man would have come out. Through so many years every trait of character would have been manifest whether the writer intended it so or not. It would be self-evidently impossible for any diarist to act a part through so long—and acting a part was not at all in harmony with the Wesley nature. Even Wesley's critics would grant that any such course would have for Wesley been out of the question. By the way, how few charges against Wesley made in his time have endured! There is a slur or two in Walpole about Wesley's hoping to get some favor from Lord Dartmouth, a Methodist; and in the first years of his preaching Wesley felt it necessary to write to the Bishop of London denying malicious reports about Wesley's alleged personal immoralities. None of this mud would stick, however. His *Journal* was his most confidential companion. He could not for a lifetime have kept secrets from that. One student, not unfriendly, has remarked that in the *Journal* Wesley's soul was on parade, by which he meant that his soul was dressed up for public exhibition. It is better for men, at least occasionally, to speak of Wesley in this fashion than in that of absolute adoration; but such comment overlooks the time through which the entries were made: through the larger part of the eighteenth century. That is too long for a parade.

In this realization of the extraordinary stretch of Wesley's life, we get the best testimony to his religious experience. How pathetic it is to see students of the highest Christian attainments searching through Wesley for single statements about distinctive spiritual climaxes! It will be recalled that Wesley never claimed to have himself reached what he called "Christian perfection." Psychologists and theologians have perused the *Journal* line by line to find some single statement on which they could themselves base a claim for such an experience for him. Some have fancied they have found, not a claim, but a proof in a passage here or there. Meantime the total stupendous record is there of an experience more important than any single crisis could ever be: decade after decade filled with no other thoughts than those of labor for the beloved societies.

The danger with any devotion to an ideal is not of some excruciating moral disaster which wrecks faith. The danger is merely that faith will die out. The temptations of long life have to do with the adjustment and readjustment to changing spiritual climates, the test being whether the life of the spirit can survive through these various stages. We look upon some lives that fade down into the commonplace in later years and sadly reflect that, if they had ceased ten years earlier, they would have left behind them memories of complete devotion to the loftiest spiritual realms. As life went on, however, it went on too long. The tragedy was that it just went on, and the enthusiasm for the ideal died out. Or, in the spiritual climate to which the life advanced, there was not enough ozone, or oxygen, and the soul suffocated. Or the life lost interest. So it was *not* with John Wesley. He ran with patience the *length* of the Christian race.

During all the phases of an abnormally long life Wesley held fast to the one ideal; held fast so tightly that he did not seem to realize that he was passing through successive phases of experience. It has been said of him that one fault which he revealed in handling children was that he always looked upon a child just as he would upon an adult. Wesley always took himself as an adult. He exacted as much of himself when he was a young man as if he had already come to full maturity, and as much of himself after he had come to old age as if he were still only at maturity. It is true that he never made as much of the relative aspects in human experience as he would have done if he had lived in an era that made more place for psychology, and for rhythm in men's lives. It is a peculiarity and danger, however, of those who study so much into the relative and the rhythmic that they make everything relative, and finally get everything washed away as in a flow, the only factor abiding being the flow itself. We live in an age that abhors anything absolute, even the word itself. It may be just as well, therefore, for us to contemplate a life that stretched through over eighty years and found something which, whether we call it absolute or not, remained much the same in the purpose of Wesley. The ideal which he pursued with an unresting quest never lost its spell over him. That ideal to which he gave himself in early life grew both in size and fineness as the years went by.

Dr. Charles E. Jefferson once put a nobly eloquent emphasis on this time-stretch of Wesley's life and of its significance as making that life a revelation of divine power and grace. Doctor Jefferson said, as already quoted, that some men die, as it were, before noon, and some in the afternoon, making a revelation of the divine indeed for which the world is grateful, but escaping some temptations and criticisms which come with longer life. Wesley, on the other hand, continued Doctor Jefferson, lived through the morning, and after-noon, and evening, and far into the night. Three generations came and went while he lived.

Wesley was probably seen and heard by more people in Eng-land than had been any other individual up to his time. Rulers draw huge crowds of spectators whenever they go abroad, but the rulers of Wesley's day seldom went far outside of London, and there were four of them in his century: Anne, George I, George II, and George III. Wesley traveled in his ministry over two hundred thousand miles and preached to over forty thousand audiences. Before the end came he was "by sight" the best-known human figure in England. He was literally a public man. Now, let the reader, if he has opportunity, dip into Wesley's writings wherever he pleases and search for any signs that Wesley was adjusting himself for an actor's part, or that he was conscious of being on a stage before all England. The reader will search in vain.

The intent to spread scriptural holiness throughout the land appears always and with equal clearness throughout the life. That intent was the absolute, always manifest through all the stages. In saying what I did about the "relative" I did not mean to slur over the facts which underlie the conception of the relative in human existence. Wesley passed through the changes which are natural to man: youth, early, full and later maturity, middle age, old age and advanced old age. He said of himself, in 1775, that he knew more of England than any other man alive, so that he faced the influence of social change as shaping even the inner destinies of individuals. The inevitable changes that come to a changing world were his also. I do insist, however, that the words which were almost his last, "The best of all is, God is with us," were the utter-ance of, and consummation of the purpose which had been his from Oxford days, and before.

I am loath to cease speaking of the length of Wesley's service. "Retirement" is a fine word, and expresses a worthy social aim, this granting a worker an evening of quiet after he has served his day and generation, conceding a vantage ground from which he who has taken off the armor may look back peacefully upon the active struggle. Retirement, however, may be a season of dullness and deadness, of disillusionment and world-weariness. We say that this is more or less dependent upon physical changes due to age; that the loss of idealism in a retired leader means nothing except that the springs of vitality have run low.

This is not always the whole truth. The fading of the ideal may be owing to the fact that the leader has compromised here or there, not on mere nonessentials but on issues more important. There is a moral ageing which does not necessarily have to do with bodily conditions, but with the sheer length of service. One man grows old—and that suddenly—by yielding a moral value because he impatiently desires a quick result. Another, for the opposite reason: he has worked so long upon ideal methods that he gives up any hope of success through them. Thus he begins to compromise, "doing," as he says, "the best I can under the circumstances." Now, John Wesley was one of the most practically-minded religious leaders the Church has ever seen. He was perfectly willing to act on what we today call the pragmatic method of testing a belief by its actual consequences. Moreover, John Wesley grew old physically, and knew it. He finally set down a description of symptoms which he knew and called the marks of old age. January 1, 1790: "I am now an old man, decayed from head to foot. My eyes are dim; my right hand shakes much; my mouth is hot and dry every morning. I have a lingering fever almost every day; my motion is weak and slow. However, blessed be God, I do not slack my labor. I can preach and work still." Yet the ageing of the body did not mean any loosening of hold on the ideal. Of course there are those who give much credit for John Wesley's success to the excellence of the body which nature had dowered him, and to a mental poise which came from physical soundness. This judgment is good as far as it goes, but it does not go far enough. There was excellence of body and there was exactness of physical balance, but body and mind acted and reacted upon each other. The mind worked upon the body; the steadiness of grasp upon Wesley's primary beliefs kept the body steady. No matter how splendidly endowed Wesley's body may have been, it could not have run so steadily for eighty-eight years if it had not been under control of a superb mind. More than once he seemed near the end because of desperate illness and came back, that too in spite of wrong methods of treating the disease, through his sheer determination to have it so.

It is relevant and necessary to lay emphasis on Wesley's length of service because of the oft-recurring tendency among those who quote him to disparage "service." In the movement to celebrate Wesley's Aldersgate experience the emphasis was twisted askew, and the impression left that the significant factors with Wesley were "experiences." We read of the futility of "service" and of the importance of getting into communion with God after the pattern of Wesley. We would not for an instant minimize the emotional stirring in the life of Wesley—Aldersgate or any other—but what was the fruit of those uplifts? What but the longest and richest sweep of service Methodism has ever seen? Those who exhort us to read Wesley to get ourselves free from all this running about, and working in committees and conferences, and striving to uplift the world, would better take the first months of their freedom to read the *Journal* and *Letters*. If they retort that all Wesley's activity came out of the "quickenings," the reply is that indeed it did, and that, if like results do not now come out of such inner happenings as those we praise in Wesley, there is no use in trying to make those re-enforcements genuinely Wesleyan. We may get puzzled as to the witness of inner assurance, and torture our minds as to just what the "witness" was to Wesley himself, but we cannot have the slightest doubt as to the witness of his experience to the world over eighty years of unceasing, unflagging performance of good deeds toward men.

We have frequently considered some of the abiding results of Wesley's work in the world; but, for the sake of showing some directions of the development of his own life, we instance two or three forms of growth which did involve change. Suppose we pick up a thread dropped in an earlier chapter and refer again to the remark of Wesley in his old age that, as he recalled how Charles and he used to preach that a man could not be saved without being conscious of salvation, he wondered that the people did not stone them. This could only mean that he came to a conviction that his earlier preaching as to assurance was extreme and absurd, as, indeed, it was. It assumed a knowledge of the working of the soul, of the forces which condition assurance, and a right to pass judgment, beyond anything vouchsafed to man. What Wesley meant by saying that the people might have cast stones at them was that such preaching was a violation of that good sense which the ordinary man is quite as likely to possess as any teacher, no matter how devout or learned. Wesley's final remark was an instance of intellectual and moral seasoning, if not ripening. The first years of the Wesley ministry carried the uncompromising spirit to the extreme. Everything had to be all or none; especially everything had to be just what the doctrine called for. Here was a lamentable lack of perspective in putting together nonessentials and essentials. The essential in salvation was to have a purpose set to do the will of God. "Assurance" and "witness" have always been confusing terms, in view of the fact that many of the finest souls in their service of men have never been willing to lay claim to any such assurance as Wesley and his early followers taught. It is much more important to have men so saved in manner and degree that the neighbors bear witness to the salvation, than to have the professedly saved man doing the witnessing himself in verbal testimony. The fundamental requisite is to do the will of God.

Now, Wesley saw this as the years went by. His words about the people and the stoning meant a firmer grasp on his truth at the latter end of his life than at the beginning. It is only one in such firm hold of his convictions as Wesley who can make such a statement as that which we have been considering. In the earlier years Wesley would probably have been afraid to speak thus: afraid of the effect on those whom he was striving to convert; afraid of the effect on himself. The oft-quoted remark did not mean that Wesley held his teaching more loosely in hand as he came into years, but that he had learned what to hold. He never ceased to preach assurance, but he ceased to be dogmatic about it.

As a further instance, there is his remark, already quoted, that he had ceased to be certain about almost everything except what he could establish by the Scriptures. Here, again, one might suppose that the life was becoming lax as its springs of energy sank lower. The tenacity of Wesley's hold increased on the things he did know. It is indeed sad and tragic when a mind, which has always been positive, becomes almost wholly negative as it draws toward its earthly close. It was not so with Wesley. His grip was closing in on what was supremely worth while. It was as if a traveler about to embark for a foreign port should discover that most of the luggage, which he had carried about with him in the land which he was to leave, would be of no use to him in the country to which he was to sail. It would be a mercy to see that it was of no further value. Take even the lapse of time; the body of formal knowledge which Wesley possessed is of slight value in this twentieth century, and our similar knowledge will have worth only to an antiquarian two centuries hence. Here is where the power to forget, both in the individual and in society, becomes a blessing. "The best of all is, God is with us." When a man tells what is best in his thought, we know pretty well his scale of values. We know what he seeks to keep and what he is willing to drop. One of the blessed privileges to a man of the Wesley type is that of dropping off the nonessentials. Otherwise the native tendency to positiveness, not to say dogmatism, would deprive the utterance of all perspective and proportion. As it was, enough dogmatism even as to the insignificant clung to Wesley to the end.

Speaking of persistence of beliefs and notions, we cannot but notice how long ideas which are false and at the same time trivial or barbarous will cling to first-rate minds, probably because those minds have taken them as of the social heritage—matters of course. There is, for example, the idea of hell, if not literally conceived, at least almost literally. One of the strangest phenomena in human history is just this: that natures naturally kindly will hold even for an hour, not to say a lifetime, notions as to punishment which would make God, the Judge, a savage. Las Casas, the apostle to the Indians, who gave the last ounce of his strength to the alleviation of the sufferings inflicted upon the American natives by the Spaniards, who called the Indians his dear lambs, spoke in the most casual fashion of the Indians who had died without the gospel as roasting in the eternal fires! Wesley did better than that, for he believed that a "heathen" who had died without hearing the gospel would be judged by his attitude toward whatever moral light he might have had. Wesley, however, for a long time seems to have assumed that children were born under the wrath of God. We ask indulgence as we record again that along toward the close of his life he saw a group of children at play and remarked that it was hard for him to believe that they were under the divine wrath— which meant, of course, that he did not believe they were under that wrath. Then there was the notion that if one breaks the law in one item, one breaks the whole law, a Pauline legalism which went unchallenged for centuries. Together with it was the accompanying idea that all unrepentant sinners went wholesale into hell without a chance for a "hearing," and the failure to protest adequately against the presentation of the gospel of love in such terms that men were to be compelled to love by the threat of virtually external and artificial penalty. All this Wesley accepted, as far as we can see, without registering much shock. He did war against the Calvinistic barbarities, but the general hardness of the orthodoxy of the time he did not declare against, at least not directly. Lecky has ground for saying that Wesley preached a religion of terrors. Yet, with his positive nature, he adopted or naturally gravitated toward the definite preaching of divine love. Even if he did take the accepted notion about hell as a literal matter of course, he himself preached something else. Probably Wesley would have been scandalized if anyone had challenged him as to his soundness on a literal hell, but nevertheless he personally made little use of it. Indeed, if we are to judge by the one hundred and fifty sermons Wesley left to us, his inheritance of the doctrine of a physical hell in which the orthodox of the time believed was something which he was practically allowing to "become atrophied by disuse," as the biologists say.

A most admirable trait in Wesley was an increasing hopefulness as to particular and general conditions as time went by. To his mother he wrote as early as 1733 that he would not give up hope of any man short of ten years effort for him, and he held fast to this belief till the end. We may repeat that he had supposed, when he began his work, that the Methodist momentum would be spent in thirty years. Before he died he declared that the force was continuing unabated because the people had learned to give so sacrificingly to Christian causes. It is true that at times the old longing for the life at Oxford came back to him that he might there seek his God in peace and without any distraction, but this was only for the moment. His satisfying joy was in his incessant activity, hardships and all—this too in the experience of one who in 1746 had written that he was tempted to be a philosophical sluggard rather than an itinerant preacher.

Wesley's determination to lead Methodism himself remained in strength to the end—if it was determination. It was indeed not so much a determination as a taking for granted. He did rule to the end. The ability to do this was an immense tribute to the hold he had won over the people and to his own powers. For, during his lifetime, the temper of the people of England, at least of the class among whom he worked, changed noticeably. When Wesley was born, the class from whom he afterward drew his followers had a habit of obedience. They seemed to like to obey. The Industrial Revolution began from the first to alter, or at least to modify this, so that, by the time the Revolution got well going, there was almost a different class in England. Those reared on farms and in villages had high respect for the station of the upper classes, and landlords were looked upon as in these upper classes. When those who would otherwise have lived out their days as tenants moved into factory towns, their old regard for position

ceased to cast a spell over them. They themselves did not quite
fit into England's social scheme. They married and reared children
in the factory towns and virtually became a class by themselves. In
spite of their hardships they came to a measure of independence in
thought and attitude. While Wesley does not say much about it
himself, it is manifest that Methodism throve best in the new industrial centers. At least he does not seem to think these classes were
in so deplorable a plight as that of the farmers. Students of the
eighteenth century have a good deal to say about the happier lot of
the worker on the farm as compared with that of the factory employee, inasmuch as the former has before him the beauties of
nature for his companions and the forces of nature for his co-
workers. That is the way it looks to a writer in a study. In truth
the farm worker, with no brighter future before him than he had
in Wesley's day, is likely to live through just the dull, spiritless
round that Wesley described as the farmer's lot. In all ages of
history the considerable proportion of those born to an agricultural life have sought to get away from it to the city, or the town,
or the sea, or to anywhere else. Anyhow, the rising class—if we can
call it that—in which Wesleyanism made its longest and fastest
strides, did not care as much for people of place, did not show as
much deference to the highborn as had the lower classes, so called,
shown at the time when Methodism took its start. It was harder
to keep things in order and in line in dealing with the industrial
groups than with any other. Yet Wesley did this, and did it by
insisting that it must be so. It is not to be wondered at that Wesley
was never willing to give up his leadership: leaders old or young are
never willing to do that. The power must be taken from the leaders
either by the working of law or by the followers refusing to follow.
The marvel is that the Methodists, more and more of whom were
coming from the industrial groups, accepted Wesley's leadership.
Of course back of that pre-eminence was fully a half century of success, but that is not always decisive with a social group becoming
more and more conscious of its own powers and possibilities. Aristo-
crat though he was, Wesley dropped remarks here and there which
revealed that he was quite aware of the power of the people, and of
the folly of courses which were not in harmony with their fundamental likes and dislikes.

Finally there was a ruthlessness which marked Wesley to the
end: his indifference to persecutions as compared with Charles;
his writing to his sister, Mrs. Hall, that "the death of your children

is a great instance of the goodness of God towards you. You have
often mentioned to me how much of your time they took up";
his willingness to break with individuals with whom he had been
associated in the work dearest to him. It was because he put the
work itself—perhaps his own estimate of the needs of the work—
above everything else. If Wesley had been a general commanding
an army, he would have been, at least in one respect, of the mould
of the Duke of Wellington of England and of General Grant of the
United States. In military concerns he would not have allowed
personal considerations to count as against what he conceived of as
the proper plan of campaign and of the execution of the plan.
Wesley's ruthlessness, indeed, was not cruelty, but it was inexorable
nevertheless. Sooner or later he broke with almost every other
leader with whom he had labored. He broke with the Moravians,
with Count Zinzendorf, with William Law, with George Whitefield,
with the first of his lay preachers, Thomas Maxfield; with George
Bell, though he tried to hold Bell back from fanaticisms; with John
Bennet and others of the preachers with whom he had been long
associated; with his wife, with Charles Wesley. As early as 1752
Charles had written to John asking for some of the money raised
by the Methodists for the support of the preachers, only to receive
the reply: "You have one hundred and fifty pounds for only two
persons. To take anything more from the classes seems unreasonable." Charles's money came by settlement at marriage. I do not
mean that these various ruptures were violent, but they were breaks
nevertheless. In all the above cases Wesley was probably acting for
the best, if his course can be called one of positive action rather
than of allowing himself to drift away from others.

The only terms on which men could work with Wesley were
his terms. He felt himself divinely called to the guidance of Methodism. He did not seek the responsibility: he felt it laid upon him.
Men like this seldom raise the question as to whether they are
ever called to let go their control. In his last years Wesley declared
that he had come to the place where he desired someone to help him
in stationing the preachers, but this was not to be taken seriously.

In two respects the leadership of Wesley fell short. He could
not, or did not, train "understudies" and he did not delegate authority. The circumstances, of course, were unique. Wesley had a distrust of his followers as to their ability to control Methodist affairs.
He ought to have seen that they would take more and more into
their own hands after he had gone, and have sought to train leaders

who could guide with some practice in such guidance gained under himself. He did consider designating John Fletcher as his successor, but here again he did not leave the impression that he actually would have made this choice if Fletcher had lived. Still, this is only our surmise, due to the frailty of Fletcher's health and to the gentleness of his character. Wesley's opinion of Fletcher, however, does indicate the surpassing importance to Wesley of having as a successor one who, in Wesley's judgment, realized in himself the type of religious character that Methodism sought to teach to the world. That to Wesley was all-important. Inadequacy in physical strength, or in knowledge of how to handle men, was secondary to the highest relation to God.

A competent executive can turn over to others whatever those others can do, and reserve to himself whatever tasks he can himself best do. One reads through the *Journal* and the *Letters* seeking for instances in which Wesley thus delegated authority, but looks practically in vain. There were, of course, the lay preachers, but even to them Wesley allowed scant liberty as to the content of their preaching. I was referring more especially, however, to administrative activity. Even when Wesley recognized that the societies in America had to go ahead after the Revolution under their own authority, he found it a strain to take his hands off and accede to the control by Asbury. How amazing this was! America had achieved political independence of England. There were three thousand miles of sea between England and America. Wesley had in the Revolution spoken most bitterly of the colonists. Nevertheless, the ruling passion was so strong in him that the American societies had deliberately to shake off his control. He never made his adjustments to American Methodists. Within three years of the end he had to shoot a little dart: "You do not know the state of the English Methodists. They do not roll in money, like many of the American Methodists."

We have looked at the qualities which remained strong in Wesley to the end of his life. We pass now to some Wesleyan consequences of Methodism which have persisted through the years.

Wesley was pre-eminently a doer of the Word. His movement must be regarded first of all for its creation of a fact-situation; it has more and more to be reckoned with in the realm of the application of the gospel to individuals and societies. It is objected, with force, that Wesleyanism has not made large, direct contribution to religious thinking. Who, however, can deny Wesley's independence?   At the outset of his ministry he declares that Luther "makes nothing out, clears up not one considerable difficulty, is quite shallow, muddy—and confused." Behmen, the mystic, teaches "most sublime nonsense, inimitable bombast, fustian not to be paralleled." What Wesleyanism did and has always done, has been to force itself indirectly at least upon the attention of all those who would understand the progress of Christianity during the past two centuries.

To begin with, the achievement of Wesley may be almost said to have been the discovery of a new world of human beings in the England of the eighteenth century.   Students of that century have commented on the little stir the philosophic and theological debates of the era made on the masses of the people.   The century has been characterized as deistic, and no doubt it was so far as systematic thinking went.   Until Tom Paine appeared, however, with his *Age of Reason,* deism was seldom heard of among the masses, to whom, before Paine, nobody had dreamed it worth while to speak philosophically.   Part of the terrific outcry against Paine was due to his ability in getting his ideas before the attention of the masses, who had been not so much purposely ignored as never thought of. Now, Wesley had been dealing with these masses long before Paine had been heard of.   He had built Methodism into a solid fact before anyone dreamed what was going on.   We have said that there is not much ground for maintaining that Wesley prevented the spread of revolutionary doctrines from France into England, but he did set limits to the spread of deism in England itself.   There may not have been much of formal controversial attack on deism by Methodism, but there was in Methodism a wall which hindered the spread of deism among the people.   The Methodists thwarted the deistic philosophy without even hearing of it.   Deism put God at a distance; Methodism brought God near and kept him near.   There is only one document in all Wesley's writings, voluminous as they were, that is a direct polemic against deism.   The limits were set by the actually changed lives among thousands upon thousands of men.   There were over seventy thousand Methodists in England when Wesley died.   The evangelism had been going on through nearly two generations, and perhaps seventy thousand others had died in the Methodist faith since Wesley's career had begun.   Now, a Methodist was a fact.   He was ordinarily a man who had been doing one quality of deed and had turned away from that quality of deed to a better.   He had ceased an evil life and was living another. These changes in the converts had transformed all the relations of their lives. Here were facts—over seventy thousand of them; here was a fact-situation created by an organized mass which deism could not account for.

A similar effect was that of the Wesleyan Movement in bringing to an end, or at least in reducing to comparative insignificance, the eighteenth century as the so-called Age of Reason. Through a philosophic trend the century had come to believe in the virtual omnipotence of human reason. In the seventeenth century John Locke had taught that the human mind was a blank tablet, *tabula rasa,* on which impressions were made through the senses. Such sense impressions were called primary. The ideas which came out of the action and reactions and interactions of the primary impressions gave rise to secondary qualities—ideas like substance, cause and effect. The practical effect of all this was to surrender the chief place to matter, though Locke did not intend to aid materialism. After Locke came Berkeley, the most powerful of idealists, who pointed out that he did not need material substance to produce the sense-impressions. If there was any way of keeping the impressions before the mind, the material substance could fall into nothingness. Berkeley maintained that there was a way of producing the impressions. They were symbols of ideas in the mind of God, which included all things in its grasp, and by its own activity produced the impressions upon the mind of men.

All this went forward, of course, under belief in reason which felt itself competent to lay hold on all the secrets of the universe. Of course philosophizing was in what might be called the upper circles. The ordinary people did not know much more about Locke and Berkeley than they do today. The conclusions reached in these upper circles led to a doubt of everything but reason itself.

Bishop Butler, in the famous *Analogy,* undertook to re-establish the foundations of Christianity by the use of reason itself. His fundamental proposition was that probability is the guide of life, and that all reasonable men order their lives by such probability. The usual experiences of men, therefore, supply illustrations and re-enforcements of the claim that what we see of the development of the human life in this present earthly existence makes it probable that the life will go on in some other phase beyond the earthly. So with other fundamental doctrines of Christianity. We are constantly acting in daily life on probabilities no more conclusive than those required in accepting the Biblical revelation as to the nature of God and man.

Butler laid stress on reason and made a noble contribution to religious defense. Wesley admired the *Analogy,* but his comment on it was significant, namely, that the argument was too abstruse for the ordinary reader to follow. The strict reasoner of the age pronounced much of the Butler reasoning loose, and especially found the "probable" as the practically likely confused with the merely possible. So that Butler was not easy enough for the plain man, and not stiff enough for the trained, virtually professional thinker. Nevertheless, Butler has undying merit. By making probability, or at bottom practical certainty, the guide of life he was doing just about what Wesley was doing. Wesley's position was that we can be as certain of God as we can of anything else, and Butler's contention was virtually the same. We would not for an instant, however, seem to imply that Butler would have countenanced any such phrasing. It was he who, as Bishop of Bristol, told Wesley that he considered Wesley's teachings of direct revelations from God as a "very horrid thing." It was he too who all but ordered Wesley out of his diocese, and it was to him also that Wesley was possibly more defiant than toward any other official of the Church of England. Butler sought to use the weapon of reason in an age of reason against the assaults of reason upon Christianity. His work has recently been admirably treated in *Joseph Butler and the Age of Reason,* by E. C. Mossner.

The powerful attack on Reason came from David Hume. We have said that Berkeley urged against materialism that, if the sensations upon the mind could be produced by any other agent, nobody needed matter to account for them. Berkeley accounted for them as produced by the immediate agency of God. With unsparing logic Hume sought to show that neither materialism nor idealism was needed. The sensations themselves are the facts; they are here with a propensity to feign substance, cause, and all other forces beyond themselves. This was skepticism of reason itself.

Hume personally was and is something of an enigma. He used to say that, as he sat down to a game of cribbage with a friend, after working on his philosophy, all his reasonings seemed strangely unreal. There is no ground for suspecting insincerity in him, but there is basis for wondering if he took his skepticism as seriously as did his readers. Professor A. E. Taylor, of Edinburgh University, feels that there are even traces of a belief in theism in much that

Hume wrote. That may be. Hume's attack was not specifically in the religious realm. The attack was not adequately met in direct reply until Thomas Hill Green, a hundred years after Hume, gave the world his definitive and decisive examination of Hume's skepticism. The most important result of that skepticism was that he "woke Kant from his dogmatic slumber," to use Kant's own expression, and Kant moved into that deeper channel of philosophic exploration which has influenced the world of abstract reflection ever since.

What has all this to do with Wesley? Just this: that Wesley had created a fact-situation which the Hume skepticism did not touch. Wesley taught a reliance upon emotion—upon feeling in its upper reaches—as the method of communion with the Divine. Inasmuch as the Wesleyan Movement was not founded upon Reason of the type which gave its name as a description to the eighteenth century, skepticism of Reason did not touch that foundation. Here, again, the defense of Christianity was not, technically speaking, a defense at all, but a witness to experience in life itself. Coming back to the figure of the seventy thousand Methodists in England at the close of Wesley's life, we may pertinently ask how many in England ever read Hume's skepticism? The most popular, as being most readily understood, of all Hume's work was his assault on the credibility of miracles. Probably not more than a few thousands of people in the England of his time ever read that. The more important work, the exposition of his thoroughgoing skepticism, was likely not read by more than a few hundreds. If Wesley found Butler too hard for the people to understand, it is interesting to speculate on what he would have said of Hume. In strict philosophy Hume was important. In the actual religious currents of his time not especially so, for the Methodists were manifestly in possession of a life-force which was changing the temper of England. To show how far the Methodist Revival was removed from abstract reasoning we need only remind ourselves that the most potent single factor in the Wesleyan success as a popular Movement was the singing of the Methodists. The content of the songs, in spite of much theological overweight, was dignified to the point of nobility, and the tunes were peculiarly fitted to mass singing. John admitted that some of Charles's hymns were "bad" and "mean, but on the whole they had justness and strength of thought and beauty of expression." They were not intended to be solos, or selections for quartets, or sextets, or choruses, but for congregations—for multi-

tudes of singing people. They did not depend upon previous training in singing. Anybody could fall in and march along. The songs
of Methodism were not purposely intended to counteract a skepti-
cal tendency in philosophy. They were the irresistible spontaneous
gushing forth of new-found springs of life, and they did create a
situation of which philosophy—or reason, to use the term current
in the eighteenth century—had to take account. The fact thus
brought forth into the life of the century could not easily be
brushed aside. "By their fruits ye shall know them." The singing
came out of lives which had been turned from transgression to
righteousness, out of despair to hope, out of dullness to alertness.
An entire social group had been spoken into newness of life. Men
had been given something to do, something to think about, something to sing about. With all his faults, Wesley was one of the
mighty forces making for a greater certainty in the eighteenth
century.

Just as there are those who insist that the Methodist Movement gave nothing to the world in the sphere of intellectual creation, so there are also those who will have it that the Movement did
not have any significance for the revelation and contemplation of
beauty. Against this may be set the judgment of the Hammonds,
who were not overfriendly to Methodism, to the effect that the
songs of the Methodists were a worthy contribution to the aesthetic
life of the bleak age. Some of the songs were genuine poetry: and
John Wesley considered himself quite a critic on such matters.
Witness his remark in the *Journal* for 1756 that "it is as impossible
to write a fine poem in French as to make fine music on the jew's-
harp"—which rather disqualifies John as a judge. Most of the
tunes had elements of stirring beauty. Words and music made a
supreme requisite as revelations of the beautiful; they satisfied
widespread cravings; they expressed moods altogether fitted to the
people and their times; they tended to carry on out into action,
without which, as William James says, the arousing of deep emotions may be worse than useless. There was a beauty about the
singing which, perhaps, we have been too slow to recognize. The
present-day interest in and emphasis on community singing is in a
measure a tribute to the singing of Methodism. If such singing
ever becomes a lost art, something irreplaceable will be lost with it,
even if we are not concerned with anything beyond the expression
of beauty. The preaching places of the Methodists could not compare with the churches, even of the villages, for beauty—certainly

not with the cathedrals—but, on the other hand, no musical expressions of that or any later day could compare in sheer moving quality of beauty with the melody of the Methodist hymns; democratic in that every one could find a place, *his* place, in it and throw into it all there was of himself. If there is beauty in the sweep of wind through tree tops, in the beat and rote of sea waves, in the roar of a cataract, much more was there beauty in the songs of hundreds of Methodists pouring forth in sheer excess of joy their vital tides of onrushing spiritual vigor and purpose.

Looking at the Methodist Movement as an outstanding social fact, or force, it may be fair to say that it was a reaction against the overemphasis on reason. This will do as a partial explanation, but only as partial. In physics, action and reaction, we are told, are equal. If we call Methodism a reaction, it was more than equal to the force of reason over against which it has been placed. It was indeed opposed to the emphasis on reason, but it was life on its own account. It is not to be explained merely as a reaction against a school of thought or tendencies in philosophy. The majority of Methodists had never heard their century called the Age of Reason. The Wesleyan Movement was not so much reaction as action.

In trying to keep our bearings as we think of Methodism as a social fact, we must not go so far as to minimize the place of reason in Wesley's own thinking. Wesley's own struggles, especially in the earlier years, were largely thought-struggles. He was himself a product of the eighteenth century. He could not write a sermon without working to an outline almost resembling the old-time scholasticism. In his speaking he was systematic to a wearisome degree. One cannot help wondering what the audiences made of Wesley's points in his sermons if he announced the numerical divisions as he printed them. It is hard enough now to tell why some of the divisions were made and numbered.

Wesley never disparaged reason as such. What he did was to recognize *data* not given by reason itself, the data, however, to be worked over and interpreted by reason. Hume used reason to overthrow reason, to establish total skepticism. Wesley used reason to make manifest the limits of reason, to bring to light something given which came from over and beyond reason. The method of Hume, whether so intended or not, was to beget skepticism; the method of Wesley, to use reason to beget faith.

Yet there is justice in the claim that Wesley's disparagement of reason did harm. The contribution of Methodism to education, especially to what we now call adult education, was immeasurable. Wesley was responsible for a lifting of the general intelligence of England, which was probably a better service than making himself clearer on the claims of abstract reasoning, but the effect of his total attitude came near being a disparagement of reason. He had a sneer at the British Museum because all the contents would be burned up at the last day. It is, of course, fair to point out that he was himself highly educated in a foremost educational institution, that he was scholarly enough to write grammars of foreign languages, including the Greek, that he was himself proficient in the solider learning of his day, but he did so put his emphasis that he practically minimized the place of reason. I am not at all speaking of his intention.

It may be that this was inevitable. Wesley did not encourage wide reading among his people. He was willing that they should read, but he virtually chose the readings. *The Christian Library,* in fifty volumes—published at a loss of fifty pounds of his own money, by the way—selections of religious literature made by Wesley himself, is a monument of pedagogical discernment so far as adults are concerned. It brought the teachings of the primitive Church through the works of leaders down to the tables of the humblest Methodists. As I write these lines, there is before me a set of the *Library* published in 1749. On the inside of the cover is a note by a good Methodist that in three years he had found time to read all the volumes through; all his reading having been done before seven o'clock in the morning. All the material in these fifty volumes is good, thoroughly orthodox, not calculated to raise question about anything in religion. There is published, for example, the classic of Baxter's *Saint's Rest.* It would never have occurred to Wesley, by the way, to publish any of Baxter's philippics against rack-renting landlords, or anything about Baxter's sufferings through persecution for his religious convictions. Some of the books he recommended for the reading of young ladies in boarding schools were a fright—Rollin's *Ancient History,* one of the terrors of my own boyhood, and Malebranche.

The truth appears to be that Wesley's impulse to leadership extended far beyond merely practical affairs. He sought to take in hand the thinking of his followers. His confidence in himself as a shaper of their ideas was supreme. From this point his leadership assumes more than a mere personal and biographical importance, and has to be regarded as a social, and in England, a national phenomenon. Here was one man practically telling tens of thousands of followers what they should read. Matthew Arnold once said of the United States, as we have already had occasion to note, that one mark of the intellectual inferiority of this nation was that so many of the inhabitants were Methodists, and that Methodists were followers of a third-rate mind.

The normal supposition is that, when a writer or an editor sets forth his views to the public, the readers can take them or leave them—as, indeed, they can. Such was not quite the situation with the Methodists. To a determinative degree the channels of their thinking were laid out before them. It is not exact to imagine Wesley as merely releasing ideas for them to take what they would.

This is to say that he seemed to distrust the ability of his followers to do any thinking on their own account. His fear of their making blunders if they sought to govern themselves—I refer especially to any self-government by Methodists as a whole—had some foundation, for they had been without political training. Whether this is true on the intellectual side is more of a question. Wesley did not encourage his preachers to speak on any themes outside what were conceived of as the specifically religious. He himself reserved the privilege to say anything he pleased about anything; but he did not have, so far as we can see, any intention of sharing this privilege with anyone. The important controversial theme in his time was Calvinism and, of course, that called forth leaders whom it was not possible to ignore. The Calvinists virtually separated themselves from Wesley.

The main question is whether Wesley's influence, in a somewhat contemptuous attitude toward reason, marked the course of Methodism in any harmful extent. We cannot resist the conclusion that it did, though this may have been inevitable. While Wesley took himself as superior to the people whom he led, he was steeped in their presuppositions and prejudices. We have had occasion before to remark on the belief of the founder of Methodism in witchcraft. It is a curious psychological question as to what this belief of Wesley in witchcraft fundamentally meant. The most casual reader of modern knowledge about the way human minds work will often raise question as to just what a man means when he says that he believes thus and so, and this too without any suspicion as to the sincerity of the professed belief. In Wesley's utterance on witchcraft and kindred themes he felt that the authority of the Bible was involved. With equal force, however, it may be avowed that the primitive tendency toward superstition, which was native to him and re-enforced by the masses among whom he worked, was speaking through him. In any event, in these and similar matters, the mighty current of Wesley's leadership moved in the wrong direction, always with qualifications. He had to cease to allow one of his first lay preachers to work in his societies because of Cennick's fear of ghosts and of seeing the devil. If he had been content to utter some beliefs as his own personal concerns, the results might have been different; but he spoke them all forth as if they were deeply significant to him. Inasmuch as the Methodist societies were almost his own private possessions, his personal beliefs fastened themselves upon his followers so firmly as to tinge darkly an entire social situation. So that it will not do to say that the criticism of Methodism as an anti-rational, not to say irrational, social force can be met by pointing to Wesley's training and scholarship. In some ways all this weight counted on the wrong side. Leadership sometimes exacts heavy social costs, especially leadership of large masses, for the followers are not and cannot always be discriminating. They are likely to take everything in the leader as about on the same plane. If a Wesley, under whom they have attained to inner peace and power, goes out and measures the extent of the harm wrought by a landslide, or what looks like an earthquake, and tells his followers that the occurrence is a threat of God against sinful men, they believe him. If he tells them that the physical contortions of men under deep conviction of sin are the direct manifestation of the presence and power of the devil, they believe that.

It requires the selection and sifting of some generations of study to reveal just what has helped men in the influence of a leader, or what in his teaching can be adapted to changing social pressures, and what has done harm. For example, Wesley told his followers to get all they could, save all they could, give all they could, by which last advice he meant: Give all to the Lord, except what was morally due to dependents. Before he died, Wesley modified this to warrant setting aside the capital which might be necessary for the conduct of any business in which the Methodist might be engaged. That opened a wide door. By the end of the first third of the nineteenth century not much was left of Wesley's threefold injunction except to earn money honestly and spend it in ways that could be employed in the name of the Lord Jesus. Practically, the directions given in the sermon on "The Use of Money" were of more consequence than the threefold adage, which is more famous, for that adage could not stand the pressure of changing social demands, especially among the Methodists.

Students of the history of the early Church tell us that the effective force in deciding what scriptures were preserved was the result of their use in the churches. Those teachers have lost all touch with actual social processes who will have it that the churches created the New Testament literature outright; but they are in close touch with those processes when they tell us that the churches determined, perhaps unconsciously, but nevertheless actually, just what should be handed down to the future. There was no longer a need, after a generation or two, for the reading of certain letters from church leaders, or for the singing of certain hymns. The same process has gone forward in Methodism, except that, through the organization which Wesley left, the standards of Methodism, chiefly the sermons, were purposely kept to the fore for over a century after their last revision by their author. Those of us who are older can remember the entire sets of the sermons that used to stand on the shelves of Methodist preachers, or of the more earnest Methodist laymen. I myself can recall farmhouses in my youth on whose shelves Wesley's sermons occupied the place of honor, except when they were in use, which was often. The good they accomplished was immense, but they did, by their overpositiveness, a positiveness which belonged as much to Wesley as his face, lead to an impatience of reasoning, reasoned though the sermons themselves were, and shut in the minds of the readers to narrow windows.

It was the selection of themes and ideas by Wesley himself that counted much with his followers. John Pawson, one of Wesley's preachers, was, as already related, that vigorous brother typical of Methodist narrowness, who saw that a volume of Shakespeare, annotated by Wesley himself, was burned after Wesley's death. Probably Wesley's notes on Shakespeare were of no special value, except for the light they might have thrown on Wesley himself; but John Pawson was just about the last man among the Methodists who should have been granted an opinion on such a question. There is nothing that we know about him that warrants the belief that he had himself ever read a line of Shakespeare. Now, this judgment is just enough, but it overlooks that what training Pawson had he got chiefly from Wesley himself. I mean that he was close enough to his leader to catch his measures and standards of emphasis. It is true that Wesley allowed himself readings and studies that he would not have permitted to his followers. From this angle of view, Pawson was probably justified in putting the notes in the fire. The faithful might not have paid much attention to them, however. They did not belong to the class of books that Wesley had trained the people to read. It is strange, however, that, after he had been at work for nearly twenty years of preaching, Wesley expelled six for reading Behman and Law.

It was the hymns of the Methodists that made the popular impression. Here the selective choice of the people was distinctly at work. The congregations kept their faith and enthusiasm alive by the singing. The dark side of the picture is that the congregations, even while singing of the great hope of the Christian, so long kept a disproportionate stress on the terrors of possible eternal loss. The saved soul indeed stood on a narrow neck of land, rejoicing in eternal salvation but remembering always the possibility of falling off into hell. Finally such hymns did sink into disuse and were allowed to drop out of memory. Then, too, a low notion of humanity, altogether out of harmony with Methodism, lasted a long time before it could be cast out. Dr. William Rice of the New England Conference, father of Professor William North Rice, of Wesleyan University, once worked on the revision of *The Methodist Hymnal*. He was instrumental in having stricken from the *Hymnal* scores of characterizations of man as a worm. Just what made that word a favorite with the early Methodists there is no telling. The term certainly did not come from the study of the New Testament. How the Wesleys came to tolerate such a word is a puzzle.

There was nothing in the emphasis of Wesley to predispose the Methodists toward the newer views of the universe which so expanded human thought in the eighteenth century. Wesley did not accept the Copernican view of the universe, which is not to be wondered at, for it took two hundred and fifty years for that view to attain at all general acceptance. Wesley did not accept Newton's more important theories. This is not to be wondered at either. Newton died in 1727, when Wesley was twenty-four years old. There was no reason why Wesley should have been especially impressed by Newton, unless it was by the experiments in optics. Newton's work was highly technical and mathematical. Naturally, it at first did not attract much attention. The Methodists would not have made much of the Newtonian theory of gravitation, not much more than they would have made of the binomial theorem and the calculus. We are likely to forget that in those days an-

nouncements of the most far-reaching changes in men's conception
of the universe only slowly made their way into the understanding
of the people. There was nothing in Wesley's utterance or attitude
that would have predisposed his followers to a friendly or even an
interested attitude toward theories of the physical universe which
are today accepted as of common knowledge. About all that can
be said is that the Methodist organization was not so ironclad as
to prove irresistible to the changes of social climate as these came
along. Wesley was as scornful as any theological dogmatist of the
claims of science, especially when these appeared to conflict with
the commonly accepted teaching of the Scriptures, let us say; but
he did not create in Methodism such a temper of resistance to the
spread of scientific ideas as to leave Methodism far in the rear, as
intelligent men accepted views of the universe which on their
first announcement seemed revolutionary. In the relation to
expanding views of the physical world Wesley left the doors of
Methodism closed but not locked.

While we are speaking of Newton, we may note that Wesley
was not more off the track in some of his views than was Newton.
The immortal mathematician, whose work remained without any
important modification till Einstein appeared a few years ago, was
through his mathematical task at a comparatively early age and
thereafter gave himself to study of Biblical matters of no moment
whatever, reaching conclusions which could be as easily ridiculed
as any of Wesley's whimsies. The difference was, of course, that
Newton was not playing any considerable part before the people of
England. Only a few, comparatively speaking, had heard even of
his laws of motion, and fewer still knew what they meant. Those
who did know of him thought of him as the Director of the Mint;
Wesley was known by sight all over England. From 1744 on to the
end Wesley complains of his workers that they do not often enough
send to him stories of remarkable conversions and remarkable triumphs of confidence on deathbeds. All this is open and above-
board, with no attempt at concealment whatever—completely sincere on Wesley's part. Wesley estimated these experiences as the
surest signs of the Divine Presence, and yet he had a keen instinct
for what was most potent in impressing the minds of the largest
number. He had an uncanny discernment of what was an extraordinary development of the ordinary, and what was extraordinary
as a departure from the ordinary. The result is that, after two

hundred years when one speaks to us of a "Methodistic" experience, we know pretty well what is meant.

We look once more at some of the limitations under which Wesley worked and some of the limitations within which his system has moved since his death.

This theme of the limitations upon the growth of institutions has never yet been given the amount of attention it deserves. Do institutions resemble organic forms, which follow laws which appear to determine the size which they shall reach? Look out over the tops of the trees of a forest and note how slight is the range variations of height reached by the mature growths. Why is it that of millions upon millions of men the range of the variation height of the adults is so small? Do men in their institutional activities move thus within limits? Wesley believed that rhythm marked even Methodism's revival efforts. In 1783 he wrote in a letter that "a swift increase is almost always followed by a decrease equally swift," and in 1787: "After an amazing flow we must expect ebb."

Without attempting any theories as to the hidden forces limiting the size of institutions, we can see some factors about whose action we need have little doubt. It is thus with Wesley's influence in Methodism. We can understand better what he did if we look at some things he did not, or perhaps could not, do.

To start with the somewhat artificial, we may note one or two geographical considerations. Wesley made over a score of journeys to Ireland. His work there has not been considered on the same plane of success as that in England or America. The *Cambridge History of the Eighteenth Century* dismisses the career of Wesley in Ireland summarily, with the remark that Wesley accomplished but little in Ireland. He accomplished enough, however, to make him think it was worth while to go to Ireland repeatedly—that, too, in spite of manifold hardship and some persecution. Through the years the work in Ireland has endured. He was not deceived as to the Irish, however. In 1750 he wrote that murder was a venial sin in Ireland.

What the criticism means is that Wesley could not achieve sweeping success in a Roman Catholic country. Even the Catholics came out in unusual numbers to hear him, but he did not win adherents to his society from them. This may have been somewhat to his opposition to toleration for the Roman Catholics in England, though in some respects and at some times, notably in 1741, he was charged with receiving large remittances from Roman

Catholics in Spain. When his nephew, Samuel, planned to join the
Roman Catholic Church, John wrote to him as if he were departing
into outer darkness. Still, it would not have been much different
if Wesley's attitude had been friendliness itself. The Roman Catholic Church has always been proof against direct persuasion by other
branches of Christianity. What has happened is that the positive
insistence upon faith, and not ecclesiastical good works, has brought
a vitality to Roman Catholic life which it might otherwise have
lacked. Many of us who think that the contribution of the Reformation to religion is to be seen only in Protestantism itself have failed
to notice that the Reformation led to the doing away in the Roman
Church of many of the abuses which called forth the Reformation,
and gave Rome herself a new lease on life.

The truth is that the Roman Church in Ireland took
hold of the lives of its believers from more angles than did the Methodist societies. It could throw around its members an atmosphere
which Methodism could not produce, at least in the early stages
of its career. The Roman Church was able to bring to bear upon
children influences which Methodism could not rival, and was
more skillful in its appeals to children than were Wesley and his
preachers.

In Scotland also Wesley did not have extraordinary success. In
1771 he wrote that McNab, one of his preachers, must be lost to
common sense to preach against perseverance in Scotland. He
wrote in 1774 that the Scots are terrible critics. He did indeed send
some of his preachers there, and even ordained two or three to
perform the rites of the Church there. Among them, John Pawson
had full clerical rights for a time. When he came back to England
and had to take off his "bands," he did so in no very pious mood.

Wesley would have denied that the Methodist labors in Scotland were a failure. "Failure" is indeed too strong a word, but
the success was limited. Here again Wesley had to meet religious
doctrines and practices which were the outcome of generations of
church experiences. The Scotch temperament did not warm easily
to the enthusiasm of the Methodists, and could not adjust itself
readily to putting religious stress on inner conviction and awareness rather than on acceptance of dogma. Wesleyan success
depended upon awakening in hearers a feeling of need—a spiritual
miracle to which the Wesleyans found themselves unequal in
Scotland.

In long-settled communities, among fixed religious institutions, Wesley could make headway only slowly. The mass of his converts came from among those whom we should call unchurched. In trying to hold his people fast to the Church of England, much of Wesley's difficulty was due to his having to deal with persons who had never had anything to do with the Church of England. The Methodist society was the only religious organization they had known. So in Scotland the religious conditions, organizationally speaking, were too firmly set for any wide effects of Methodism.

The success of Methodism in the American colonies, and afterward in the new lands to the American west, was due to the movement's getting into new fields where the institutions were not too solidified. The persistency of religious institutions is remarkable. Where in America the first settlers were Congregational, or Baptist, or Episcopalian, or Roman Catholic, there these types of organization abide in more or less of strength to this day. In America George Whitefield did not make any appreciable gains for Methodism as such. His work was in re-enforcing the churches already established.

I am not thinking of the Methodism which is now an established institution in America, which moves along as other churches do, chiefly through holding children born in Methodist homes and in winning those brought in through the church school, but of the movement in the days when it still had on it the impress which made it most fitting to call it Wesleyan.

Here it may be appropriate to say that looking at the characteristic Methodist procedure, if not policy, which "spreads" rather than concentrates, leading to results often superficial, we cannot fail to see that the superficiality of the work of Methodism was to be expected in a religious effort whose avowed aim was to "spread." The result has been to cover a wide extent of thin cultivation, leaving to the after times to dig more deeply into the soil. Now, this predominantly extensive result was foreign to the spirit of John Wesley. He did not have overmuch of missionary spirit in the present-day almost technical sense. As late as 1783 he called the preachers together to discuss missions to the East Indies and "decided there is no call thither yet." When he said that the world was his parish he meant he would speak wherever he pleased. In whatever part he was he would declare salvation. He was thorough in his own search for the highest possible type of religious experience and in his insistence upon such search by his followers. Nobody can look through the earlier years of Wesley's life and fail to see

the desperate thoroughness with which he sought perfection.   If
anything, the criticism could be urged that he tried to carry the
spiritual quest too far into details, often getting his accent on trifles
of no moral consequence.

The same thoroughness marked him as an organizer.   He
knew nothing of what present-day ecclesiastical criticism calls the
padding of statistics.   He would ask for the lists of the members of
the Methodist society wherever he went, and then, by personal
visitation of the members, would determine whether he ought to
continue to carry names upon the lists where no fruit of righteous
living was manifest.   He was altogether open in declaring results
that must have been disheartening.   Ardent as was his devotion to
the preaching of what he called Christian perfection, he admitted
time and again that the results were so meager as to cause him to
ask whether the preachers should not cease preaching upon this
theme.   No matter what we may think about Wesley's idea of perfection, we cannot help a tinge of the feeling of pathos as we read
in his last writings how few there were among the Methodists who
could be said to have achieved any conspicuous success in the search
for the highest religious experience.   How significant it is that Wesley knew their number with almost absolute exactness!

There is some reason to believe that Wesley planned the
spreading method, for the sake of getting a given area covered as
soon as possible.   He seldom planned anything far ahead, but he
could not help seeing the significance of the response of numbers
as such.   He had to give himself to the message that would reach
the most hearers.   Take just one item: the worth of every individual soul in the sight of God, his surpassing achievement when
masses did not know whether they had any souls or not, or whether
those souls had any significance before whatever God there might
be.   Wesley never spoke of the Methodists as being other than a
minority group, with a limited and restricted aim, in the midst
of a larger group.   If this seems to introduce a divisive spirit into
the Church, let it be remembered that nothing is more divisive
than a uniformity and sameness which finally breaks, or at least
cracks, of its own weight.   The limitations under which Wesley
was willing to work indicated that the best course for a society is
to get its own view and practice out into full expression.   If the
united Church, when it comes, is made up of societies as con-
stituent organs, each organ will have to serve the whole by being
fully what it is and by cherishing, as Wesley did, a charitable spirit

toward other organs. In the days to come the united Church, if it renders service at all in the social realms, will have to find place for prophetic voices coming out of minorities, which will disturb the peace of the Church as a whole. Wesley knew that making his society as radically distinctive as it was, insisting on its running true to itself, maintaining that those who could not fit into Methodism were free to go elsewhere, he had to recognize like rights in other groups. All this means that the founder of Methodism pointed the way toward any church union worth having. Wesley avowed that he was not a dissenter, though his ancestors had been spirited dissenters. Dissent meant opposition to the Church, and Wesley believed in and was loyal to the Church. He felt that the English Church was failing just because it was not welcoming the society which could do it the most good. Wesley's narrowness was that merely of the cutting edge. It had to have weight back of it to give the edge drive and penetration. By his being himself the center around which Methodism could so largely mass itself, he found the needed weight.

One other limitation I have already mentioned more than once: the limitation which came out of the class to whom Wesley preached. He did not get far with the more privileged groups. I put here an excerpt from Horace Walpole, which shows the temper of the upper classes toward Methodism:

> To the Earl of Strafford
> Strawberry Hill, July 5, 1761.
>
> My dear Lord,
> . . . The apostle Whitefield is come to some shame: he went to Lady Huntingdon lately, and asked for forty pounds for some distressed saint or other. She said she had not so much money in the house, but would give it him the first time she had. He was very pressing, but in vain. At last he said, "There's your watch and trinkets, you don't want such vanities; I will have that." She would have put him off: but he persisting, she said, "Well, if you must have it, you must." About a fortnight afterwards, going to his house, and being carried into his wife's chamber, among the paraphernalia of the latter the countess found her own offering. This has made a terrible schism; she tells the story herself—I had not it from Saint Francis, but I hope it is true. Adieu, My dear Lord!

The longer Wesley worked among the lower groups, the more surely he saw that he had to confine himself to those groups. There is not much ground for doubt that the remark of one of the better privileged to the Countess of Huntingdon in protest against the preaching of the Methodists as putting men all together as sinners without regard to their positions in this world, represented the feeling of the higher-placed groups in England in the eighteenth century. There was a class complacency which it was hard to disturb. Wesley would not do anything, or countenance anything which would slow down the vigor of Methodism. If this was limitation, he made the most of it.

One of the forces most certain to cut into the driving power of any socially forward-looking movement is support by the more favored groups. It was a sure instinct in Wesley that made him frown upon the presence of the well to do among his societies. If, now, Wesley had been the head of a Church, he would have had no warrant for thus throwing barriers in the way of rich men's becoming Methodists, for he would have had to concede the right of the rich to place in a Church. Not so, however, in a society whose aim was militancy. Making all allowance for the inevitable exceptions, it is next to impossible to fit those who have much of this world's goods into aggressive Christian tasks when those tasks look beyond the personal inner religious experience.

Movements of the Wesleyan stamp are seldom understood in their own day. William Hogarth, the artist, painted the more degraded aspects of English life in the eighteenth century. Hogarth was probably stirred by a genuine moral disgust against the evil which he saw around him. To get an impression of the extent to which Wesley was taken as of the same type of persons whom he himself was striving to save, we have only to remember that Hogarth produced a print which was one of the bitterest slurs on Methodism ever perpetrated. The picture was made in 1762 and was entitled: "Credulity, Superstition, Fanaticism—a Medley." The scene is in a tabernacle—a Methodist revivalistic meeting. Under the preacher's gown is a harlequin's jacket; his head is that of a Roman Catholic priest. Part of the audience is wild to the verge of insanity. In one pew a devil is whispering in the ear of one of the audience. Another devil stands on the edge of the pulpit. A frenzied fanatic—a woman—sprawls on the floor. A Turk, looking in at the window, thanks God that he is not a Methodist. A witch on a broomstick is just above the preacher. There are other symbols literally too numerous to mention—the whole done with Hogarth's genius and with his power to depict the horrible.

In the above paragraph I have followed the key to the symbols given by Marjorie Bowen in her *William Hogarth, the Cockney's Mirror*. Miss Bowen is a sympathetic student of Hogarth, but declares that there is no reason to suppose that Hogarth knew anything about the "tenets" of Wesleyanism. Yet the picture gives a hint of the extent to which Wesley was supposed to have connected himself with the lower human strata. The truth is that he paid chief attention, after the Movement began to show its strength, to the lowlier classes: though there is no justice in Hogarth's description as applied to Wesleyanism.

Wesley called himself a Tory and a High Churchman. He was sure that those favored like himself were under obligation to help those not so favored. Yet, with the exception of a few, among them John Fletcher and Thomas Coke, he did not attract to himself men of higher "birth" whom he put into positions of responsibility. There is not much indication that he tried to attract the better born and better bred. There may be many reasons for this, one of them that he was not likely to get on with men on a plane of culture as high as his own unless they would obey him to the last detail. Whatever the reasons, the instinct was probably sound. The Methodists had mostly to be led by leaders from among themselves. How futile is the question itself as to the alleged futility of Wesley's work on the ground that he was not an outright originator! Some have said that the mystery of Wesley is that there is no mystery, that the means used were so commonplace that all mystery vanishes. Yet this brings the mystery back: which is that with so little so much could be done; that with the ordinary so extraordinary gains could be won; that with the natural so much of the supernatural could be revealed; that with the earthy so much of the heavenly could be attained.

I think I have mentioned the chief features in the career of Wesley that are commonly reckoned as especially strange. We need to remind ourselves that there is much that is puzzling in any career as far back in time from us as Wesley now is. There are always shreds and patches of peculiar times clinging to any historical character no matter how enlightened. Men in one day accept much which will seem absurd to later days without thinking about it at all.

I have already more than once mentioned Richard Baxter, because he was the outstanding religious figure in England of the seventeenth century as Wesley was of the eighteenth; a man who excelled in profundity of intellect as did Wesley in reach of will activity. Baxter lived until within a dozen years of the birth of Wesley. He had many of the same superstitions as Wesley, relying, for instance, for the cure of a troublesome illness on moss taken from the inside of a human skull. He too gave himself to practicing medicine with about the same queer cures as Wesley's. The two men talked in about the same fashion about diseases. It was not they who were talking but the times in which they lived. Scientific control of disease had not yet begun. In all such realms the world was just about what it had been for a thousand years. A single scientific discovery will change a course of human procedure within a quarter of a century, a course which has been traveled by hundreds of thousands of human beings from time immemorial.

Wesley was a child of his time. In spite of the radiance of the Methodist message there was about it a weight of tragedy. It broke through the tragedy in its opposition to Calvinism, but it accepted as a matter of course a dark background for its message, perhaps darker than Calvinism itself, for Calvinism was a comfortable belief to those who held it. No Calvinists, as previously suggested, contemplated themselves as lost, whereas Methodists lived in fear of such possibility. I refer to such notions as that men are born under wrath. Here, again, the darkness came out of the time and was an age-old inheritance. The times were tragic—indeed all history had been tragic. If men were to think at all of a divine Kingdom, they painted it as like unto the earthly kingdoms which they knew: resting on force, on arbitrary decrees, on favoritism toward the powerful. Traits like this inevitably colored the notion of the rulership over the world. One disadvantage about the doctrine of the divine right of kings was that it seemed to suggest the kind of sway that the Divine King exercised over men.

We must not, however, take the gloom of the age too seriously, though it was now and again subject to strange terrors, as from the so-called French prophets who suffered from a lunacy from a belief in inspiration, which students of the time have pronounced responsible for the century's dread of "enthusiasm." Human nature has a way of adjusting itself to what seems to men of a later time like intolerable tragedy. The men of the eighteenth century did not take their troubles so gravely as we fancy they did as we look back to the formal catalogues of their beliefs. Nevertheless, the beliefs were bad enough. It was bad enough to have to make adjustments to such gloomy religion. It was like becoming callous to evil. Getting used to a theory which taught of children as born in wrath was about as bad as the fact of such birth would have been—if there had been such a fact.

There are some pictures—indeed, some of them actually painted—which aim to set out the significant meanings of Wesley's life. One is that illustration of the "brand plucked from the burning." Copies of that steel engraving used to decorate Methodist walls by the score. The picture was not excellent from the artistic angle except in its suggestion of the fury of the flames. It leaves the impression that the rescue of young John could have been easier than the narrative makes out. Then there is, or once was, the picture of Wesley preaching on his father's tomb, which has dramatic merit suggesting the futility of the stupid injustice against Wesley wherever the English clergy got their chance. There is also a picture of Wesley's death which seems to aim at making the event as public as possible—a crowd in a room which could not possibly have held so many persons. Indeed, at least some of the persons in the picture were not present when Wesley died.

Passing away from these actual attempts at setting Wesleyan scenes before us, there are one or two lifelike strokes which call up Wesley very vividly. First is the fact that Wesley was about five feet five inches and never weighed more than one hundred and twenty pounds. There is Sir Leslie Stephen's remark that he looked like a "human gamecock." This is not altogether reverent, but it is graphic: a man trained down to the bone; all vigor and alertness. There is also the swift phrase of Horace Walpole, who for an instant saw and heard Wesley speaking in a street: the one word "actor," which gives us Wesley's perfect self-command and his control over his audiences, a control so absolute that a noted psychologist of our time has told us that it can only be accounted for on the supposition of hypnotism. A white-haired actor, of long familiarity with what he had to say, suggests much.

There are one or two other scenes which we can readily put before our imaginations. Take one, often enough described. On one of his horseback journeys Wesley came into a company with a horseman who fell to talking Calvinism. Not knowing who his companion was, this horseman freed his mind on the preaching and character of John Wesley. Whereupon Wesley revealed himself. The Calvinist put spurs to his horse and sought to flee, but the Arminian of his own free choice and self-determination would not be put off. So away they went, uphill and down dale to the next town. What this picture signifies it might be a little hard to say, but it becomes pleasanter the longer one thinks of it. Probably Calvinism was never more forcibly attacked than in the phrases which Wesley shouted at his companion from horseback. Surely, under the circumstances, the discussion could not have been pronounced academic, or abstract, or verbose.

Still another picture is the portrait which shows Wesley walking along in company with two fellow Methodists, Wesley in the center. The portrait could not have been painted so as to put Wesley at less advantage so far as his stature was concerned—the companions appearing notably tall, far overtopping their diminutive associate. Yet something about the picture suggests the superiority of Wesley unmistakably. Little men seem to take a queer pleasure in stretching themselves up to their full height, and thus succeed only in showing how small they are. Not so with Wesley. There is something about that picture as he walks along with the two tall men which suggests intellectual and moral height.

Another picture suggested by Wesley's own statement could be that of his riding along on horseback, with the bridle reins lying loose on the horse's neck. Wesley used to say that a horse under reins thus loose and picking his own path, would never stumble. Whether this is correct or not, the writer is not horseman enough to say. It is tolerably certain, however, that, if one held the horse with a tight rein, one could not do much reading. It is a fair surmise also that Wesley could easily become so absorbed in his book as not to be aware whether his horse stumbled or not.

Still another picture could be most interesting: that of the coach transformed into a traveling study. After Wesley had come far into years his friends presented him with a coach, to lighten the wear and tear of travel. He boarded up one side of it and filled that side with book shelves. Then he put in a table so that he might write as much as he liked. One who knows anything of the strain of writing on the smoothest moving Pullman today can only marvel at writing done in Wesley's coach, especially after people began to refer "to the rumbling old carriage." It is said that Wesley finally abandoned this writing in the coach for fear that such continued effort might injure his eyes—this when he was well past seventy years of age!

Further material on which we can let our imaginations paint a picture is Wesley's account of how in the early days of their evangelistic journeys he and Charles read together as they walked. They would walk in single file, almost like a convict lockstep. The one behind did the reading. The one in front broke the force of the wind for the reader and selected the path, stepping around the holes or the stones or the mud. This enabled the reader to give his whole attention to the book. Of course they took turns in reading. One cannot help wondering whether it was not better to let John do the reading on windy days, for his short stature would not have done much to shield Charles when it was the turn of Charles to read. How can we match this plan for ingenuity, energy, and persistence?

Probably the best picture is the one we do not see: Wesley alone on the roads of England. It would not be accurate to say that Wesley was lonely, but he must have been alone quite as much as any public man of his century in England. Doctor Johnson used to complain that Wesley would never have his talk out, and some have likewise maintained that he was too busy even to think his thought through. Wesley had time enough to carry his thought through, but he gave himself so much to the practical that he did not create any theological system as such. What was he thinking of on the roads of England? Probably of his societies by name, of preachers by name, of followers by name. One last glimpse of the Evangelist is left to us from the pen of Crabbe Robinson.

October 18th, 1790.

Dear Brother:

. . . I felt a great Satisfaction last Week, on Monday, in hearing (excuse me now) that veteran in the Service of God, the Rev. John Wesley. I was informed in the Afternoon that he was in Town and would preach that Evening. Unfortunately a sick Man had sent to have his Will made directly, and it was given to me to write. But Mr. Francis, seeing how mortified I appeared, gave it to some one else, and I went to the Chapel. At another time, and not knowing the Man, I should almost have ridiculed his figure. Far from it now. I lookt upon him with a respect bordering upon Enthusiasm. After the people had sung one Verse of a hymn he arose, and said; "It gives me a great pleasure to find that you have not lost your Singing. Neither Men nor Women— you have not forgot a single Note. And I hope that by the assistance of the same God which enables you to sing well, you may do all other things well." A Universal Amen followed. At the End of every Head or Division of His Discourse, he finished by a kind of Prayer, a Momentary Wish as it were, not consisting of more than three or four words, which was always followed by a Universal Buzz. His discourse was short—the

Text I could not hear. After the last prayer, he rose up and addressed the people on Liberality of Sentiment, and spoke much against refusing to join with any Congregation on account of difference in Opinion. He said, "If they do but fear God, work righteousness, and keep his commandments, we have nothing to object to." He preached again on Tuesday Evening, but I was out of Town with Mr. Francis all day, holding a Court Baron. . . .

I remain, etc.,

H. C. R.

I wish to express my gratitude for the attention Arnold Lunn has drawn to a letter which seems to me to be one of the highest notes Wesley ever struck. If I were to think one last thought about Wesley, or say one last word about him, I should prefer above all else to read the letter which I here print in full. The introductory note in Telford's edition of Wesley's *Letters* tells that William Shent, a Methodist worker, had fallen into sin and had been forsaken by the Methodists.

To the Society at Keighley

London, January 11, 1779.

I have a few questions which I desire may be proposed to the Society at Keighley.

Who was the occasion of the Methodist preachers first setting foot in Leeds? William Shent.

Who received John Nelson into his house at his first coming thither? William Shent.

Who was it that invited me and received me when I came? William Shent.

Who was it that stood by me while I preached in the street with stones flying on every side? William Shent.

Who was it bore the storm of persecution for the whole town and stemmed it at the peril of his life? William Shent.

Whose word did God bless for many years in an eminent manner? William Shent's.

By whom were many children now in Paradise begotten in the Lord, and many now alive? William Shent.

Who is he that is now ready to be broken up and turned into the street? William Shent.

And does nobody care for this? William Shent fell into sin and was publicly expelled the Society; but must he also be stoned? Must he with his gray hairs and all his children be without a place to lay his head? Can you suffer this? O tell it not in Gath! Where is gratitude?

Where is compassion? Where is Christianity? Where is humanity?
Where is concern for the cause of God? Who is a wise man among you?
Who is concerned for the Gospel? Who has put on bowels of mercy?
Let him rise and exert himself in this matter. You here, all arise as
one man and roll away the reproach. Let us set him on his feet once
more. It may save both him and his family. But what we do, let it be
done quickly. I am, dear brethren

Your affectionate brother,

JOHN WESLEY.

INDEX

351